The Education of the Young Child

A Handbook for Nursery and Infant Teachers

Second Edition

Edited by David Fontana

Basil Blackwell

© Basil Blackwell Ltd 1984

First published 1978 by Open Books Publishing Limited
Second edition 1984
Reprinted 1985

Basil Blackwell Ltd
108 Cowley Road, Oxford OX4 1JF, UK

Basil Blackwell Inc.
432 Park Avenue South, Suite 1505,
New York, NY 10016, USA

British Library Cataloguing in Publication Data
Fontana, David
    The education of the young child. — 2nd ed.
    1. Education, Pre school 2. Education of children
    I. Title
    372   B1140.2

    ISBN 0-631-13584-7
    ISBN 0-631-13585-5 Pbk

Library of Congress Cataloging in Publication Data
Main entry under title:

The Education of the young child.

    Includes indexes.
    1. Education, Preschool. 2. Child development.
I. Fontana, David.
LB1140.2.E325   1984   372'.21   84–12478
ISBN 0-631-13584-7
ISBN 0-631-13585-5 (pbk.)

Typeset by Cambrian Typesetters, Aldershot, Hants.
Printed in Great Britain by Bell and Bain Ltd, Glasgow

Contents

Preface to the Second Edition

Since its publication in 1978, *The Education of the Young Child* has established itself as one of the most widely recommended books on education in the United Kingdom. This success has been particularly gratifying to the book's contributors since our aim was to provide something of positive use to those preparing for or involved in nursery and infant teaching, a book that would cover both the psychosocial development of children during the nursery and infant school years and the practical skills and techniques required in teaching them.

The chapters in this new edition have been revised and up-dated by the original contributors, and the opportunity has also been taken to commission work from four additional authors. Sohan and Celia Modgil are responsible for a completely new chapter on cognitive development (an area in which there have been important recent developments), and Steven Tyler and Teresa Smith write respectively on assessment and on working with parents (two topics which experienced teachers indicate are of great importance in the work of nursery and infant schools). The aim of this second edition remains the same as that of the first. We have written it in the hope that it will be of practical benefit to those responsible for the demanding and delightful business of teaching young children.

A word of caution: the contributors have reluctantly adopted the personal pronoun 'he' to refer to 'the child' throughout the book (to avoid awkward he/she and himself/herself repetition). However, the reader should understand that 'the child' refers to both boys and girls unless specific sex differences are given. Likewise, 'the teacher' is referred to throughout as 'she'. While this is statistically more likely in current nursery and infant education, it should not be taken to preclude the male teacher of young children.

Acknowledgements

The author and publisher would like to thank Behaviourdelia Inc., Kalamazoo, Michigan and the *Journal of Applied Behaviour Analysis*, Lawrence, Kansas for material contained in Roger McIntire's chapter. Grateful thanks are also due to Patrick Taylor of Open Books, who published the first edition of this book.

Contributors

Maurice Chazan is Professor of Education, University College, Swansea

Derek Cherrington is Reader in Educational Studies, City of Birmingham Polytechnic

Dennis Child is Professor of Educational Psychology, University of Leeds

Avril Dankworth is a professional musician and teacher

Ronald Davie is Director, National Children's Bureau

David Fontana is Senior Lecturer in Educational Psychology, University College Cardiff

Peter Horner is Senior Lecturer in Education, Rolle College Exmouth

Alice Laing is Senior Lecturer in Education, University College Swansea

Sheila Lane was formerly Headmistress of Tidemill Primary School, London

Barbara Lewis is HM Inspector of Schools

Roger McIntire is Professor of Educational Psychology, University of Maryland, USA

Geoffrey Matthews was formerly Shell Professor of Mathematics Education, University of London

Celia Modgil is Senior Lecturer in Educational Psychology, University of London

Sohan Modgil is Reader in Educational Research and Development, Brighton Polytechnic

Henry Pluckrose is Headmaster of Prior Weston Primary School, London

Teresa Smith is Lecturer in Applied Social Studies, University of Oxford

Jim Tanner is Professor of Child Health and Growth, University of London

Joan Tough is Senior Lecturer in Education, University of Leeds

Steve Tyler was formerly Research Fellow in Pre-School Education, University of Keele

Alice Yardley was formerly Principal Lecturer in Curriculum Studies, Trent Polytechnic

Introduction

DAVID FONTANA

Despite the many changes in educational theory and practice that have taken place in recent years, there is still little doubt that early learning and early experience remain crucial to later development. During the first seven years of life the child masters an extraordinary range of skills unparalleled in complexity and scope by anything that follows during a comparable period of time. Language, socialisation, attachment, number skills, self-awareness and self-concepts, early reading and writing skills, discrimination of colour, form and sound all combine to transform the world of the newborn baby into the highly organised and controllable world of the seven-year-old. Were we not, as teachers and parents, so habituated to this process we could not fail to stand in awe of it as one of nature's major miracles.

We cannot argue, of course, that it is impossible to compensate later on – to some degree at least – for social and educational deprivation during the early years. But such compensation is difficult and uncertain and demands a rare level of dedication and skill in the teachers and caretakers responsible for it. For most children today, it is fair to say that learning opportunities withheld or poorly presented during the early years can lead to escalating social and academic problems throughout childhood and indeed into and throughout adult life.

Such a state of affairs places a special responsibility upon all teachers of young children, and it is unfortunate that a misinterpretation of research evidence has led some authorities to question the long-term effectiveness of what these teachers (in particular nursery school teachers) are trying to do. This is evident in the doubts that have been expressed as to the benefits accruing from programmes (such as the American Head Start programmes) designed to provide children from socially and culturally deprived backgrounds with compensatory pre-school education. Critics of these programmes claim that in spite of all the resources the programmes receive there is little evidence that children gain much identifiable long-term benefit; and, inevitably, certain of these critics have broadened their attack to challenge the value of all forms of nursery education. The weakness of the arguments advanced by these critics is fully explored by a number of writers (see the survey in Sylva, 1983) and the most redoubtable and vocal of these, David Weikart (for example Schweinhart and Weikart 1980), even demonstrates that money invested in a child's education at the pre-school stage can show a fourfold return for society in the shape of (a) reduced expenditure on later remedial education, (b) reduced expenditure on the legal processing of delinquent behaviour, and (c) increased eventual employment prospects for participants (see also Breedlove and Schweinhart, 1982).

The evidence quoted by Weikhart and his colleagues is based upon findings in the USA but, allowing for differences in education and employment patterns, these findings are likely to provide a valid guide to what happens in the UK and other developed countries. Weikart indicates that for the group of severely underprivileged children studied by him from pre-school age to 19 years the pattern given in table 1 emerged.

Table 1 *Findings of Weikart among severely underprivileged children (adapted from Breedlove and Schweinhart, 1982)*

	With pre-school education (%)	Without pre-school education (%)
Arrested for delinquent behaviour	22	43
Left high school at earliest opportunity	35	55
Attended college or job training scheme	38	21
Currently in employment	48	29
Currently self- or spouse-supported	45	24
Years in special education classes during schooling	1.8	3.8

It is difficult to argue with figures of this kind, or to doubt the benefits they represent both for the community and for the individual. They constitute a powerful case for making nursery education available to all those from underprivileged or deprived backgrounds, and indeed to all those who in the view of their parents would be enhanced by it.

Inevitably, of course, this raises the question 'what *kind* of nursery education?'. There are wide variations between the practices adopted in one nursery school or unit and another, between one nursery teacher and another. Should nursery education be seen as a downward extension of infant education, for example, or should it be allowed to develop its own separate method and ideology? Should nursery training be separate from infant training, or should the nursery and the infant teacher both have a clear knowledge of what the other is doing, and in fact be able to swap roles as and when inclination or necessity demands it? Is a break at the age of five a good thing, or is it simply wished on us by historical accident and by the fact that many children are still denied formal education before they reach this age?

The purpose of this book is to try to answer these questions by examining, first, the psychosocial development of the nursery and infant school child and, secondly, the curriculum and methodology of good nursery and infant school practice. It will become clear as we proceed that while contributors take the view that the years from three to seven should be studied as a unit, with both nursery and infant teachers fully aware of what goes on throughout, there are nevertheless identifiable differences between the work attempted respectively by nursery and infant teachers. Nursery work is not a diluted form of infant work, and infant work is not a concentrated form of nursery work. The contributors therefore draw careful distinctions throughout between what we can expect from (and what we should be doing with) nursery school children and what we should be seeking from (and doing with) infant school children. Nevertheless, there is no suggestion that the break between schools should be an abrupt one. Children do not change suddenly at the age of five. There should instead be a smooth transition from the final term in the nursery school to the first term in reception infants, with teachers working closely together to ensure that the child benefits to the full from the work done within each context.

In order to examine both psychosocial development and curriculum/methodology the book is divided for convenience into two parts, with part I concentrating on the former and part II on the latter. The chapter divisions in part I need no lengthy justification and provide a conceptual framework helpful to both readers and contributors. Children's behaviour does not consist, of course, of separate units called language, intelligence and so on, and the child must ultimately be thought of as a whole. However, when we are faced with a complex range of information, we try to make sense of it by sorting and categorising, keeping sight, where necessary, of the fact that such categorisation is in the interests of clarity and coherence, and must not be interpreted too rigidly.

These arguments apply equally to part II, but here some further justification is needed since the division into chapters follows what might loosely be called 'subject' boundaries (e.g. music, art and craft, reading), and against this it can reasonably be contended that the aim of nursery and infant school teachers is to provide children with integrated learning experiences rather than to fragment these experiences into subject-based areas. The rationale behind the divisions adopted in part II, however, is that although no teacher of young children observes clear subject boundaries in her work, these boundaries, flexibly interpreted, nevertheless provide effective ways of conceptualising this work and of monitoring children's progress. For example, although reading and musical experiences might perhaps be drawn from the same set of activities, the teacher can only select and plan these activities to best advantage if she bears in mind the distinctive sets of skills which reading and music respectively involve.

The alternative approach to the education of young children, i.e. that we should start from the 'needs' of the children themselves, has been examined and found wanting by a number of educational philosophers. Dearden (1969) argues that the concept of children's 'needs' is too vague and imprecise to be a useful starting point for the curriculum, while Peters (1969) also attacks the muddled thinking of these 'child-centred' theories. The point is that once we have satisified the basic biological needs of children (food, drink, shelter, affection and the like) anything else becomes a matter of opinion. Traditionalists argued that the child 'needed' discipline in order to develop his character, while progressives argue today that he 'needs' free expression. To add to the confusion, the economist might well argue that the child 'needs' to become numerate and literate if he is one day to contribute significantly to our industrial survival. The conception of a child's needs depends very much on the sort of theories that one holds about the kind of person the child should one day grow up to be.

Fundamentally, 'child-centred' theories would have us think of the curriculum, to use the well-known phraseology of the Hadow Report (Consultative Committee, 1933), 'in terms of activity and experience rather than of facts to be stored and of knowledge to be gained'. But as Bruner (1976) points out, what kind of knowledge and for what? The Hadow Report's statement, so potent an influence upon nearly half a century of educational thought, confuses means and ends. Activity and experience may be all very well as means, but the ends which they serve must surely involve some of the very 'facts' and 'knowledge' which the Report postulates as an inferior alternative to them. Bruner suggests that this means–end muddle stems from misplaced theories about the:

> impact of experience in the early years upon experience later in life. It is reflected most clearly in the progressive refrain that education is to be considered as life itself, and not as a preparation for later living. It is a view that risks being blind to. . . the subtle and indirect ways in which the child becomes father to the man.

Rather than subscribing to these misplaced theories, Bruner has it that our concern should be with what 'our practices are doing to children whom we commit to educational institutions'.

Bruner's views do not imply, of course, that we should abandon any thought of progressive education. What they really mean is that all the experiences encountered by a child have a potential influence upon his long-term development. Thus these experiences cannot be viewed simply as ends in themselves, but should be seen within the context of this development, and should be chosen by the teacher with an eye to those forms of development which society considers to be most worthwhile.

I have argued elsewhere (Fontana, 1976) that if we wish to make early experience contribute most effectively to long-term ends, then the curriculum in the first school can best be thought of in terms of a number of areas of skills, in each of which the child must undertake appropriate learning tasks.

Many of these areas are covered by the material discussed in part I of this book, but those associated with what might loosely be called the formal curriculum lie within the province of part II.

In discussing the curriculum, however, the contributors to part II do not concern themselves only with 'knowledge to be gained and facts to be stored'. They take account, in addition (and here our conflict with the child-centred theories goes some way towards successful resolution), of the child who has to do the learning. In doing so, they are thus discussing both the content of the curriculum (which as we have suggested is related to educational ends) and the methods which can best be used to teach this content to young children (i.e. the means by which these ends can best be served).

Turning to Bruner once more, we find him making the now classic statement (1960) that 'any idea or problem or body of knowledge can be presented in a form simple enough so that any particular learner can understand it in a recognisable form'. In other words, without simplifying a subject to a point where it ceases identifiably to be that subject, part of the knowledge which it contains can be taught to the young child at school, no matter how immature his cognitive processes may appear to be. The secret lies in the way in which this knowledge is presented. The teacher's job, Bruner suggests, is to provide a learning context appropriate to the child's level of understanding. Where learning fails to take place, the fault lies not in the nature of the subject to be taught, nor in the child himself, but in the form in which the learning experience is presented. The discussion on methodology in part II is an attempt, for the subject areas concerned, to help us all to get this form right.

References

Breedlove, C. and Schweinhart, J. (1982) *The Cost-effectiveness of High Quality Early Childhood Programs*. Ypsilanti, Mich.: High-Scope Educational Research Foundation (Report prepared for the 1982 Southern Governors' Conference).

Bruner, J. S. (1960) *The Process of Education*. Cambridge, Mass.: Harvard University Press.

Bruner, J. S. (1969) The styles of teaching. *New Society*, April.

Consultative Committee (1933) *Report on Infant and Nursery Schools* (the Hadow Report). London: HMSO.

Dearden, R. (1969) *The Philosophy of Primary Education*. London: Routledge & Kegan Paul.

Fontana, D. (1976) Formulating objectives in nursery education. *Journal of Curriculum Studies* **8**, 27–34.

Peters, R. S. (1969) A recognisable philosophy of education. In Peters, R. S. (ed.) *Perspectives on Plowden*. London: Routledge & Kegan Paul.

Schweinhart, L. J. and Weikart, D. P. (1980) Young children grow up: the effects of the Perry Preschool Programme on youths through age 15. Ypsilanti, Mich.: *Monographs of the High Scope Educational Research Foundation no. 27*.

Sylva, K. (1983) Some lasting effects of pre-school provision – or, the Emperor wore clothes after all. *Education Section Review* **7**, 10–16.

Part I

1

Physical Development from Three to Seven

JIM TANNER

The years from three to seven are years of steady and unspectacular growth, a smooth passage across an open sea. Amongst a group of children there is little change in position, and what there is occurs, as it were, in slow motion, one at the rear of the flotilla moving ever so gradually through to the middle. There are no sudden spurts, no critical jockeyings such as occur later in the squally weather of adolescence. This is not to say that growth in these years is passive, a sort of coasting after the initial push. The orderliness proceeds from a high degree of regulation amongst the enormous number of processes which underlie the final result. Each endocrine gland, each enzyme, has to be switched on in an exact sequence, turned on to an exact amount. It is like the weaving of a complex tapestry; the plan lies implicit in the hereditary material of the genes, but the correct supply of thread must be assured, and the loom itself must function without hesitations or hitches. We understand quite well the nature and amount of thread necessary to make human beings and we begin to understand the way the plans are drawn, but about the functioning of the loom we are still woefully ignorant. It is probably here, however, that the teacher's care and understanding may have their impact in assuring a steady uninterrupted realisation of the particular pattern that is peculiar to each child.

The curve of growth

We will look first at the whole growth curve of a child, from birth to maturity, to see the location of our particular period within it. Figure 1 shows the most famous of all records of human growth. It concerns the height of a single boy, measured every six months from birth to 18 years. So far as we know it was the first such record ever made, and it remains, even now, one of the best. It was published in Buffon's *Histoire Naturelle* in the eighteenth century and made by his close friend and collaborator, Count Philibert Guéneau de Montbeillard on his son.

In figure 1*a* the height attained at successive ages is plotted; in 1*b* the increments of height from one age to the next, expressed as the rate of growth per year. If we think of the growth of a child as the passage of a railway train along a line to its destination, we can liken the upper curve to the distance travelled and the lower to the speed or velocity of the train. The velocity, or rate of growth, generally reflects the child's state at any particular time better than the distance covered does, which depends largely on how much the child has grown in the preceding years. Thus in monitoring the growth of a given child (a subject to which we shall return below), it is the velocity of · growth to which we should give most attention – although the child himself, of course, will be more concerned with his 'distance', relative to the 'distance' of all the others.

Figure 1*b* indicates that in general the velocity of growth decreases from birth (and actually from as early as the fourth month of fetal life) but that

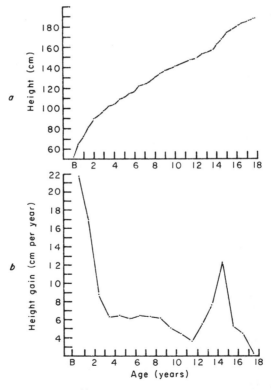

Figure 1   *The curve of height growth for a single boy measured from birth to maturity. a, Height attained at successive ages; b, rate, or velocity of growth (Tanner, 1962).*

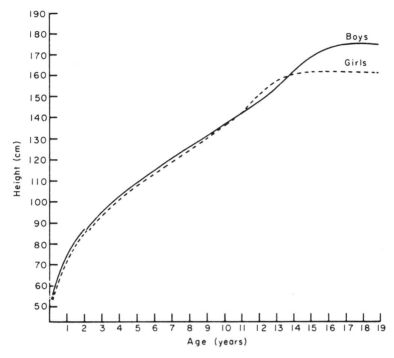

Figure 2   *Curve of height attained for the average boy and average girl (Tanner et al., 1966).*

this decline is diminished very markedly from about the age of six to eight, and then spectacularly interrupted shortly before the end of the growth period by the so-called 'adolescent growth spurt', which in de Montbeillard's son took place between the ages of 12 and 16 years.

There is a difference in growth between girls and boys (or rather, between the average girl and the average boy, since there is overlap in growth curves just as there is overlap in stature, some girls being taller than some boys). Figure 2 shows the distance, height-for-age, curve for the average or typical girl and boy in Britain, and figure 3 the corresponding velocity curves. The average boy is slightly longer at birth than the average girl, and his height remains a little greater until, at about the age of eleven, the girl's earlier adolescent growth spurt carries her past him for a couple of years, till his own larger but later spurt carries him past her again. (The break in the curves in figure 2 at two years of age represents the difference between measurements taken lying supine, and measurements taken standing up; the average child is about 1 cm longer when supine.) Figure 3 shows the difference between the sexes more clearly, at least in terms of the process of growth. Immediately after birth boys are growing a little faster than girls, but they decelerate more, and by about seven months girls, on average, are growing faster. The difference in velocity is small, however, and practically

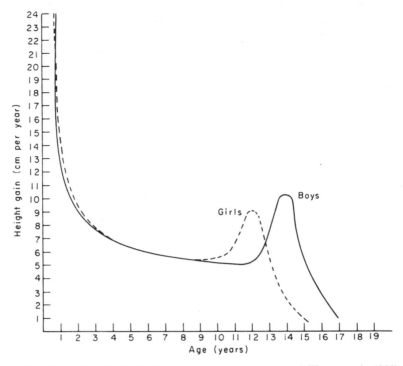

Figure 3   *Curve of height velocity for the average boy and average girl (Tanner et al., 1966).*

disappears at about the age of three; during the period with which we are concerned, boys and girls grow at identical rates. Then, on average at about ten, the girls' adolescent spurt begins. It reaches its peak at 12 years, two years before the peak of the boys' spurt. The girls' peak is smaller in magnitude, however, as can be seen in figure 3. This is due to the different endocrine gland arrangements in males and females; testosterone, the sex hormone peculiar to males, is secreted by boys when the testes grow at puberty, and is responsible for the extra amount of growth.

Developmental age

The difference in growth between the sexes becomes striking at adolescence, where in a class of boys and girls of approximately the same chronological age, say 12+, girls are within sight of physical maturity and boys are for the most part entirely prepubescent. But the sex difference is not something which arises for the first time at adolescence. It is present from birth, and indeed from late fetal life. It is a difference in the *tempo of growth*. Girls pass through the same sequence of changes as boys, more or less, but they travel faster, right from the beginning. They play out their growth *allegro*, boys *andante*. Even in the nursery and infant school the average girl is more physically mature than the average boy.

Such differences in tempo also occur between different children of the same sex. Again, they are most spectacularly seen at adolescence, where amongst a group of 12-year-old girls or 14-year-old boys one finds all stages of puberty represented, from individuals yet to begin to individuals who are fully mature. These differences also arise much earlier; the early-maturing adolescent has, as a rule, been advanced in physical development in the infant school. We know this from the considerable number of studies which have followed individual children from birth to maturity (so-called longitudinal studies) using a measurement of their *developmental* or *physiological age* on successive occasions, as well as the usual measurement of chronological age.

Developmental age may be measured in various ways. In all it signifies the percentage of adult status reached at the age considered; thus at age of entry to infant school one boy may have reached 55% of his adult height; another, who is going to finish growth two or three years earlier, 65% (corresponding figures for girls would be 60% and 70%). Height itself, of course, is not a measure of developmental age because individuals differ in their mature height. Thus tallness may signify either a rapid tempo of growth in a child who will be of average height when adult or an average tempo of growth in a child who is going to be tall when adult. Age at entry to the various stages of puberty is a valid measure of developmental age, since all normal children pass through and complete the same stages; but we require a measure applicable to earlier ages also.

The measure most generally used in research is *skeletal maturity* or *bone age*. This is a measure of how far the bones of an area, usually the hand and wrist, have progressed towards maturity, not in size, but in shape and in their relative positions one to another, as visualised by x-ray. Each bone begins as a small centre of ossification and then passes through various stages of enlargement and shaping, acquiring in some cases new pieces; all these changes can be readily seen. All normal children pass through the same stages and reach the same final state, that of complete ossification. Thus bone age, introduced into the study of children's growth in 1904, enables us to categorise children as advanced or delayed at all ages since individual differences in relative advancement of the bones begin in fetal life. The actual bone age is assigned to a child by comparing his radiograph with those obtained from a sample of normal children. The average child of the standardising sample, by definition, has a bone age of 10.0 'years' when he is chronologically aged 10.0. If a given child's radiograph matches that of the average standardising child of chronological age 9.0, then that given child's bone age is 9.0 'years', whatever his chronological age. At nursery and infant school the variation in bone age is already considerable. At the age of three the range of bone ages covering 95% of pupils runs from one and a half to four and a half 'years', and at the age of four from two to six 'years'.

Other measures of developmental age (e.g. the number of erupted teeth or the appearance of the tooth roots on x-ray) give different ranges, but the point remains the same: large differences in degree of physical maturity exist amongst any group of nursery or infant school children, with girls more advanced on average than boys, but with overlap between the sexes.

Regulation of growth: sensitive periods and catch-up

Growth is a product of the continuous and complex interaction of heredity and environment. The plan of possible growth is laid down in the genes; whether it comes to fruition depends on the environment providing precisely what is called for in the plan at each successive stage of development. Since every child's genes are different from every other child's (except in the case of monozygotic, or identical, twins), it follows that in the ideal sense every child requires some slightly different succession of environmental stimuli for optimal development. This is, perhaps, impossible to achieve in any society, but the principle is important. Modern biology gives no support to the notion of treating children alike, only to that of supplying them with the widest possible choice of interactions.

In many animals such interactions are highly specific. When a greylag goose hatches from its egg, it has an inborn reaction to follow the first large moving object it sees. Normally this is its mother. But, as everyone knows, it will follow Dr Konrad Lorenz (1952) just as well if he should creep by first, and it will forever after treat him as mother. The distinction between environment and heredity is a man-made one, and evolution makes or ignores it according to the laws of Darwin rather than Aristotle. Animals are born into expected environments; some occupy niches of exquisite precision and negligible width; others, like man, are relatively polyvalent and can interact, with varying success, with a wide variety of environments. An example of a necessary environmental interaction is provided by work on the vision of kittens. If an adult cat's eyes are covered for a few weeks and then the covers are removed, the cat is a bit clumsy for some minutes, then normal. But if a kitten's eyes are similarly covered, and for as little as a week from the time it normally begins to use them, then the kitten never develops the ability to see properly; the cells of the brain concerned with vision fail to develop their full characteristics. The genes bring the cells to the point in time where light is expected. Then the interaction must occur or disaster follows. The experience of seeing is necessary during what is called the *critical* or *sensitive* period.

Such sensitive periods are very common in growth, although most of the ones we know about concern internal relationships in the growing organism rather than external relationships with the environment. For the correct development of the male genitalia, for example, male sex hormone has to be secreted by the fetal testes from ten to 13 weeks after fertilisation. If this fails to occur, later secretion of testosterone is without the proper effect.

During fetal life similar sensitive periods occur in the growth and development of the brain. Most of the examples known so far concern the differentiation of the part of the brain concerned with reproductive behaviour, but it is certainly possible that areas concerned with the development of motor and intellectual skills may also be subject to the same mechanisms. If so, there is no particular reason to suppose that they cease to operate after birth. There may indeed be periods, as some educationists insist, when failure to present material or ideas to the child results in a permanent deprivation.

All young organisms, however, have an inborn capacity to recover lost ground after some sorts of environmental catastrophe (the catastrophes normally encountered in the evolutionary life of the animal, that is, which do not include Dr Lorenz). Figure 4 shows the distance and velocity curves of a girl with starvation due to an inability to absorb foodstuffs because she suffered from coeliac disease, in which a type of allergic reaction to wheat-derived foods destroys the cells lining the upper part of the gut. In this child the usual symptoms of indigestion were muted, and the disease was not diagnosed till the age of 11, by which time growth in height and weight had been severely affected, as figure 4 shows. At this time the proper diet, which omits all the offending foods, was started, and a marked increase in growth

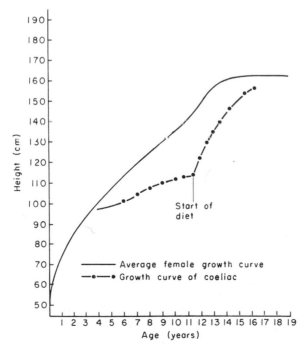

Figure 4   *Growth of girl with coeliac disease to show catch-up on dietary treatment.*

took place, the velocity reaching to well above the normal levels, a phenomenon named catch-up growth. Such catch-up may be sufficient to enable the child to recover completely and reach an entirely normal adult stature, as in this girl's case. Catch-up is also a universal principle in growth; expectedly so, for man did not evolve in Hampstead Garden Suburb but in small nomadic groups of hunter-gatherers living from one famine to another, always on the edge of starvation. In such circumstances a young animal has to be able to stop growing until times get better.

To what extent catch-up can occur in brain growth or in intellectual abilities is uncertain. We know that deprivation of necessary substances at the time cells are dividing usually results in a permanent later deficit of cells. In man this means, essentially, the first six or seven months of fetal life, with the addition of the first year after birth for certain tissue-supporting cells in the brain. Thus, disorder of the placenta may result in a small child at birth who cannot catch up later. But when the cell division phase of growth is over, children have a remarkable ability to catch up even after very severe starvation. In 1945 certain parts of Holland were subjected to extremely severe starvation for six months, resulting in an average reduction of birthweight of 9%. Yet when these children were measured on induction into the Dutch army as adults, they were no shorter and scored no lower in aptitude tests than their contemporaries from parts of Holland outside the famine area (Stein et al., 1975). Catch-up was apparently complete. These children, when the famine was over, grew up under excellent conditions of food and care, and this is probably the most important factor to be stressed. From the point of view of the nursery and infant teacher, children arriving from a deprived background may be expected to show catch-up to the degree that home circumstances, as well as school ones, support it.

Thus physical growth provides us with solid models both for sensitive periods wherein developments must occur or be forever lost, and contrastingly, periods in which catch-up is possible, allowing ground apparently lost to be made up in full. Just where in this spectrum any particular combination of age, deprivation and missed skill fit is a subject for test in the particular case. The only safe generalisation is that the earlier the deprivation and the longer it persists the less the chance of catch-up, even in optimal circumstances.

Growth of the brain

The brain is an organ of particular interest to teachers, and its growth is in one way very different from that of most of the rest of the body. The brain, together with the skull covering it, and the eyes and ears, is ahead of the rest of the body in terms of its developmental age. Thus at the age of three it has reached 65% of its adult weight and at the age of seven, 90%. Height at similar times has reached only about 55% and 70%, and weight 25% and

40%. This comparison shows us not only that the brain is advanced in maturity, however. It is also growing very rapidly during the nursery and infant years, adding 25% of its final weight, whereas height and body weight in the same time increase by only 15%. No new neurons, or nerve cells, are made; they have all been present since the middle of fetal life. No supporting cells, or neuroglia, are made either; they have all been present since a year or so after birth. But both sorts of cells enlarge greatly, develop longer processes and new connections by means of the small processes called dendrites. Though the relation between mental ability and brain structure is anything but clear, the richness of the connections between different cells does seem to be the most important factor that we can invoke at present. During the nursery and infant years, 'connectivity', as it is called, is increasing enormously, at a rate much greater than at any time later in childhood. Though it is not now believed that the brain is entirely 'hard-wired', that is, that connections once made are permanent and exclusive, it must certainly be easier to build on a good existing scaffold than on a faulty or poorly developed one. Thus the period we are considering must be one of great importance for brain development. What the teacher can do to help no biologist can yet say, for we do not know what causes connections to be made or what influences from outside the brain can cause one form of connection rather than another. In general, however, it seems to be that connections are established by use; the passage of impulses across them keeps them from decline, just as in the case of the kitten's eye. Perhaps by taking thought one can add a few million dendrites to the brain, even if not a cubit of one's stature.

The various areas of the brain develop in a clearly defined scale of advancement, right from fetal life. (In the same way the hand is at all times nearer completion than the forearm and the forearm nearer than the upper arm.) During the first two years after birth, the areas in the brain subserving the inception of movement and the reception of sensory stimuli are ahead of the 'association' areas. These latter are areas in which linking up between the incoming and outgoing stimuli occur and in which elaboration ('consideration' in mental terms) takes place. This predominance of the primary areas· gradually fades during the period we are considering. Even by the age of three or four, however, some fibre tracts in the brain are still not fully functional. An example is the series of tracts linking the cerebellum at the back of the brain to the cerebral cortex. These tracts are responsible for the fine control of voluntary movement, and it is following their maturation that the physical skills of the nursery school child develop so strikingly. In the same way the cells and fibres of the sound-receiving system, though they begin to develop very early in fetal life, hang fire till quite late and become fully mature only in the fourth year. Their tempo, as Yakovlev and Lecours (1967) suggest, may be linked to the development of language.

The comparative study of growth reinforces the importance of the years three to seven in the development of the human brain. All primates (that is man, apes and monkeys) have growth patterns that are basically similar, and very different indeed from the growth patterns of rats or mice or domestic animals. All primates are born at about the time when the weight velocity curve reaches its first peak. The curve then falls (like the height velocity chart) until eventually it rises again in the adolescent growth spurt. In monkeys the time between the two peaks is quite short, a matter of about four years; in apes it is longer (about seven years in the chimpanzee) and in man, at 12 to 14 years, it is longer still. Thus puberty is progressively delayed as we move up the primate scale to man, presumably to give the brain time to mature and provide a period for learning before the individual comes into competition with adults. It is precisely the years we are considering that have been sandwiched in between birth and puberty as a specialisation of the human.

Growth as a monitor of health

The rate of growth of a child is a remarkably good indication of the child's state of health; indeed, it is probably the best single monitor of health that we have. This applies to growth in height, and not in weight, in which excessive growth is all too often productive of, or produced by, disorder. Even for height it is the regularity which is most important, though the actual amount of growth is indicative also, provided it is considered in relation to parental height.

In healthy children growth in height is very regular; it does not proceed, as used to be said in some of the old textbooks, by fits and starts. It will not appear regular, however, unless very careful attention is paid to the manner in which height is measured. The child's positioning is all important. He is told to stand up straight, heels in contact with the backboard of the apparatus or the wall or door (buttocks, shoulders and head not necessarily so unless they fit this way). His head is aligned carefully so that his ear-holes are in the same horizontal plane (i.e. plane parallel to the floor) as the lower border of his eye-sockets (not, therefore, a nose-in-air stance). He is urged to make himself as tall as possible, and aided in doing so by gentle upward pressure applied to the bony prominences under the ears (on both sides equally). All this is to straighten out his back and prevent slumping due to tiredness or boredom. The technique reduces to a couple of millimetres the otherwise considerable diminution in apparent height that takes place during the day for postural reasons. The ideal apparatus has a counterbalanced board which rests always lightly in contact with the child's head, so that the measurer can simply call out the height when the position is correctly achieved. The apparatus can also have a rack and pinion gear activating a counter so that the numbers are simply read out. This is a refinement, however. Height can be perfectly well measured by means of a triangular block of wood, not less than 15 cm broad, brought down on to the top of the head by a second observer, with one face of the triangle against the wall or door, against which the child stands, and the other on top of the head. The wall can be marked or a ruled board can be fixed permanently to it. Such a method is preferable to the use of the floppy little arms attached to some weighing scales, which bend, are too narrow and fail to permit proper positioning.

The height should then be plotted on a chart such as that shown in figure 5. The lines represent 'centiles' of height at successive ages from two to eight.

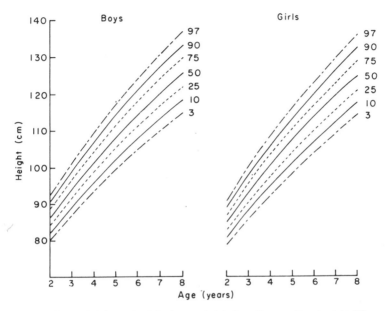

Figure 5   Centiles for height attained for boys and girls from the age of two to eight (Tanner et al., 1966).

The meaning of each centile is straightforward: 3% of normal children are below the third centile in height, 10% below the tenth, 25% below the 25th, 50% below the 50th (which is thus the average value), 75% below the 75th, 90% below the 90th, and all but 3% below the 97th. Thus a child's height can be at once judged in relation to the heights of other children. Individual children stay on or close to the same centile during the period three to seven; some move gradually and slightly upward through the centiles, travelling a little faster than the others, and some move gradually down, with a velocity slightly slower. But over this age range the changes in position are very minor. If a child sinks considerably, say from the 50th to the tenth, then something is wrong and a full investigation should be undertaken. In figure 6 the centiles for velocity of height growth are given, which permit a more

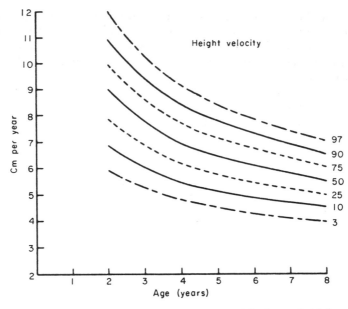

Figure 6   *Centiles for velocity of height growth from two to eight; boys and girls have approximately the same centiles. Centiles appropriate for velocity over whole year period (Tanner et al., 1966).*

accurate assessment, provided only that the measurements have been taken with the utmost care. Two errors of measurement enter into the calculation of velocity, one at the first time of measurement, the other at the second. They may summate; hence the importance of minimising them. The velocity chart is couched in terms of cm/year. A rate of this sort can be calculated for any period of time; thus a gain of 3.2 cm over a six-month period would be a rate of 6.4 (3.2 ÷ 0.5) cm/year. But the centiles other than the 50th are only accurate if the velocity has been measured over approximately a whole year. Over shorter periods, not only are the unavoidable errors of measurement of proportionately greater importance but also a seasonal variation in growth rate affects the values. Most children show some difference between their rates of growth in spring and in autumn, and in some the difference is quite large, the velocity in the six months including spring being twice as much as in the six months which include autumn. Thus on the generally regular curve of growth there is superimposed a small but noticeable seasonal undulation.

The height charts of figure 5 show the position of a child in relation to other children in the population, but given a good environment children take after their parents in the height they attain, being equally influenced (despite all rumours to the contrary) by mother and father, whether they themselves are boys or girls. Naturally, one takes a different view of a child at the third centile for height if he has two parents at the third centile than if his parents are, say, at the 90th centile. It is possible to allow for the height of the parents in assessing a child, but the charts for doing so take us beyond the scope of this chapter. They will be found in *Foetus into Man* by Tanner (1978).

The causes of a falling off in height growth are many, and any diminution in velocity to below the tenth centile should alert the teacher to obtain further advice. Endocrinological disease, of the thyroid or pituitary glands, causes a diminution in growth rate, often combined with increasing fatness. Mal-absorption of food causes a diminution in rate, allied with loss of weight or at least increasing leanness as the child grows. Kidney disease may be responsible. Over-enthusiastic treatment of asthma or eczema with steroid hormones – even ones applied as creams to eczematous skin – is a very potent cause of short stature. Unhappiness may cause a diminution of growth rate too, either in the obvious way by causing the child to reduce his intake of food, producing a thin small child or, in much rarer instances, by causing an actual switching off of the secretion of human hormone, a hormone necessary for normal growth, secreted by the pituitary gland. In this case the child may be small and not thin at all. Such children are rare, and usually show other signs of their very disturbed family background.

The point for the teacher, however, is that regular measurement and plot-ting of height and, less importantly, weight is probably the best simple way of keeping a check on a child's health and well-being, and serves too as a point of contact with the parents and the family doctor. Weight standard charts are given in figure 7; their chief importance at present is probably as a warning of

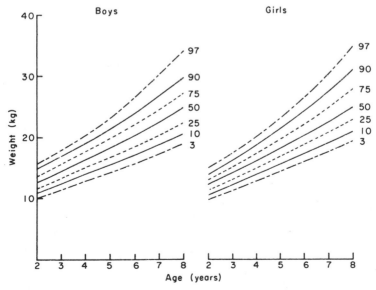

Figure 7   *Centiles for weight attained for boys and girls from the age of two to eight (Tanner et al., 1966).*

excessive fatness. The centile for weight should be compared with that for height; if there is more than a single channel difference either way (e.g. 90th weight at 50th height, or tenth weight at 50th height), then further inquiries should be made to establish whether the child has a rather extreme but perfectly healthy build, or whether he is becoming obese or excessively lean.

References

Lorenz, K. Z. (1952) *King Solomon's Ring: New Light on Animal Ways*. London: Methuen.

Stein, Z., Susser, M., Saenger, G. and Marolla, F. (1975) *Famine and Human Development: the Dutch Hunger Winter of 1944–45*. New York: Oxford University Press.

Tanner, J. M. (1962) *Growth at Adolescence*, 2nd ed. Oxford: Blackwell Scientific.

Tanner, J. M. (1978) *Foetus into Man*, London: Open Books.

Tanner, J. M., Whitehouse, R. H. and Takaishi, M. (1966) Standards from birth to maturity for height, weight, height velocity and weight velocity; British children, 1965. *Archives of Diseases in Childhood* **41**, 454-71; 613-35.

Yakovlev, P. I. and Lecours, A. R. (1967) The myelogenetic cycles of regional maturation of the brain. In Minkowksi, A. (ed.) *Regional Development of the Brain in Early Life*. Oxford: Blackwell Scientific.

Further Reading

Tanner, J. M. (1978) *Education and Physical Growth*, 2nd ed. London: Hodder & Stoughton.

2

The Development of Thinking and Reasoning

CELIA MODGIL and SOHAN MODGIL

Although there have been attempts to describe the processes of thinking since the days of Aristotle, the past few decades have seen an upsurge of interest in cognition. Studies of cognition (or mental activities) are concerned with how the individual acquires, stores, retrieves and uses knowledge. This 'cognitive revolution', as it has been termed, marks an awareness of the inadequacies of the behaviourist approach which concerns itself with outward behaviour and views humans as passive, waiting to copy and be moulded by significant persons in their environment. The cognitive approach emphasises individual initiative and activity in acquiring information and achieving coherence.

The cognitive processes are all interrelated, and it is important to realise that thinking and reasoning cannot function without input from other cognitive components: perception, memory, imagery and language. A general definition of thinking can include three basic ideas (see for example Mayer, 1983): (1) Thinking is *cognitive*. It occurs internally, in the mind or cognitive system, and must be inferred indirectly from behaviour. (2) Thinking is a *process* that involves some manipulation of or set of operations on knowledge in the cognitive system. (3) Thinking is *directed* and results in behaviour that 'solves' a problem or is directed toward solution. Reasoning can be considered a subset of thinking, occurring when the individual draws inferences or goes beyond the information given. Reasoning is therefore involved in problem-solving and involves thinking logically.

Owing to our inability to observe mental processes directly, several explanations of how thinking occurs can seem equally likely, and it is not possible to rely entirely on one theory and reject all others. Researchers tend to focus on different aspects: for example, approaches concerned primarily with perception, memory and processing skills are termed 'information-processing' approaches to cognition. In general, information-processing approaches have not attempted to describe how cognition changes according to age. By contrast, theorists concerned with studying how cognition develops emphasise that there are different ways of interpreting the environment (and of manipulating such interpretations) which correlate with a sequence of stages in development. A young child, for example, has a qualitatively different representation of the world from that of the mature adult. Further, cognitive-developmentalists argue that thinking processes depend on how an individual represents his experiences and on his developmental competence in manipulating his internal representations of those experiences.

Inspired by the profound insights of Jean Piaget, the problem of how cognitive processes develop in children has been the focus of prolific research (Modgil and Modgil, 1976). Most consequent writings on cognitive development have been presented entirely within Piaget's framework or consist of critical analyses of aspects of his thoery. For a number of years, therefore, interpreting cognitive developmental phenomena has predominantly involved agreement or disagreement with Piaget (Modgil and Modgil, 1982; Modgil et al., 1983). However, there are recent indications of attempts to integrate the cognitive development and general cognition areas; for example, by complementing and supplementing Piagetian theory with the information-processing approach.

Piaget calls internal mental structures, or representations, 'schemes', and he refers to the ways they are manipulated when thinking as 'operations'. However, Piaget emphasises that schemes do not remain static; they are continually developing in quality. Concern with the development of thinking and reasoning therefore requires that the schemes (mental structures) and the operations (internal activities) demonstrated by problem-solvers should be defined throughout the developmental sequence.

It is axiomatic that an understanding of the development of thinking and reasoning is of crucial importance to the teacher, especially to teachers of young children. Such an understanding influences the provision of educational materials; the general structure of the learning environment; the nature of the interaction between child and teacher during the learning experience, particularly discussion and the posing of stimulating questions to enhance learning; and the expectations of the teacher concerning the individual child's development and the recording of learning progress. Perhaps the main educational impact of all the research into the development of thinking and reasoning has been in making teachers aware of the need to observe children more carefully, to listen to their mental expressions more intently and to be generally more analytical in their approach, the teacher always providing the stimulus to which the child responds in a predetermined mode. Teachers increasingly take into account the child's own orientation toward, and current understanding of, situations and experiences. Such awareness requires teachers of young children to possess the highest levels of professional and academic expertise: a requirement not traditionally associated with the teacher of the young child.

The cognitive developmental approach to thinking and reasoning

The basic premise of the cognitive developmental approach is that motivation for cognitive growth is intrinsic. Piaget was first a biologist with philosophical interests in the origins of knowledge. His main biological interest in the adaptation of living things to their environment was applied to the study of the nature and origins of human knowledge. His resulting theory sees the individual as striving to survive and function successfully by taking in information in interaction with his environment. The individual's view of the environment is not passively registered, but is actively constructed throughout his lifespan by continually relating new information to existing knowledge. There is a continual interaction within the individual between the need to have organised knowledge (accommodation) and the need to seek further information (assimilation), which disturbs the current organisation which thus requires reorganisation. Information which is widely discrepant with existing knowledge will not be recorded because it cannot be related. Information which is similar, but not identical, to knowledge already stored by the individual will be assimilated by the existing mental structures. Changes in mental organisation will then take place to accommodate the new knowledge, leading on to the ability to assimilate even more complex knowledge. The individual's mental schemes, and consequently his representations of the world, therefore change systematically with development (for further discussion see Appendix in Donaldson, 1978).

Piaget describes four main stages in cognitive growth which can be identified in all persons. These stages are based on the two aspects of cognitive development already referred to, namely mental structures and operations, and represent progressively better cognitive structures accompanied by more efficient cognitive operations. Although the speed of progression through the stages may vary, the order of progression is consistent for all.

Thinking and reasoning from birth to two years

It may be considered inappropriate to focus on the first two years of life, a period of time not traditionally associated with the teacher. However, insight into these early stages is of crucial importance in demonstrating the processes involved in the development of thinking and for understanding how new experiences are related to existing ones. It is also expedient for the teacher to be aware of the amount of experience that the young child has already had in processing information and thinking before coming to school. It is the teacher's concern to *continue* this process rather than to set it into motion, and this will depend on a knowledge of the initial years.

The newborn and young babies have increasingly become subjects for psychological study, and the most sophisticated researchers are involved in exploring their abilities without embarrassment. Much of this current focus can be attributed to Piaget's pioneering work in providing the earliest and most extensive description of infant cognitive development under the name 'sensorimotor intelligence'. As Boden (1979) has pointed out, Piaget:

> does not claim merely that an account of human knowledge should, for completness's sake, include an understanding of how a baby learns the things that at birth she did not know. He claims that the basic organising principles of logic and science start developing well before language. They are evident in and generated by the baby's sensory and motor actions, whose adaptive interactions with each other and with the environment become increasingly differentiated, coordinated and skilled.

The term 'sensorimotor' means that during this period the baby learns to coordinate his senses with motor behaviour: for example, adapting the sucking reflex to search for a nipple before sucking, coordinating hand to mouth and visually following a moving object. At this stage, therefore, the child represents the world in terms of actions – sucking, kicking, reaching, dropping and shaking – thereby performing operations on actual objects rather than on internal mental representations. Piaget associates the first two years of life with the sensorimotor period.

Phillips (1981) usefully summarises Piaget's interpretations of how the child constructs his knowledge of an object:

> To know an object is not merely to register a copy of reality (its figurative aspect) but to *transform* it through assimilation to operative structures. . . The construction begins when the infant starts to coordinate various action schemes – for example, hearing and looking at the same object; reaching and grasping the same object; seeing, reaching and grasping the same object; reaching, grasping and sucking the same object. In order to construct the object scheme from those experiences, he must abstract from them the one feature that they all share – the one *invariant* among many experiences – namely, the special configuration of experiences that is characteristic of that particular object. In the initial stages of that coordination, each object with which the child interacts is to him merely a temporary node in a network of sensorimotor activities.

In this way, the very young child acquires rudimentary knowledge of objects.

Object permanence

During the sensorimotor period, the very young child demonstrates the progressive development of the concept of object permanence. At birth, the baby is dependent on the sensory stimulation of the object: when an object is removed from the visual field, the baby does not pursue it further and switches his attention to something else: apparently for him the object no longer exists. Later, the concept begins to develop and a young child will actively search for a vanished object, but cannot yet follow a contrived sequence of displacements, designed to test this interesting phenomenon. If an object is hidden in one place and then visibly moved to another hiding place, the very young child looks for it in the original place of disappearance. His object concept has not yet been sufficiently constructed to relate to a variety of context in space.

Gradually the child is able to follow displacements of an object if he witnesses all the moves, but if the object is concealed while it is moved, he will again look for it where it first disappeared. For example, Piaget reports that when a celluloid fish containing a rattle was put in a box, the box placed under a rug and then shaken so that the fish was heard in the box and then the box was removed without the fish, the infant searched energetically for the fish. However, the search was mainly in relation to the box and involved the box being turned over in all directions, followed by looking around generally. The rug received some visual attention but no attempt was made to raise it to look underneath (Piaget, 1955). The growing competence of the child's response to this problem of constructing objects when the displacements are not all visible (and involve even more complex sequences) led Piaget (1955) to conclude:

> In general terms it can be said that the child has become capable of directing his search by means of representation. Sometimes he takes note of the invisible displacements of the object and shows himself able to deduce them as well as to perceive them, sometimes, through thought, he masters a series of incasements too complex not to give rise to a true awareness of relationships.

Space

This formation of the concept of objects is related to the organisation of space. Gradually, the young child begins to move objects about and experiment with the relations between objects, rather than being totally concerned with the object itself. Piaget also provides a detailed analysis of children's development in the spatial field. For example, for a baby of approximately six months, he cites the general difficulty of conceiving of the relation of objects with one another (in contrast to the relation of objects with the subject himself). It is this general difficulty which prevents the child from realising that two objects can be independent of each other when the first is placed upon the second. To illustrate: the infant tries to grasp a matchbox, but when he is at the point of reaching it, the experimenter places it on a book; the infant immediately withdraws his hand, then grasps the book itself. He remains puzzled until the box begins to slide off the book and thanks to this accident he dissociates it from its support (Piaget, 1955).

Late in this sensorimotor stage, children are able to represent spatial interrelations and represent displacements of the body itself. Piaget cites an example of a young child throwing a ball under a sofa. The child was able to realise that the ball had passed beneath the sofa, and accordingly set out to go behind it, circumnavigating barriers which caused her to turn her back on the place where the ball had disappeared and yet she finally arrived behind the sofa at the right place. She had therefore followed an itinerary different from that of the object and had mentally represented the invisible displacement of the ball and the detour to be made in order to find it again. Piaget's writings abound with such fascinating examples, and although his theoretical commentaries involve heavy reading, a perusal of some of his observations add greatly to an appreciation of the child's developmental challenges (Piaget, 1953, 1955).

Time

The notion of permanence implies also a dimension of time; so, together with object permanence and space, the young child develops an early awareness of time. Time, like space, is constructed little by little and involves the elaboration of a system of relations. 'Time presupposes space, for time is nothing other than the forming of relationships between the events which fill it and those which require for their formation the concept of object and spatial organisations' (Piaget, 1955). As early as his reflex activity and the formation of his first habits, the baby knows how to coordinate his movements in time and to perform certain acts before others in a regular order. For instance, he knows how to open his mouth and seek contact before sucking, how to steer his hand to his mouth and even his mouth to his thumb before putting the thumb between the lips.

By the end of this sensorimotor period, the young child is able to extend the temporal series to representations and becomes 'capable of evoking memories not linked to direct perception, (succeeding) by that very fact in locating them in a time which includes the whole chronology of his universe. This does not in the least imply that this chronology is as yet well seriated or that the evaluation of duration is correct. . .' (Piaget, 1955). Nevertheless, the child becomes capable of locating in time the action of the self amidst other events. For example, Piaget recounts how the child of 19 months while sitting on the terrace of a mountain chalet is able to locate (by pointing) a range of persons named, taking into account their recent movements (Piaget, 1955).

Causality

It is not until near the end of the first year that the child demonstrates behaviour that can be attributed to an appreciation of causality (Piaget, 1955):

Up to this time the child's own activity – to the extent that he has remained incapable of attributing it to a self separate from the external world – has been conceived as the center of production of the movements of the universe. But now, that activity is not only established as limited in power by a totality of actions independent of the self, but is also recognized as subject to pressures emanating from an external universe. More precisely, the child ceases to place his own activity in the center of the world and instead conceives of it as maintaining relations of mutual dependence with objects.

He becomes a mere cause among other causes and his acts depend on external factors. However, the child is not yet capable of a representation of causality; he perceives causes, but does not yet know how to evoke them when only their effects are given.

In the latter half of the sensorimotor period, Piaget identifies the child's ability to invent, that is, to invent new means through mental combinations. 'Invention through sensorimotor deduction is nothing other than a spontaneous reorganization of earlier schemata which are accommodated by themselves to the new situation, through reciprocal assimilation' (Piaget, 1955). The child does not simply evoke the operations already performed but combines or compares the various images in his imagination. A good example is furnished in an observation which Piaget records of a child opening her mouth while looking at a slit to be widened, thus revealing the representative combinations she is in the process of realising. The child was confronted by a slightly open matchbox containing a chain. She first tried to grasp the chain through the opening. Not succeeding, she simply put her index finger into the slit and succeeded in getting out a small fragment of the chain, which she then pulled until she had completely solved the problem. When the opening of the box was reduced to 3 mm, the child tried to put her finger inside, but of course, failed. (She possessed only two preceding schemata: experience of turning the box over to empty it of its contents and sliding her finger into the slit; she was not aware of the functioning of the matchbox.) She looked at the slit with great attention; then, several times in succession, opened and shut her mouth, at first slightly, then wider and wider! Apparently she understood the existence of a cavity subjacent to the slit and wished to enlarge the cavity. 'The attempt at representation which she thus furnishes is expressed plastically, that is to say, due to inability to think out the situation in words or clear visual images she uses a simple motor indication as "signifier" or symbol' (Piaget, 1955). By opening her mouth she thus expressed or reflected her desire to enlarge the opening of the box.

This schema of imitation constituted for her the means of thinking out the situation. Soon after, she unhesitatingly put her finger in the slit and, instead of trying as before to reach the chain, she pulled so as to enlarge the opening and grasped the chain. She was, however, in later experimentation, unable to open the box when it was completely closed. The child found herself in a new situation which required unforeseen and particular adaptation. The behaviour pattern appeared to operate by sudden invention controlled by mental combination, the child foreseeing which manoeuvres would succeed. 'Moreover, the procedure conceived as being capable of succeeding is in itself new, that is to say, it results from an original mental combination and not from a combination of movements actually executed at each stage of the operation' (Piaget, 1953).

Imitation

In the above example, Piaget has identified the importance of imitation. He interprets the baby's mouth movements as an imitative representation of the opening of the box. In a primitive sense it symbolises the action which will eventually be performed on the box, apparently substituting for it mentally in the internal representation and planning of intentional action. However, motor imitation will have occurred before this, but will have been initially limited to movements that the child can already make and can see herself making. Later the child will be able to mimic actions for which she does not already possess full schemes and cannot see herself doing, implying a relative freedom of the imitative scheme from current perception. This ability leads to imitation in purposeful problem-solving. Piaget also reports incidents of the young child imitating actions which have just occurred in an attempt to understand them. Imitation of absent objects (deferred imitation) is important because it marks the beginning of the ability to use internalised imagery or verbal thought, the external imitative movements being suppressed or bypassed. Piaget also identifies the importance of play.

More recent advances in knowledge of sensorimotor thinking

It is generally agreed (Flavell, 1977; Boden, 1979) that Piaget's pioneering account of the sensorimotor period (based on just his own three children) has held up well on further investigation. A number of subsequent researchers, using larger samples of children have observed the same patterns, occurring in the same sequential order. However, recent experimentation indicates that Piaget may have been over-influenced by the young child's limited motor behaviour, thereby inferring that cognitive capacities are similarly inhibited. Using more refined experimental methods and laboratory equipment, it has been determined that the young child's perceptual capabilities particularly have been underestimated: he is in fact able to perceive the world a lot more efficiently than he can act on it. For example, the young child shows himself capable of recognising and discriminating between visual patterns presented to him. Further, he stores his experiences in the memory and they then influence his future visual responses, for example, the infant responds to novel figures and habituates (becomes bored) with unchanging familiar patterns.

In an interesting series of experiments, Fantz (1961) invented 'visual preference apparatus' on the premise that if infants were shown two patterns together and revealed a preference for one in relation to the other they must have discrimination ability, and demonstrated that babies aged between one and 15 weeks showed a clear preference for more complex patterns (concentric and chequered). In an attempt to explore their acuity (i.e. their ability to see fine detail), Fantz then required the babies to discriminate among grey and striped cards, on the expectation (demonstrated in the earlier research) that if a baby could identify a pattern he would orientate towards it. Even at less than a month, infants could see ⅛in stripes, distinguishing ¹⁄₁₆in stripes at six months. Fantz (1961) therefore supports the position that some degree of form perception is innate. Bower (1977) also illustrates the auditory and visual capabilities of the newborn and further demonstrates both their ability to perceive the difference between objects and holes and their existing awareness of the intermodal properties of objects (i.e. seen objects can be touched, heard objects can be seen and touched etc.) In addition, he shows their ability to recognise object, size and shape constancy when presented with objects in varying orientations.

A number of studies report the abilities of young infants to learn through conditioning. Siqueland and Lipsitt (1966; cited in Bower, 1977) demonstrated a baby's ability to discriminate between two stimuli and to respond appropriately. The baby was successfully conditioned by a sugar solution to turn his head to the right only when a bell sounded, not in response to a buzzer, and was even conditioned to reverse the proceedings. Flavell (1977) summarises these phenomena as follows. The baby's:

> . . . obvious motoric helplessness – his inability to manipulate his environment with his hands, to explore it by moving himself through space etc. – tends to give the mistaken impression that little cognitive learning and development could be taking place. But if he can, in fact, connect actions to reinforcements (be conditioned) and can perceptually process and retain environmental events at this tender age, he may well know more than even a Piaget could discern by naturalistic observation. . .

Flavell further usefully cites Charlesworth (1968) in relation to the infant's perceptual versus motor precocity:

> . . . early organizations of information in the form of knowledge of the environment may take place before trial-and-error motor involvement even occurs. When motor activity does take place, it is assimilated to pre-existing structures laid down by perceptual learning processes. In other words, the infant's visual system (and auditory system too, I would add) provides the initial matrix upon which later

acquisition based on tactual contact and kinesthetic, proprioceptive feedbacks are mainly built.

However, these recent insights to not deny the importance of the child's actions in enabling him to construct the external world of objects, together with their properties and functions, and they further (as Boden, 1979 comments) endorse Piaget's claim that babies are born already possessing structures with which to organize their experience. But Butterworth (1981) concludes that there is evidence for objective perception before the development of the constructive processes considered necessary by Piaget, and 'that there appears to exist a pre-established harmony between sensory perception and actions'. Piaget 'may have been wrong to rule out direct sensory experience as a means of gaining access to information which may form one of the foundations of knowing.'

Johnson-Laird (1983) in further criticism of Piaget, posits the question: 'if thought is internalized action then what is it that controls such action in the first place? . . . Moreover, what is the underlying mechanism for this mysterious process of internalization? An ability to internalize events might turn out to be nothing else than the ability to think.' However, whatever the point of origin, the tracing of developmental change is important. Butterworth emphasises the importance of moving forward to a synthesis which would include studies placing biologically given information-processing systems within a modified Piagetian framework. Papers by Bullinger, Mounoud and Vinter and by Lock and Brown (in Butterworth, 1981) reinforce 'Piaget's insistence on the qualitative transformations of early cognitive processes as the basis for development' and re-emphasise 'the continuity between structures of knowledge and their foundations in human biology'.

Considerable attention has been given in this chapter to the sensorimotor period in an attempt to initiate the teacher into the processes which appear to operate in the origins of thought and in early thinking activity, and to present the individual as an active information-processor, attempting to make sense of his environment (aided by some preprogramming), organise his experiences and have an effect upon them. It should be emphasised again that the child has had a vast amount of thinking experience before entering the formal educational context, and that it is the teacher's concern to continue rather than to set this process into motion. Within the acknowledgement of the shortcomings of Piaget's theory, the detailed documentation of the very young child's encounters with his environment provides stimulation and profound insight for anyone concerned with the development of children's thinking and reasoning.

Thinking and reasoning in early childhood

In alignment with the Piagetian developmental sequence, the characteristic thinking and reasoning of early childhood (from two to seven years) is termed the 'preoperational stage'. Piaget divides the stage into two sub stages: 'preconceptual' and 'intuitive'. However, as the stage is generally one of increasing symbolic functioning, characteristics of the stage as a whole will be dealt with rather than a chronological account.

The key feature of this stage is the child's achievement of a rudimentary ability to manipulate symbols which represent the environment. Bruner (Bruner et al. 1966) refers to this stage as the 'iconic' stage, focusing on the manipulation of images (icons) in the child's thinking at this age. Phillips (1981) usefully paraphrases Piaget's analysis of the qualitative transformation during this stage:

> The preoperational child has signifiers (such as words and images) in his repertoire, and can differentiate them from significates (internalized 'representations in the broadest sense' of earlier experiences to which the words or images may refer), whereas the sensorimotor child apparently perceives the signal and the rest of the situation as a single unit – for example, 'tinkle-on-blow-taste-of-soup', or 'hat-on-mother-go-away' or even 'pillow-thumb-sleep'. Piaget sometimes refers to such a signal as an index. An index is an undifferentiated part of a total situation. . . In each case, the subject responds to the index as if it *were* the total situation. The 'signal meaning' of the sensorimotor period is of that kind. The preoperational child, on the other hand, can make an internal response that represents an absent object or event. And he can differentiate that signifier (an internal process that represents tinkle-on-bowl, hat-on-mother, or pillow and thumb-sucking) from its significate (the process that represents taste-of-soup, mother-go-away, or going-to-sleep).

Piaget emphasises that the first signifiers are not linguistic signs (words) but unique private symbols which do not have words, e.g. opening and closing of the mouth represents opening and closing of the matchbox in the example given above. This is an imitation and when imitations become internalised, Piaget refers to them as images. Images are the initial internal signifiers, whereas the significates are the unique individual meanings they have for an individual child. Words (capable of being communicated and socially agreed) are then assimilated into the child's individual systems of significates, which continue to expand through the processes of assimilation and accommodation. However, notwithstanding such mental advance, the child's thought remains qualitatively different from that of the older child and adolescent.

Of particular note is Piaget's description of a prevalent form of thinking during these years which he refers to as 'transduction'. The preoperational child reasons from particular to particular, instead of following the accepted laws of reasoning associated with the mature thinking processes of deduction (moving from the general to the particular) and induction (proceeding from the particular to the general). Piaget (1951) defines transduction 'as an inference that is non-regulated (non-necessary) because it bears on schemas which are still halfway between the individual and the general'. Children draw implications – if x, then y – without there being any reliable relationship between the two occurrences. For example, amongst the many protocols given, Piaget (1955) cites the child as concluding that ' "Daddy's getting hot water, so he's going to shave" (2 years 4 months); "She hasn't got a name"(of a little girl a year old) – "Why?" – "Because she can't talk" (2 years 9 months); an afternoon when she had not had her nap: "I haven't had my nap so it isn't afternoon" (4 years 10 months).' The implication drawn from hot water is shaving; not talking implies no name and no nap results in no afternoon. Piaget suggests that this kind of reasoning occurs because the child has only preconcepts with which to make the inferences: he has only a limited, personal concept of shaving and hot water which have not been incorporated into general organised structures of classes and relations. Piaget generally regards this stage as a semilogical or prelogical stage.

Piaget focuses on a number of further limitations which he has identified at this stage. It is here proposed to follow Flavell's (1977) categorisation of these limitations and to adopt his strategy of contrasting what is distinctive about thinking in early childhood with that of the accomplishments of middle childhood. The limitations as categorised by Flavell, derived from Piaget's developmental account, include: 'perceived appearances versus inferred reality'; 'centration versus decentration'; 'states versus transformations'; and 'irreversibility versus reversibility'. As a simple illustration, Piaget's classic 'conservation of liquid quantity task' will be selected. Piaget devised a multiplicity of tasks which he administered to identify the qualitative differences in children's thinking at different ages (concerned with number, logic, quantity, time, velocity, space etc.). The conservation of liquid quantity task involves the child agreeing that two identical glass containers hold identical amounts of water. The water from one container is poured into a third, taller and thinner container, while the child watches. The child is then asked if the two amounts of water remain identical, or whether one container now contains more water than the other.

In relation to 'perceived appearances versus inferred reality' the younger child generally concludes that the taller and thinner container has more water in it than the other container. This response is made apparently because the younger child makes judgements on 'the basis of the immediate, perceived *appearances* of things'; being 'prone to accept things as they seem to be, in terms of their outer, perceptual, phenomenal, "on-the-surface" characteristics'. The older child is able to go beyond appearance to infer that the two quantities remain the same: he makes an inference about underlying reality. Flavell (1977) adds the proviso that this does not suggest that young children never make inferences about unperceived states of affairs, but there is a general propensity in this respect, identifiable within early childhood.

As regards 'centration versus decentration', the younger child apparently concentrates solely on one aspect of the task and fails to pay attention to other relevant factors. He is apparently most influenced by the respective heights of the liquid within each container. The older child is capable of 'decentring' and relates the height differences to the differences in widith of the containers. He therefore takes into account all the relevant factors in his thinking before making a judgement. O'Bryan and Boersma (cited in Flavell, 1977), using a special camera to record eye movements, gave further credence to Piaget's identification that the younger child fixes on the dominant part of the visual presentation and that the older child demonstrates a range of eye movements covering the range of factors inherent in the task.

'States versus transformations' refers to the partitioning of the events occurring in the liquid quantity task. There is an initial state, when the two containers contain equal quantities of water, and a final state, when two containers of differing shape contain identical amounts of liquid, although the perceptual appearance confuses the reality of the situation. Intermediate between these two states is a transformation which links the two states together. Piaget identified the tendency in younger children to focus on the states rather than the intermediate transformations between the states. Their thinking during problem-solving is generally not capable of retaining all the earlier states of the problem and is not sufficiently developed to anticipate further states or events. Their attention is focused on the present and the immediate. As can be anticipated, the older child is able to take all the events into account and arrive at a reliable solution.

The above examples imply a lack of flexibility in the thinking of the young child, and 'irreversibility versus reversibility' refers to a further limitation in early thinking processes. Piaget discusses the reversibility of thought which is discernible in the older child. He is capable of recognising that the final state of the liquid quantity task can be negated by pouring the liquid back into the original container and further he can relate the increase in height of the liquid to the decrease in width, thereby demonstrating an ability to provide compensation-type explanations and deal with invariance amid transformations (better known as the ability to conserve).

Piagets' publications testify to the limitations in the thinking of the young child within a wide range of thinking situations. He gives lengthy accounts of the young child's inaccurate responses to a variety of tasks. As a result, Piaget has been accused of presenting the mind of the younger child primarily in negative terms. However, Flavell (1977) attempts to redress the balance by making reference to some of Piaget's lesser known and non-translated works in which, together with co-workers, he has focused on the preoperational child's ability to cope successfully with some invariants. Under the categorisation of identities and functions, Piaget and co-workers describe the preoperational child's abilities to cope with some 'qualitatively describable constancies, consistencies, recurrent environmental regularities, predictable covariations among actions, objects and events. . .' (Flavell, 1977).

Subsequent evaluation of the thinking of the young child

As Boden (1979) emphasises, 'the main thrust of Piaget's work is not to make essentially negative points about what children cannot do'; he views progression 'not as the passage from an absence of understanding to its presence, but as the evolution of a superior, better-differentiated form out of a more lowly one'. However, Piaget's work in relation to the young child has been considerably challenged. Donaldson (1978) particularly questions Piaget's methodology and his notions of the 'egocentricity' of the young child. She considers that the tasks which Piaget administered to children which relate to his emphasis on the egocentricity of the young child are incomprehensible to young children (particularly the 'mountains task' which concerns the ability to take account of what someone else will see who is looking at the same object as oneself from a different viewpoint). According to Donaldson, the 'mountain task' is abstract in the sense that it is devoid of all 'basic human purposes and feelings and endeavors'; she comments:

> One obstacle that stands in the way of better understanding is that those who study such topics are, for the most part, accustomed to abstract and formal modes of thought to the point where they find it hard to appreciate that degrees of abstractness which present no kind of difficulty to them may render a task senseless and bewildering to a child. [The research worker] may often fail to decentre!

Donaldson cites methodogical experimentation by Hughes, Maratsos and Lloyd which shows children to be more able to 'decentre' or appreciate someone else's point of view than Piaget has suggested when the methodological context is less formal. Donaldson (1978) is not claiming that egocentrism is not present in childhood, but that it is present throughout life and that the developmental significance in early childhood is overstated.

Donaldson (1978) focuses on further methodological experimentation which suggests that the child's interpretation of experimental tasks is not the same as the experimenter's: the child can apparently have different expectations about the questions which are being asked dependent upon the experimental materials. The child's understanding of the language used within the experimental context can also be questioned in relation to whether it corresponds with the experimenter's intent. Donaldson considers that it makes more 'human sense' to use familiar materials to produce a task, rather than the standard Piagetian tasks. She draws a distinction between 'embedded' and 'disembedded' thought: 'embedded thought' deals with people and things in the context of fairly immediate goals and intentions and familiar patterns of events; 'disembedded thought' operates outside 'the supportive context of meaningful events' (see Modgil and Modgil, 1982).

Bryant (1974) presents evidence which suggests that young children can make inferences even though they may have some difficulty in gathering the information on which inferences can be based. Bryant's 'most important result' was the 'complete failure of children younger than six years to use the inference principle "spontaneously" '. Piaget saw this as a clear indication that young children cannot make inferences. Bryant found that they can make inferences where they are given the information which they then have to combine establishing that young children have 'the logical basis to do so'. Boden (inspired by Flavell) reiterates: 'One of the methodological problems is to decide when a child's failure is due to a lack of Piagetian structures or general principles of thinking, and when it is due to other factors (such as ignorance, incomprehension or short memory-span).' Donaldson (1978) however concludes that it does not mean that Piagetian theories about the growth of thinking are wrong in their entirety; nor that because children turn out to be in some respects closer to adults than has been supposed, they are really just like them after all: 'it may simply be that we have to look for differences elsewhere'.

It would certainly seem to be the case that more of the evolutionary richness of the young child's thinking remains to be discovered and more naturalistic longitudinal records, together with further experimental procedures, are needed for analysis. Research has been influenced by Piaget's work to such an extent that a new analysis may need to be made outside the framework and particular intents of Piaget. Young children display a great deal of thinking ability; as in the case of the six-year-old who, on noticing a disabled sign on a car parked on double yellow lines and being told that such a situation is allowed, said: 'It's not very nice to be disabled but you can park on double yellow lines.' What a wealth of knowledge and understanding this statement involved and what a profound interpretation was made, together with a demonstration of the ability to project into the position of the other person. The same is true of the child of just six who, when discussing the relative attractions of different forms of long-distance travel, concluded that flying was safer as travel by ship might involve sinking. He elaborated that air travel was safer as there were fewer vehicles in the air, the sea being cluttered with so many fishing boats. Certainly the reasoning continues to show evidence of pre-concepts but nevertheless demonstrates considerable profundity of thought and early attempts to relate variables to each other. Developmental differences can be seen in quite small aspects, for example the four-year-old who, describing the making of scrambled egg, said 'you get three eggs' (because that described her experience) and was challenged by the six-year-old: 'It doesn't have to be three eggs!' Questions are another form of revelation of children's thinking processes.

There would seem to be little doubt that methodological weaknesses exist in the Piagetian work and that children do not always respond reliably to the intentions of the experimenter. In everyday situations in school children with intentions to please make desperate attempts to come to terms with the confusing world emanating from the adult, as in the case of the six-year-old who responded to the question 'What is the difference between eight and three?' by replying 'Three you have to go round twice and eight you have to do an 'S' but join it up.' However, it is possible to note in all young children spontaneous occurrences to many of the behavioural phenomena recorded by Piaget. In relation to his observational approaches, similar examples are easily catalogued: the young child can indicate many instances of trans-ductional reasoning. After having a special cake for her birthday, the three-year-old continued to question any subsequent attractive cake with: 'Is it for my birthday?'. And whenever she saw a long expanse of high fence adjacent to the pavement she said 'This is Helen's house' since Helen's house had previously been noted as having a long stretch of fence included in its approach.

Conservation phenomena were demonstrated spontaneously in the example of the five-year-old who found it difficult to eat breakfast when under pressure to get to school on time and responded favourably only to eating a whole slice of bread and butter spread with marmite and cut into four triangles. One morning he decided in favour of having the whole piece cut in half so that he did not 'have to eat so many pieces'. This is an illustration of the difficulty young children may have in quantifying in relation to transformation of states. The child of approximately three years who, looking from a distance at cows standing adjacent to each other but facing in opposite directions said 'Look at that cow with two heads', demonstrated the propensity (at least initially) to be influenced by the immediate perceptual appearance. The difficulties of the concept of time can be demonstrated in the statement of the preoperational child who, while watching a favourite television programme and needing to go to the bathroom, asked the remaining children not to 'let the programme finish before I come back'. Such everyday occurrences which can be noted in young children's thinking provide further credence to Piagetian notions, although the inadequacies of his theory have to be acknowledged.

Thinking in middle childhood

The older child has a quantitative attitude towards many cognitive tasks and problems. Around seven years of age, the construction of operational structures gives the child the means to know the world within the systems of logical classification, seriation, numbers, spatial and temporal coordinates and causality. These systems and operations include such acts as those of compensation and of identity and reversibility.

An illustration of these 'concrete operations' concerns the classification of objects according to their similarity or difference. This is accomplished by including the subclasses within larger and more general classes, a process that implies inclusion. During the stage of concrete operations, mobile and systematic thought organises and classifies information. Thought is no longer centred on a particular state of an object: it can follow successive changes through various types of detours and reversals (as demonstrated earlier) but the operations remain tied to practical concrete situations (concrete operational stage) and can only project into the hypothetical as an extension of the present and the actual. Seven-year-olds can demonstrate initial difficulty in dealing with such less demanding projections into the hypothetical as: 'The day before yesterday was Tuesday, what day will it be tomorrow?'

Other theorists and the relation of language to thinking

Other theorists of cognitive development have concerned themselves more than Piaget with the role of language in thinking. A major change in the child's thinking apparently occurs at about the time that language is becoming proficient. It has yet to be determined how these two events are related: is internal representation made possible through the emergence of language or is it only with the ability to represent the environment internally that language has a meaning? A further possibility is that the two have little interrelation, and are not causal to each other but develop separately, at least initially.

According to Piaget, cognitive development does not depend on language; cognitive development begins early in life long before children can formulate words. Piaget has been accused of not according sufficient attention to language, although he emphasises its importance in the later stages of thinking. Boden (1979) points out that Piaget insists that before understanding can be internalised linguistically it must exist in a practical form. Drawing on Sinclair (1971), Boden writes:

> Piagetians see the baby's sensorimotor action patterns as essential developmental conditions for the acquisition of syntax – and criticise Chomsky's stress on the 'innateness' of grammatical structures accordingly . . . Just as sensorimotor coordinations provide the structural seeds of logic so they allow for the development of abstract linguistic relations such as word-order, noun and verb, subject and object, and recursively embedded phrases; it is because the stage-5 baby has developed many levelled goal-hierarchies that she has the structural basis for assimilating sentences like 'Put the teddy with the brown eyes on the table'. And these primitive sensorimotor coordinations are further developed by practical action in the preoperational stage.

Russian theorists maintain that thought and speech have different routes. According to Luria (1961), in the early stages speech is only a means of communication with others; subsequently, it becomes a means whereby the individual organises experience and regulates his actions and gradually becomes more significant in the control of behaviour. Vygotsky (1934) emphasises the significant role that language may play in the development of internal representational ability and places importance on the labelling process in the formation of concepts; however, the issue of the causal relation between language and thought is not resolved.

Bruner (Bruner et al. 1966) concludes that language and thought have separate roots, language emanating from biological origins and thought from experience. At approximately six or seven years, the child's thinking catches up with language, and language begins to be used in effective problem-solving. Bruner therefore accounts for the progression in cognitive processing that occurs at Piaget's concrete operational stage by emphasising the role of language development, rather than Piaget's stress on reversibility and other mental representations. Bruner suggests three different modes of representing the world rather than Piaget's four periods of cognitive development: 'enactive' (synonymous with sensorimotor); 'iconic' (synonymous with preoperational) and 'symbolic', which is similar to operational thinking but which emphasises the use of language and symbols (see also chapter 4).

Modifications of Piaget's theory

Attempts have been made to 'recast cognitive-developmental psychology into the language and methods of modern information processing' (Mayer, 1983). The information-processing approach (influenced by computer technology) aims to develop a detailed account of the actual cognitive activities underlying the child's problem-solving performance rather than the general structural explanations provided by Piaget (influenced by biological concepts). Mayer (1983) cites the work of Case in promoting the cognitive components of strategies and working memory as requiring modification within Piaget's theory. Influenced by earlier work, Case emphasises the acquisition of information-processing strategies in cognitive development in terms of the number of different pieces of information the child can hold in active memory at one time. In relation to the development of strategies, simple strategies become more automatic with frequency of use, gradually becoming modified into more powerful strategies.

Case reports the results of an experiment which reveals four basic strategies ranging in number of steps and number of items to be held in working memory, and correlating with the increasing age of the child. As Mayer (1983) comments:

> In Case's revision of Piagetian theory, the level of the child's strategy depends on the amount of attentional energy available in working memory – what Pascual-Leone calls M-space (Case, 1974). Early in development, even a simple strategy requires much attentional energy because each step must be monitored. Thus a child does not have attentional energy available for holding many items in working memory. However, once a strategy has become automatic, through much practice, it no longer requires as much attention. Thus, there is

more attentional energy available for holding more items in working memory so a child may move on to a more complex strategy, and so on. Increasingly sophisticated strategies develop because simple strategies become automatic, freeing space in working memory for more use in monitoring more complex stragegies.'

Siegler (1976, 1978, cited in Mayer, 1983) is another authority who has suggested that cognitive development may be explained in terms of the acquisition of more complex strategies of information processing, while debate continues as to whether the increased holding capacity that comes with age is due to improvements in memory or to increased ability to group items usefully (chunking).

The teaching of thinking

Piaget's stages emerge in a fixed order but the speed of development can vary. Much attention has been focused by subsequent researchers on attempts to accelerate progression through the stages. Improvements have been demonstrated in attempts to train children to deal with Piagetian tasks, although in a number of studies it is reported that effects are most marked for children who already give indication of transition to the next stage. Kemler (1982), however, recently stated that 'Although not everyone would agree. . ., training successes are starting to outnumber reported training failures in the literature. Thus, . . . the position that the older elementary school child has qualitatively different concepts from the younger child is far less secure than it seemed several years ago.'

Siegler's work (1976, 1978 cited in Mayer, 1983) in a more information-processing context demonstrated that the giving of feedback and training in encoding helped children to develop more adequate strategies. This again was most beneficial for children already showing signs of movement to more sophisticated levels. Siegler's work further suggested that rudimentary scientific thinking is possessed by young children: his observations (see Kemler, 1982) indicate that young children:

> . . . apply rules to the solution of problems. Their predictions are guided by systematic hypotheses. Moreover, through observations that disconfirm their hypotheses, children can learn more sophisticated or more correct rules. But not just any opportunities for feedback will benefit the child. The instructor must be sensitive as to whether or not the child encodes (attends to) the critical properties of the new information that is to be learned from. If the child does not, then specific training to pay attention to these properties of the situation must precede the opportunity to learn from feedback.

There is then the growing suggestion that performances in thinking by the younger child are a function of strategies, skills and specific knowledge which can be modified rather than viewed as fixed limitations. 'The ability to perform any task is, in principle, a function of three factors: strategies, factual knowledge and capacity. Both strategies and factual knowledge are modifiable. They are nonfixed attributes of the performer susceptible to training. Capacities are not modifiable by experience. Capacities can change over time, but only as a function of maturation' (Kemler, 1982). A distinction between fixed and non-fixed limitations therefore has to be made. A further complication is that knowledge, strategy and capacity limitations must interact with each other. As Kemler (1982) elaborates:

> Executing certain strategies may depend on having particular know-ledge (e.g. recording the digit string 1963 as the year that John F. Kennedy was assassinated) or having sufficient capacity (e.g. being able to hold 1-9-6-3 in memory while simultaneously retrieving an event associated to the year 1963). Moreover, as the skill in executing strategies increases, the demand that the strategy makes on current capacity decreases. The relation works the other way around, too. The more capacity, the easier it is to acquire and to produce sophisticated strategies. The conclusion, then, is that we can rarely pinpoint one or another type of limitation as the focus of a child's difficulty in a particular task.

The particularly discernible quality that older children have when compared with younger children is the acquisition of a strategy to use strategies. 'What distinguishes younger and older children is the degree to which such routines are brought under conscious control and are available for self-selection and self-monitoring, so that they can be deployed flexibly and efficiently, (Kemler, 1982). A more metacognitive approach is perhaps called for to make the thinker sensitive to the limitations of his own cognitive routines, although such routines will naturally expand and develop through the school years and ultimately call on levels of abstract thinking which are still generally considered the thinking province of the adolescent and adult.

Implications for teachers of young children

Educational approaches would seem to need to take account of the propensity within the child to self-regulate and structure cognitive processes. As Boden (1979) reflects:

> Piaget's concept of intrinsically motivated exercise (functional assimil-ation) applies to the schoolchild no less than to the baby. It implies that children are not naturally motivated primarily by external rewards or Skinnerian 'reinforcements' (excessive use of which in schools may warp their spontaneous development) and it implies also that each child will develop gradually at her own rate, having a natural tendency to differentiate her intellectual powers but little interest in learning

strings of unstructured – and so largely unintelligible – facts. Premature teaching may be worse than useless since it may mask radical incomprehension by a spurious 'understanding' and so divert both teacher and child from the imminent structural developments that should be claiming their attention.

Piaget has replaced the traditional view of the child as a passive respondent to environmental pressures with one of the child as an active seeker of solutions to problems.

Piaget's focus on the importance of assimilating new information to existing structures implies that initial school learning should be based on experiences that children have already acquired before coming to school. Learning needs to be similar but not identical to these experiences; if it is too widely discrepant it cannot be related. Subsequent work has suggested that young children respond best to informal context in which materials have familiarity, progressively generalising to more objective contexts; see Donaldson's (1978) distinction between embedded and disembedded thought. The development of thinking and problem-solving strategies would therefore seem to take place best within the context of the children's general learning environment. That is, it should be related to the basic provision of a range of representational materials (dramatic, constructional and other media); scientific and mathematically orientated materials; collections of all kinds (natural science; objects made from various materials; collections on the basis of a variety of criteria), all of which provide unlimited opportunities for grouping, classifying, class inclusion, seriating, relations, invariance in relation to transformational states and all the aspects of operational intelligence given credence by Piaget. Teachers of young children need to prepare activities in relation to the thinking opportunities inherent in such environmental provision, based on knowledge of children's thinking development. More spontaneous use can also be made of all the points of individual and general interest which arise within the daily lives of young children. Thus, the concrete nature of the child's thinking is taken into account: thinking being based on concrete activities with opportunities to act upon objects for eventual mental representation, the teacher guiding the child to attend to structurally significant aspects of the situation.

Piaget has emphasised that understanding can only occur in a linguistic form if it is based on practical experience: emphasis on spoken language alone does not develop intelligence. Piaget would, however, acknowledge the importance of language to support thinking, and it would seem essential for teachers therefore to encourage children to discuss their activities and to introduce relevant language in an active context. It is important to remember though that language is not always a reliable guide to conceptual development: children's understanding of words changes with time and is dependent on ever-widening experience, with concepts that are being constantly modified.

Analysis of children's responses to materials and environmental problems together with an examination of their limitations and 'errors' provides insight into their thinking processes and their current view of the world. Teachers need to spend time observing young children's responses and sensitively assessing their current thinking levels in order to determine further relevant problems to pose and accompanying questions to ask. More recent work on children's thinking and problem-solving would suggest the necessity of supporting cognitive development with relevant use of language, together with assisting the child to process relevant information and cues and encouraging the development of more efficient strategies (e.g. organisation strategies to help memory performance, effective routines for approaching thinking situations and for generalising them to other similar situations). These forms of assistance should occur within the everyday learning environment and be based on the teacher's knowledge of the development of thinking and on her analytical record-keeping in relation to each child. An individual approach would seem essential therefore, and it is obvious that more research work is needed in this area, particularly in relation to task analysis in the context of young children's thinking.

We can question, with Donaldson (1978), whether we must accept it as inevitable that only a small minority of people can ever develop intellectually to a high level of competence. Children come to school already skilled in thinking and the use of language and can deal effectively with 'real-life' situations. But, as Donaldson (1978) comments, the child 'has only a very limited awareness of the means that he uses for coping and he does not reflect upon them in abstraction from the contexts in which he employs them. . . he cannot call them into service deliberately when the compelling purpose has gone.' It can be stated (as Donaldson does) that education as it has developed requires the child to tackle problems which do not arise out of his familiar framework and which are presented in 'abrupt isolation' by a person 'whose purposes are obscure'. Once the importance of this is recognised, Donaldson states, and we develop an 'understanding of what is involved in moving beyond the bounds of human sense and learning to manipulate our own thinking in the new disembedded modes. . . we shall be able to help many children to become competent thinkers in these new modes if we choose to do so.'

References

Boden, M. (1979) *Piaget*. London: Fontana.
Bower, T. G. R. (1977) *A Primer of Infant Development*. San Francisco: W. H. Freeman & Co.
Bruner, J. S., Olver, R. R. and Greenfield, P. M. (1966) *Studies in Cognitive Growth*. New York: Wiley.
Bryant, P. (1974) *Perception and Understanding in Young Children: an Experimental Approach*. London: Methuen.

Butterworth, G. (ed.) (1981) *Infancy and Epistemology: an Evaluation of Piaget's Theory.* Brighton: Harvester Press.

Donaldson, M. (1978) *Children's Minds.* London: Fontana.

Fantz, R. (1961) The origin of form perception. *Scientific American* **204**, 66-72.

Flavell, J. H. (1977) *Cognitive Development.* New Jersey: Prentice-Hall Inc.

Johnson-Laird, P. N. (1983) Thinking as a skill. In Evans, J. B. T. (ed.) *Thinking and Reasoning: Psychological Approaches.* London: Routledge & Kegan Paul.

Kemler, D. G. (1982) Cognitive development: foundations and directions. In Worell, J. (ed.) *Psychological Development in the Elementary Years.* New York: Academic Press.

Luria, A. R. (1961) *The Role of Speech in the Regulation of Behaviour.* Harmondsworth Penguin.

Mayer, R. E. (1983) *Thinking, Problem Solving, Cognition.* New York: W. H. Freeman & Co.

Modgil, S and Modgil, C. (1976) *Piagetian Research: Compilation and Commentary.* Windsor: NFER.

Modgil, S and Modgil, C (eds) (1982) *Jean Piaget: Consensus and Controversy.* London: Holt, Rinehart & Winston.

Modgil, S., Modgil, C. and Brown, G. (eds) (1983) *Jean Piaget: an Interdisciplinary Critique.* London: Routledge & Kegan Paul.

Phillips, J. L. (1981) *Piaget's Theory: a Primer.* San Francisco. W. H. Freeman & Co.

Piaget, J. (1951) *Play, Dreams and Imitation.* London: Routledge & Kegan Paul.

Piaget, J. (1953) *The Origin of Intelligence in the Child.* London: Routledge & Kegan Paul.

Piaget, J. (1955) *The Construction of Reality in the Child.* London: Routledge & Kegan Paul.

Vygotsky, L. S. (1934) *Thought and Language,* 1962 ed. Cambridge, Mass: MIT Press.

Further Reading

Boden, M. (1979) *Piaget.* London: Fontana.

Bower, T. G. R. (1977) *A Primer of Infant Development.* San Francisco: W. H. Freeman & Co.

Donaldson, M. (1978) *Children's Minds.* London: Fontana.

Flavell, J. H. (1977) *Cognitive Development.* New Jersey: Prentice-Hall Inc.

Modgil, S., Modgil, C. and Brown, G. (eds) (1983) *Jean Piaget: an Interdisciplinary Critique.* London: Routledge & Kegan Paul.

Phillips, J. L. (1981) *Piaget's Theory: a Primer.* San Francisco. W. H. Freeman & Co.

3

The Growth of Intelligence and Creativity in Young Children

DENNIS CHILD

Perhaps one of the most intriguing capacities possessed by the human race is that which enables it to examine and solve problems, theoretical or practical, symbolic or real, with or without (in some cases) the need to handle the 'raw material' of the problem. We can devise and shape tools which extend our bodies (amplifiers, lenses, levers, agricultural equipment) and express ourselves symbolically (words, numbers, musical notes, paintings), thereby creating new objects and ideas from old ones. We can do more than just survive: we can adapt to many kinds of novel situations; we can scheme and make provision for the future in the comfort of a cave or a living room. It is this ability to comprehend and reason, enabling us to adjust ourselves to our environment, that has intrigued philosophers and psychologists from early times, and we still know very little about it. But the desire and need to study the capacities that it represents are obvious and necessary for a race so dependent upon the exploitation of the environment, and no course of study in education would be complete without a consideration of the issues relevant to the nature and nurture of these capacities since much of our formal educational system is devoted to developing and exercising them.

There are many considerations possible in the study of reasoning and problem-solving (learning, motivation, temperament and so on) which are mentioned elsewhere in the book. Here we shall concentrate on those aspects involving the assessment of mental functioning ('higher mental processes') which are thought to accompany reasoning. Ideally, psychologists have sought some measure of an individual's general and specific competence across the whole range of problem-solving situations as well as trying to map out the developmental aspects of intellectual growth. But the best we have been able to do so far is to produce tests which sample an unknown fraction of this competence or to give qualitative descriptions of the stages through which we pass *en route*. Most readers will already be familiar with these so-called 'intelligence' tests. Those who have not been on the receiving end as candidates for selection at 11+, work, college or university will doubtless have read about them. Their use in school-selection is declining rapidly, but they continue to find a place in many primary and secondary schools where teachers like to have some baseline knowledge of a child's capacities. They are also used by the School Psychological Service as one of a number of clues to the analysis of intellectual and behavioural problems for clinical and educational purposes. Job selection and research programmes can also involve measures of intelligence. The importance of this subject for those concerned with the very young stems from the fact that the early years are crucial in the extent and direction of intellectual development, and it has become increasingly recognised that many older children's achievement problems arise from deviant or delayed development in pre-school or early school years.

The other area with which this chapter is concerned, namely creative talent and its exploitation in the young, has received impetus from recent interest in measuring 'creativity'. While the concept of creativity and its connection with intelligence are still hotly debated, it seems appropriate to tackle the problems of definition, discuss the work done to identify creative capacity and pinpoint some of the research into encouraging creativity in the young.

Defining intelligent behaviour

Psychologists, along with other behavioural scientists, are notoriously poor at finding definitions with which they all agree. This is in the nature of their subject, and reflects the complexity of the concepts which it contains. Intelligence is no exception. Indeed, part of the price paid for making the term as commonplace as it is today is that it has become subject to two major over-simplifications. The first is the notion that intelligence is a quality of exact size which starts at birth, grows to about 15 years of age and degenerates thereafter. The second is that intelligence tests will tell us this 'size' very accurately. Such over-simplifications will remain unavoidable if psychologists persist in attaching figures to concepts, and in using such circular definitions as 'intelligence is what intelligence tests measure'. To avoid the dangers of regarding an abstraction as if it were a possession of precise dimensions (reification), Miles (1957) recommends that we drop the term intelligence altogether and replace it by the term 'intelligent behaviour'. The latter term helps to emphasise the active nature of the concept. For present purposes, however, we shall asume that readers are fully aware of the dangers, and consequently the expressions 'intelligence' and 'intelligent behaviour' will be used synonymously.

As psychologists are not agreed on a single definition for intelligence, probably because of the differing emphases which they place on the attributes which can justifiably be regarded as intelligent behaviour, we must look for certain trends behind the various definitions which they advance and see if we can group them. One useful classification of definitions is given by Vernon (1960) who divides them into (*a*) biological (*b*) psychological and (*c*) operational. Briefly, the biological definitions stress adaptation to the environment and actions which are of survival value. The idea of man as a successful member of the animal kingdom (Darwin's survival of the fittest) is evident in these views. However, they are really too broad and not as yet capable of being reliably tested. Psychological definitions are mainly to do with reasoning, relational thinking and with what Terman calls 'capacity for abstract thinking' (see Vernon, 1960). Agreement about the kinds of item which might tap this capacity has never been reached, and the wide range of problems found in intelligence tests is evidence of this lack of agreement. Operational definitions are very much the province of the behaviourist school in psychology, which makes no assumptions about internal mental processes but only observes the outward manifestations of what is defined as intelligent behaviour. 'Operational' means 'definable in observable ways'. If it is decided, for example, that spatial orientation of shapes constitutes an intellectual skill, then the behaviourist simply designs items which allow people to demonstrate that skill.

No test has ever been devised which incorporates all the requirements of the above three groups of definitions, particularly of the biological group. However, a definition which comes close to a compromise and has a 'commonsense' feel about it is one provided by Heim (1970): 'intelligent activity consists in grasping the essentials in a given situation and responding appropriately to them'. However, even here there still remains the problem of deciding what is to be regarded as intelligent activity, and finding valid ways of identifying its presence.

The crucial question, then, is what do we regard as intelligent behaviour and how can it be assessed? The answer requires value judgements. Is musical composition intelligent behaviour? Does success in business or the speed at which a baby learns its mother tongue count? All these activities involve reasoning of one kind or another: grasping essentials and responding appropriately. In the design of any assessment of intelligence should we expect to find questions relating to all these and the many other activities we could include? In fact, up to now, tests have been based upon the debatable assumption that a general level of mental proficiency in all these activities can be estimated from performance in only a small sample of them. Those readers who have taken, or seen, an intelligence test will recall that this sample usually contains items on memory, spatial relations, analogies, number problems and verbal reasoning. These are indeed the specific abilities thought by most psychologists to contribute to a general fund of intelligence which underlies any activity involving Heim's 'grasping the essentials in a given situation and responding appropriately to them'.

The nature of intelligence: Hebb's view

All the definitions above reflect speculations about the nature of intelligence, but it is to Hebb (1948) that we owe recognition for a developmental theory of intelligence. (Piaget likewise has a considerable amount to say about cognitive development, but this has been covered in chapter 2.) Hebb's basic proposition is that intelligence is a function of the central nervous system. This he calls 'Intelligence A', genetic potential (resulting from the possession of a brain and central nervous system or CNS) which forms, retains and reorganises sensory input. He then goes on to define 'Intelligence B' as the mental proficiency arising from the opportunities afforded by environmental circumstances in the exercising of Intelligence A. Both Hebb and Piaget lay great stress on the sensorimotor activity of the young in acquiring intelligent behaviour patterns. Thus, sensory deprivation in early childhood is a grave disadvantage for later performance. As the CNS and brain are still developing during childhood, it is considered essential to give the widest sensory experience at this time. Evidence (Hebb, 1948) from brain-damaged children and adults supports the view that in childhood the brain is in the process of building up schemata (patterns of actions – mental or physical – resulting from experience).

Intelligence A is a theoretical construct. There is no way we can assess it with certainty because the influences of the environment (pre- or post-natal) are effective from the moment of conception. Some psychologists, however, (notably those who have worked on the relative contributions of heredity and environment such as Eysenck, Cattell and recently Jensen) believe it is possible to 'partial out' the respective influences of heredity and environment either by using statistical procedures or 'culture fair' tests. The latter are said to overcome the cultural–educational influences chiefly by using non-verbal problems. Whilst this is an extremely contentious area, it is nevertheless an important one for teachers. If we knew for certain the relative influences of nature or nurture, it would have a corresponding impact on our educational arrangements. If 80% of the variation in intelligence between children was a matter of inheritance, it would certainly produce a different educational programme from the one which would obtain if the figure of 80% was the result of the environment.

Intelligence B, which operates in all activities involving reasoning, is, as we indicated in the last section, only *sampled* by intelligence tests. Vernon has suggested that this sampling of Intelligence B measured by these tests should be given the name 'Intelligence C'. The designers of intelligence tests operate on the assumption that intelligence test scores (Intelligence C) will give an indication of the outcome of the interaction between A and B. Therefore, what we measure is more an *effect* than a *cause*. A similar theoretical stance proposed by Cattell (see Horn, 1967) in his theory of 'fluid' and 'crystallised' intelligence has been used to devise tests claiming to measure Intelligence A and B. Fluid intelligence (g_f) is relatively independent of cultural experience (and thus corresponds to the Intelligence A of Hebb) and 'flows' into most intelligent human behaviour. Crystallised intelligence (g_c) 'precipitates out' from the accumulation of experience, interacting with fluid intelligence (and thus corresponds to Hebb's Intelligence B). In contrast to Vernon's Intelligence C, Cattell takes his argument a step further by suggesting tests which distinguish between g_f and g_c. As a result, culture-free tests have been devised which give g_f scores (based on inductive reasoning, span of apprehension etc.) and g_c scores (based on verbal comprehension, number facility etc.) separately. We shall return to this later.

One widely held view amongst psychologists who have specialised in the study of human ability is the belief that intelligence can be expressed either as a general ability (Spearman called it g) or specific abilities (s) or both (however, see Heim's comments, 1970). The basis for this belief is the moderately high positive correlation which exists between the items most frequently chosen for test design. The earliest pioneers in this country (Spearman, Burt) preferred to concentrate on g as the most useful measure, whilst in America, Thurstone, Guilford and others found the specific abilities most practicable (Thurstone's 'primary mental abilities'). Most modern tests concentrate on these latter (although they will, if required, yield a general score) because detailed profiles are of greater value in diagnostic work in educational achievement or employment.

The assessment of intelligence

From the turn of the century, when Binet conducted his famous researches into intelligence testing, to the present day, a number of theoretical models of intelligence have been converted into practical assessment devices. It would be impossible and is unnecessary to go through these here (see Butcher, 1968; Child, 1981; Pyle, 1979 for details), but a few key contributions will be mentioned because they have, by and large, given rise to most contemporary forms of assessment. We shall concentrate on those tests which have been designed for use with the young child.

There are several methods of classifying tests of intelligence according to whether (a) an individual or group design is used; (b) age is a consideration; (c) general or specific abilities (or both) are needed; and (d) pencil and paper (verbal, numerical, spatial etc.) or performance tests (manipulation of objects, toys, movement skills) are appropriate. In the age range covered by this book, individual tests are undoubtedly more appropriate because young children require careful handling to sustain motivation and attention and to ensure that the level of communication is suitable. Fatigue soon sets in so that timing is crucial. Children also need to get to know the tester well for a good rapport to be established. Testing young children is a most exacting and skilled task, requiring both patience and sophistication to get the best from them. For these reasons, pencil and paper group tests are out of the question: the best media of communication are visual and auditory observation of actions and sayings.

Thus, the basic question posed for the would-be designer of tests of intelligence for young children is what can these children reasonably be expected to do in terms of their physical, mental, linguistic and social competence and development? Some tests (Bühler and Hetzer, 1935; Gesell and Amatruda, 1947; Griffiths, 1954; McCarthy, 1972; Uzgiris and Hunt, 1975) were essentially concerned with providing a developmental scale rather than fixed measures which purported to be predictive of future performance. This approach has much to commend it, because it is widely recognised that the very young have erratic spurts of growth in mental (as well as in physical and social) skills which render tests of little predictive value below the age of four or five (Bloom, 1964). For the two-to-three-year-olds, the tests mentioned above in fact placed less emphasis upon mental than upon locomotor, sensory and social performance. For example, in Griffiths' scale such activities as kicking, walking, smiling, reaction to sights and sounds, eye–hand coordination and grasping appear and can be carefully monitored from birth onwards. One importance distinction between the assessment methods available rests upon whether observations of an individual's performance are compared with others of a similar age or with a specified content such as a range of physical or mental activities. The former is known as 'norm-referencing' because performance is judged by reference to what is regarded as normal for a particular group. The latter is 'criterion-referencing' because performance is judged by reference to criteria of performance, i.e. whether a person can or cannot do a particular task irrespective of age. Norm-referencing emphasises the products of actions in relation to each other (how much); criterion-referencing is concerned with analysing processes of actions (how) (Satterly, 1981). Some of the better established tests are mentioned below.

The Binet–Simon and Terman–Merrill scales

Binet's task in 1904 was to select those children who would not benefit from an ordinary school education. He and Simon devised the first individual test for the age range two to twelve years. A version is still in use today, although more recent devices are rapidly replacing it. Therefore, only a brief account is given here. They selected many tasks which they thought would distinguish the defective and severely retarded from other children. Each item was tried out for difficulty, and graded according to the proportion of children able to answer it at a particular age (in months), thus establishing norms for the items, i.e. norm-referencing. In this way a profile for each child taking the test could be built up in terms of his competence relative to these norms. This profile became known as the child's 'mental age'. Thus a child whose chronological age, for example, was seven years exactly, but who could only answer those test items normally answered by a six-year-old, has a mental age of six years. The profile was frequently converted into a mental ratio, or the now famous 'Intelligence Quotient' or IQ, in the following way:

$$\frac{\text{Mental age}}{\text{Chronological age}} \times \frac{100}{1}$$

This formula is now rarely used. Instead the child's results are expressed as a deviation score (i.e. as a deviation from the norm for his age).

The kinds of items used by Binet and Simon for children in the age range two to seven years cover such activities as building with blocks, naming drawings (or models) or objects, using formboards (putting shapes into their corresponding slots) and tracing between parallel lines. Note the emphasis on performance rather than pencil and paper responses. The most up-to-date form of the original Binet–Simon scale is the Terman–Merrill modification of the Stanford–Binet intelligence test (Terman and Merrill, 1960).

Goodenough's 'draw-a-man' test

Anyone familiar with children's drawings cannot fail to have noticed the obvious improvement in sophistication with the child's advancing age. Apart from the purely mechanical improvement resulting from holding and manipulating crayons, pencils or brushes more surely, there is an increase in the complexity and proportion introduced into the drawings. This has been observed by many psychologists, and it was one of the earliest areas of exploration (Harris, 1963). In 1926, Goodenough showed a substantial relationship between measured intelligence and children's drawing of a man. Further advances have taken place by using a parallel test (draw-a-woman) and a third task (draw yourself) which is also used as a projection technique in the analysis of self-concepts (Harris, 1963). In the draw-a-man test, children are asked to draw the best possible whole man they can. The outcome is marked using 73 criteria (e.g. neck present, mouth present, fingers, shoulders etc.). One point is awarded for each inclusion, and, as with the other tests we have discussed, the child's results are compared with the norm for children of the same age. The final score is expressed as a deviation score (that is, as a deviation from the norm, either positive or negative) as with modern IQ scores. The correlation between the deviation scores of the Goodenough test and the Terman–Merrill score for each child is quite good (ranging between +0.4 and +0.9).

Physical and mental development scales

The long and patient researches of Ruth Griffiths (1954), using a detailed observation of children from birth to two, resulted in a mental development scale which fills the gap of the first two years of life left by the

Terman–Merrill scale. Like Piaget and Gesell, Griffiths firmly believed in a maturational theory of mental development, i.e. that there is a progression and orderliness in the unfolding of actions construed as intelligent, with babble and understanding of speech preceding talking for example, and sensorimotor activity progressing in a fairy well defined sequence (see chapter 2). If this maturational theory is correct, it should be possible to plot the steps of a child's development at particular ages, and use the results as a means of comparing the developmental rates of individual children. This is a combination of norm- and criterion-referencing.

Griffiths considered that a child's developmental rate is very largely dependent in the earliest stages upon social background and related circumstances, and that maturation reaches its fullest potential only under favourable socio-psychological conditions. Griffiths regarded (a) attainment of erect posture, (b) manipulative skills and (c) speech as the three crucial lines of progress. They are all, in the first place, motor skills, speech being the most refined and complex of the three, and they progress side by side. The rate of development is very rapid and Griffiths endeavours in her scale to provide an age-linked progression chart for five functions, i.e. locomotor (lifts chin when prone at one month; can kick a ball at two years), personal–social (regards person momentarily at one month; helps actively to dress and undress at two years), learning and speech (startled by sound at one month; names four toys at two years), eye and hand (follows a moving light with the eyes at one month; makes a brick or toy walk at two years), performance (grasps tester's hand at one month; can open a screw top at two years).

These development profiles have been used to derive a General Intelligence Quotient by using a calculation with mental and chronological ages similar to the example given in the description of Binet's work.

McCarthy (1972) has compiled the McCarthy Scales of Children's Abilities (MSCA). It is standardised for the age range two and a half to eight and a half years and will give a diagnostic profile in various verbal, spatial, memory and motor abilities. An overall score can be obtained if needed: the General Cognitive Index. Until recently, only American norms were available, but an anglicised version with norms has now been produced for the younger ages (Lynch et al. 1982). More recently, another American scale by Uzgiris and Hunt (1975), using the criterion-referencing method, has been devised for the first two years of childhood. Ordinal scales of behaviour are based on a developmental hierarchy largely in the Piagetian tradition (see chapter 2). Six areas of developmental assessment form the scales. They are the development of visual pursuit, means for obtaining desired events, imitation of voice and gesture, causality schemes for relating to objects and how objects relate in space.

The British Ability Scales

The most recent tests to emerge within the general field of intelligence are the

British Ability Scales (Elliott et al. 1983). These again are criterion-referenced and are the first scales for individual administration designed and standardised in Britain. They contain several innovations intended to give a wide profile of special abilities for children in the age range two to sixteen years. Table 1 gives some idea of these sub-scales. Notice the introduction of Piagetian type sub-scales for formal operational thinking, number concepts and social reasoning. Also of interest is the inclusion of verbal fluency (perhaps linked to creativity), verbal tactile matching and a speed test.

There are a few other scales for individual testing covering the age range from five years onwards, but they have not been used and standardised so extensively in Britain. Chief amongst these are the Wechsler Pre-school and Primary School Intelligence Scale (four to six and a half years) and several diagnostic tests in word recognition and reading.

Table 1 *Sub-scales for the British Ability Scales (from NFER-Nelson's* Catalogue of Clinical Tests and Procedures)

Organisation of the British Ability Scales Speed of information processing		Items	Age Range
1 Speed of Information Processing	4 disposable booklets of simple number exercises, differentiating between children's abilities in terms of time, not power.	40	8-17
Reasoning			
2 Formal Operational Thinking	Reasoning exercises based on illustration of pairs of boys and girls.	13	8.17
3 Matrices	Children are required to draw the correct solution in the blank square of a matrix.	28	5-17
4 Similarities	Children listen to three words (e.g. orange, strawberry, banana) and explain why they are similar.		
5 Social Reasoning	Children evaluate stories told to them from the manual. Their responses are categorised in terms of four development stages.	7	5-17
Spatial imagery			
6/7 Block Design Level and Power	Children reconstruct two-dimensional patterns using blocks. The children can be scored in two ways: for accuracy (level) and for accuracy and speed (power).	16	4-17
8 Rotation of Letter-Like Forms	A small wooden doll is placed on the opposite side of the stimulus design from the child, who has to visualise how the design appears to the doll and then select from six alternatives.	10	8-14

9	Visualisation of Cubes	Matching patterned blocks to one of four alternative pictures	18	8-17

Perceptual matching

10	Copying	Children are required to copy designs and letter-like characters while the design is in front of them.	19	4-8
11	Matching Letter-Like Forms	Matching a stimulus figure to one of six representations of it viewed from different angles.	10	5-9
12	Verbal-Tactile Matching	Two bags are used from which children are asked to select: (i) objects with certain characteristics (ii) named items.	19	2½-8

Short term memory

13	Immediate Visual Recall/	A card showing 20 objects is shown for 2 minutes. The child has to recall the objects verbally at once, and then after 20 minutes.	19	5-17
14	Delayed Visual Recall			
15	Recall of Designs	The child draws a design from memory after being shown it for 5 seconds.	19	5-17
16	Recall of Digits	Digit strings are presented at the rate of 2 digits per second and the child is asked to repeat them in the correct sequence.	36	2½-17
17	Visual Recognition	Drawings of toys and non-representational figures are shown to children for 5 seconds. They then have to select these from a number of alternatives shown on a second card.	17	2½-8

Retrieval and application of knowledge

18	Basic Number Skills	A new scale combining the original Basic Arithmetic and Early Number Scales, with the addition of 28 new items. It focuses on the number skills which will lead to a basic competence in arithmetical calculation.	68	2½-14½
19	Naming Vocabulary	Naming objects in the room or on picture cards.	20	2½-8
20	Verbal Comprehension	Children are asked to carry out operations using toys in response to verbal commands.	27	2½-8
21	Verbal Fluency	A creativity test comprising a variety of activities: object naming; deducing consequences from events; ink blot tests. This scale is scored solely on the number of distinct ideas the child produces.	6	4-17
22	Word Definitions		37	5-17
23	Word Reading		90	5-14

Convergent and divergent thinking

As mentioned above, the emphasis tends to have been on what is done rather than on *how* it is done. We present a person with tasks such as verbal reasoning, memory, number problems, and assume from the total correct responses that he or she has such and such a level of competence in comparison with others. This emphasis on products of thinking rather than processes is understandable. Products can be observed, processes cannot. We can only infer them from the products or from introspection (i.e. from a person's own description of what has gone on in his or her head during a process such as problem-solving). From the earliest days of psychology, schools of thought have been generated which show preferences for one or other end of the process–product continuum. The cognitivists (crudely, those interested in the mind and thought processes) have tended towards the process end, while the behaviourists (those interested in observing stimulus and response) have tended towards the product end. In recent years there have been signs that the cognitivist approach is beginning to attract increasing interest, and a compromise between this approach and that of the behaviourists is to be found in the model presented by Guilford (1950) in which he considers the interaction of process product and content variables in problem-solving. The model is complex, involving, according to Guilford, 120 intellectual factors, but two processes of special interest are convergent and divergent thinking.

Convergent thinking is assumed to take place when a person solves a problem having one clearly obtainable solution from the information given. This kind of strategy would certainly be used on conventional intelligence test items, multiple choice questions and most mathematical problems. Divergent thinking, on the other hand, is assumed to take place when a person answers a question having many equally acceptable answers, as, for example, when he is asked to state as many uses as possible for a spade.

Divergent thinking has been identified, largely by American psychologists, with 'creativity' (see, for example, Torrance 1962.) But the questions of the relationships between creativity, divergent and convergent thinking are so complex that we could not do justice to them here. However, four questions will be considered. These are (*a*) does divergent thinking relate to creativity? (*b*) What attempts have been made to measure divergent thinking? (*c*) Does divergent thinking relate to intelligence (or convergent thinking)? (*d*) What attempts have been made to stimulate divergent thinking in young children?

'Creativity' is such an elusive concept that it is hardly surprising to find so little agreement about how to identify it. At a commonsense level, we want to encourage children to be sensibly self-sufficient, to be capable of exploring problems and finding solutions; we want to educate them in such a way that they actively seek for as many options as possible rather than becoming trapped in mental *cul de sacs*. But whether this can be regarded as creative thinking is a source of debate. Our problem is still one of contexts. How do we correlate the inventive activities and output of a famous scientist, a famous artist and a small child? Each produces something novel, but in terms of particular media (abstract or concrete) and levels of discovery. The scientist is concerned with novelty in relation to known scientific knowledge. In a different medium, the artist (writer, poet, painter, musician) is also striving for novelty, although here the criteria are as much dependent upon the emotional effects on others as upon whether the output is novel in the world of art. For a child, the rate of development is so rapid that almost every action brings something new to his repertoire, but this is novelty in terms of the individual's previous performance and not the society in which he lives. Thus, we have levels of original performance which may be judged from personal, cultural, societal or global standpoints.

Most people have the capacity for novel, adventurous thinking. Whether we can measure individual differences in, or enhance, creative thinking is quite another matter, however, and the relationship between such measures as we have managed to devise so far and the creativity of scientists and artists has yet to be proved.

Methods purporting to measure children's creative output have been with us for at least 50 years. Some of the earliest work by McCarty (1924) relied on the analysis of drawings; this was, in fact, an extension of Goodenough's work in which the unusualness of the drawings counted as creative. Methods in the 1930s included imaginative play, dramatisation, fantasy stories, use of language, leadership and aesthetic appreciation. More 'quantitative' methods concentrating upon fluency, flexibility and originality of ideas have appeared through the work of Guilford (1950) and Torrance (1962). These methods are open-ended, and for the youngest children consist either of completion tasks or oral description. Examples are (a) the Incomplete Figures Task in which children are asked to turn a number of lines and squiggles into complete drawings (figure 1); (b) Circles and Squares, in which the child is confronted with a sheet of circles or squares and is asked to make as many objects as possible by adding lines to the circles and squares and saying what each object is; (c) the Ask-and-Guess-Test, in which several pictures taken from the Mother Goose prints (e.g. 'Tom the Piper's Son', 'Little Boy Blue', 'Pussy in the Well') are presented to the child, who is then asked to think of all the questions he can about what is happening in the pictures; (d) Product Improvement Tasks in which the child is presented with model animals (dog, monkey) and asked 'to think of the cleverest, most interesting and most unusual ways you can for changing this toy dog so that boys and girls will have more fun playing with it'.

Such open-ended questions give rise to numerous possible responses. Most often there is a time limit, although this has been criticised by those (Wallach and Kogan, 1965) who regard creative activity as requiring, in some cases, time for incubation, and who thus feel that a time imposition may staunch original responses. The child's responses are scored according to the number of responses made in the given time (fluency), the variety of response

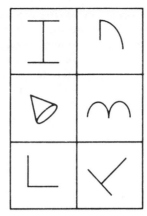

Figure 1   *Incomplete Figure Task. Instructions are given orally: by adding lines to the six figures above, sketch some object or design that no one else will think of. Try to add as much to each drawing as you can. Make up a title for each of your drawings and tell me what it is.*

(flexibility) and the uniqueness of response in terms of the total number of times a particular response has been given by the rest of the children in the sample being tested (originality).

Another set of research instruments designed by Startweather (1971) consists of formboards, a target game and an originality test. The formboards (four in number) contain scenes familiar to most children of pre-school age, such as a tree, house, playground and barnyard. Many selections can be made of objects to go with the scenes, and Startweather uses these choices to assess conformity. The other two tests are intended to assess respectively the child's willingness to attempt difficult tasks (assumed by Startweather to be a mark of the creative person) and the originality of these attempts.

The relationship between divergent thinking as measured by the kind of tasks outlined above and intelligence as measured by conventional IQ tests is a source of dispute amongst psychologists. In the greater part of the research so far, the evidence supports a relationship; most correlational studies show positive and statistically significant results (Butcher, 1968). The inference from the research seems to be that intelligence is a necessary, though perhaps not a sufficient, possession for creative behaviour. The first major work was conducted by Getzels and Jackson (1962), who in addition to obtaining only small correlations found that children scoring high on divergent thinking but relatively low on IQ ('high creatives') were characterised by nonconformity, over-achievement and a sense of humour when compared with children who scored high on IQ but relatively low on divergent thinking ('high intelligents'). This work has been savagely criticised on both statistical and methodological grounds, and reworking of Getzels and Jackson's data gives a higher value for the relationship between divergent and IQ scores. Wallach and Kogan's (1965) work deserves mention because they managed, by using a different approach, to obtain much smaller correlations. If we accept that creative activity requires time and a relaxed atmosphere, then it follows that divergent thinking tests should be presented untimed and more as a game than as a test. This Wallach and Kogan did, and by scoring for originality using only unique responses they obtained a more obvious distinction between the scores.

However, it is generally true to say that when the mathematical technique known as factor analysis is used the evidence for a relationship between factors of creativity and factors of intelligence is strong. The factor of divergency obtained so far which correlates most conspicuously with factors of intelligence is verbal (and in some researches non-verbal) ideational fluency (Sultan, 1962; Dacey et al., 1969). This factor, indeed, occurs strongly in many of the divergent thinking tests now in use, and we are therefore left wondering along with Burt (1962), whether divergent thinking tests do any more than 'form very satisfactory additions to any ordinary battery for testing the general factor of intelligence'.

A recurring theme in this area is the impact of personality on creative production. Roe (1953), MacKinnon (1961), Catell (1963) and Hudson (1966, 1968) are but a few of the researchers who have looked at the personality profiles of creative people. Such people *tend* to be single-minded, stubborn, self-assured, reserved, nonconformist, persistent, tolerant of ambiguity, and prepared to take risks. Several researchers have emphasised (Butcher, 1968) that the role of personality is indeed quite influential enough to account for an appreciable proportion of the variation which occurs in the divergent thinking scores. Whether the personality characteristics of creative people outlined above also appear in those who score well on divergent thinking tests has yet to be confirmed.

Hudson (1966) has also made the point that performance on convergent thinking (IQ) and divergent thinking tests may reflect preference and facility for particular types of problems. Thus it seems science students do much better on convergent tests than arts students, and the explanation could be the preference of science specialists for convergent types of problems. The stress has therefore been changed by Hudson from divergent thinking tests as measures of creativity to their use as measures of ability in, and preference for, thinking styles. The case for an arts–divergent thinking link is not as well founded (Nuttall, 1972).

For the teacher of young children, perhaps the most crucial question is the role she can play in developing *both* styles of thinking. Torrance is deeply concerned about the tendency of our formal system of education to foster conforming and limited intellectual perspectives. The emphasis upon traditional school subjects taught in a 'this is the right way' style may result in an over-production of convergent thinkers. To counteract this effect, several teaching schemes have been prepared. One, by Torrance and Myers (1970), is aimed at teachers who, amongst other things, want to be made aware of 'practical ways of going about the business of enhancing the creative functions of their students'. The programme is aimed at helping teachers to acquire an ability to present children with a progression of ideas from the commonplace to the unusual or strange, to free children from fear of criticism when they are being inventive, to invite children to let their ideas run free and to help children pose questions (either for the sake of gaining information or simply for thought provocation). These principles and techniques follow very much the 'brain storming' techniques proposed by Osborn (1963) and Parnes (1967), the 'psychodrama' of Moreno (1964) and the 'synectics' (or systematic brain storming after a period of concentrated research) of Gordon (1961, 1966).

A second line of approach in Britain has been elaborated by Edward de Bono (1967, 1968, 1969). De Bono is concerned to produce practical methods of teaching thinking 'in as deliberate a manner as mathematics, or history, or French'. He concentrates on process rather than content, thus making the quest for improved thinking strategies a more deliberate affair. The steps are too numerous to list in full, but they include exercises in looking for positive, negative and interesting points about ideas, searching for alternatives to more obvious solutions, looking at the consequences of decisions and so on. The idea is to break children's thinking habits so that they do not take any one process of problem-solving for granted. De Bono claims that his scheme has a marked effect on ability and attitudes.

The development of intellect

Finally, and doubtless most problematically, we must look at research and theorising about the development of intelligence. Bound up with this topic are the unanswered questions about the relative impact of inheritance and environment. Genetic and maturational theories of intelligence stress the place of genetic endowment in the unfolding of ability from the helpless child to the competent adult, while the place of the home, school and locality in directing intellectual potential is stressed by the environmentalists. In the absence of reliable evidence [see Kamin (1975) for a strong attack on much of the work linking intelligence with inheritance] about the relative contributions, it is advisable to keep our options open and assume that both nature and nurture are involved. The evidence for both is overwhelming.

Bloom (1964), in a summary of research into the stability of several human characteristics, concludes that:

> in terms of intelligence measured at age seventeen, about 50% of the development takes place between conception and age four, about 30% between ages four and eight, and about 20% between ages eight and seventeen. These results make it clear that a single early measure of general intelligence cannot be the basis for a long-term decision about an individual.

Notice also the changing rate of development, with as much change occurring in the first four years of life as in the next thirteen. One other conclusion of Bloom's is worth noting, namely that much more research is needed into the creation of descriptive accounts of environments as they affect the growth of intelligence. We do not as yet know the consequences of particular environments other than the most extreme, i.e. *marked* impoverishment or enrichment in physical and mental resources.

Beyond the age of seventeen, there is much evidence to show a continuing change in intelligence, a change which is more obviously a consequence of environmental conditions. For example, those who move on to further education tend to display increased measured intelligence, while old age brings a certain deterioration, in some people at least.

Research by Horn (1967), using Catell's theory of fluid and crystallised intelligence (see above), is of interest in that it presents a model which goes some way towards separating out the relative contributions of heredity and environment. Horn argues that as *fluid* intelligence is postulated as having its origins in biological mechanisms, it follows that it will deteriorate along with the physical deterioration which comes with old age. On the other hand, *crystallised* intelligence, being substantially a function of accumulated wisdom (i.e. of environment), can continue to grow throughout life.

Figure 2 is instructive in several ways. The overall measure of intelligence spoken of by writers such as Bloom (1964) is assumed by Horn to be the *sum* of fluid and crystallised intelligence ($g_f + g_c$ in figure 2). g_f develops alongside g_c into adolescence, but in adult life the two curves become increasingly differentiated (i.e. they get further apart). The g_c curve remains level, while g_f deteriorates with age. This illustrates Horn's thesis nicely, but we must remember, of course, that this graph is an average for a large group of individuals. A graph for one person could well be far more irregular as different influences in life dominate or recede. In addition, a graph for a person involved in an academic profession, who is called upon to use his or her intelligence during much of his or her working life, might well show a steeper rise in g_c than would a graph for a person involved in a more manual occupation.

One thing is certain. With early environmental stimulation, measures of intelligence are increased. Several research projects have shown this; a careful study by Garber and Heber (1977), known as the Milwaukee Project, was a particularly impressive example. They took 40 Black boys whose mothers all had IQs of less than 80% and lived in very poor areas. Twenty in the experimental group were given a concentrated programme for seven hours a day, five days a week intended to improve sensorimotor, language and thinking skills. The mothers were also given a programme in home-making, child care and vocational training. The programmes ran from three months to six years of age. The contrast between this and the control group which had normal upbringing on IQ scores was marked. At 12 months the scores were close but at 18 months the control group fell behind. Between two and four and a half years the mean scores were 123 (experimental) and 95 (control). By eight to nine years the experimental group had dropped to 108 and the control was 80. The experiment has not been completed yet and interest is concentrated on the extent to which this large difference of about 30 points will be maintained.

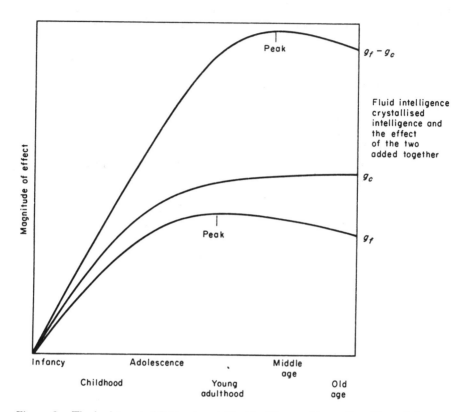

Figure 2   *The development of fluid and crystallised intelligence with age (from Horn, J. L. (1967) Intelligence – why it grows, why it declines.* Trans-action **5**, *31).*

These studies still leave some critical questions unanswered, such as what are the most favourable experiences in infancy and childhood which enhance the development of crystallised intelligence? Which child-rearing (pre- and early) school practices must we avoid as damaging to it, and which must we emphasise? How permanent is the effect of special programmes? Finally, and for teachers perhaps most fundamentally of all, how do we actually go about creating the most potent learning environment for intellectual growth once we have discovered what that environment is? The answers to this question will emerge in part II.

References

Bloom, B. S. (1964) *Stability and Change in Human Characteristics.* New York: Wiley.

Bühler, C. and Hetzer, H. (1935) *Testing Children's Development from Birth to School Age.* London: Allen & Unwin.

Burt, C. (1962) Critical notice of *Creativity and Intelligence* by Getzels and Jackson. *British Journal of Educational Psychology* **32**, 292-8.

Butcher, H. J. (1968) *Human Intelligence: its Nature and Assessment,* London: Methuen.

Cattell, R. B. (1963) The personality and motivation of the researchers from measurements of contemporaries and from biography. In Taylor, C. W. and Barron, F. (eds) *Scientific Creativity.* New York: Wiley.

Child, D. (1981) *Psychology and the Teacher,* 3rd edn. Eastbourne: Holt-Saunders.

Dacey, J., Madaus, G. F. and Allen, A. (1969) The relationship of creativity and intelligence in Irish adolescents. *British Journal of Educational Psychology* **39**, 261-6.

De Bono, E. (1967) *The Use of Lateral Thinking.* London: Cape.

De Bono, E. (1968) *The Five Day Course in Thinking.* London: Penguin.

De Bono, E. (1969) *The Mechanism of Mind.* London: Cape.

Elliott, C., Murray, D. J. and Pearson, L. S. (1983) *The British Ability Scales.* Windsor: NFER–Nelson.

Garber, H. and Heber, F. R. (1977) The Milwaukee Project. In Mittler, P. (ed.) *Research to Practice in Mental Retardation.* Baltimore: University Park Press.

Gesell, A. and Amatruda, C. S. (1947) *Developmental Diagnosis.* New York: Hoeber.

Getzels, J. W. and Jackson, P. W. (1962) *Creativity and Intelligence.* New York: Wiley.

Goodenough, F. L. (1926) *Measurement of Intelligence by Drawings.* New York: Harcourt, Brace & World.

Gordon, W. J. J. (1961) *Synectics: the Development of Creative Capacity.* New York: Harper.

Gordon, W. J. J. (1966) *Making it Strange.* Cambridge, Mass.: Synectics Inc.

Griffiths, R. (1954) *The Abilities of Babies.* London: University of London Press.

Guilford, J. P. (1950) Creativity. *American Psychologist* **5**, 444-54.

Harris, D. B. (1963) *Children's Drawings as Measures of Intellectual Maturity.* New York: Harcourt, Brace & World.

Hebb, D. O. (1948) *The Organisation of Behavior.* New York: Wiley.

Heim, A. (1970) *The Appraisal of Intelligence.* Slough: NFER.

Horn, J. L. (1967) Inteligence—why it grows, why it declines. *Trans-action* **5**, 23-31. Reprinted in Child, D. (ed.) (1977) *Readings in Psychology for the Teacher.* Eastbourne: Holt-Saunders.

Hudson, L. (1966) *Contrary Imaginations.* London: Methuen.

Hudson, L. (1968) *Frames of Mind.* London: Methuen.

Kamin, L. (1975) *The Science and Politics of IQ.* Potomac, Md.: Lawrence Erlbaum.

Lynch, A., Mitchell, L. B., Vincent, E. M., Trueman, M. and Macdonald, L. M. (1982) The McCarthy Scales of Children's Abilities: a normative study on English 4-year-olds. *British Journal of Educational Psychology* **52**, 133-43.

McCarthy, D. (1972) *The McCarthy Scales of Children's Abilities.* New York: Psychological Corporation.

McCarty, S. A. (1924) *Children's Drawings: A Study of Interest and Abilities.* Baltimore, Md.: Williams and Wilkins.

MacKinnon, D. W. (1961) Characteristics of the creative person: implications for the teaching-learning process. *Current Issues in Higher Education,* 89-92, National Educational Assoc., Washington. Reprinted in Child D. (ed.) (1977) *Readings in Psychology for the Teacher.* Eastbourne: Holt-Saunders.

Miles, T. R. (1957) Symposium: contributions to intelligence testing and the theory of intelligence. *British Journal of Educational Psychology* **27**, 153-210. Reprinted in Child, D. (ed.) (1977) *Readings in Psychology for the Teacher*. Eastbourne: Holt-Saunders.

Moreno, J. L. (1964) *Psychodrama*, Vol. 1. New York: Beacon.

Nuttall, D. L. (1972) Convergent and divergent thinking. In Butcher, H. J. and Pont, H. B. (eds) *Educational Research in Britain*, Vol. 3. London: University of London Press.

Osborne, A. F. (1963) *Applied Imagination*, 3rd edn. New York: Scribner.

Parnes, S. J. (1967) *Creative Behavior Workbook*. New York: Scribner.

Pyle, D. W. (1979) *Intelligence*. London: Routledge & Kegan Paul.

Roe, A. (1953) A psychological study of eminent psychologists and anthropologists and a comparison with biological and physical scientists. *Psychological Monograph* **67**. no. 2.

Satterly, D. (1981) *Assessment in Schools*. Oxford: Blackwell.

Startweather, E. K. (1971) Creativity research instruments designed for use with pre-school children. *Journal of Creative Behavior* **5**, 245-55.

Sultan, E. E. (1962) A factorial study in the domain of creative thinking. *British Journal of Educational Psychology* **32**, 78-82.

Terman, L. M. and Merrill, M. A. (1960) *Stanford–Binet Intelligence Scale*. Boston, Mass.: Houghton Mifflin.

Torrance, E. P. (1962) *Guiding Creative Talent*. New York: Prentice-Hall.

Torrance, E. P. and Myers, R. E. (1970) *Creative Learning and Teaching*. New York: Dodd Mead.

Uzgiris, I. C. and Hunt, J. McV. (1975) *Assessment in Infancy: Ordinal Scales of Psychological Development*. Urbana Ill.: University of Illinois Press.

Vernon, P. E. (1960) *Intelligence and Attainment Tests*. London: University of London Press.

Wallach, M. A. and Kogan, N. (1965) *Modes of Thinking in Young Children*. New York: Holt, Rinehart & Winston.

Further Reading

de Bono, E. (1969) *The Mechanism of Mind*. London: Cape. Reprinted by Penguin Books.

Nuttall, D. L. (1972) Convergent and divergent thinking. In Butcher, H. J. and Pont, H. B. (eds) Educational Research in Britain, Vol. 3. London: University of London Press.

Pyle, D. W. (1979) *Intelligence*. London: Routledge & Kegan Paul.

Satterley, D. (1981) *Assessment in Schools*. Oxford: Blackwell.

Torrance, E. P. (1962) *Guiding Creative Talent*. New York: Prentice Hall.

4

How Young Children Develop and Use Language

JOAN TOUGH

What is language?

Using language is a part of human behaviour that makes man different from all other animals. The term 'language' is often used to refer to speech behaviour, to the act of using language, but it is used more specifically to refer to those systems of signs through which people communicate with one another. We shall use the term with this second meaning. The systems we refer to here are those based on the use of the voice in the articulation of patterns of sounds that are established through use as signs representing particular elements of experience. We will use the term 'speech' to refer to the articulated patterns of sounds and 'talk' to refer to the use of speech to represent elements of experience, that is, meanings. These systems of language include words that make up a vocabulary or lexis, and a set of rules that governs the way in which words are ordered and how they relate to one another, that is, a grammar. Speech is the medium through which children first learn to use language; later, they meet a graphic medium as they learn to read and write.

Language is the most versatile means through which people can communicate with one another. Communication can and does go on by other means; for example, we all use gesture, and ideas are often expressed through mime, music, movement, drama, drawings, paintings and other media. None of these forms of expression, however, can support an interaction between people that has the possibility for immediacy and explicitness that using language provides. We are here using the term communication to refer to the transmission of meanings between people in such a way that there is agreement between the meaning intended and expressed by one and the meaning received and interpreted by the other. Although language has the best potential of all media for communicating complex meanings, we do not always communicate successfully when we use language and frequently we misunderstand one another. Even so, language provides the best means through which we can try to reach understanding.

The development of language

Much of the basic research that helps us to understand how young children use language was carried out between 1930 and 1960. In Britain, M. M. Lewis made a major contribution through close studies of the way in which young children learn to talk and the factors that affect this development (Lewis, 1963).

Even in his first days, the baby turns his head in response to the human voice, a movement that brings equal input of sound to both ears, but also brings the baby's eyes to look at the face of the speaker. During the next two months, the baby begins not only to differentiate what he sees, but also begins to distinguish between the sounds he hears. He begins to distinguish a familiar voice from an unfamilar one, and responds to the tone of voice: he cries when the voice is harsh, and smiles if the familiar voice is pleasant.

As the baby grows, he seems to take pleasure from increasing control of his movements as he kicks and grasps, seemingly with intention. He also begins to gain some control of the movements of his throat, tongue and mouth, and becomes aware of his own voice as he takes pleasure in the babbling that is characteristic of this period. As people respond and talk to the baby, a conversation-like exchange is built up; the baby pauses to listen and then vocalises in his turn, apparently with intention. Clearly, the baby is aware of the exchange and some meaning begins to develop as his part is being established in the kind of social interaction that is essential if language is to develop.

As the baby gains more control of his hands and limbs, his attention seems to be concentrated on his own mobility and on grasping and bringing objects to his mouth. At the same time his babbling seems to diminish. The sounds he makes seem to express pleasure, surprise, protest or need for attention. By ten months he often uses his voice to accompany his actions, for example, as he bangs a spoon on his plate. Some of the baby's vocalisations begin to resemble words, and parents and others respond to these articulations as though they are words, imitating the baby's vocalisation, offering objects and matching actions to them. By the child's first birthday one or more baby words have been established in this way.

From about the age of 15 months the baby begins to imitate sounds intentionally with some success, an essential skill if he is to develop speech. Now it becomes clear that the child intends to communicate something through the sounds he utters as well as through his gestures and actions. The intonation of his utterances gives some indication of his intention: he may appear to be demanding, complaining, directing or to be showing pleasure and approval. His vocalisation may resemble words, but it is not likely to carry specific meaning, rather meanings that relate to whole situations. Utterances of this kind have been referred to as 'holophrases'. Halliday (1975) has provided us with a fascinating study of his son from the period during which he used holophrases through to their differentiation into groups of words.

Towards the end of his second year the child begins to use two or three words together. They are content words, that is, they refer to objects and actions, but the embedding features are missing, for example 'want dolly', 'go daddy', 'doggy gone'. Each word has a clear reference and they are combined in a sequence that matches the child's action or the direction of his attention. This kind of utterance has been termed 'telegraphic', since it appears as a reduction of a grammatical utterance to content words only. We should not assume, however, that the child is aware of the missing embedded features. It is true that he often seems to understand them in the talk of others, but usually he is helped by many clues present in the situation.

Gradually, the child fills out his telegraphic utterances as his mother and others repeat and extend what he says, offering him the mature form for him to imitate. Most children by the age of three have learned to use languages in a form that is quite near to that of the adult. The child may make mistakes in grammar, his voice will be immature, he may have some problems of articulation, but by the age of three he is likely to use a wide range of constructions and to be rapidly building up his vocabulary.

The norms of language development

Many early studies of the language used by children were concerned with establishing norms of language development, that is, with constructing a picture of 'average' achievement for each age. Several studies, for example those by Gesell (1943), looked at a large number of children at each age and assessed their development in a number of different areas including physical, social and intellectual development. Frequently in such studies language development was one of the areas in which measurements were used.

Other normative studies have concentrated on aspects of language used by children at different ages. An aspect given much attention in early studies was the size of vocabulary used by children at different ages. The work of Watts (1948) is particularly well known. From a number of such studies it seems that we can expect normal children to have three words at 12 months, 20 words at 18 months, 300 words at 24 months, 900–1000 words at 36 months, and at least 2000 words by the age of five and 4000 by the age of seven.

A study in America by Templin (1957) was perhaps the most extensive of the normative studies, and concentrated exclusively on several aspects of language development. In this study, 24 000 utterances from children aged from three to eight years of age were analysed. These analyses included the length of children's utterances, the grammatical complexity and accuracy of utterances, the parts of speech used and the articulation of sounds.

This study found that as children grew older they tended to use more complex forms of utterances, and fewer that were structurally incomplete. Many of the earlier studies had found differences between boys and girls, suggesting that girls are usually more advanced in language development. The Templin study, however, did not find any significant differences in language development between boys and girls, but showed some differences between children from different socioeconomic groups.

The concept of norms of development underlies the construction of observation schedules, for example, those devised by Sheridan (1973), and tests of language skills, for example, the Reynell Developmental Language Scales (Reynell, 1969), since these are usually based on evidence from normative studies.

Theoretical views of language acquisition

In recent years there has been increasing interest in children's development of language and in theoretical explanations of the fact that children learn to use language when they are so young that they cannot understand what language is, let alone any explanations of grammatical rules. Among the theories that have developed are those that most strongly stress innate factors (that is, that the child has a genetic disposition for using language), and therefore consider that maturational processes offer the best explanation. Others see language development as an inherent part of cognitive development, and lay emphasis on the role of language in structuring the child's thinking. Other theories lay stress on the child's experiences, particularly on the social uses of language within the family.

The view that language development arises as the result of innate mechanisms has led to, and supports, the concept of generative grammar, that is, grammars that explain how particular linguistic structures of any utterance arise. The most important contribution to our thinking here has been that of Noam Chomsky. His conclusion is that the child's development of language can only be explained by assuming the existence of an innate language capacity with mechanisms that come into operation at particular stages of development. He concludes that humans are endowed with a hypothetical 'language acquisition device' (LAD) which permits them to process linguistic matter and so produce the grammar of the language (Chomsky, 1965).

The child's acquisition of language, Chomsky argues, must depend on the child being able to operate rules. Since all children seem to learn language in the same way, the underlying rules of all language must be the same. Thus, he puts forward the notion of a set of language universals to explain why the early stages of language acquisition are the same for all children, whatever language they are exposed to and whatever the characteristics of its grammar. Children the world over, it seems, learn to speak first using holophrases, then use telegraphic utterances. The innate concepts of language, the language universals, then come into play and form the essential basis of any language: these universal concepts include the categories of noun and verb and those that distinguish between present, past and future action. The sentence is seen also as an innate concept, providing a formula for linking and ordering words. Every utterance, it is argued, has an underlying sentence structure, which is an active proposition consisting of a noun, phrase and a verb phrase. This is referred to as the 'deep structure'. Every language is based on the innate deep structure, and has ways of elaborating on this deep structure by a process of transformations. Each language has its own vocabulary and its own set of transformations which, when applied to the underlying deep structures, produce utterances that are unique to that language.

Chomsky's theory has stimulated a number of studies, both of children's early development of structure and of their problems in applying grammatical rules at later stages. The study of Brown et al. (1970) is well known. They recorded all the talk of Adam, a two-year-old boy, during several days. By analysing the recordings, they worked out the rules the child was operating as he put together two- and three-word utterances, and predicted the new utterances that Adam would produce next. As the predicted utterances appeared in Adam's talk, so their inferences about the rules were confirmed and Adam was shown to be constructing his utterances according to the rules of a simple grammar.

McNeill (1970) has applied similar techniques to a study of children's acquisition of language from the time of the appearance of two-word utterances to the establishment of the adult grammar. He shows that the child progresses towards the adult form through a sequence of simple grammars that are established and applied until another rule is learned and the grammar consequently changed. This notion helps us to understand how the child progresses step by step, establishing one rule after another, until he has learned all that is required to operate the language system in much the same way as the adults who talk with him. However, a study by Carol Chomsky indicates that the age at which certain structures are used and understood may be later than is usually assumed, and that there are some structures that children find difficult to use even at the age of ten (Chomsky, 1969).

The function of language

The view of language as a set of acquired rules, as elaborated by Chomsky and others, has brought great insight into the nature of language itself, but according to Bruner (1975) it has led to the neglect of important considerations about the functions of language. In particular, Bruner argues, the view of the child's acquisition of language developed by McNeill (1970) overlooks the basis of action and meaning from which the child's language emerges. He comments that McNeill begins his book with the following assertion: 'The facts of language acquisition could not be as they are unless the concept of a sentence is available to children at the start of their learning.' Bruner would see this statement as a more credible one if it read: 'The facts of language acquisition could not be as they are unless fundamental concepts about action and attention are available to the children at the beginning of learning' (Bruner, 1975). This expresses the view that the growth of language is part of an overall cognitive development that arises from the child's own operations upon objects, and from his experiences of interaction with others.

Although the study of development of linguistic structures has raised many issues of interest, it has not proved to be of great practical value. Theoretical elaboration of the view that language arises in order to serve particular purposes offers teachers more insight into the role of language in communication and learning in the classroom. Piaget's early work, based on the classification and functions of the language of six children whose talk he recorded, is well known (Piaget, 1954). The main divisions he recognised were those of 'egocentric' and 'socialised' language. Egocentric language is that which serves to maintain the child's own position, and includes threats and criticisms of others. A characteristic of egocentric language is that it takes into account only the child's view; even though the child may be responding to others, he fails to take into account their needs as listeners, and therefore does not give information that is needed if communication is to be effective. In addition, his interpretations of his own experiences are limited by his inability to project beyond the immediate concrete situation. Thus, his interpretations are also egocentric. As the child grows older he becomes more aware of the listener and projects into his needs, giving information and explanations. His language is adapted to the other's needs as listeners and becomes 'socialised'.

Vygotsky (1934), a Russian psychologist, put forward the view that all children's language is social in origin, since it arises in interaction between the child and others. Thus, in the first place the child's language is both the *result* and a *part* of social interaction. This view is supported by more recent work, particularly by Halliday (1975) and Bruner (1975) in their studies of the period of development during which the child passes from using helophrases to the use of telegraphic speech. Halliday's study of the child's development of holophrases shows clearly that the child's use of intentional communication grows as the result of social interaction. Bruner's account of this period shows even more clearly how the holophrases grow out of collaborative actions between the child and his mother or another adult. The very use of language is a social act, and there is no doubt that the development of language is dependent on the child's interaction with others.

An interesting debate has arisen from what is often interpreted as conflict between the views of Piaget and his many associates and the view expressed by Vygotsky and further developed by Luria and his colleagues (Luria and Yudovich, 1971). The argument perhaps arises because Piaget has convincingly shown that basic concepts arise from sensorimotor information, particularly from the child's own actions upon objects. This work shows that terms for reference to concepts can have little meaning for the child until they are underpinned by understanding that arises from the development of the concept through the concrete experience. This seems to be an unassailable position, but does not necessarily conflict with the view that the child's experiences of using language (and of the talk that others have with him) lead him to give attention to certain aspects of his experiences, place value on some experiences and so prompt him to view the world from a particular standpoint. The view taken by Vygotsky and Luria is that the experiences of talk that a child has with adults about familiar everyday experiences are crucial, not only for building up knowledge of the language, but also for the child's awareness of particular ways of thinking and of interpreting his own experiences. They emphasise how the use of language helps the child to place a structure on his experiences and to organise the meaning they have for him. They emphasise, too, the role that language plays in helping the child to think about his own thinking.

This argument is essentially about the functions of language, the purposes which language serves for the child. Until relatively recently this question has not been prominent, but now it is being studied from several different viewpoints. Halliday, as a linguist, has been concerned to show how the holophrases advance the development of the child's meaning, and how, as a meaning is differentiated, holophrases give rise to linguistic structures as the child begins to acquire a grammar. The linguistic structures then have a potential for expressing particular meaning. This clearly is the case, but it is also clear that the potential for meaning may or may not be taken up by a speaker. For example, the use of 'because' does not necessarily mean that a causal relationship will be expressed. Frequently, young children give an answer of the type 'because it is,' 'because it does' which certainly does not take up the potential that the use of 'because' holds. Halliday's classification of language functions is based on the potential for meaning that language structures hold (Halliday, 1973), but we cannot assume that the purposes for which children use language reflect that potential to the full.

Bruner's approach to the study of young children's earliest development shows quite clearly that the early stages are characterised by action. In discussing the notion of the innateness of linguistic structures he makes the point: 'What may be innate about language acquisition is not *linguistic* innateness but some special features of human action and human attention that permit language to be decoded by the uses to which it is put' (Bruner, 1975).

In a study of the language of three-year-olds (Tough, 1977a) I also tried to answer the question, 'To what uses does the child put language? What does the child use language for?' In analysing the recorded language of 48 three-year-olds, a classification of children's use of language was devised. When the children were three they used language mainly for self-maintaining, for directing themselves and others, for reporting on present and past experiences and for imagining; at the ages of five and seven there was more evidence of reasoning, predicting and projecting. At each age some differences were found between groups of children in the study, differences that were associated with the occupational status of their parents.

The environmental view

Many studies of children's use of language have produced evidence of differences between the language used by children from different sections within the population. Early studies by Smith (1935) and Davis (1937), for example, indicated that children from lower social groups scored less on several measures than children from upper social groups. These studies all relied on the use of linguistic measures, for example, the mean length of children's utterances, the complexity of utterances, elaboration within the noun phrase and the extensions of the verb. Later, Templin's study (1957) found that increasing complexity was associated not only with increasing age and higher intelligence, but also with social groups. Since this work, many other studies have brought forward similar evidence.

An important study of differences in the language used by children from different social groups is that of Professor Bernstein and his associates at the Institute of Education, London University. This original work has led towards an understanding of the relationship between language and learning and the effects of early experiences (Bernstein, 1971).

Bernstein's view of language is very much influenced by the work of Whorf and Sapir. Whorf's original work (1955) was based on a study of the Hopi Indians and the structures of language used to indicate meaning of a particular kind. He examined the way in which the Hopi Indians refer to aspects of time and space, and compared the devices in the Hopi language with those of standard European languages. His findings showed that the possibilities for representing aspects of time and space in the Hopi language were more restricted and less discriminating. Because the Hopi Indians also displayed less awareness of space and time, Whorf argued that the structure of languages they learned as children constrained their conceptualisation of these dimensions. In other words, the language used by a group of people expresses not only cultural values, but also ways of viewing the world, and thus results in the maintenance of the culture of the group. Sapir (1921) also argues that the way in which we view our experiences is built through the language habits of the group. As the child comes to use language in the home and neighbourhood, so we can expect him to assimilate ways of thinking expressed by the group.

Although this original work focused on the differences between languages, Bernstein was amongst the first to see that the same relationships could be seen in the different ways in which the *same* language was used. Members of any group convey the meaning they set on their experiences through their use of language. A child growing up in a particular group will learn to use language in the way of this group, and this will have a major influence on his thinking. Moreover, relationships are expressed in the way language is used. In this way the culture of the particular group and relationships between members of the group are maintained and reproduced.

Bernstein has applied his thesis to an examination of the differences between groups of children described as lower working class and middle class. The parents of these two groups tend to be differentiated by the extent of their education as well as by their occupations.

Since the methods Bernstin employed for comparing the language used by children from these two backgrounds relied on measures of linguistic structures the differences that emerged were described in these terms. Two codes are distinguished, the 'elaborated' and 'restricted' codes, and these were defined in terms of the linguistic structures that were predominant in the language used by middle-class and working-class children respectively. Many have since accused Bernstein of suggesting that the lower working-class child is in some way deficient in language and unable to think in complex ways. Others, like Labov (1970), see the elaborate code as superficial and unnecessary verbosity, and accuse Bernstein of neglecting the fact that complex thinking can be expressed in dialects other than standard English. In a subsequent paper, Bernstein explains that his work should not be interpreted as indicating that lower working-class children are inferior in their potential for thinking, but only in the expression of their thinking (Bernstein, 1973a).

Language and thinking

Bernstein's work has stimulated a debate that centres on the relative value of different forms of language. A major question that must be taken into consideration in such a debate is whether experiences of particular ways of using language constrain or extend the development of children's thinking. Piaget has demonstrated convincingly that the basis of children's thinking is formed by their own operations upon concrete situations. His view is that 'the roots of logical operations are deeper than linguistic connections' (Piaget, 1962). Many experiments support this view. For example, in a group of children who performed a series of conservation tasks, there were those who conserved and those who did not. Some children were given specific training in the language needed for expressing the concepts underlying these tasks, but they performed no better than those who had had no training (Inhelder et al., 1966).

Other evidence that must be considered is that from studies of deaf children. Furth (1966) compared the performances of deaf and hearing children on tasks that related to the recognition of sameness, symmetry and apposition. The deaf children were able to deal with the first two concepts as well as the hearing children, but they were not as successful with the third concept. Furth concludes from this that the influence of language on concept formation is a facilitating but not a necessary prerequisite for abstracting and generalising. Vygotsky (1934), however, puts forward convincing evidence to support the view that the very naming of particular attributes aids concept formation. His well-known experiments showed that children were helped in a classification task, using blocks of different shapes and colours, when particular concepts were designated by nonsense syllables. The use of naming helped the children to search for similarities and differences. Vygotsky concluded that the use of words guides the intellectual operation by centring attention, abstracting certain characteristics and synthesising them in the meaning of the sign, that is, the word. Thus, he argued, words are central to the process of forming complex concepts.

But there are ways of thinking that do not involve the development of new concepts, and thinking that involves judgements, decisions and values cannot depend solely on concrete evidence from a situation. Such thinking may be much more influenced by the experiences of using language. The concept of coins and understanding of relative value may be abstracted from the actual use of coins, but thinking about the use of money may be much more influenced by ways of thinking made evident in the language used by others.

How does the experience of using language with others affect the development of children's thinking? Evidence from studies of retarded twin boys is put forward by Luria and his associates. At the age of five the speech of these children consisted of a small number of words, and some additional words and sounds through which they communicated only with one another. These twins were then separated in a nursery, and one was given speech training in addition to exposure to language in the classroom. Separation caused a need to speak with others, and their speech improved rapidly. The crucial issue then was whether their mental processes had also improved. Observation showed marked gains in both children in a range of mental processes, and the one who had received special training surpassed his brother. Luria and Yudovich (1971) conclude from this that the acquisition of language brings about the development of more complex mental processes.

The debate continues. Bruner's (1964) notion of 'instrumental conceptual-isation' is leading to a synthesis of the several different aspects of language that we have discussed so far. He is concerned with ways of representing experience, and how past experience is organised through language for use in the future. He is further concerned with the impact of culture on development, that is, with the push from the child's inner maturation with the pull of the child's environment. The child represents his experiences for a purpose, and uses actions (referred to as the enactive mode of representation), images (referred to as the iconic mode of representation), and the symbolic mode, which is predominantly the use of language.

Bruner's view is that our knowledge of the world is based upon our models of reality which we construct through, and which are limited by, our neuromuscular system. These inner models of reality are shaped through the way in which they are used by a particular group, and so by the individual within that group. Further, Bruner argues, since our culture is a technical one, we are pressed to bring action, image and language into a coherent relationship, resulting in a predominantly linguistic model that is symbolic and abstract. Children exposed to our culture inevitably grow towards the establishment of such a model.

Language experience in the home

We can see, then, that the way in which parents talk with their young children will have an effect from the earliest days. From the point at which the child moves towards the mature form of language, communication through language begins to play an important part in shaping his view of the world and his expectations about the ways of using language. If there are differences in the experiences offered by families to their young children, these are likely to become evident in the way in which children learn to use language.

What evidence have we that parents do provide such different experiences for children? Evidence of this kind is not easy to obtain. It is rarely possible to sample the conversation that goes on within the child's home. There have been attempts to do this; for example, a study by Wooton (1974) of children talking with their mothers at home shows that some mothers are much more directive and less explanatory than others in their dealings with children, and are less likely to respond to the child's own initiatives.

There is further evidence from a study by Hess and Shipman (1965) of Black American mothers helping their children to understand how to carry out a simple task. In this study, middle-class mothers tended to help their children understand the principles underlying the task and gave careful, explicit explanations and general encouragement. The working-class mothers tended to direct children without giving explanations, and were less encouraging and did not make any of the possible elaborations of meanings that were inherent in the task and situation. Hess and Shipman (1965) suggest that such children are being deprived of meanings that could be made available to them.

Other evidence about the nature of the interaction in the home comes from Bernstein (1973b) and his associates. In this work, mothers of young children were interviewed and asked about issues that had some direct bearing on the experiences they were providing for their children. For example, they answered a questionnaire on their view of toys, how they would control their children and how they would answer children's questions. There were significant differences between the lower working-class and the middle class mothers' answers, and this revealed important differences in the way in which they viewed their children.

Sestini (1975) interviewed a group of mothers when their children were seven, asking them questions that were intended to reveal how they viewed their children, what their priorities were in controlling them, the kind of activities they engaged in with them and how they viewed their education. There are major problems in using interviews as a means of discovering how people behave, and the picture gained may not fairly represent what actually happened in their homes, but differences in the way in which mothers viewed the questions and set about answering them seem likely to reflect to some extent the kind of experiences of using language they will give their children. The major differences were distinguished in the values mothers expressed, in the way in which they organised and modified their answers, the extent to which they were reflecting on what they were saying and their awareness of possible interpretations. The mothers who had had extended education showed reflective behaviour more frequently than those who had had minimum education; these latter mothers tended to give categorical answers with little qualification or indication of reflection on the meaning of what they were saying. It seems likely that differences of this kind would also relate to differences in mothers' use of language in the home.

Evidence from such studies offers us some insight into the causes of the differences between children's skills in using language when they first come to school. It is often suggested that some children have too little experience of using language, and that this results in inadequate development of language. All the children studied by myself (Tough, 1977a) had developed a wide range of language structures. All the children used complexity in all the features measured on some occasions. The main differences were in the frequency with which such complexity appeared.

The children from the educationally advantaged homes used language significantly more for reporting on recalled events, and for referring to detail and sequence and related aspects. They more frequently looked for and gave explanations, and referred to causal and dependent relationships. They more frequently projected into other people's feelings and conditions, anticipated events and predicted the outcome. They looked for possible solutions, and above all they reflected on the answers they were giving and modified their meaning in some sense. They were learning to think in different ways.

When the children were seen at the age of seven and a half, the differences were more clearly marked, and were due to the children's interpretation of situations and their expectations of their role in giving answers. The children from non-advantaged homes tended to give minimal responses, even though relationships with adults seemed good. Yet, with encouragement and persistence, and given some clues about what was expected, many of these children showed they could give more extended and appropriate answers

(Tough, 1977a). This seems to indicate that their restricted responses were not due to deficient knowledge of language, but to lack of experience of using language in certain ways.

Fostering children's use of language

What can we learn from studying children's development of language? Perhaps the most important aspect that emerges is that talk is itself an important part of children's experiences, one that is having a continuing and pervasive effect. The talk in which parents and others involve children provides children not only with experiences of using language, but also of ways of thinking. All children are gaining experiences of using language in their homes, but the purposes for which they learn to use language, and their disposition to think in certain ways, largely depend upon the kind of linguistic experiences offered to them. How, then, can we extend the development of children's use of language and of thinking?

In different parts of the world attempts have been made to devise experiences for young children that will extend their skills in using language. In the United States many experimental programmes were devised and used as part of the Head Start policy, and some have shown that children do improve, both in the use of language and in their general attainment. However, so far there is little evidence to show that such gains continue to have an effect during the first years in school.

These programmes have different emphases, but all tend to assume that the child is deficient in some way, and aim to teach a range of cognitive skills. Some see the teacher as lacking in skills, and so provide materials to be used in set, daily lessons. Some see rejection of the child by his teacher as the main reason for failure, and so devise situations to be enjoyed and in which success can be assured. The Peabody Language Development Kit combines all these features.

Although such programmes are intended to provide materials for lessons that go on in a spirit of enjoyment, they make assumptions about the way in which language is learned. All set out to teach particular language skills through repetition and formal drills. Even if the atmosphere of fun can be maintained and the child's confidence can be increased, there seems to be no justification for assuming that this is the way in which children learn to use language. Nor should the only motivation be to express ideas to the teacher. The child needs language as a tool for exploring ideas and experiences, and this can only happen if children meet situations in which experiences are explored through the use of language. But, more than this, the greatest advantage that using language brings is to free communication from the concrete and the present. Language enables us to communicate about the past and the future, and to consider concrete situations in their absence.

Blank and Solomon (1968) have proposed a method of extending children's thinking and use of language that assumes that the child is failing to use language to organise his experiences, and that this failure can be remedied by individual tutoring through the use of dialogue involving particular techniques of questioning. A controlled experiment showed that children involved in such a programme made impressive gains in general ability, and also changed their attitudes to learning quite dramatically.

The essential experience for promoting the development and use of language appears to be the talk into which a child is drawn, and which helps the child to structure and set value on his experiences, and to reflect on his experiences, and think about them in certain ways. The aims of education for young children must surely include helping children to think in ways that will support their learning and understanding. Several recent studies have shown that interaction between children and teachers in the classroom tends to restrict rather than extend children's thinking. A study carried out in British nursery classes has shown that teachers and nursery assistants may spend little time talking with individual children: when they do, it is likely to be with children who already have the most extensive use of language (Tizard et al., 1976) In a mjaor longitudinal study of children in their homes and in school, Wells (1979) has found that children may have less opportunity to extend ideas through talk with adults in school than they do at home. Yet it is clear that the innate potential for developing and using language may not be fully realised by children if they do not meet, in their homes or at school, interaction which calls that potential fully into play.

Teachers of young children might play a crucial role in influencing children's development and use of language if they were aware of the kind of help needed by each child and were able to provide appropriate experiences for all the children in the class. The Schools Council *Communication Skills in Early Childhood Project* puts forward the view that teachers need to observe each child's language behaviour closely in order to build a picture of the ability each has in using language and to appraise the needs of all (Tough, 1976). With such knowledge the teacher might recognise opportunities for talk with children in situations which have a potential for promoting particular ways of thinking. Through dialogue with the teacher, the child can be helped to become familiar with a range of uses of language and ways of thinking that can provide a basis for his continuing education (Tough, 1977b).

References

Bernstein, B. (1971) *Class, Codes and Control*, vol. I. London: Routledge & Kegan Paul.

Bernstein, B. (1973a) A brief account of the theory of codes. In *Social Relationships and Language*. London: Routledge & Kegan Paul.

Bernstein, B. (1973b) *Class, Codes and Control*, vol. II. London: Routledge & Kegan Paul.

Blank, M. and Solomon, F. (1968) A tutorial language programme to develop abstract thinking in socially disadvantaged pre-school children. *Child Development* **39**, 379-90.

Brown, R., Fraser, C. and Bellugi, U. (1970) Explorations in grammar evaluation. In Brown, R. (ed.) *Psycholinguistics*. New York: The Free Press.
Bruner, J. (1964) Course of cognitive growth. *American Psychologist* **19**, 1-5.
Bruner, J. (1975) The ontogenesis of speech acts. *Journal of Child Language* **2**, 1-19.
Chomsky, C. S. (1969) *The Acquisition of Syntax in Children from Five to Ten*. Cambridge, Mass.: MIT Press.
Chomsky, N. (1965) *Aspects of the Theory of Syntax*. Cambridge, Mass.: MIT Press.
Davis, E. J. (1937) The development of linguistic skills in twins, singletons with siblings and only children from age five to ten years. Institute of Child Welfare Monograph Services, no. 14.
Furth, H. (1966) *Thinking without Language*. Illinois: The Free Press of Glencoe.
Gesell, A. (1943) *Infant and Child in the Culture of Today*. London: Hamish Hamilton.
Halliday, M. (1973) *Explorations in the Functions of Grammar*. London: Edward Arnold.
Halliday, M. (1975) *Learning How to Mean*. London: Edward Arnold.
Hess, R. D. and Shipman, V. C. (1965) Early experience and the socialisation of cognitive modes in children. *Child Development* **36**, 4, 867-86. Reprinted in Cashdan, A. and Grugeon, E. (eds) (1972) *Language in Education: A Source Book*. London: Routledge & Kegan Paul/Open University.
Inhelder, B., Bovet, M., Sinclair, H. and Smock, C. D. (1966) On cognitive development. *American Psychologist* **21**, 160-84.
Labov, W. (1970) The logic of non-standard English. In Cashdan, A. and Grugeon, E. (eds) (1972) *Language in Education: A Source Book*. London: Routledge & Kegan Paul/Open University.
Lewis, M. M. (1963) *Language, Thought and Personality*. London: Harrap.
Luria, A. R. and Yudovich, F. I. (1971) *Speech and the Development of Mental Processes in the Child*. Harmondsworth: Penguin.
McNeill, D. (1970) *The Acquisition of Language: the Study of Developmental Linguistics*. New York: Harper and Row.
Piaget, J. (1954) Language and thought from a genetic point of view. *Acta Psychologica* **10**, 88-98.
Piaget, J. (1962) *Comments on Vygotsky's Critical Remarks Concerning 'Language and Thought of the Child' and 'Judgement and Reason in the Child'*. Cambridge, Mass.: MIT Press.
Reynell, J. K. (1969) *The Reynell Developmental Language Scales*. Slough: NFER.
Sapir, E. (1921) *Language: an Introduction to the Study of Speech*. New York: Harcourt, Brace and World.
Sestini, E. (1975) Maternal values and modes of communication. Unpublished M Phil thesis, University of Leeds.
Sheridan, M. (1973) *Children's Developmental Progress from Birth to Five Years: the Stycar Sequences*. Slough: NFER.
Smith, M. E. (1935) A study of some factors influencing the development of the sentence in pre-school children. *Journal of Genetic Psychology* **46**, 182-212.
Templin, M. (1957) *Certain Language Skills in Children*. London: Oxford University Press.
Tizard. B., Philps, S. and Plewis, J. (1976) Staff behaviour in pre-school centres. *Journal of Child Psychology and Psychiatry* **17**, 21-23.
Tough, J. (1976) *Listening to Children Talking: A Guide to the Appraisal of Children's Use of Language*. London: Ward Lock.
Tough, J. (1977a) *The Development of Meaning*. London: Allan & Unwin.
Tough, J. (1977b) *Talking and Learning: a Guide to Fostering Communication Skills in the Nursery and Infant School*. London: Ward Lock.
Vygotsky, L. S. (1934) *Thought and Language*. Cambridge, Mass.: MIT Press.
Watts, A. E. (1948) *The Language and Mental Development of Children*. London: Harrap.

Wells, G. (1979) Variations in child language. In Lee, V. (ed.) *Language Development.* London: Croom Helm.

Whorf, B. C. (1955) *Language, Thought and Reality: Selected Writings of Bejamin Lee Whorf,* ed. J. B. Carroll. Cambridge, Mass.: MIT Press.

Wooton, A. J. (1974) Talk in the homes of young children. *Sociology* **8**, 277-95.

Further Reading

Cashdan, A. and Grugeon, E. (eds) (1972) *Language in Education.* London: Routledge & Kegan Paul/Open University.

Luria, A. R. and Yudovich, F. I. (1971) *Speech and the Development of Mental Processes in the Child.* London: Penguin.

5

How Children Learn

ROGER W. McINTIRE

Opportunities for a young child to practise his growing capacity for learning are essential. When we see learnt improvements in his behaviour, our encouraging reactions are crucial because they support and further extend these improvements. Sometimes, however, when the child has difficulties in learning, he needs more intensive and carefully planned help.

Understanding the changes in learning

Since Robert (six years old) came into his new class he has had a lot of trouble. In the past he needed little discipline and did adequate work, but this year he has been very disruptive: fighting frequently and doing poor work. Is there a practical explanation for this sudden turn for the worse? Can remedies be suggested that a teacher can apply? We need, first, to take a careful look at the changes that have occurred in his behaviour.

Changes in behaviour that take place as a result of experience with the environment, are called 'learning' even when the changes are not for the better. For example, Robert may be fighting in order to defend himself against teasing. Perhaps he is learning that he can intimidate the people who are teasing him. Changes taking place in a child are reflected in the way the child behaves. Such changes in behaviour may reflect maturity in cognitive or emotional development, or they may reflect changes that occur as a result of the child's interaction with the environment. The exact process by which learning occurs is not known, but we do have a great deal of evidence concerning how learning can be facilitated or retarded, and about the way in which it sometimes relates to cognitive insights (e.g. 'They stop teasing me when I let them know I'll hit them'). We also know that sometimes it is closely linked with maturation in that certain kinds of learning can only reliably take place when certain maturational levels have been reached. But however learning occurs, it usually evidences itself through changes in behaviour. Thus, progress in learning can be assessed by systematic observation of behaviour.

The teacher has control only over Robert's experiences within the school; factors such as maturation (including inheritance) and the environment connected with the child's home are not controllable. Robert tries out some behaviour within school hours, and the teacher reacts to that behaviour: by encouraging it, discouraging it or ignoring it altogether. The teacher can also influence the opportunities that Robert has for trying out behaviour; for example, by the scope that she gives him to be creative, to mix with others, to have access to appropriate learning materials and to offer answers, comments and questions. All these things will influence learning because they determine the amount of possible practice.

Allowing the practice of needlessly disruptive behaviour or flippancy is just as much a learning experience as practising the lesson in the book. It therefore becomes important to pick out certain behavioural changes as goals that can be set for practice by the child. If we know the child's capability from observation and our knowledge of developmental stages, then we know where to begin the practice. In Robert's case, we may have to begin quite far back. If we can define the goals for the learning task that is facing Robert, we can know both where to begin and where we are going. With the starting and finishing points set, we can examine the help (called 'behaviour modification'), step by step, that we can give Robert in solving his problems.

Catching Robert being good

Suppose you are Robert's teacher. Where could you begin? The complaint is that he is being disruptive and doing poor work. That is a good starting point, but before proceeding you will want some specific information. The first step therefore (step 1) is to make the complaint of 'disruptive' and 'poor work' more specific. Perhaps Robert hits others in class and talks to them at inappropriate times. Perhaps his work is always late and incomplete. Step 1 is a good start because it specifies in an objective way what Robert does that causes others to complain about him. It does so without blaming him, or his parent's genetics or his early childhood experiences. Putting the blame on such factors may be partly true, but it is an unproductive approach because these factors are not changeable. After step 1 of specifying Robert's unwanted behaviour as observable events in the classroom, we can plan reactions to these events by proceeding to the second step (step 2), sorting out the reactions that control classroom learning.

We have already seen that the explanations for behaviour can take many forms, some useful and some not. With step 1 accomplished, we can now seek an explanation for behaviour in the results of that behaviour. We ask why Robert acts the way he does: hitting others, talking at the wrong times, always late and incomplete with his work, and we answer the question by observing what follows on from the behaviour. We thus take the view that the most helpful explanation for behaviour is one based on the reactions, the consequences, of that behaviour. Robert does whatever he does because of consequences, good ones and bad ones. In step 2 we need to make some careful observations in order to discover just what these consequences are.

Some speculation and exploration may be necessary to discover the consequences that are supporting the behaviour. The praise and compliments a child receives for tentatively suggesting an answer in a classroom lesson will encourage future answers. Robert's practice in adjusting to his classroom, or attempting to do so, and his experience of the results of these attempts, are the crucial aspects of the learning exercise.

What happens next for Robert? His hitting may bring objections from you, the teacher, and from others. You react to his inappropriate talking with objections and reprimands, but occasional interest and pleasant reactions may come from others. His procrastination may also bring reprimands from you, the teacher, but, in the short run, procrastination has its own reward: immediate free time for more pleasant things.

The third step (step 3) is to try to change the consequences that follow Robert's hitting, talking and procrastination. You could ignore the bad activities as much as is practical while focusing attention on his small movements of good behaviour. This would improve Robert's expectations of acknowledgement for his successes. With less encouragement for poor behaviour and more for his successes, learning is likely to improve as well as general behaviour. In the following study, some formal observations show that the 'catch them being good' approach can have surprising effects.

Broden et al. (1970) selected two boys who were troublesome in class and poor learners. The first boy, Greg, had been kept back a class because of poor academic and social behaviour. The second boy, Edwin, was also a problem in class and a slow learner. As a team, they were enough to drive an otherwise sane teacher into early retirement.

Observers, making judgements of each child every ten seconds for 30 minute sessions, found that the boys attended to appropriate classroom activities only 30% of the time. The teacher was then asked to give special attention to Edwin when he was paying attention and not fooling around. She was not to change her reactions to Greg until the next phase of the experiment when it would be Greg's turn for the special attention. Special attention meant not only recognising, praising and encouraging good behaviour, but also completely ignoring bad behaviour. In the last phase, the teacher gave special attention to both boys.

The graphs in figure 1 show the dramatic improvement when the teacher moves from the initial observation period to giving special attention for good behaviour. Even when the praise is directed to only one boy the other seems to have benefited.

As a first attempt at step 3, you could catch Robert being good as the teacher caught Greg and Edwin. You could plan to provide attention and praise on those rare moments when Robert attends his work and then more

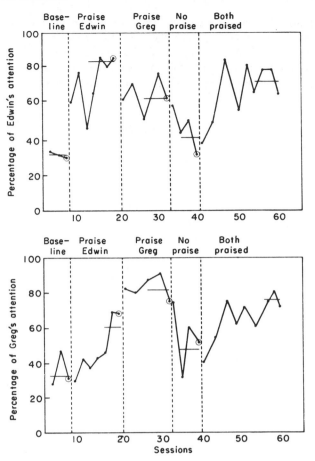

Figure 1   *Percentage of time Edwin and Greg paid attention during experimental sessions.*
(Adapted with the permission of the Journal of Applied Behavior Analysis *from Broden, M.,*
Bruce, C., Mitchell, M. A., Carter, V. and Hall, R. V. (1970) Effects of teacher attention on
attending behaviour of two boys at adjacent desks. Journal of Applied Behavior Analysis **3**,
201. Copyright 1970 by the Society for the Experimental Analysis of of Behavior, Inc.)

easily ignore the bad moments. Of course, you cannot watch Robert all the
time. Other children deserve your attention and you will miss many
opportunities with Robert. However, if you support only one in every five or
ten good performances, you will add a pleasant reliability to Robert's life.
While trying to encourage Robert as often as you see an opportunity, you will
catch him being good often enough to produce a change. Notice the very
small level being suggested for step 3 action. We settle for very brief victories
over undesirable, behaviour and we keep a watch for occasional moments
when we can *catch Robert being good.*

If you would like to encourage a little help from home for Robert's problem, you could follow a procedure used by Drew et al. (1982). Two seven-year-old boys, David and Jeff, had a long history of difficulty in completing assigned classwork. Both showed above average intelligence when tested, yet in class they performed poorly. The new procedure used a daily report card for mathematics work. A 'yes' on this card meant that all problems assigned had been done and 76% or more were correct. If either boy returned from school without his daily report card or with a 'no' on the card, his mother would not allow any outside play that afternoon. If he returned with a 'yes', he was praised for his success and allowed to play outside. The percentage of work completed each day went up from 0 to 100 for Jeff and from 30 to 100 for David. The percentage of correct work went up from 0 to 80 for Jeff and from 30 to 80 for David. Possibly Robert could benefit from a similar incentive. Some more strategies to help Robert will be suggested later in this chapter, but for the moment let us consider a friend of his who is not disruptive but too quiet instead.

Getting the learning started with a low responder

Unlike Robert, Anne (also six years old) is never a problem of discipline in class. She tries hard but somehow seems unable to learn concepts and new words as quickly as other children. If there are items to learn or events to remember, Anne contines to go over them with little success. The complaint about Anne is easily dealt with in step 1 (translating the complaint into a description of classroom habits and reactions). We would like Anne to be able to speak up and answer correctly when asked questions in class.

Step 2 (the identification of consequences) may also be easy: it seems she would be social enough to respond well to teacher praise and recognition. Step 3 (implementing a plan) is where the difficulty begins. Suppose you are Anne's teacher. You would be happy to encourage and support Anne's success in speaking and answering if only she gave you an opportunity, but her success rate is near zero, perhaps because she is intimidated and afraid of embarrassment (possibly from past failures). In order for experiences, practice and consequences to do their work, some level of success must be initiated. The more Anne refuses to respond the less opportunity you have to encourage her.

For Anne, therefore, a quiet non-competitive situation is needed, where you can allow a long time and many opportunities for Anne to work out answers to fairly easy questions. We need to maximise chances for encouraging Anne not only by 'catching her being good', as in Robert's case, but also by removing the competition, the interruptions and the impatience she has to contend with from others so that she will have many opportunities for her tentative and infrequent answers. As she gains success with your encouragement, she will gradually deal with more competitive and disrupted situations without withdrawing.

We may not be able to change Anne's native intellectual capacity, but we can arrange the environment, and its responsiveness, to give her every chance to develop her potential.

Advantages of a practical approach to learning

People often wonder if it is ethical or even in the child's best interests to plan consequences for learning. However, we are all engaged in such plans to some extent every day. The children in your class will do something and you will react, i.e. provide a consequence which will have its influence. It is suggested here that some situations in teaching need thoughtful plans for particular behaviours using specific consequences. For the sake of the troubled child, let us list some of the advantages of providing these consequences.

The advantages of reliable consequences

The first advantage of reliable consequences is the frequence reinforcement of confidence. Given consistently, such frequent feedback encourages both the rate and quality of learning. Robert needs to be told something good about his behaviour in a concrete and uncomplicated message.

A second advantage is the reliability to which Robert can adjust. His teacher will also have a feeling of more consistency and sense of purpose in a reliable plan of response to Robert's good behaviour as well as his poor behaviour. Robert will come to know the rules, not just the stated ones of the school but the expectations and reactions of his teacher. Most importantly, he will come to like most of the consistencies because they have to do with pleasant reactions of his teacher to his successes. Anne will also benefit by coming 'out of her shell' as she comes to trust the consistency of praise for success. Even with the most diligent teacher she will be encouraged only part of the time, but occasional encouragement, given consistently for the same good behaviour, will provide Anne with the reliability she needs to gain confidence.

The motivation and incentive provided by the generosity of their teachers will, of course, be a third benefit to both Robert and Anne. Both want to be successful and both want to be told about their successes. Generous teachers who provide great amounts of social incentives usually have a more pleasant day for themselves and provide a better day for the children around them.

Rewards and punishment

The overall amount of encouragement versus punishment in the classroom will influence the range of behaviours the child is willing to risk. A punishment strategy tends to suppress not only the bad behaviour it is aimed at but other behaviour as well, and in consequence the teacher's opportunities to encourage will also be reduced.

A second problem arising from a punishment strategy is that it tends to destroy the reliability of the learning environment for the child because, paradoxically, the teacher is too humane to use it strictly. The punishment rule should say: 'If the wrong behaviour occurs, then punishment will be strictly applied'. Unfortunately, due to our love for our children we tend to give them 'the benefit of the doubt' and let them off with warnings. The electric shock received from a wall socket is an effective punishment because a wall socket is not a loving teacher. It does not think that the child touching it looks cute or that it has already been too hard on him today; a wall socket is inhuman and cold-blooded. The rule is simple, and few people touch wall sockets. Since none of us is a wall socket however, we find cold-blooded rules hard to administer.

From our loving attitude comes a further disadvantage of punishment: the warnings and inconsistencies themselves are a kind of encouragement to the child to make mistakes rather than avoid them. They provide him with verbal attention and a challenging game in which he may take certain risks in order to feel the accomplishment of having taken the risk but avoided the punishment. This kind of encouragement leads to further deterioration in behaviour. In addition to these disadvantages is the problem of keeping the child in the situation where punishment threatens. This is not possible as some of his behaviour naturally takes place out of our sight, and he will quickly learn additional strategies of subterfuge.

Returning to our problems with Anne and Robert, we must avoid some pitfalls which might reduce their occasions for good behaviour or reduce our inclination to react positively when this good behaviour occurs. Pitfalls that reduce occasions for good behaviour are: (a) not allowing enough practice and (b) suppressing too much behaviour with punishment. Pitfalls that reduce our inclination to be encouraging even when good behaviour occurs are (a) losing track of the behavioural objectives and (b), a related habit, focusing on catching errors rather than catching children being good. Giving encouragement and making opportunities for encouragement are the two most important principles and they are dependent on each other: you must have opportunities to be generous *and* must be generous to have opportunities.

Some rules to learn by

The 'do' rule

The first important rule is to provide as much opportunity for children to practise desirable behaviour as possible. It seems obvious when teaching someone to play a musical instrument or when coaching someone in a sport, but the rule tends to be lost in the more verbal and written lessons of the classroom. One needs repeated practice in order to play the piano well, and practice is essential to be proficient at golf; but when it comes to academic subjects we sometimes hope students can just look and listen and thereby learn.

Recently, the recognition of the error of this distinction between learning in music and sport and learning in academic subjects has led to an emphasis on 'getting involved'. The children are more often asked for their opinion, to present their ideas or to construct their own application of the principles in the lesson. This opportunity to behave, to 'act out' and practise the principles, has become one of the most gratifying steps forward in the modern educational approach.

The imitation rule

As Anne casts about to find solutions to her problems of learning and classroom adjustment, what will she try? It seems likely she will mimic her teacher, particularly in attitude, disposition and social reactions. If the teacher is quiet, moody and unsociable, then Anne and her fellow students are likely to respond in kind. If the teacher is positive, loving and sociable, they are likely to develop the same temperament when they are in class. As one teacher put it to me, 'I've become very tough with those children, but they are still nasty and tough themselves!' Manners, disposition and inclinations to reward or to punish are contagious.

How easily and how frequently do you react to the children around you? Everyone has seen parents and teachers who are nagging children all the time: 'Sit down', 'Tuck in your shirt', 'Don't touch', 'Walk faster', 'Walk slower' and so on. The pleasantness and the friendliness of a person's disposition may be measured by his or her tendency to support, encourage, agree with, or in other ways give rewards frequently. Jovial and approachable people seem to have a rule that says, 'When in doubt, reward. Hardly ever punish.' To the extent that you correct, contradict, reprimand and punish, you lose this friendly air. The reason a child would rather go outside with friends than stay home or in his classroom is that there is a greater likelihood outside that his behaviour will be accepted (and thus rewarded). As much as a child may dislike a nagging disposition, however, his own disposition is usually a copy of it. This copying is almost always rewarded by adults through example because it accords with their own preferred behaviour.

The shaping rule

To have opportunities with Anne in the very beginning you will need to express encouragement for the little successes. As a beginning, you could select a behaviour which occurs so frequently that your success in finding an opportunity to be rewarding is absolutely guaranteed. With that success behind her, Anne will be more willing to attack more difficult problems.

In Robert's case, we may have to look very hard to find the first shaping level: some little social reaction done pleasantly, some small victory over a part of a lesson. We are all aware of the need for gradual learning, but we often miss the importance of a low starting place: it is important not only because the child is immature but also because we must be looking for an opportunity to encourage his first successful efforts.

One study demonstrating the value of gradual learning was performed by Corey and Shamow (1972). In the Robin Bird Nursery School 12 children were trying to learn to read their first words. The words were shown to each child individually by 'Happy the Clown', a face on a slide projector screen, and the children were asked to tell 'Happy' the words as they were presented on slides. Each slide also had a picture representing the word (i.e. apple, ball, horse, dog, elephant, book). Each time the children were correct Happy's nose would light up, and occasionally a mechanism would give the child a sweet. The words were all presented six times, but for half the children the helping picture slowly faded out of view as the slides continued to be presented. The other six children saw the helping picture clearly until the last presentation of the words when the pictures were abruptly absent.

On this last presentation when the pictures were absent those children who had had the pictures faded out over preceding trials showed nearly perfect word identification. Those who had the pictures removed for only the last test could only average one out of six correct. A gradual 'shaping' change in the demands of learning adds an additional guarantee of success.

The 'one-shot' rule

'Robert and Anne, if you don't settle down and get this lesson right, neither of you will go on the outing next week!' There! That ought to produce some results! But, if they still fail, should the children be warned again? Should the teacher be an ogre and disallow the outing as promised? Or should she give in and allow them to go if they do only a bit better? And what about the day after the outing? Some new threat?

Such threats are called 'one-shots'. The threatened consequence can only be applied once; it is short-lived, and forces the teacher to threaten a great deal in order to 'use' the consequence for all its worth. The teacher falls into a situation where some small improvements will not be rewarded and mistakes are met with many warnings about the 'one-shot'.

Consequences should be made up of the small, repeatable teacher reactions that children can come to expect as a consistency in their lives, such as teacher praise or trying again at a poor piece of work. Let the children have the big things like outings and Christmas plays, and hope everyone enjoys them. Do not try to make rewards or punishments out of events that cannot be repeated frequently.

The extinction rule

Extinction is a word used when consequences are withheld or removed. One might consider putting Robert 'on extinction' for his poor behaviour (i.e. ignoring it altogether). This might remove a social incentive discovered in step 2 where we searched for the reasons for the behaviour. The extinction rule can be a useful one but it requires three important cautions.

First, by itself, the extinction rule lowers the total amount of encouragement Robert receives for bad as well as good behaviour. The addition of the 'catch him being good' rule is most important here and should be applied at the same time as the extinction rule in order to avoid creating a situation that is totally discouraging to Robert.

Secondly, Robert's first reaction to extinction is likely to be to intensify his bad behaviour: 'If a little trouble no longer produces any fun, try some more!' Possibly Robert will start throwing tantrums in frustration. It will take some courage on the part of the teacher to keep these new reactions 'on extinction' also, and yet continue the 'catch him being good' rule.

Thirdly, the extinction rule can produce an adverse reaction. The empty time with lack of attention or reaction from the teacher might be filled with repetitive and annoying activities continuously performed as a reaction to boredom and disappointment. Such reactions are called 'adjunctive behaviours' because they are not directly supported by consequences, but are a reaction to the lack of consequences. Examples might be nail biting, pen clicking, aimless scribbling and harassing other children. In some cases, these types of behaviour are reduced by extinction because they may have been attention-getting, but on other occasions, when they are adjunctive, they may be *increased* by extinction. In this last case, more general attention by the teacher would be the remedy for these annoying habits.

An extinction rule, then, has the danger of increasing adjunctive behaviours. Again, the remedy is to include with the extinction rule an accompanying effort to increase positive encouragement for other desirable behaviours. A study by Madsen et al. (1968) was quite successful using a combination of the extinction and the 'catch them being good' rules.

Cliff and Frank were in Mrs A's top infant class. Cliff spent nearly all his time playing with objects in or on his desk. He frequently bothered others around him. He wrote on his shoes or arms and threw kisses to the girls. The other children had stopped paying attention to him so all this behaviour looked rather lonely. A sign he made for his desk said 'Do you love me?' Frank's behaviour was also a problem. he fought at break time, and like Cliff he often disrupted class by running around, talking and bothering others. Reprimands and discipline had no effect.

In Mrs B's class there was a further child, Stan, who was very wild. He ran from place to place grabbing and biting others, stealing when he could and swearing profusely.

Observers began cataloguing the behaviour of these three boys. Inappropriate behaviours were: getting out of one's seat, running, making a noise with objects or feet, grabbing other people's belongings, biting, fighting, talking when asked not to, whistling, screaming, ignoring the teacher etc.

Appropriate behaviours were: working as assigned and following instructions for ten seconds.

After some preliminary observation, the teachers were asked to make some very exact rules to be placed on their classroom notice boards such as: 'Don't run in class' or 'Sit quietly while working'. Teachers read these rules to the class about five times a day.

In the next phase of the study a few weeks later, Mrs A and Mrs B were asked to ignore all the inappropriate behaviour of these boys. Instead of saying, 'Cliff, you know you are supposed to be working' or 'Frank, will you stop bothering your neighbours', 'Stan, you have been at the window a long time', 'Cliff, don't sit on your. . .', 'Frank, stop chewing your. . .' etc., the teachers were asked to ignore all of these instances of bad behaviour except when they thought someone was about to be hurt.

After some weeks, praise was added. Mrs A and Mrs B were to 'catch the children being good', give praise, a smile or attention instead of letting the good behaviour go unnoticed as in the last phase. This helped Mrs A and Mrs B with the ignoring rule because they could now turn their attention to one child saying, 'I like the way you're working, Cliff' or 'That is a very good job, Stan' or 'Frank, you're doing that very well!'

The graphs in figures 2 and 3 show that improvement was best under the last condition. Mrs A said, 'I was amazed at the difference and became convinced that a positive approach to discipline is the answer'. Mrs B reported that, 'Stan has changed from a sullen, morose, muttering, angry

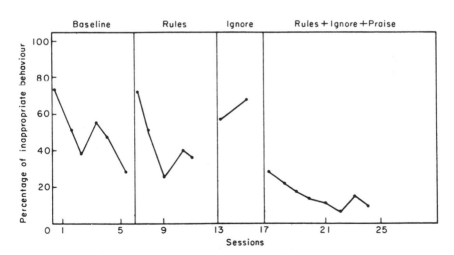

Figure 2   *Percentage of intervals in which inappropriate behaviour occurred under different rule conditions for Cliff. (Adapted with the permission of the* Journal of Applied Behavior Analysis *from Madsen, C. H., Becker, W. C., Thomas, D. R. (1968) Rules, praise and ignoring: elements of elementary classroom control.* Journal of Applied Behavior Analysis **1**, *146, Copyright 1968 by the Society for the Experimental Analysis of Behavior, Inc.)*

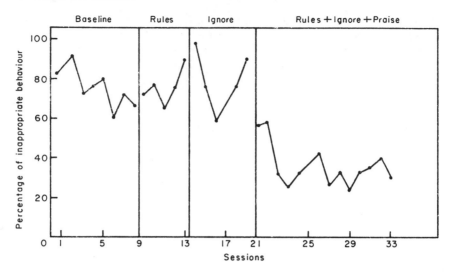

Figure 3   *Percentage of intervals in which inappropriate behaviour occurred under different rule conditions for Stan. (Adapted with the permission of the* Journal of Applied Behavior Analysis *from Madsen, C. H., Becker, W. C., Thomas D. R. (1968) Rules, praise and ignoring: elements of elementary classroom control.* Journal of Applied Behavior Analysis **1**, *147. Copyright 1968 by the Society for the Experimental Analysis of Behavior, Inc.)*

individual into a boy whose smile seems to cover his whole face.' Even the teachers were beginning to enjoy their classes again!

The 'applying too many rules' rule

As the number of rules increases, the inclination to punish increases. 'The children are doing so many things wrong and there are so many of them, I have all I can do just to keep the peace.' Consider carefully the need for rules concerning trivial matters; will a few mistakes justify imposing a rules that produces a great deal of unpleasant punishment? Does the rule possibly infringe upon basic rights of the children's freedom? Possibly a little disorder and individuality in getting their coats on is better than a rigid rule enforced by unpleasantness.

The need for a rule limiting the number of rules can be obvious even in a short visit to the headteacher's room. While waiting with the troublesome Robert, one teacher demonstrated the problem even before it was discussed. Robert had come in first and sat on a convenient chair; the teacher chose to sit at the opposite side of the waiting area. 'Sit over here', she said. 'Don't swing your foot', she said. Robert picked up a book from the table. 'Be careful with that', she said. He made a noise turning a page. 'Shhh', she said. Had the teacher ever thought why Robert should be made to sit next to her?

When asked later, she said she had not. Why had she instructed him to do so? After some thought, she said she was afraid he would 'do something wrong over there'. It was just habit with a little reprimand built in. A psychological leash had been put on Robert and it was jerked regularly.

To break the habit of using a psychological leash, a good rule to include in your strategy is one you would use with adult friends: 'Don't correct or instruct without a specific purpose.' This is a rule all adults expect you to apply to them, and children deserve as much of your faith as adults. Train yourself to hesitate before giving a reprimanding consequence or correction. Is the child doing something wrong or just being given no benefit of the doubt?

The following study by Herbert and Baer (1972) demonstrates how two mothers improved their children's behaviour by heeding the 'applying too many rules' rule.

Frankie and Hannah (aged five) had been troublesome in school for many reasons including hyperactivity. They were suspected of having serious physical and emotional problems. Their mothers had successfully used steps 1, 2 and 3 in improving mealtime, bedtime and playtime behaviour, but they still attended to much bad behaviour and missed opportunities for rewarding good ones.

Observers conducted sessions for one hour each day, five days a week, for six months. The observer sat quietly on a small stool and did not speak to the mother or child after initially greeting them and telling the child, 'I'm just a worker.' Every ten seconds the observer recorded the occurrence of inappropriate behaviour by the child (breaking or throwing objects, damaging furniture, snatching food, screaming, kicking, pinching people or animals etc.). Also annoying verbal habits were recorded, such as repeating the same phrase over and over again. The mother's attention was also recorded, 'uh-huh, 'good', 'stop that', grabbing, hitting or restraining the child etc. In addition, the order of these behaviours was recorded.

After initial observations, each mother was given a wrist counter and told to keep a count of the times she gave attention to her child for *good* behaviour. Praise, instruction and hugging were given as examples. After counting attention for good behaviour, the experimenters asked the mothers to stop counting for a few sessions. Then Hannah's mother was asked to count 'wrong' attention (attention for bad behaviour), and Frankie's mother was asked to go back to counting attention for good behaviour.

In the final phase, both mothers were asked to count attention for good behaviour, and then counting was faded out by removing the counters for some sessions. As can be seen from the graphs in figures 4 and 5, when mothers pay attention to their own behaviour, the good behaviour of their children improves. When the mothers were not required to count or were distracted by having to count attention for bad behaviour, they begin to fall behind the growth of good behaviour and this growth slows. Overall, when the mothers limited their rules to good behaviour, these behaviours not only

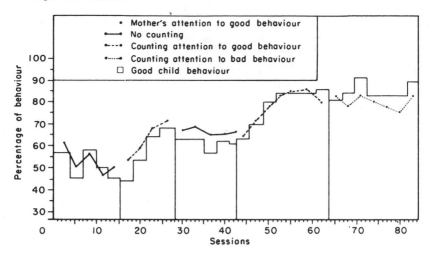

Figure 4   *Percentage of maternal attention following appropriate behaviour and the percentage of Frankie's behaviour recorded as appropriate across no-counting and counting conditions. (Adapted with the permission of the* Journal of Applied Behavior Analysis *from Herbert, E. W. and Baer, D. M. (1972) Training parents as behavior modifiers: self-recording of contingent attention.* Journal of Applied Behavior Analysis **5,** *144, Copyright 1972 by the Society for the Experimental Analysis of Behavior, Inc.)*

improved they remain improved! Such change in the behaviour of a parent or teacher is partly a result of the give and take of consequences with the child. In the next example by Sherman and Cormier (1974), changes in the teacher's behaviour are particularly apparent.

Mrs Z, a teacher, was asked to imagine a scale from 0 to 100 and picture 100 as a score given to the most irritating child she could think of. A child who caused no trouble was represented as 0. Using these guidelines, she assigned a number to each child she had in her class.

From these results, Robin and Karen were selected by the experimenter to help change Mrs Z's behaviour. Robin was 11 years old and was one of the worst behaviour problems in school. He was sent to the headteacher's office almost every day. Karen, also 11 years old, had a similar reputation and a very poor rating on Mrs Z's behaviour scale.

Mrs Z was asked to make two lists of classroom behaviours: appropriate and inappropriate. She listed appropriate behaviours as 'following instructions', 'paying attention', 'having necessary materials', 'raising hands rather than talking out of turn'. Inappropriate behaviours were defined by Mrs Z as 'talking back', 'touching items on the teacher's desk', 'being out of seat', 'talking out of turn', and 'inattention'. Observers counted all of these behaviours and the reactions of the teacher as well. The teacher's reactions were divided into 'praise', 'reprimands', 'neutral remarks' and 'instructions'.

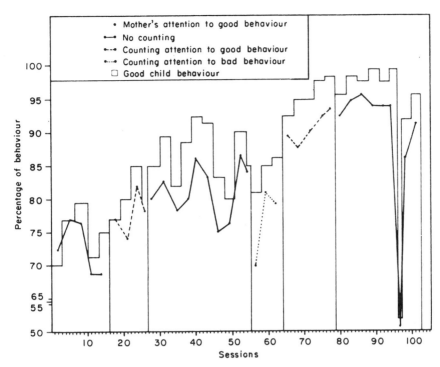

Figure 5   *Percentage of maternal attention following appropriate behaviour and the percentage of Hannah's behaviour recorded as appropriate across conditions (Adapted with the permission of the* Journal of Applied Behavior Analysis *from Herbert, E. W. and Baer, D. M. (1972) Training parents as behavior modifiers: self-recording of contingent attention.* Journal of Applied Behavior Analysis **5**, *146. Copyright 1972 by the Society for the Experimental Analysis of Behavior, Inc.)*

    The appropriate behaviours of the children, and therefore of Mrs Z as well, were low during initial observations. The situation remained poor even when the children were instructed outside class on just how to get good ratings from the observers. However, when rewards (in the form of toys or records) were offered for each two-day period in which less than two inappropriate behaviours occurred, the children's behaviour improved. (See figure 6.) Mrs Z's behaviour also showed great improvement even though she was not told which children were being observed or rewarded or that she herself was being observed.

    When Robin was told the experiment was over and rewards were discontinued, his appropriate behaviour dropped by 50%, but Mrs Z's appropriate behaviour dropped by 100%! Her behaviour with Karen remained good while Karen remained good. So who was controlling whom?! Of course, the answer is that teachers control children some of the time, and

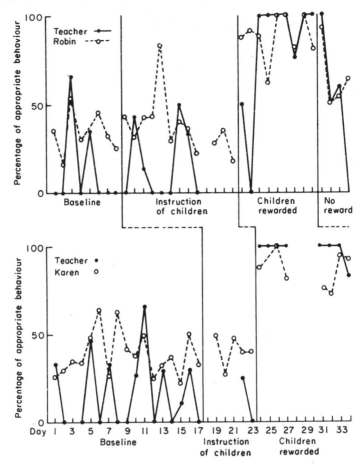

Figure 6· *Percentage of Robin's and Karen's appropriate behaviour and the teacher's behaviour in using consequences. (Adapted with the permission of the* Journal of Applied Behavior Analysis *from Sherman, T. M., and Cormier, W. H. (1974) An investigation of the influence of student behavior on teacher behavior.* Journal of Applied Behavior Analysis **7**, 16. *Copyright 1974 by the Society for the Experimental Analysis of Behavior, Inc.)*

children control teachers some of the time. And each can do better with a little help from the other.

The 'do' rule applied to teachers

The 'do' rule also applies to adults. Perhaps teachers can get together and help each other practise good reactions and benefit from the feedback. An informal programme with a small group of teachers will allow each teacher a new view of his or her own classroom activities. For example, you could visit each other's lessons occasionally with a chart in hand such as the one in figure 7.

If you are to be the visitor remember you are to record what the *teacher* does. Select two ten-minute periods and tally each reaction of the teacher under one of four headings: (*a*) appropriate encouragement; (*b*) inappropriate encouragement; (*c*) appropriate discouragement; and (*d*) inappropriate discouragement. Whenever your fellow teacher encourages children's work e.g. 'This looks very good!', tally one mark under 'appropriate encouragement'. If the teacher says, 'You boys come and sit down', to two rowdy boys, you have a little interpreting to do. Possibly this reaction should be tallied as 'appropriate discouragement', but if there is a suspicion that the boys *intended* to be scolded, you might want to tally the reaction under 'inappropriate encouragement'. The observing teacher may also wish to gather recordings concerning the reactions of the working teacher with respect to a specific child.

With the totals entered, the active and observing teachers should meet and discuss the circumstances of the observations. Were the ten-minute intervals typical? In what ways do the remarks show special circumstances? Are both teachers thinking of the categories in the same way? Refrain from reaching any conclusions on the bases of these first few charts. It is not fair to single out a ten-minute period, or even four or five, as a basis for advice or generalisations. As a matter of fact, advice of that sort is not likely ever to be welcome or used. Rather, each teacher can draw his or her own conclusions while reviewing and totalling their own results.

Such tallies of teacher behaviour are not new. David Brook, (1982) in a recent review of 'commonsense' (i.e. behavioural) practices for teachers, describes a useful measure suggested by Withall (1949), and known as the

Day _____ Time _____ Activity _____

	Encouragements		Discouragements		Total	Total
	Appropriate	Inappropriate	Appropriate	Inappropriate	Encouragements	Discouragements
1st. 10 min. for class						
2nd. 10 min. for class						
Student of special interest #1						
#2						
#3						
#4						

Figure 7   *Chart to be used by the visiting teacher for classroom observation.*

'socioemotional climate index', which measures the ratio of the teacher's pleasant rewarding remarks to her unpleasant, criticising or punishing ones.

Discussion between teachers of the results of classroom observations is best centered on the specific children with whom the teacher has been observed. Here we have clear evidence of classroom problems which allows teachers to discuss the merits of specific teacher strategies, for example, those strategies listed in this chapter and others that will occur to you as your observations accumulate. Such informal discussion allows a fresh look to be taken at the general frequency of teacher rewards and punishments and the circumstances under which they are given. It takes only a little time and provides a basis for the adoption and development of more appropriate strategies, which lead in turn to a change in behaviour in teachers and children alike.

References

Broden, M., Bruce, C., Mitchell, M. A., Carter, V. and Hall, R. V. (1970) Effects of teacher attention on attending behavior of two boys at adjacent desks. *Journal of Applied Behavior Analysis* **3**, 199-203.

Brook, D. J. (1982) Behaviour modification and teachers' 'common sense' practices. *Educational Psychology* **2**, 313-16.

Corey, J. and Shamow, J. (1972) The effects of fading on the acquisition and retention of oral reading. *Journal of Applied Behavior Analysis* **5**, 311-15.

Drew, B., Evans, J., Bostow, D., Geiger, G. and Drash, P. (1982) Increasing assignment completion and accuracy using a daily report card procedure. *Psychology in the Schools* **19**, 540-7.

Herbert, E. W. and Baer, D. M. (1972) Training parents as behavior modifiers: self-recording of contingent attention. *Journal of Behaviour Analysis* **5**, 139-49.

Madsen, C. H. Becker, W. C. and Thomas, D. R. (1968) Rules, praise and ignoring: elements of elementary classroom control. *Journal of Behavior Analysis* **1**, 139-50.

Sherman, T. M. and Cormier, W. H. (1974) An investigation of the influence of student behavior on teacher behavior. *Journal of Behavior Analysis* **7**, 11-21.

Withall, J. (1949) The development of a technique of measurement of social and emotional climate in the classroom. *Journal of Experimental Education* **17**, 347-61.

Further Reading

Harrop, A. (1983) *Behaviour Modification in the Classroom.* London: Hodder and Stoughton.

Stone, D. R. and Nielsen, E. C. (1982) *Educational Psychology: the Development of Teaching Skills.* New York: Harper and Row.

Alberto, P. A. and Troutman, A. C. (1982) *Applied Behavior Analysis for Teachers: Influencing Student Performance.* New York: Charles E. Merrill Publishing Co.

6

Personality and Personal Development

DAVID FONTANA

Man has been interested in the study of personality since the time of the ancient Greeks, and probably for thousands of years before that. Few people, however, are more professionally concerned with personality than the teacher. Her concern takes two closely related forms; first, a desire that children should be helped to make the best of themselves as people (i.e. that they should learn to express their wishes and their feelings in a confident, acceptable manner, and be able to relate warmly to others) and, secondly, an interest in the extent to which children's personalities influence their ability to tackle school work satisfactorily. But she faces an immediate problem as human personality is so complex. We are each of us many faceted. We behave differently with different people and in different circumstances. We suffer from moods. Our attitudes change, our standards alter, our goals in life fluctuate. At times, we may even seem virtual strangers to ourselves. And at no stage in life is all this more apparent than in early childhood.

The complexity of human personality has raised particular problems for those who have attempted to provide an all-embracing definition of the term. Some of the efforts that have been made range so widely that, as Allport (1961) says, they seem to include practically everything that interests us about people. Such imprecision is difficult to avoid, since even in everyday life it is almost impossible to think about someone's personality without being influenced by considerations of how intelligent he or she is, how creative, how physically adept and so on. However, in an attempt to introduce some rationality into the field, psychologists have tended in recent years to exclude from the term 'personality' cognitive attributes such as intelligence and physical attributes such as motor skills. A good example of the kind of definition that emerges as a result is that of Eysenck et al. (1975), who suggest that: 'Personality is the relatively stable organisation of a person's motivational dispositions . . . The term refers chiefly to the affective and conative traits, sentiments, attitudes, complexes and unconscious mechanisms, interests and ideals, which determine man's characteristic behaviour and thought.' This definition is the one to which we shall be working in this chapter.

The origins of personality

The teacher is particularly interested to know how a child comes by his unique personality. Does he inherit it or does he acquire it as the result of experience? Obviously, the more dependent it is upon experience, the greater the teacher's potential influence over it. Unfortunately, like all nature versus nurture controversies in psychology, the answer to this question is by no means clear cut. From birth—and even from conception—onwards, inheritance and environment interact with each other in the formation of the child's personality so intricately that it is very difficult to separate the relative contributions of the two.

Nevertheless, the results of modern research help us to go some way in this direction. Taking inheritance first, we know from biology that genetic defects can lead to abnormal behaviour patterns in children. For example, Down's syndrome (mongolism) seems linked to chromosomal defects. From this we can infer that if inheritance is linked with *abnormal* behaviour patterns, it may also play a part in *normal* ones. We also know from selective breeding studies with animals that in a few short generations it is possible to breed strains manifesting markedly high or low aggression levels and other such characteristics. Again, we possess a number of studies (Eysenck, 1967; Shields, 1962) which suggest that identical twins (who receive the same genetic endowments at conception) are significantly more alike in personality than are non-identical twins (who are no more alike genetically than any other siblings). Finally, there is some evidence that certain kinds of personality seem to go with certain kinds of physique. The American psychologist William Sheldon in a number of studies (e.g. Sheldon et al., 1969) has produced findings that indicate that most men and women fall predominantly into one of three personality types: the fat (the endomorph), the muscular (the mesomorph) and the thin (the ectomorph). The personalities of endomorphs seem to show some tendency towards tolerance, complacency, sociability and dependency, while those of mesomorphs are inclined towards aggression, tough-mindedness, competitiveness and dominance, and those of ectomorphs towards restraint, withdrawal, studiousness and anxiety.

These research results have been criticised on methodological grounds and are not completely conclusive. Identical twins may be more alike than non-identical not because of inheritance but simply because they are treated more alike by their families and friends, while muscular people may be more aggressive than thin people simply because their experiences in life allow them to get away with aggression more often. Extreme environmentalist arguments of this kind are admittedly unlikely to fit all the facts revealed in the above investigations, but they remain as possible alternative explanations to many of them. This is less true, however, of those findings produced by investigations into personality in the very early weeks of life, at a time when environmental factors have had little chance to make much significant impact. One of the most revealing of these studies is that of the American paediatricians Thomas, Chess and Birch (1970). Taking a sample of 141 children at only 12 weeks of age, Thomas and his colleagues found that on such measures as activity levels, regularity of bodily functions (e.g. feeding, sleeping, excreting), adaptability, sensitivity to stimuli (i.e. reaction to things such as loud noise) and disposition (cheerful, cranky etc.) 65% of the children could be assigned to one of the following three groups:

1 The *easy* group, characterised by regular bodily functions, adaptability, a positive approach to new people and to new events, and a
   normal reaction to stimuli (40% of sample).
2 The *difficult* group, characterised by irregular body functions, low
   adaptability levels, a negative response to new people and situations,
   an over-reaction to stimuli, and negativity of mood (10% of sample).
3 The *slow to warm up* group, characterised by low activity and
   adaptability levels, an inclination to withdraw when confronted by
   new people and situations, mild reaction to stimuli, and by a slight
   negativity of mood (15% of sample).

Even in very young babies, these characteristics seemed to the investigators to be identifiable evidence of the existence of personality. Their next step was to follow the sample of children through into adolesence to see how persistent these characteristics were, and although the methods of assessment have obviously had to be altered to remain in keeping with the children's advancing age, findings indicate that membership of the three groups has remained remarkably constant. So much so indeed that Thomas and his colleagues are prompted to conclude that it looks very much as if the personality we have at adolescence is already apparent in essentials from the early weeks of life. They also note that of the children belonging to the 'difficult' category no less than 70% have developed behaviour problems, as opposed to only 18% of the 'easy' group (Thomas and Chess, 1977).

Of great interest to the teacher is the contrasting reactions shown by the three groups of children to the business of starting school. The 'easy' children took to school readily, adapting quickly, joining in activities and learning rules with a minimum of fuss. The 'difficult' and 'slow to warm up' children posed much more of a problem, with the former group showing particular reluctance and contrariness. Obviously, by the time children are of school age, environment has had some time in which to shape behaviour, but in examining the background of each of the children the investigators found that the parents of children in the three respective groups did not differ significantly from each other in the way in which they brought up their children. All three groups contained similar proportions of authoritarian and permissive parents, and the inescapable conclusion was that it was innate characteristics rather than parental behaviour that still, at school age, determined to which of the three groups individual children belonged.

This must not be taken to suggest, of course, that it does not matter how we bring up children. There were no really bad (i.e. neglecting or over-punitive) parents in any of the three groups. Had there been, then doubtless even the easiest of children would have become a behaviour problem. It was also significant that children from the 'difficult' and 'slow to warm up' groups were much more successful at coping with their potentially troublesome natures if they were blessed with parents who were extra patient, consistent and objective in their manner. The 'difficult' children, in the face of parents who were none of these things, or who were unnecessarily rigid, tended to become even more negative and awkward, while those who were 'slow to warm up' were prone to show an ever decreasing disinclination to act with initiative or to participate if they had parents who tried to force them into novel situations or who failed to provide them with encouragement. These children seemed at their best when given ample opportunity for new experience, but allowed time to adjust to this experience against a background of keen parental interest and guidance.

We could summarise this section on inheritance and personality by saying that individuals seem to inherit the raw material of their personalities (their 'nature' or 'temperaments' for want of better words), with environment influencing the way in which this raw material develops. Obviously, researchers such as Thomas, Chess and Birch are not suggesting that their threefold classification of temperament is the only one, or that the measures which they used to arrive at this classification are exhaustive. But such a classification provides a useful guideline for both parents and teachers, and helps to emphasise the extent to which both groups of adults must be sensitive to the child's inherited tendencies.

Environment

Having said that environment influences the way in which temperament develops, we can now look at how this happens. And we can best begin by considering an example of what the result is when a young animal is isolated from appropriate adult care. Harry Harlow at the University of Wisconsin (Harlow and Harlow, 1966) has shown that rhesus monkeys reared in isolation for the first six months of life are permanently unable, when allowed subsequently to mix with their own kind, to relate to them satisfactorily either socially or sexually. Neither are they able, in the rare instances when they achieve parenthood themselves, to care for their own young. Since rhesus monkeys mature more rapidly than humans, and the first six months of their lives are roughly equivalent to the first three years of a child's, Harlow's findings led him to suggest that it is parental deprivation during these three years that is likely to have the most permanent and damaging effect upon the development of human personality. The ill effects of deprivation during the first month of the money's life (equivalent to the first six months of the child's) seem to be reversible given adequate subsequent care, but after this critical point has been passed, the chances of reversal appear to become increasingly poor.

Of course, no child is subjected to the complete isolation that Harlow imposed upon his infant monkeys, but even though a child may be cared for physically, he may be deprived of any real show of parental love and concern. Brought up by a rejecting or a neglecting mother, he may be denied the warm human contacts and the all-round environmental stimulation necessary if he is to have a secure base from which to explore the world around him and to offer and receive friendship.

All children, it seems, need a generous minimum of care by a mother or mother substitute if they are to develop their temperamental potential to best advantage. By 'care' is meant not just the satisfaction of physical wants but affection, acceptance, encouragement, patience and sufficient contact with the kind of environment capable of arousing and maintaining the child's interest in the way in which people and objects in the outside world behave. It is true that children are resilient creatures, and that with appropriate support in later childhood the effects of severe deprivation in the early years can to some extent be overcome (Clarke and Clarke, 1976). But it is a sad fact that the child who is deprived in the first five or six years of life often remains deprived throughout childhood, and thus has little chance to make up for his poor start. Indeed, since this poor start often means he is unable to relate appropriately to teachers or to school learning, satisfactory development in subsequent years normally becomes increasingly hard to achieve.

Personality in the pre-school years

The American psychologist Erik Erikson (1965) sums up many of the points contained in the above section when he writes that the first 'task' facing the child's personality is to learn to *trust*. The child who receives the necessary quota of parental care learns as a result that the world in which he finds himself is a place to be trusted. He knows that his physical and emotional wants will be satisfied adequately, and this frees him to turn his attention to all the other things going on in his immediate environment. Where he is deprived of the opportunity to learn to trust, he either becomes hostile and over-aggressive and tries to take what he wants from the world by force, or withdraws more and more into himself and shows little readiness to engage himself in the activities happening around him.

Having gained a sense of trust, Erikson (1965) considers that the child is now able to tackle the next task facing his personality, that is, to learn to express *autonomy*. In the second and third years of life, his growing physical and mental powers enable him to become potentially much more independent of the adults in his life. Since over-dependency is a bad thing, this burgeoning capacity to assert autonomy is to be encouraged, but it is not without its problems. It often results in the child's going through a particularly 'negative' stage, especially during the third year of life, a stage in which he seems impelled to disagree with even the simplest of adult requests, and often to engage in tantrums and general awkwardness if thwarted in what he wants to do.

It is important, however, that adults avoid making the mistake of seeing this awkward behaviour as simply disagreement for disagreement's sake. A child who is met by a head-on clash of wills with parents every time he tries to assert his growing independence is likely to get the impression that the world is a sort of conspiracy to stop him from ever doing as he wants. The resulting feeling of frustration is likely to make him assert himself even more aggressively or, if that is the way he is temperamentally inclined, to give up the attempt altogether and lapse into a docility which, later on, adults will condemn in him as a lack of spirit. Either way, the experience of a constant conflict between what he wants to do and what his parents will allow him to do leads to a sense of self-doubt and uncertainty. Since he is unable to view the situation objectively, he cannot escape the feeling that his lack of ability to control his own behaviour is something of which he should be deeply ashamed. Further, he may feel a sense of inadequacy at never being allowed to make his own decisions. Control and decision making, it seems, are things which are always imposed upon him from outside, things which he either has to capitulate to meekly or resist with the kind of extreme temper tantrum that only confirms to him even more fully his own lack of self-control.

Although his theories are far too many and involved to explore deeply, it is worth mentioning that one of the most influential of all personality theorists, Sigmund Freud, saw the conflict between what the child really wants to do and what the world will actually allow him to do as being the root cause of neurotic and maladjusted behaviour later in life. The child is born, Freud claimed, with a reservoir of instinctive energy, termed the *id*, which lies below the level of conscious thought and seeks throughout life to gratify its own very basic needs. Chief amongst these needs are the need for self-preservation (which includes the need for self-assertion and for food and drink) and the need for preservation of the species (i.e. the sex drive). Due to its instinctive, biological nature, the child cannot turn off, so to speak, the needs of the *id* (i.e. he cannot stop himself feeling hungry, sexually aroused or aggressive in the furtherance of his own needs), and instead of making him feel ashamed of these needs or frightened of them he should be helped to bring his methods of expressing them more and more under the control of his conscious thought processes (termed by Freud the *ego*). Thus the child should not be made to see himself as naughty or wicked for feeling angry with those who thwart him, but should be helped to realise that it is what he does with his anger that matters. In practical terms, this means that the child should be helped to channel his aggression (which is an essential part of the self-preservation mechanism) into socially acceptable forms such as determination and productive endeavour, instead of being made to bottle it up inside him, and even deny its existence to himself until extreme frustration makes it explode into a guilt-provoking outburst.

A key factor here, of course, is the development of the emotions and of the child's ability to understand and regulate them. Recent research by Lewis and Michalson (1983) shows that enduring emotional patterns (or 'profiles') are clearly present in children in the second year of life, with positive correlations present between for example anger and fear, and negative correlations present between these variables and more desirable ones such as happiness, affiliation and competence. Since learning and socialisation appear to play an important part in determining how the child relates to his emotional life, it is important for teachers and parents to provide the young child with an environment which avoids the unnecessary arousal of negative, destructive emotions and enhances opportunities for positive, creative ones.

Furnishing such an environment makes considerable demands upon adult patience and understanding, of course, since it means adults should avoid head-on clashes with the young child wherever possible, and attempt to answer tantrums or aggression with calmness rather than with equal displays of temper. This does not mean, however, that the adult should constantly give in to the child. The child must learn that the world in which we live is not the kind of place in which he will be allowed to go through life ignoring the legitimate rights of others in order to serve his own ends. Parents, teachers and other children have rights too, and it is part of a child's socialisation that he comes to appreciate this, and to give others their due consideration. The key to helping this aspect of the child's socialisation, while at the same time helping him to come to terms with his own feelings, is to demonstrate to him that while some of his behaviour may be unacceptable, it is not he as a *person* who is being rejected. Thus, while telling him that a particular action must be discontinued, the adult avoids labelling the child as 'bad' or 'naughty' for wanting to do it. And she backs this up with an explanation of *why* the particular action cannot be allowed ('the other children haven't had their turns yet', 'you might hurt yourself', 'you wouldn't like it if someone did that to you'), and suggests wherever possible an alternative, acceptable activity.

To return to Erikson's (1965) work again, we find him suggesting that the constant frustration of a child's growing need for autonomy and self-expression leads to a distortion of the balance within him between 'cooperation and wilfulness, between self-expression and its suppression'. Only by learning the self-control that comes through the measured expression of autonomy can the child, argues Erikson, gain 'a lasting sense of goodwill and pride', as opposed to 'a lasting propensity for doubts and shame'.

Personality at school age

The period we have looked at so far in the development of the child's personality spans the years from birth to his first year or so in the nursery school. By the age of four, he should have gained the emotional security that comes through a trust in others, and should have learnt to exercise his developing independence within a framework of realistic self-control and a growing understanding of the rights of others. If he has learnt these early lessons, he should, by the time he is ready to move on to the infant school, be reasonably free of the need to cling too closely to adults, and of the kind of aggressive behaviour that stems from constant frustration or from inadequate socialisation. He should be ready to take part in group activities, to offer and receive friendship and to show no undue timidity in the face of new experiences. The child who fails to show these signs of healthy adjustment should attract the teacher's special concern, and methods for helping him are dealt with in chapters 7 and 8.

We must not lose sight of the fact, however, that even to the best adjusted child, starting school, whether it be at the age of three or five, can be an intimidating experience. He is plunged from the small familiar world of home into the much bigger and less personal one of school. He is called upon to learn his way around a new physical environment, to mix with new children, to take his instructions from strange adults. The sense of bewilderment (and even of betrayal) at being left by his mother in these new surroundings can sometimes be very real. The busy teacher is often, naturally enough, tempted to assume that new children will quickly 'settle', and to make light of the 'silliness' of those who seem to be taking longer than usual to do so. But the experiences of early school life can often play an important part in determining not only a child's longer term attitude to school, but also his attitude to new experiences in general. For the first two weeks or so of his school life, his mother should be even more welcome in school than usual, and should be allowed to accompany him into the classroom if necessary, disengaging herself gently from this habit as he gets to know his teacher and the other children and shows less need for her presence. The abrupt break between child and mother, often advocated by an earlier generation of infant school teachers, had little to commend it beyond a doubtful administrative convenience.

During the nursery and infant school years, the child is faced with the task of consolidating his autonomy and, again in the language of Erikson (1965), going on to learn the lessons first of initiative and then of competence. Initiative refers to the child's ability to think for himself, to manifest originality and to assume ever greater responsibility for his own school work and behaviour. One of the main arguments against the old, over-formal school regime was that it presented the child with a too tightly controlled and regimented environment. There was too often only one way of doing things and that was the teacher's way, and it was hardly surprising that the child frequently failed to use what is loosely termed his 'commonsense' or to act responsibly when the teacher's back was turned.

Essentially, the growth of initative is best fostered in an atmosphere in which the child is made to feel that his ideas are respected, in which he feels confident of being listened to and, where practicable, is drawn into the business of classroom decision making. We mean by this, however, a measure of classroom democracy and not of classroom anarchy. At no point is it of much value to present children with an environment lacking in the kind of structure that comes from a clear recognition by the teacher of her educational objectives and a clear knowledge of the means by which they can best be achieved. Schools are society's formal attempt to influence the behaviour of the next generation along socially agreed lines, and they are only likely to succeed in their task if the teacher presents the children with a carefully planned framework of activities, each designed to foster identifiable skills: a framework within which there is ample opportunity for exploration and the exercise of initiative certainly, but a framework which guides the child away from unproductive pursuits, or from those which present insufficient stimulus to his particular level of ability.

Following on from the growth of initiative comes the growth of competence. In the infant school, the child becomes very conscious that certain levels of performance are expected of him by his teachers, and begins to compare his own attempts at achieving these levels with the kind of success met with by other children. Should these comparisons consistently go against him, he begins inevitably to experience a sense of failure and ultimately of inferiority. As on earlier occasions when he has not been enabled to master one of the necessary stages in personality development, his response to this inferiority, dependent upon temperament, may take one of two extreme forms. Either he may show a passive acceptance of it and a disinclination to try new things in the future, or he may rebel against it and show a rejection of all the school activities that remind him of it (saying, in effect, it is not *I* who am at fault, it is the things that I am asked to do). In both instances, there is also likely to be an attempt, through such activities as tears, sulks, tantrums or wild and irresponsible behaviour, to gain the attention and prestige which his lack of success at school work denies him.

One of the most interesting pieces of research into the self-confidence that goes with the acquisition of competence is that of the American psychologist Stanley Coopersmith (1968). Coopersmith followed a group of boys from primary school to early adult life and found that, on the basis of tests and of self- and teacher-ratings, they divided consistently into three groups which he calls 'high', 'medium' and 'low' self-esteem respectively. High self-esteem boys were from the beginning of the research found to be active and expressive, with a willingness to participate in activities and to communicate freely with others. For the most part successful both academically and socially, the boys were self-assured, not unduly disturbed by criticism and were generally good judges of their own abilities. The medium self-esteem boys shared many of these qualities, but tended to be much more anxious to win the approval of adults, and much readier to follow the lead of others. The low self-esteem boys, by contrast, were what Coopersmith called a sad little group, isolated, fearful, self-conscious, reluctant to participate, over-sensitive to criticism and likely consistently to underrate their own abilities.

In searching for reasons for these differences between the three groups, Coopersmith (1968) found no significant evidence of variations in intelligence or in physical attractiveness. The root cause seemed to lie in the way in which the boys were treated by their parents. The high self-esteem boys came from homes in which they were regarded as significant and interesting people, and in which their views were invited and listened to. Parental expectations were consistent and were higher than in the other two groups, while discipline, though firm, depended more upon the giving and withholding of approval than upon corporal punishment. The boys, significantly, also considered their parents to be fair in their dealings with them. The low self-esteem boys, on the other hand, came from homes in which their parents seemed to take little real interest in them. They were given little consistent guidance, and standards of discipline varied from extreme permissiveness to extreme strictness, even within the same families. Not surprisingly, the boys regarded their parents' behaviour as unfair.

What seemed to be happening was that the high self-esteem boys had parents who made them feel they mattered. They were made to understand what was expected of them and encouraged to aim as high as their abilities realistically allowed. They were confident of their parents' interest, support and affection, and their attempts to achieve their aims in life were not inhibited by excessive fear of failure or by uncertainties as to their own worth. By virtue of their accurate assessment of their own capabilities, they were less deflated by criticism and less dependent upon the unqualified approval of all and sundry. The low self-esteem boys had none of these advantages. They lived in an environment in which they were made to feel much less sure of themselves. Their parents treated them unpredictably, and they were denied the security of knowing that they were worthy of their parents' interest and concern.

Although Coopersmith's work was concerned with parent–child relationships, it contains lessons of direct practical concern for the teacher. Young children take their ideas about themselves largely from the opinions that adults have about them. If these adults show them, by word and deed, that they count as people, that their interests are of sufficient value to arouse those of the adults too, that their efforts are worthy of praise and encouragement, then it is likely that they will respond by taking an equally positive view of themselves. Few things are more dispiriting than the child who consistently underrates himself, who declines to take part for fear of failure, whose achievements are consistently below the level of which he is capable. Yet by failing to ensure that all children experience success at their own realistic level, by failing to confront them with consistent standards, the achievement of which brings a sense of reward and fulfilment, and by failing to reassure them of their own worth, we do much to bring about this very state of affairs.

One gap in Coopersmith's work was that it was concerned only with boys from middle-class homes. However, there is reason to believe that the lessons to be derived from it are applicable to all children. Indeed, the problem is exacerbated amongst working-class families in that we know from other pieces of research (Rosenberg, 1965) that children from these families, as a social group, are lower in self-esteem than are children from middle-class homes. This may be because working-class parents more frequently exhibit the parental styles associated with low self-esteem in children (though we must be careful here: many working-class parents show far more genuine involvement in their children than do many middle-class parents), or it may be because working-class children as a whole are given the impression that society often rates them of less importance than middle-class children. Working-class children often live in the least attractive housing and go to physically the least attractive schools. The trappings of success, it seems, are less readily available to them and their kind.

Low self-esteem in working-class children, however, seems less often associated with the symptoms of withdrawal and defeat found in Cooper-smith's middle-class boys than with aggression and hostility, impulsive and uncontrolled behaviour. The working-class child, coming it seems from a subculture that many sociologists see as actively prizing attributes like 'toughness' and 'smartness', is prone to try and protect his self-esteem by rejecting the standards for which the school stands. Evidence exists to suggest (Conger and Miller, 1966) that a high percentage of children who become delinquent are drawn from amongst these low self-esteem working-class children.

Sex roles in personality development

Just as adults strongly influence children's self-concepts during the nursery and infant school years, so they also influence their ideas of the kind of role appropriate to the respective sexes. That some part of sex roles is probably genetically determined is suggested by research which shows, for example, that in primates generally the female is less inclined to engage in aggressive and boisterous behaviour than the male (Smith, 1974). Research shows further that, in animals at least, these inter-sex differences are significantly decreased if females are born to mothers who have received injections of male hormones during pregnancy, suggesting that the presence of these hormones may play some part in determining such differences. Nevertheless, there can be little doubt that a large part of the sex role is culturally created. Violent activity is more readily countenanced by adults in boys than in girls, while expressions of timidity are more readily accepted from the latter. Certain pastimes are regarded as the prerogative of boys, others as that of girls, and the child who fails to observe these conventions is often made to feel different and odd.

Perhaps because of their traditional role in the home, girls are frequently encouraged to be less independent than boys. Lewis (1972) shows that this process is noticeable from at least the second year of life onwards, and that it continues through into adolescence, while Davie et al. (1972) show that girls are generally more anxious for parental approval than are boys, while boys are more concerned to gain the approval of their peers.

Clearly, the teacher of young children cannot ignore completely the different sex roles demanded by society from boys and girls. Children will learn these roles outside school whatever she may try to do inside it, and it would be quite wrong of her to encourage forms of girlish behaviour in boys and boyish behaviour in girls that would only hold them up to ridicule in the home. However, she must insist that neither sex is 'better' than the other, that all school activities are open equally to both sexes and that different standards in the performance of these activities are not frequently expected from them. She must also try to avoid the polarisation into monosexual groups which usually commences early in a child's school life, and must gently discourage signs of excessive prudery or shyness shown by children in the face of members of the opposite sex.

The maladjusted personality

We have said enough throughout this chapter to suggest that the cause of personality problems in children lies largely in the unsatisfactory relationships that they have with adults, particularly in the early years of life. We have suggested that some children may be temperamentally more vulnerable to the ill effects of these relationships than others, and that temperament will also play a part in deciding what form the resultant problems take, but largely we have laid stress on the overriding importance of correct relationships between adults and children if the latter are to develop into the confident, well-adjusted persons we wish them to be. We have also said enough to suggest that in dealing with the personality problems that inevitably she encounters from time to time among her children the teacher should try to reverse the processes that originally caused them, i.e. she should offer acceptance in the place of rejection, concern in the place of indifference, consistency in the place of inconsistency and encouragement in the place of discouragement.

However, in conclusion, it is fair to point out that the teacher cannot be expected alone to redress the balance of the adverse home circumstances that have given rise to these problems. Such problems, which often cause children to be designated maladjusted, require specialist help. The Underwood Report (1955), in its official definition of the maladjusted child, described him as 'developing in ways that have a bad effect on himself and on his fellows, and cannot without help be remedied by his parents, teachers, and other adults in normal contact with him'. Where she suspects a child to fit this description (and remember the description covers the extremely withdrawn child as well as the over-aggressive and disruptive one), the teacher must quickly, through the head of the school, seek the assistance of the School Psychological Service. Admittedly, she will find that some school psychologists are reluctant to diagnose maladjustment while children are still of nursery and infant school age, knowing that many children simply learn the rules of socialisation more slowly than others, and that seemingly intractable problems often clear up in the friendly, structured atmosphere of such schools. Nevertheless, many do not, and by seeking expert help the teacher can ensure that the child's progress is carefully monitored.

Finally, where she suspects that a child is being ill treated at home, the teacher has a duty to see that the headteacher is informed so that the social services department of the local authority may be alerted. A qualified social worker can then visit the home and make recommendations on the best course of action. Often, nursery and infant teachers are the best placed to notice evidence of ill treatment in children, and promptness in bringing this evidence to the attention of those whose job it is to take the appropriate action is the best way of avoiding long term mental and physical harm to the child.

Conclusion

Personality is such a vast topic that in one short chapter it is not possible to provide more than the most general of introductions to it. The arguments given here would probably be agreed by most psychologists, but it is relevant to point out that the reader who pursues the subject further will find a considerable divergence of opinion amongst psychologists in many of the deeper aspects of the subject. How important, for example, are unconscious processes in determining personality? And to what extent are we able usefully to measure some or all of its many aspects? For those who do want to read further, some suggested texts are listed below.

References

Allport, G. W. (1961) *Pattern and Growth in Personality*. New York: Holt, Rinehart and Winston.

Clarke, A. M. and Clarke, A. D. B. (1976) *Early Experience: Myth and Evidence*. London: Open Books.

Conger, J. J. and Miller, W. C. (1966) *Personality, Social Class and Delinquency*. New York: Wiley.

Coopersmith, S. (1968) Studies in self-esteem. *Scientific American* February.

Davie, R., Butler, N. and Goldstein, H. (1972) *From Birth to Seven*. London: Longman.

Erikson, E. (1965) *Childhood and Society* 2nd ed. Harmondsworth: Penguin.

Eysenck, H. J. (1967) *The Biological Basis of Personality*. Illinois: C. C. Thomas.

Eysenck, H. J., Arnold, W. J. and Meili, R. (1975) *Encyclopedia of Psychology*, vol. 2. London: Fontana/Collins.

Harlow, H. F. and Harlow, M. (1966) Learning to love. *American Scientist* **54**, 244-272.

Lewis, M. M. (1972) State as an infant-environment interaction; an analysis of mother-infant behaviour as a function of sex. *Merrill-Palmer Quarterly in Behavioural Development* **18**, 95-121.

Lewis, M. and Michalson, L. (1983) *Children's Emotions and Moods: Developmental Theory and Measurement*. New York: Plenum.

Rosenberg, M. (1965) *Society and the Adolescent Self-Image*. Princeton, NJ: Princeton University Press.

Sheldon, W. H., Lewis, N. and Tenney, A. (1969) Psychotic patterns and physical constitution. In Sankar, D. (ed.) *Schizophrenia: Current Concepts and Research*. New York: PJD Publications.

Shields, J. (1962) *Monozygotic Twins*. London: Oxford University Press.

Smith, P. K. (1974) Ethological methods. In Foss, B. (ed.) *New Perspectives in Child Development*. Harmondsworth: Penguin.

Thomas, A., Chess, S. and Birch, H. (1970) The origins of personality. *Scientific American* August.

Thomas, A. and Chess, S. (1977) *Temperament and Development*. New York: Brunner/Mazel.

Underwood Report (1955) *Report of the Committee on Maladjusted Children*. London: HMSO.

Further Reading

Fontana, D. (1977) *Personality and Education*. London: Open Books.

Hall, C. S. and Lindzey, G. (1970) *Theories of Personality*. New York: Wiley.

Mischel, W. (1981) *Introduction to Personality*, 3rd ed. New York: Holt, Rinehart and Winston.

Mussen, P. H., Conger, J. J. and Kagan, J. (1979) *Child Development and Personality*, 5th ed. New York: Harper and Row.

7

Social Development and Social Behaviour

RONALD DAVIE

Various aspects of the development of young children are dealt with in different chapters of this book. Inevitably, there will be some overlap between them but in a chapter devoted to social development and social behaviour there are particular difficulties in establishing the boundaries of our territory. This need not concern us unduly. Indeed, it may serve to remind us that, although it is often helpful to think about human development under separate headings (physical, cognitive etc.), this is only a convenient abstraction. In the real world outside the textbook and the psychologist's laboratory, children are indivisible wholes. Furthermore, the wholes are more than the sum of their parts; each facet of development is continually interacting with every other. Physical development is probably the most isolated in this respect but even here there is evidence, for example, that a child's growth rate can be adversely affected by emotional deprivation, and that bodily movements will often reflect psychological tension. Social development is almost certainly the least isolated in this context; in some of its aspects it is virtually indistinguishable from other, nominally separate, facets of development, and at all times it can be seen as a context for emerging intellectual, emotional and physical maturity.

The developing child

Until quite recently, it was not considered useful to discuss the social development of children in their earliest weeks and months. The very young baby was thought to be a bundle of largely instinctive reflexes, responding to his environment, if at all, in a rather mechanistic fashion. Indeed, as recently as 1976, an official notice which was being sent to British doctors and child health clinics for display to mothers mentioned (wrongly) that the new born baby cannot see. On the contrary, we have known for some while that from birth babies can not only see but are perceptually alert and capable of paying attention to visual (and other) stimuli.

Social development, then, can be said to start within the first few moments as the baby begins to respond selectively to the sight, sound and touch of those around him. Of course, at this stage the baby still has a long way to go, not only because there is much to learn about his social world but because his capacity for such learning is as yet relatively limited. For example, even at two months old a baby will smile at two dark blobs on a white card, simulating a pair of eyes. For some time after this, too, he will tend to smile at unfamiliar faces as well as familiar ones.

From a social standpoint, the baby's first year of life is one of a developing awareness of the people around him and, in particular, of a growth in his understanding of their significance for him (Leach, 1983). At first, this process involves associating certain recurring sights and sounds in the immediate environment with the fulfilment of the basic needs for food, warmth, sleep and physical comfort. Towards the middle or end of the year, as the baby is able increasingly to differentiate between the people around him, he will begin to develop attachments (Bowlby, 1975) to those whom he sees most frequently and who satisfy his psychological and bodily needs. Almost always, one of these attachments will be stronger than the others and this will usually be to the mother. However, it is interesting to note that one study has indicated that, in as many as a third of cases, the closest bond by the age of 18 months will be with some other member of the family or even someone outside the family (Schaffer, 1977).

Whether this closest of bonds merely differs in degree from the others or whether it also differs in kind is still not established (Rutter, 1981). This is an important issue since it relates to the still vexed question of the psychological effect upon a child of separation from his mother or the person to whom he is most closely attached. This in turn relates to other question such as the custody of young children in the event of family break-up and the effect of working mothers, residential care etc. We shall return to some of these issues later.

What is beyond dispute is that the quality of these early attachments and the security which the young child derives from them is important for him in two main ways. First, it provides a firm base for sound emotional development. Secondly, it gives him growing confidence to explore his environment. This exploration will enhance his social development, as he interacts with a widening circle of people. It will also provide a stimulus for physical development both in gross motor movements and in the fine coordination of hands and fingers needed in grasping and manipulation. The new experiences which such physical exploration make possible are, in part, the building bricks of cognitive growth; and the social and linguistic interactions which normally follow comprise the mortar. Here we can see the essentially dynamic interrelationship of the various aspects of development.

If attachment is an important element (some would say *the* important element) in the very early social development of the child, the next phase can perhaps best be characterised as one of progressive disengagement from parents and others. The word 'phase' here should not be taken to imply a changed situation which is either sudden or which entirely supplants what has gone before. On the contrary, new attachments may still be made and the existing ones will continue to be important for very many years to come, perhaps in different ways throughout life. However, the second year of life normally sees the beginnings of a process in which the child appears to be striving for some disengagement from those closest to him. Exploration from a secure attachment forms an important part of this disengagement and it can be seen as clearly in young animals as in young children (Harlow and Harlow, 1969). If curiosity about the world is a vital ingredient of this, a quest for independence or autonomy is another. The child, even in his second year, will be clearly indicating his wish to do things for himself and, when he has the language, 'Me do it' will become a familiar phrase. This quest for independence will also take the form of *not* wishing to do particular things; and the word 'no' will also assume a favoured place in his limited early vocabulary.

The relationship between children's need for attachment (love, security etc.) and their need to disengage from their parents is an interesting one and mirrors important aspects of the socialisation process. On the one hand, as we have seen, the needs are complementary in that the more secure a child feels, the more he will feel able to break away. On the other hand, the needs can be seen as conflicting in that they are focused on the same adults. Certainly, an important element of conflict is often present when an adult is preventing the child from doing what he immediately wishes to do, or, conversely, insisting on the child doing something which he does not wish to do. The conflict arises if the target for the child's consequent displeasure (or even rage) is an adult to whom the child is also strongly attached. This situation is certain to arouse anxiety and, as the child's capacity for self-reflection grows, it may be associated with feelings of guilt.

It is important to recognise that the areas of conflict which arise are not only inevitable but are essential for healthy development. The child will meet with conflict and frustration in varying degrees throughout his life and he has to learn to deal with these. Such learning is a gradual process, however, and healthy development will be set back if the conflicts are too frequent or too extreme. A crucial factor, of course, is how the adult deals with the situation, and we shall consider this later.

The growth of language

One aspect of development which greatly facilitates social development and can 'lower the temperature' in situations of potential conflict is the growth of language. Young children's increasing understanding of speech makes it possible to explain to them in simple terms why something must or must not be done or perhaps to explain that something can be done 'soon' or 'in a minute'. One of the most valuable uses of language in this context is to distract a child in order to avert a potential conflict. Of course, this may be done non-verbally, too, but the possibilities for employing this strategy are greatly increased once a comprehension of everyday words and phrases has been established. Furthermore, we should not forget that young children's growing command of verbal expression enables them to communicate their wishes more effectively so that the chances of misunderstandings are diminished and the possibilities for compromise enhanced. Finally, where anger and hostility are generated, the spoken word provides the child with another outlet for their expression, either immediately or later in fantasy or in play (see also chapter 4).

Play

The role of play is destined to become increasingly important not only as an outlet for anger and other emotions but also as a rehearsal strategy in which the child unself-consciously practises new skills and consolidates older ones (see also chapter 16). In very early childhood, these skills will inevitably centre on motor activities and perceptual development, but with the growth of language in the second and third years, play becomes a valuable medium for the development of social skills. Even solitary play may involve the re-enactment of past events or active experimentation with new, imagined social situations. Toys or make-believe persons may either represent themselves or be made to assume the role of the child whilst he steps out of himself, as it were, to become the parent or another figure. Often these roles will alternate rapidly in the rich interplay of the child's fantasies. Such play not only performs an important function in the rehearsal of social and other skills, it also increases the child's understanding of social situations and will enable him to begin to appreciate the standpoints of other people. It may also help to lessen tension as, for example, when a frightening, or potentially frightening, situation is re-enacted in fantasy.

Of course, play is most often a social activity. Even in early childhood, parents, other adults and siblings will interact with a child in play or make-believe situations. The very young child is egocentric and cannot yet engage in cooperative activity with children of his own age. However, by the end of the second year and into the third year, cooperative play between two young children will begin to emerge. At first this will take place only for brief periods as the children's egocentricity reasserts itself. Then, gradually, genuinely shared activity in which there is an element of give and take can be sustained for a longer time and may involve three or more children. We should remember, however, that children's capacity for cooperative play is dependent not only upon their maturity but also upon opportunities for this capacity to develop. The necessary social skills and attitudes have to be learnt. Many children will arrive at a play group, a nursery school and even at an infant school lacking these skills, and will need help in adjustment. All children at these ages have still much to learn about sharing and cooperation and can be greatly helped by a skilled and sensitive adult. However, perhaps the most important component of this adult skill is judging when *not* to intervene.

Identification

Another important aspect of social development is children's tendency to identify with people around them, especially those to whom an attachment has been made. The concept of identification is derived from psychoanalysis and was originally introduced by Freud. It is a 'process by which the child comes to think, feel and behave as though someone else's characteristics belonged to him. He gets pleasure from the other person's success, shares his misery and learns to value the same things' (Rutter, 1975). One fairly simple explanation for this tendency is that as children spontaneously imitate the actions of those around them, these imitations will please, and even flatter, the models. This overt pleasure reinforces the child's imitations, which are therefore more likely to recur. The imitations will initially be of specific actions or speech but as the tendency is reinforced and increases it will become more generalised and stronger, so that the psychological boundary between the child and his model becomes blurred.

It seems likely that this explanation is a valid one, but whether it is sufficient to explain all aspects of the process is not yet clear. Whatever the explanation, and whatever we call this tendency, there is no doubt that it can readily be observed in children of four years of age and older. Although the identification is not normally exclusive to one person, it is usually strongest for the parent of the same sex.

This process is clearly of considerable importance in children's socialisation. Not only do they aspire to behave like their model in trivial and often amusing ways, but in a more generalised and fundamental way it helps them to assimilate a whole way of life and to acquire moral and other standards. Freud suggested that the child's internalisation of adult moral standards through identification was the genesis of our feelings of conscience.

The maternal role

We have so far considered the parents almost as a kind of backcloth to the child's social development. We must now move them nearer to the centre of the stage in order to examine in more detail the impact of their relationship with the child upon his personality and social skills (Richards, 1974;

Schaffer, 1977). Inevitably, our first thoughts centre on the mother, whose rapport with the child is normally of crucial importance, particularly in early childhood (Wall, 1975):

> In the first few months mother and child form a close biological unit and baby's security depends upon the mother's attitude and upon her physical handling. . . For the child's subsequent mental health, the essential is the development and reinforcement of his sense of security, his feeling of always being loved and acceptable.

It has not been established, nor does it seem plausible, that any particular method of child rearing is better than others, although there is evidence (both in primitive cultures and in modern industrialised societies) that different patterns of child rearing tend to be associated with different kinds of behaviour and personality in the children. Nevertheless, 'it is not primarily upon the methods used that his mental health depends but upon the meaning which the incidents of his daily life have for him; and more than anything else this will be conditioned by the mother's attitudes as he senses them' (Wall, 1975).

The important features of the mother's attitude towards her child are that she should value him 'unconditionally and for his own sake, irrespective of his sex, appearance, abilities or personality; that this love is given without expectation of or demand for gratitude' (Pringle, 1980a). She will show this attitude in all kinds of ways, some obvious, some subtle: in the way she handles him, how she responds to his smiles and his babblings and how she talks to him. However, a frightening picture is sometimes painted for young mothers of the 'ideal Mum', who is always patient and kind, never tired or irritable and is always responsive to her child's needs. Sometimes, 'experts' inadvertently create this impression; more often it is peddled by advertisers wishing to sell the instant passport to this happy state, whether it be a new labour-saving device or some form of medication. The truth is that children are incredibly resilient creatures and provided the mother's basic attitude is right, they can and do tolerate her occasional lack of interest or irritability with at most a short-lived flurry of tears or a cry of protest. In fact, it might be said that the mother who is always patient and attentive (if she exists) would provide the child with very inadequate preparation for the harsher, less predictable world outside.

The maternal role is sometimes considered, conceptually at least, as if it were somehow independent of the child. However, babies differ greatly from birth in their temperamental characteristics (see chapter 6) and, for example, in their response to feeding. Some mothers (and fathers) seem to have a relatively easy time from the beginning. The baby is placid, does not cry much, feeds easily and his sleep pattern is consistent. Others are driven to distraction by a baby that cries a great deal, wakens at frequent but irregular intervals during the night, quite often brings his food up and so on. It is impossible to attribute such wide differences to the mother's handling of the situation.

However, mothers certainly differ a great deal in their capacity to cope with broken sleep and frequent crying. In extreme cases, such pressure may result in the mother attacking the baby violently and, in an unknown yet probably quite large number of cases, the mother comes very close to this state (Kempe and Kempe, 1978; Lee, 1978). But under many normal circumstances, a mother who may adequately meet the psychological needs of an 'easy' baby may be less than adequate for a very 'difficult' one. The pattern of interaction which occurs is rarely one of simple acceptance or rejection. Most often, a baby which responds well strengthens the mother's confidence in her own ability and reinforces her positive feelings for him. This enhanced confidence and warmth produces more stability and contentment in the baby, which is turn further strengthens the mother's confidence and so on. By the same token, a difficult baby may undermine the mother's confidence, particularly if it is her first child, and give no reinforcement for her positive feelings. The spiral of interacting responses may now continue in a negative direction unless some intervention halts this process.

The paternal role

The paternal role has until quite recently received very much less attention than the maternal role (but see Beail and McGuire, 1982; McKee and O'Brien, 1982). This is because under most circumstances the role of the father is normally taken to be less important for the child's development than the mother's, especially in his early years. This is not an inescapable biological or psychological fact. It is almost certainly a by-product of the maternal and paternal roles which most societies expect and to which most parents therefore conform. If the mother spends more time with the baby than the father, expects to handle him more and, generally, to have a closer relationship, it is hardly surprising that this is what happens. And under these circumstances the maternal role will be more important for the baby. However, there is no evidence that parents with different expectations cannot reverse their roles. Certainly, maternal and paternal roles could move closer together than they are at present and there is already a significant move in this direction in many countries, particularly in middle-class families (Lamb, 1981; Lewis et al., 1982).

However, under most circumstances, particularly if the father is at work all day and the mother is at home for part or all of the day, the father's role when the child is very young will mainly be that of a supporting actor. In part, this support will be to his wife in her role as mother, particularly since, as we have seen, caring for a young baby can be a very stressful experience. This may take the form of reassurance, suggestions or just listening to an account of the day's happenings. In addition, his wife may need reassurance in her role as a marriage partner. (This need may be a mutual one but for different reasons.) Finally, the father's support will usually take more

F

tangible forms such as helping with chores and, in particular, standing in for the mother in attending to the baby's needs. In this situation, there is, of course, no reason why he should not be as warm and responsive towards the baby as his wife, unless it be that his own perception of the paternal role precludes such behaviour (Pilling and Pringle, 1978).

Later on, the father's role in relation to the child will become more sharply focused as he provides another powerful, valued but different adult model with which the child may identify. This is valuable in itself for the child's social development but of particular importance for a boy, who can assimilate some of the characteristics of sex-typed behaviour in this way. The father's relationship with his daughter is important in this context, too, in that it helps her more clearly to distinguish between male and female behaviour and attitudes. For both son and daughter, the behaviour and attitudes of their parents towards each other will have a powerful influence upon their emerging social skills because of the strong identification with both parents, and will probably help to mould the children's expectations of their future marriage partners.

The family unit

In considering separately the maternal and paternal roles it is not always possible to keep them apart. This is because, although the child's relationship with individual members of his family will be different, the impact of the family unit as a whole upon his emotional and social development adds a further dimension (Mussen et al., 1979). For example, as the relationship between the parents will provide a model for the child's behaviour and attitudes, where this relationship is a tense and unhappy one, and particularly where there is open hostility, the child's development is likely to be adversely affected. If, in addition to these circumstances, there is rejection of the child, the prognosis is much worse. On the other hand, there is some evidence that a good relationship with only one of the parents can mitigate to a large extent the effects of even severe parental disharmony (Rutter, 1975).

Leaving aside the question of abnormal and discordant family situations, it is clear that the nature of the family unit, its size and composition, its overt and covert methods of control and of communication, and the quality of the relationship within it, play a large part in shaping the social development of each child. That the children may show quite substantial individual variations in their social development reflects in large measure the dynamic nature of the family influence. The family unit is a different social experience for each child. As we have seen, mothers may respond differently to initial differences between babies and there is likely then to be a build-up of mutual interactions. This is also true of the family unit as a whole, although the checks and balances in a group will make the more extreme responses of outright rejection and hostility or overprotection less likely. Nevertheless, the 'scapegoating' of an individual child is not uncommon in disturbed family situations.

The family unit will differ in significant ways for each new child. The most obvious characteristic which changes is its size and there is evidence that children from large families are as a group somewhat disadvantaged in a number of directions, including their social adjustment in school (Davie et al., 1972). The reasons for this are not clearly understood but it has been suggested that in part it may be a reflection of the adult time and attention available for each child. Another changing characteristic for each succeeding child is the parents' experience and confidence in handling their children. The most marked difference here will be between the family environment of the first child and that of any subsequent children. Thus, first-born children have been shown in a number of studies to be, generally, 'more adult orientated, more conscientious and prone to feelings of guilt, more achievement-orientated, more affiliative, more concerned with being co-operative and responsible, more conforming to social pressures. . . They also appear somewhat more likely to encounter psychological problems than younger siblings' (Mussen et al., 1979).

Mention has already been made of the child's need for a secure and stable relationship with his mother. The family as a group has a part to play here, too, in providing a coherence and a consistency which will further buttress the child's feeling of security and provide a base for social contacts outside the family. The parents obviously set the pattern for older siblings (Mussen et al., 1979).

The way in which the parents deal with the children's disengagement from parental attachment, supervision and authority will have far reaching effects upon their children's personal and social development. Persistent attempts to inhibit this tendency, for whatever reason, may result in timidity and lack of confidence or in emotional overdependence or disturbance. On the other hand, they may spell the beginnings of parent–child conflict which explodes in rebellion or antisocial behaviour at adolescence or earlier. Too much autonomy and independence too soon can, of course, mean increased risk of physical injury from scalding kettles, live electric plugs or busy traffic. They can also result in a selfish, egocentric child who makes unreasonable demands upon others and who largely ignores the needs and rights of people around him, and perhaps ultimately in an adult with these same characteristics.

However, provided the extremes of child-rearing practice are avoided, there is no evidence that the line to be drawn between contrasting approaches is very narrow or critical for satisfactory emotional and social development. What does seem clear is that it is not so much *what* parents do to or with their children as *how* they do it, which is important for emotional and social development. There is a great deal of difference between an authoritarian parental control which is accompanied by underlying hostility and negative feelings and one which, while firm (perhaps even rigid) leaves the child no room for doubt that he is loved and accepted for his own sake.

Sex roles

In considering the process of identification, we noted the tendency of children to identify most strongly with the parent of the same sex and, therefore, to move towards thinking, feeling and behaving like this parent. Given that the parent's social behaviour and attitudes are broadly what would be expected in most societies of a man or a woman, identification clearly plays an important part in moulding the sexually differentiated social development of boys and girls.

However, differences in the behaviour of the sexes emerge well before the age at which identification is normally assumed to start, so that we must look for additional explanations. It is virtually certain that some of these behavioural differences are biologically determined. This is not to say that they cannot be modified or that they are always present with equal strength in each individual. Nevertheless, some temperamental differences between boys and girls even in early infancy, and a tendency for males in general to be more aggressive, more assertive and show more vigorous activity, do seem to be independent of social or cultural conditioning (Hutt, 1972). One of the reasons why biological determinants of sex-typed behaviour are so difficult to isolate in humans is that this conditioning starts so early in life. It would be by no means unusual, for example, for the mother of a four-week-old baby boy to explain his vigorous and demanding crying with the comment, 'He's a proper boy!' Such comments are often made half in jest but there is enough substance to indicate that the mother's responses, tolerance etc. may be influenced by her prior expectations of sexually differentiated behaviour even at such an early age.

At later stages of babyhood and into infancy these expectations will usually be more clearly discerned in the behaviour not only of the parents but of other siblings and almost every adult the child meets. This will be manifested, for example, in the kind of toys given but also in more subtle ways such as adult comment on clothing, appearance and performance (e.g. 'Isn't Amanda a pretty girl?' 'Isn't John clever with his hands?').

Later on, more robust and messy play and a greater challenging of adult authority may be tolerated from a boy than a girl. A national study showed that, by the age of seven years, boys (as reported by their mothers) were more likely to have temper tantrums and show reluctance to go to school, had more difficulty in settling to anything, were more destructive and disobedient, fought and were bullied more often. Girls, on the other hand, were more likely to have had difficulty in getting off to sleep, were more faddy, had poorer appetites and were more prone to thumb-sucking and nail-biting (Davie et al., 1972). It should be added that these types of behaviour were only present in a small minority of children. Nevertheless, the pattern of sex differences is mostly predictable and consistent with adult male and female behaviour.

The past decade or two has in most Western countries seen a narrowing of the gap between the sexes in terms of behaviour, attitudes and educational and vocational aspirations. This (together with the struggle for women's rights) has highlighted the fact that much sexually differentiated behaviour is conditioned by the social and cultural milieu in which boys and girls grow up. Whether this realisation by tomorrow's parents will accelerate the process remains to be seen (Pilling and Pringle, 1978; Pringle, 1980b; Wilkin, 1982).

Influences of social class

There is a great deal of evidence in Britain and elsewhere that children's social development and, perhaps even more markedly, their educational achievement are related to the social class of their family. The term 'social class', it should be noted, is normally used in a British context to denote the occupational group of the father or male head of the household, as defined by the Registrar General for census and similar purposes.

Davie et al. (1972), for example, showed that seven-year-old children from homes where the father's occupation is less skilled (or required less formal education) tend to show more deviant behaviour in school, as reported by their teachers, and at home, as reported by their mothers, using the behavioural descriptions already mentioned above in relation to sex differences. In the same study, children whose fathers had professional occupations were five times more likely to 'express themselves well' (teachers' rating) than were children whose fathers had unskilled occupations. The former children were five times as likely to be described as 'avid readers' and three times as likely to have 'extremely good facility' in number work. For every one child from a professional family who was thought by the school to be in need of special schooling by the age of seven, there were 45 children from unskilled homes judged to have the same need (see also Wedge and Prosser, 1973).

In trying to interpret such results, it is necessary, first, to put the problem into proportion. It must be stressed that the great majority of children from unskilled homes do not show deviant behaviour in school and over half of them have average educational attainment or better. Nevertheless, the social class differences are sufficiently wide to be of educational and social significance. Furthermore, they are not restricted to the two occupational groups at the extremes; typically, a more or less regular trend is seen in the intermediate groups. Of course, the occupation of the father is of no particular relevance in itself but in our society it will tend to be related to the way he and his family live outside his working environment. Within broad limits, his occupation will be related to his income, to the kind of house he can buy or rent and to the area he chooses to live in. It will be more directly linked to his qualifications, level of skill and training and to his level of education. More importantly for our purpose, the occupational level of the father is likely to be related in a variety of ways, some obvious, some subtle, to his lifestyle and that of his wife and children in the home. The importance of this fact, educationally, is twofold. First, those children whose lifestyle at home is consonant with the social environment of their school are likely to find the initial transition from home to school relatively easy and will continue throughout their schooldays to live in the same world, as it were, although in two different contexts. Other children will have a more difficult adjustment to make.

This is not simply a matter of adjusting to different social environments, however. There is a second and deeper level of similarity and difference between home and school. This is related to what may perhaps better be described as a way of life rather than a lifestyle, if by the latter we imply relatively superficial norms of behaviour, ways of speaking, dressing and so on. The expression 'way of life' can be taken to encompass ways of thinking, values, attitudes and aspirations, one's perception of oneself and one's expectations of others and of life. At this level, it is inappropriate to think of a gap between schools and some homes which can be bridged by an *adjustment* on the child's part. The bridging operation to be complete may need a fundamental *reorientation*.

It is not suggested that in Britain the schools and certain more privileged homes share a somewhat rarefied subculture or way of life, which is exclusive to them and rigidly demarcated from a more popular subculture. The reality approaches nearer to a continuum than to a sharp dichotomy. Nevertheless, the differences at the extremes may be considerable and will include aspects of child-rearing practice, ways of behaving, attitudes towards authority, perception of the purpose and value of work, the perceived status of literacy and numeracy and the use of verbal and non-verbal communication. Bernstein (1971) has contributed greatly to our understanding of the relevance of language in this context (see chapter 4).

Some part of the social class differences in educational attainment can probably be attributed to hereditary factors but it seems likely that the ethos of the school can present a considerable barrier to some children. It is important for schools to recognise this, especially with young children, for adverse attitudes to education may lead to alienation later. It is important, too, to acknowledge that some reorientation on the part of the school may be essential. This will involve, first, a recognition that even in a relatively homogeneous society like Britain important subcultural differences exist and that these run deep. Secondly, the particular subculture which tends to characterise schools is not in any absolute sense the right one and should in some directions at least be considered different from, rather than better than, others. If these two points are accepted, schools and individual teachers will need to question more closely than most have done hitherto which aspects of their own norms of behaviour and values are essential to the educational process and which are more peripheral. The high value which schools place upon literacy and numeracy, for example, seems central to education, at least as we know it today, although the context in which they are taught may for some children be reappraised. On the other hand, attitudes to cleanliness, aggression, religion and to the value of work as an end in itself may be felt to be less central.

Answers to such questions will not be easily found because they are embedded in an integrated system whose parts are rarely examined in isolation. Teachers are used to thinking about their curriculum but we are referring here to what has sometimes been called 'the hidden curriculum', i.e. all those influences which schools and teachers bring to bear but which do not form a part of the formal curriculum. However, despite the difficulty of finding definitive answers, asking the questions could be an extremely valuable and significant first step. The school which considers itself to be an oasis of civilisation in some kind of subcultural desert is unlikely to make optimal progress in catering for the social and educational development of those children whom it often most wishes to serve.

Atypical family situations

Mention was made above, in discussing children's attachments, that although one attachment (usually to the mother) was typically stronger than the others, there is still some disagreement as to whether this attachment differs from the others in kind as well as in degree. Rutter (1981), in a reassessment of the evidence on the effects of children of maternal deprivation, concludes that the attachment to the mother is not by its nature qualitatively different from other attachments. This is not to say that a sudden, traumatic or lengthy separation may not have adverse effects upon a child's social and emotional development but rather that this is not necessarily so. One has to distinguish here between short-term consequences and more permanent effects. Short-term, overt distress is very common under such circumstances, particularly with younger children, but the longer-term effects are more difficult to predict and depend on many factors, including the particular circumstances surrounding the separation, the prior relationship with the mother, the number, strength and nature of other attachments and whether these latter can be maintained.

A great deal has been written about the effects on children of, for example, residential care (Prosser, 1976), foster care (Prosser, 1978), bereavement (Anthony, 1973), divorce (Wallerstein and Kelly, 1980), living in a one-parent family (Ferri, 1976) and step-parenthood (Ferri, 1984). The evidence is quite clear that such circumstances, whether or not they involve separation from the mother, place children at risk of subsequent emotional and social difficulties. However, evidence in recent years has tended to reveal that it is not these circumstances *per se* which are likely to have an adverse effect but other factors which are often found in association. For example, the deleterious consequences of divorce are much less likely to be linked to that event than to the family discord which preceded it. Some children's emotional and social adjustment may improve after the divorce as a result of the lessening of tension. Again, a single parent coping with a family alone may well suffer financial hardship and the family may be living in crowded or sub-standard accommodation. Such material factors and their psychological and social consequences may be more important considerations in certain circumstances than the absence of a parent. Contrary to many teachers' belief, research on the children of working mothers has tended to show few, if any, adverse effects (Davie et al., 1972). Here again, though, other factors, notably the quality of substitute care, are likely to be important (Pilling and Pringle, 1978).

Most studies which have looked at age effects have confirmed that young children are more vulnerable to these kinds of stress than older children. However, it has sometimes been suggested that the effects of early adverse events on children are irreversible. Clarke and Clarke (1976) have attempted to redress the balance by pointing to methodological shortcomings in a number of research studies and quoting evidence that some children have made apparently good recoveries from even extreme and damaging events in early life. Inevitably, some (Pringle, 1976) feel that the Clarkes have gone too far and that their arguments in turn show inconsistencies. However, the greater vulnerability of young children seems in no serious doubt in the present state of our knowledge. What is becoming increasingly clear is that the effects of early damage may be due to the chain of self-perpetuating circumstances which can follow the apparently critical event as well as to the particular circumstances in which it took place, and those which preceded it. Although we have much to learn about the nature and effects of these interacting factors, and much to learn about strategies of effective support or intervention, the assumption must be made by all who have the care of children that any effects of psychological or social deprivation or damage are not irreversible and can be ameliorated, minimised or eradicated altogether, given the right kind of psychological, educational or social treatment.

References

Anthony, S. (1973) *The Discovery of Death in Childhood and After*. London: Penguin.

Beail, N. and McGuire, J. (eds) (1982) *Fathers: Psychological Perspectives*. London: Junction Books.

Bernstein, B. (1971) *Class, Codes and Control*, vol. 1. London: Routledge & Kegan Paul.

Bowlby, J. (1975) *Separation: Anxiety and Anger*. London: Penguin.

Clarke, A. M. and Clarke, A. D. B. (1976) *Early Experience: Myth and Evidence*. London: Open Books.

Davie, R., Butler, N. and Goldstein, H. (1972) *From Birth to Seven*. London: Longman.

Ferri, E. (1976) *Growing Up in a One-parent Family*. Windsor: NFER.

Ferri, E. (1984) *Stepchildren*. Windsor: NFER–Nelson.

Harlow, H. F. and Harlow, M. K. (1969) Effects of various mother–infant relationships in rhesus monkey behaviour. In Foss, B. M. (ed.) *Determinants of Infant Behaviour*, vol 4. London: Methuen.

Hutt, C. (1972) *Males and Females*. Harmondsworth: Penguin.

Kempe, R. S. and Kempe, C. H. (1978) *Child Abuse*. London: Fontana/Open Books.

Lamb, M. E. (ed.) (1981) *The Role of the Father in Child Development*, 2nd ed. Chichester: Wiley.

Leach, P. (1983) *Babyhood*, 2nd ed. Harmondsworth: Penguin.

Lee, C. M. (ed.) (1978) *Child Abuse*. Milton Keynes: Open University Press.

Lewis, C., Newson, E. and Newson, J. (1982) Father participation through childhood and its relation to career aspirations and delinquency. In Beail, N. and McGuire, J. (eds) *Fathers: Psychological Perspectives*. London: Junction Books.

McKee, L. and O'Brien, M. (eds) (1982) *The Father Figure*. London: Tavistock.

Mussen, P. H., Conger, J. J. and Kagan, J. (1979) *Child Development and Personality*, 5th ed. New York: Harper and Row.

Pilling, D. and Pringle, M. K. (1978) *Controversial Issues in Child Development*. London: Elek.

Pringle, M. K. (1976) Rights of adults or needs of children? *Times Higher Educational Supplement* 23 July.

Pringle, M. K. (1980a) *The Needs of Children*, 2nd ed. London: Hutchinson.

Pringle, M. K. (1980b) *A Fairer Future for Children*. London: Macmillan.

Prosser, H. (1976) *Perspectives on Residential Child Care*. Windsor: NFER.

Prosser, H. (1978) *Perspectives on Foster Care*. Windsor: NFER.

Richards, M. P. M. (ed.) (1974) *The Integration of a Child in a Social World*. London: Cambridge University Press.

Rutter, M. (1975) *Helping Troubled Children*. Harmondsworth: Penguin.

Rutter, M. (1981) *Maternal Deprivation Re-assessed*, 2nd ed. Harmondsworth: Penguin.

Schaffer, R. (1977) *Mothering*. London: Fontana.

Wall, W. D. (1975) *Constructive Education for Children*. London: Harrap.

Wallerstein, J. S. and Kelly, J. B. (1980) *Surviving the Breakup*. London: Grant McIntyre.

Wedge, P. and Prosser, H. (1973) *Born to Fail?* London: Arrow Books.

Wilkin, M. (1982) Equal opportunity and achievement. In Reid, I. (ed.) *Sex Differences in Britain*. London: Grant McIntyre.

Further Reading

Davie, R., Butler, N. and Goldstein, H. (1972) *From Birth to Seven*. London: Longman.

Clarke, A. M. and Clarke, A. D. B. (1976) *Early Experience: Myth and Evidence*. London: Open Books.

Pilling, D. and Pringle, M. K. (1978) *Controversial Issues in Child Development*. London: Elek.

Pringle, M. K. (1980) *The Needs of Children*, 2nd ed. London: Hutchinson.

Rutter, M. (1975) *Helping Troubled Children*. Harmondsworth: Penguin.

Schaffer, R. (1977) *Mothering*. London: Fontana.

8

Young Children with Special Educational Needs

ALICE F. LAING AND MAURICE CHAZAN

What are special educational needs?

There are very few among us who do not need help at some time or other with particular problems. It may be that we need a helping hand to steady our wobbly balance, a finger to point out something we have not seen, an offer to repeat or explain information which we have not understood and so on. Yet these needs are not very often considered as in any way out of the ordinary. Suppose, however, that we wobbled even on flat ground, or never could read the small print or found most of what people said to us had little or no meaning. At what point would such problems become out of the ordinary? One way of trying to answer this question would be to consider the effect that such difficulties appear to have on the functioning of the individual. With young children we might consider especially the effect which their developmental difficulties appear to have on their ability to learn. Broadly speaking, if their response to learning opportunities is adversely affected, then we could say that such children have special educational needs. Perhaps there may be special needs which do not have educational implications but it is surprisingly difficult to list them. For example, if a child can see the board perfectly well when wearing glasses, does her short sight have educational implications or not?

Children with special educational needs, it can be said, have more difficulty in learning in general or in specific aspects than would normally be expected or they may be unable to make full use of the facilities of the normal school (Education Act 1981). They may require specific provision to be made for them, by way of special equipment or resources or structural modifications, or a special or modified curriculum to be provided or both (Department of Education and Science, 1978).

Many of the learning needs of these children are, however, the same as those of all children. They need opportunities to explore their environment and to come to terms with it, under guidance from adults who can help to increase their comprehension or understanding by structuring these opportunities and matching them to the children's abilities. The normally accepted aims of nursery and infant schools would appear, therefore, to be well suited to children with special needs. According to the Gittins Report, 'Nursery education is designed to help young children to adjust easily and happily to children and adults outside the family circle, to give opportunities for a variety of experiences of play situations, to build up muscular control, co-ordination and skill, and to enable the child to find out about people and things' (Central Advisory Council for Education, Wales, 1967). Nursery teachers themselves see the nursery programme as appropriate to the needs of children with special difficulties and place them high in priority for receiving nursery education (Taylor, et al., 1972). Referring to rather older children, Blackie (1967) says, 'The allowance made for individual variation in need, speed, interest and capacity by the modern primary school, makes it far better adapted to cope with the less able or the difficult child than the traditional school.' Research (Galton et al., 1980) may call for a much more critical examination of the effectiveness of some approaches to teaching which claim to be based on child-centred principles, but an emphasis on individual differences in 'need, speed, interest and capacity' must mean, when taken in conjunction with the aims quoted from the Gittins Report, that the possibility of providing for children with special educational needs exists in the normal provision made for young children. It might, at this point, be helpful to look more closely at different kinds of difficulty and to consider some of the special educational needs associated with each subdivision.

Sociocultural disadvantage

For children who fall into this category, it is the misfortune of being born a member of an underprivileged group which causes difficulties. From birth, adverse environmental circumstances restrict their opportunities to explore, to learn alongside adults, to develop and understand the subtleties of language or to see themselves as acquiring some form of successful control over their lives. Adverse environmental circumstances include poverty, colour, race, large family size, minimal parental education coupled with low job aspirations or, more frequently, some combination of these. Children growing up in such circumstances enter the educational system ill prepared to take advantage of it (Mortimore and Blackstone, 1982). Teachers may expect too much or too little of them (Goodacre, 1968) and may have difficulty in ensuring, within the freedom of choice offered, that each child is deriving maximum benefit from the learning opportunities available in the school. Special programmes may have to be implemented to give such children the skills which will increase their chances of educational success in the present system. Even so, radical changes in the content and methods of education may be required before these particular difficulties, partly imposed by society, are reduced.

Low intellectual ability

Discussion of the learning needs of children who are limited in the intellectual area of their development is complicated by the fact that they may be judged to be of low ability for different reasons. Some children are genetically programmed to be shorter in physical height than others, so some are born less well endowed intellectually than others. In other cases, limitations in ability are the result of brain damage either before, during or after birth. In yet other cases, inadequacies in the functioning of the sensory organs reduce the environmental stimulation and feedback which are essential for cognitive development. Indeed, if the learning opportunities in the early environment are not used effectively by the child and the adults closest to him, as is the case with the disadvantaged children discussed above, cognitive development is again restricted.

In this area of difficulty in particular, there is an absence of clearly marked boundaries. The groupings within limited intellectual ability described above merge into one another, just as normal intellectual development merges into that which could be considered as below normal. Careful assessment (Mittler, 1970) is essential to determine the degree and effect of the handicap and to monitor subsequently planned programmes for every type of learning retardation, whether or not its cause is known (Kirman, 1968).

From an educational point of view, the critical issue is whether the learner is able to respond to, and profit from, the experiences offered in normal schools or whether special provision is necessary. The differences are likely to lie not so much in the content as in the greater degree of direction and structure which has to be provided (Priestley, 1973). The greater the handicap, the more direction and structure will be required and the slower the progress. It should be borne in mind, however, that the majority of cases in the category of mental handicap show mild retardation (Edgerton, 1967) and only a small number (approximately 3.7 per 1000 population) (Forrest et al., 1973; Kushlick and Cox, 1973) are considered to be severely handicapped. It would, therefore, seem reasonable, especially in the early stages of education, to consider adapting the normal school programme in most cases. For those children who are severely mentally retarded (and these cases are usually easily identifiable because of their extreme slowness of development) early and carefully planned specialised help is essential.

Physical handicap

Two broad categories can be distinguished in this group of children: those whose condition is associated with neurological impairment (e.g. cerebral palsy, epilepsy) and those whose condition involves no damage to the brain (e.g. asthma, orthopaedic disorders, heart disease). Children who are blind, partially sighted, deaf or partially hearing can be placed in either category depending on the nature of the diagnosis. Obviously some handicaps are more incapacitating than others, and some show periods of remission or improvement while others do not.

The presence or absence of neurological impairment is a major factor determining educational progress (Anderson, 1973) and social adjustment (Rutter et al., 1970a). Where no neurological impairment is present, the child tends to be more successful academically and not so seriously disturbed. It should be noted, of course, that these judgements are relative. Physical impairment is likely to restrict the opportunities for learning available to all physically handicapped children, and to interfere with their acceptance of themselves and by others. Both groups of physically handicapped children are, therefore, at risk of educational retardation and behavioural disorder, the neurologically impaired being particularly vulnerable. But there is no common pattern in their learning or adjustment difficulties, and the majority of cases show little psychiatric disorder (Rutter et al., 1970b). The severity of the conditions does not wholly determine success in learning or adjustment; important factors appear to be the child's level of intelligence, the number of children in the family and the emotional stability of the parents (Anderson, 1973).

Early diagnosis and constructive guidance are particularly important for children with physical disorders. Not only is extra effort required for these children and their families (with a consequent need for extra support by society), but decisions have to be made as to the best school placement for them. Such decisions are often hotly debated, and can only be satisfactorily resolved if care is taken to match the children's assessed strengths and weaknesses with a suitable learning environment. Suitability here involves safety, correct facilities and easy access to medical and therapeutic services, as well as availability of individually tailored programmes, of accepting adults and of a willingness on the part of teachers to understand the implications of the individual child's condition, its treatment and prognosis.

Boarding education or separate day provision has in the past been thought appropriate for many physically handicapped children. As research studies (Mittler, 1970) gradually extend our knowledge of specific conditions, however, the move to integrate as many physically handicapped children as possible into ordinary schools is increasing, and the provision of schools specially designed for physically handicapped children is now aimed chiefly at the severely multiply handicapped (Jackson, 1975). This move is in line with the view expressed by Younghusband et al. (1970) that placement depends on the child's developmental needs rather than on the handicapping condition. Teachers in normal schools must be prepared for the additional responsibilities resulting from this change in policy, and should not be left to cope unsupported.

If physical dysfunction is mild, it is easy to overlook its existence. Children may learn to compensate to some extent for their difficulties, so that they appear to function as physically normal but are judged to be dull, clumsy, careless or uninterested. Sometimes brain damage can be shown to be present, but often clinical examination reveals no neurological explanation (Francis-Williams, 1970; Becker, 1976). Slight motor or perceptual impairment is a highly frustrating condition, as the children so affected struggle to understand environmental stimuli or orientate themselves adequately in space, only to be told on many occasions that they are not trying hard enough. Writing of children with visual perceptual difficulties, Langan (1970) says, 'What these children lack is the ability to interpret a seen stimulus into a meaningful concept or even, in some cases, to see the whole at all.' For children with motor dysfunction, education is a succession of blots and spillages, with difficulties in transmitting information obstructing progress.

Behavioural disturbance

Children who are experiencing learning difficulties are also likely to face problems of adjustment, for no one enjoys the feeling of failure. Alternatively, the behavioural problem itself may be the cause of the learning difficulty, if it inhibits learning potential. Behavioural distubance may well accompany the other difficulties discussed in this chapter (Rutter et al., 1970b; Chazan and Jackson, 1971, 1974). Teachers play an essential role in ensuring that children whose behaviour shows signs of disturbance or inappropriateness do receive the help they require (Chazan et al., 1983).

In cases where behaviour is consistently and persistently strange, no adult who knows such children could fail to feel puzzled and concerned. Psychotic behaviour of this kind in young children is described by Rutter (1968) as being of two kinds:

1. psychosis, which is probably a form of chronic brain disease, occurring in early childhood (three–five years) and showing such symptoms as general regression, loss of speech and marked over-activity.
2. autism, which has a slightly earlier onset, and which is characterised by disruption of personal relationships through withdrawal, loss of speech or the emergence of abnormal speech patterns, peculiar or excessive movements, unusual reaction to sensory stimuli, and acute resistance to environmental change of any kind.

The incidence of these two conditions is small. Teachers are much more likely to be faced with behavioural difficulties which get in the way of the child's educational progress, such as aggression, anxiety, solitariness, withdrawal, immaturity or a mixture of one or more of these (Chazan and Laing, 1982; Richman et al., 1982). Sensitivity, ingenuity and imagination on the part of the teacher can do much to alleviate the immediate difficulties, but it is essential with children under the age of eight years for contact to be established with the parents, and for other agencies, such as the School Psychological Service, to be alerted.

Communication difficulties

In the very early years, children learn from their own active exploration of the environment. Language, however, is always of value in directing attention and providing a general climate of encouragement. Where children's speech develops normally, language becomes more and more important, both widening and refining understanding, as well as strengthening social relationships. Children who are deprived of suitable language experiences will, therefore, suffer other limitations in development.

Language difficulties may be receptive or expressive, although these two aspects are so interrelated as to be almost inseparable. An alternative classification is into difficulties which are primarily of a decoding nature (i.e. understanding incoming messages) and those which are primarily encoding (i.e. responding in age-appropriate language), although again each affects the other. It is also useful to distinguish disorders which result from neurological or structural abnormalities (e.g. brain lesions, cleft palate, tongue-tie) from those which are secondary to other factors, such as mental retardation, hearing loss, psychiatric disorder or an adverse environment. It can be seen, therefore, that not only does language disorder or delay cause problems, it is also a clear pointer to other possible difficulties. Assessment, either in the clinic or in the classroom, is complicated, and it is probably best to record carefully the children's reponse to, and use of, language over a period of time, as Mittler (1970) suggests, so as to get a picture of their present level of competence and its relationship to other aspects of their development. Special programmes can then be devised.

Multiple handicap

The various subdivisions of learning difficulties discussed so far are not, in practice, clearly differentiated. Often there are other related difficulties. In cases of severe mental or physical handicap, several developmental aspects may be involved. It is also possible for a number of mild problems to combine to present a major learning difficulty for the child concerned (Brennan, 1974). The category of multiple handicap can, therefore, be defined so widely as to include almost every child with special needs or so specifically as to include only those children with more than one identifiable primary handicap (e.g. the partially sighted child with cerebral palsy).

What is important, however, is not so much how the problem is defined, but the decisions which are based on the subsequent categorisation. The alternative definitions given above could be seen as compatible by suggesting that defining categories and labelling children accordingly are productive exercises only if undertaken with a view to deciding appropriate educational placement. Discussions as to the nature of the condition would then be of less importance than consideration of how the immediate problems can be tackled in the light of the child's learning potential. At the same time, the learning difficulties children have provide the basis of their special needs and may make separate special educational provision essential.

The legislation which is now in force (Education Act 1981) calls for a shift of emphasis from the categorisation of conditions to the specification of needs. Decisions can then be taken as to how these needs can best be met and where the necessary educational provision can be made. Careful discussion of each child is necessary and, in some cases, a written statement is drawn up about the child incorporating information from a variety of sources and showing decisions taken. In addition, the rights of parents to be consulted about their child and to have access to the statement and its accompanying records are upheld.

Special educational provision

For children with moderate or severe learning difficulties up to the age of eight years, educational provision is varied and patchy. While the variety of provision may have merit, lack of provision certainly has not. Since 1971, local authorities have had a statutory obligation to provide education for all children over five years of age, however handicapped they may be, so that for this age group there should be no lack of places. For pre-school children, however, no such obligation at present exists, although a considerable extension of nursery school places was officially proposed (Department of Education and Science 1972a) at least on a part-time basis.

It is not easy to be precise about the number of children with special needs. The above discussion on how needs might be defined reveals the pitfalls which prevent precision. The Warnock Report, however, indicates that it is a fair assumption that 'about one in six children at any time and up to one in five children at some time during their school career will require some form of special educational provision' (Department of Education and Science, 1978). This figure is rather higher than previous estimates (Pringle et al., 1966) because of the deliberate broadening by the Report of the concept of special educational needs to include children with mild problems, whether physical, intellectual or emotional. If it is accepted that 20% of children may have some form of learning difficulty, then clearly most of them are to be found in ordinary groups. Relatively few five- to seven-year-olds are offered special school places and an even smaller number are admitted to special pre-school units.

Special schools, concentrating usually on one particular handicap, have been established in Britain over a number of years (Pritchard, 1963). While those catering for the visually handicapped have long accepted pre-school age children, most of the others have a later age of entry on average, especially those which, because of decision or location, are residential. Special schools are small, often purpose-built (or specially adapted), and a number of the staff have additional training specific to the handicap concerned. These conditions obviously benefit the children who attend such schools (127,157 pupils in maintained and non-maintained special schools in England and Wales in August 1980 according to Department of Education and Science, 1981 statistics), but special schools do have disadvantages such as those arising out of possible isolation from the normal community.

Current policy is to keep pupils with learning difficulties in the ordinary school as long as their special needs can be adequately met there. Where it is felt to be necessary, special classes or special units can be set up within the ordinary schools to fulfil a variety of functions. For children in their first school, the specialised function is often one of assessment, carried out in the context of an educational programme designed to show in practical terms the nature of the learning and adjustment needs of the individual pupils (Department of Education and Science, 1972b, 1973). With careful planning and the cooperation of the whole of the school concerned, genuine integration can result. Such placement can also help to avoid the twin dangers of labelling children too soon, before they have had a chance to come to terms with the demands of the educational system, or of postponing identification of special learning needs for too long, so that bad habits and wrong attitudes become established.

In identifying and assessing special educational needs, and in planning subsequent programmes, a multi-professional approach is in most cases useful and sometimes essential. Inter-professional cooperation, especially where young children are concerned, is supported by all the professions involved (medical, nursing, therapeutic, educational, psychological and social services) but does not always materialise because of time pressures, lack of staff or inadequate lines of communication. The emergence in some areas of district handicap teams, as advocated by the Court Report (Department of Health and Social Security, 1976), shows the possibilities, and at times the inherent difficulties, of cooperation across the professions. For those children whose needs are such that they are the subject of a written statement, multi-professional consideration is required (Education Act 1981), and it is possible that this requirement will lead to the emergence of many more teams. Teachers have a considerable contribution to make to these deliberations.

The teacher and the child with special educational needs

Whether young children with learning or behaviour difficulties are educated in a special unit or in an ordinary class or school, the teacher has a complex and often difficult task in meeting their needs. In some cases, even in spite of good potential, the child's progress will be so slow that the lack of feedback may be discouraging to the teacher; in others, the child's impaired mobility or hyperactivity, for example, may put a severe strain on the patience of the most tolerant person. Children showing emotional or behavioural disturbance may be so provocative that an unsatisfactory rather than a therapeutic teacher–child relationship may develop. Many physically and mentally handicapped children take a long time to loosen the bonds of almost complete dependence on adults and may see the teacher primarily in the role of mother-substitute, demanding maternal rather than pedagogic behaviour on her part.

In dealing with children with special educational needs, it is easy for a teacher to become over-involved emotionally or else for her to feel that little can be achieved with a particular child. There is, consequently, always a danger that the educational implications of any difficulty may be exaggerated or distorted. As teachers' attitudes and expectations influence the course of a child's development in subtle ways (Rogers, 1982), it is important that the abilities of children should not be underestimated. It is important, too, that teachers of children with special educational needs, while being fully aware of the problems facing them, should adopt a positive attitude towards these problems (Webb, 1967). In spite of the difficulties, teaching these children can be very challenging and rewarding. If realistic goals are set, considerable satisfaction can be gained from seeing a child take even small steps in a forward direction.

The main role of the teacher of children with special educational needs is to ensure that they are provided with opportunities for appropriate learning and social experiences, and the problems relating to the selection of special educational programmes for specific needs are discussed below. However, teachers of young children also have a part to play in the identification and assessment of need, and in linking with a variety of agencies, external to the school, concerned with the welfare and treatment of children with difficulties.

As far as identification is concerned, the more serious cases of mental and physical handicap will have been recognised long before the child is placed in any kind of educational unit. Nevertheless, the teacher may in other cases be the first person to suspect a hearing loss or to draw attention to a speech problem. She has a particularly valuable contribution to make in the identification of less obvious or milder disabilities which may adversely affect progress in school (e.g. slightly impaired vision or relatively poor motor coordination without gross physical handicap), as well as of children educationally at risk for a variety of other reasons (Wedell and Raybould, 1976). Increasing emphasis has been put on the key role of the teacher in early identification of the effects of social disadvantage (Evans and Ferguson, 1974) and also of poor emotional adjustment. Westman et al., (1967), for example, concluded, on the basis of a study in the USA, that the observations of sensitive nursery school teachers can make a significant contribution to mental health screening. Largely as a result of the recognition of the value of early identification, a growing number of local education authorities are using some form of screening procedure, mainly involving observation by teachers, at the nursery or infant school stage in order to identify children at risk educationally (Leach, 1981).

The assessment of educational needs will also depend to a considerable extent on the observational skills of the teacher, and her ability both to make use of the reports provided by the specialists concerned with the child and to pass on school-based information to relevant external agencies. Although provisional diagnoses may have been made, before placement in school, the assessment of children's needs should constantly be reviewed in the light of the accumulating knowledge of their development, and not least their response to education.

The multiplicity of agencies involved in the assessment, care and treatment of young children has given rise to problems of communication which are not easily resolved but, if the full potential of the child is to be realised, the teacher will need from time to time to have direct links with a number of specialists. These include doctors, health visitors, educational psychologists, social workers, speech therapists and physiotherapists. The School Psychological Service will often adopt a coordinating role in the assessment of the child's educational needs, and should work closely with the teacher to ensure that an appropriate programme is planned. In the more serious cases of emotional and behavioural disturbance referral to a Child Guidance Clinic, where psychiatric help is available, is advised. In all cases, the teacher should have close links with the child's parents (see below for a discussion of the role of the parents of children with special needs), and very often the school will find it useful to make contact with the local or national headquarters of the various voluntary bodies concerned.

As the Warnock Report (Department of Education and Science, 1978) emphasises, more adequate preparation for understanding and teaching children with special educational needs is required for every teacher. Over the past 25 years, an increasing number of universities and other institutions have provided one-year full-time courses in special education for serving teachers, but these courses cater for only a small proportion of those teachers wishing to specialise in this field. Most initial teacher-training courses include some reference to special education. However, as all teachers in nursery and infant schools are likely to have some contact with special educational needs, it is essential that they should have the opportunity of attending at least a short course or workshop dealing with the education of children with learning difficulties. Local authorities and teacher-training establishments already offer a variety of courses of this kind, lasting for varying periods up to a term, and it is important that this in-service training should be extended.

Special programmes

When working with children with special educational needs it is more often the case that selections and adaptations have to be made than that existing programmes can be implemented in full. The following is therefore offered only as a guide to some of the material available, particularly in this country.

Motor and perceptual programmes

In encouraging and shaping motor development, physiotherapy is obviously of major importance, especially in the very early years when natural 'milestones' may be delayed and the parents are unsure how to handle abnormal development (Finnie, 1971; Hughes, 1972). Somewhat older children may present marked unevenness of development in hand–eye coordination, visual or auditory perception and visual or auditory discrimination because developmental difficulties have restricted environmental explorations and subsequent feedback. They may also have failed to form adequate body images and be poorly orientated in space. Programmes aimed to improve these abilities, vital to coping with learning situations, have been devised by Kephart (1960), Delacato (1963), Frostig and Horne (1964), Tansley (1967) and Cratty (1970). All of these are built upon an initial testing procedure, aimed at indicating specific areas of difficulty. Sequenced exercises to develop motor and perceptual skills have also been developed by Haskell and Paull (1973) and by McInnes and Treffry (1982) for young children with visual and auditory impairment.

While it is necessary to train some children to attend to stimuli, others are constantly reacting to everything going on around them, whether relevant to their activities or not. High distractibility and hyperactivity causing poor attention and concentration have been associated with children suffering from brain damage (Wedell, 1973; Winchell, 1975) and cerebral palsy (Francis-Williams, 1964). Emphasising relevant cues and minimising possible sources of distraction when tasks demand careful attention seem appropriate measures. At the same time, children should be helped to inhibit their tendency to over-reaction under normal conditions as they cannot exist in an unstimulating environment all the time. Behaviour modification techniques may be helpful here, as they are in improving performance in many other areas.

Behaviour modification techniques involve a gradual shaping of behaviour so that the existing undesired behaviour is replaced by a more acceptable pattern. Praise, adult attention or even tangible rewards are given, first of all for the nearest approximation to the desired behaviour which is produced, and then for closer and closer approximations until the acceptable pattern is achieved. Careful observation of the original behaviour is therefore required, along with a detailed breakdown of the steps between that baseline and the goal, and the selection of a reward which the individual concerned regards as satisfying. Behaviour modification has been used successfully in many different circumstances (Neisworth and Smith, 1973; National Society for the Study of Education, 1973). A number of books are available to help staff wishing to implement a behaviour modification approach (see Kiernan and Woodford, 1975; Westmacott and Cameron, 1981; Chazan et al., 1983).

Language development programmes

Since the development of linguistic and cognitive skills is so closely related, there has been concern over a number of years to promote language development through the use of specially devised programmes. A diversity of approaches has been advocated, generating considerable controversy as to which is the most effective, an argument which can only be resolved when agreement can be reached as to what is meant by 'effective'. Does it mean increasing vocabulary (O'Connor and Hermelin, 1963), promoting conceptual growth (Blank and Solomon, 1968), developing cognitive efficiency (Luria, 1961) or equalising educational opportunity (Bereiter and Engelmann, 1966)? The targets for language programmes differ, therefore, and so do the methods advocated for reaching them.

In working with severely mentally handicapped children, the aim may be much simpler than any of those above, namely the establishing of a recognisable form of verbal communication (Jeffree and McConkey, 1974, 1976; Gillham, 1979; Leeming et al., 1979). As has been said before, a careful analysis from observation, followed by an individually tailored programme, is essential for success here. Behaviour modification techniques (Bricker, 1971; Yule et al., 1973) seem to be more productive than exposing the child to a rich language environment, as the latter may not have any meaning to a child who has not learned to sort out auditory or verbal input.

Even with children who have acquired some of the decoding and encoding skills necessary for adequate linguistic communication, merely surrounding them with language may not help them to make good their deficiencies. It is better policy to pinpoint these deficiencies either from careful and continuing assessment or from the use of standardised tests, such as the Illinois Test of Psycholinguistic Abilities (Kirk et al., 1968) or the Reynell Developmental Language Scales (Reynell, 1969), which are administered by educational psychologists. Programmes (Chazan and Cox, 1976) can then be selected with confidence as to their suitability.

Amongst the variety of programmes which might be considered are the Peabody Language Development Kit (Dunn et al., 1968), an approach involving 180 sequenced lessons covering receptive, expressive and thinking skills; an informal 'games' approach occupying a short spell of time each day (Gahagan and Gahagan, 1970); Piaget-based approaches with particular emphasis on moving the child from the stage of sensorimotor intelligence to the beginnings of conceptual thought (Sonquist and Kamii, 1967); a highly structured, almost drill-like approach aimed to increase vocabulary and to extend syntactical competence (Bereiter and Engelmann, 1966); a careful ordering of the conventional British methods of promoting language skills (Shiach, 1972); a developmental programme linking a variety of linguistic and non-linguistic activities (Cooper et al., 1978); and, based on a detailed analysis of the children's problems, *Language Assessment, Remediation and Screening Procedure* (LARSP) (Crystal et al., 1976).

None of these approaches will be helpful unless the teacher believes it to be worth the time and effort involved in reaching a full understanding of the method and the principles behind it (Quigley, 1971), and unless the parents, too, support it. Indeed, the crucial importance of the early years in the development of communication means that programmes to be carried out by parents will be particularly useful.

Behavioural adjustment programmes

As with the other areas of difficulty which have been discussed, decisions as to possible approaches depend on whether new patterns of behaviour have to be encouraged or inappropriate reactions have to be changed. Teachers of young children have always accepted that they have a major contribution to make in the first category, and have unobtrusively shaped children's interactional behaviour or speech or personal competence towards increased maturity and independence. Teachers are, therefore, the main instigators of procedures which might prove useful in the classroom (Chazan et al., 1983), working in close conjunction, of course, with parents. With severely mentally handicapped children, the educational programme has to be constructed largely around the development of competent and appropriate social behaviour. Gunzburg (1968) shows how important for acceptance in the community is the acquisition of socially competent behaviour, and suggests ways by which it might be promoted. Behaviour modification techniques are also likely to be productive in this aspect of development (Thompson and Grabowski, 1972; Watson, 1973; Kiernan et al., 1978).

Changing of inappropriate reactions may also have to be tackled. There is continuing debate over the extent to which young children who show extremely disturbed behaviour require, and can respond to, clinical therapeutic approaches (Bender and Gurevitz, 1955). Bentovim (1973) reports on therapeutic work carried out at a day centre with young children and their families, the presenting problems including acute management difficulties (e.g. aggression, severe temper tantrums), high anxiety, abnormal speech development and abnormal reactions to toilet training. The main value of the centre appeared to lie in its 'containing' function, so that opportunities could be given for anxieties to be expressed, and to some extent worked through, in a supportive setting. The question of which severely disturbed children can profit from therapeutic help and what type of therapy is appropriate remains an open one.

Not a great deal of evidence is at present available as to how effective these various programmes are. Where they have been tried with severely handicapped children, progress is inevitably slow as well as difficult to measure accurately and usefully. With the less severely handicapped, the outcome is more encouraging. Measurable progress, however, as well as depending on the potential strengths of the child (cognitive, physical and emotional) is most likely to occur under the following conditions:

1 If objectives are clearly defined. For example, with socially disadvantaged children, programmes aimed at a fairly undifferentiated enrichment of the environment have been shown to be less successful than those carefully structured to reach preselected goals (Weikart et al., 1978). These goals should not be exclusively cognitive, but should take account of weaknesses in other areas of development.

2 If there is continuity in the educational experiences offered to the children. This continuity means a carrying over of programmes and methods from one stage of educational provision to the next (Cleave et al., 1982), so that any progress made is consolidated and extended.

3 If teachers see the full implications of the programme and believe in the principles on which it has been constructed.

4 If parents are involved. For young children, the main focus of learning is in the experiences which they encounter at home. Different answers to the questions of the extent and level of parental involvement in special educational programmes may be necessary for different problems, but all require that parents understand and support them.

Parents and the child with special educational needs

Parallel with the recognition of the value of early educational experiences for children with special educational needs in a group setting (Department of Education and Science, 1972a, 1975), understanding has increased of the contribution which both mother and father can make to the child's development, cognitive as well as social and emotional.

The primary role of the parents is to provide a secure home base where they enjoy a warm and affectionate relationship with their child. It is rarely easy for parents to make or maintain this kind of relationship with a handicapped child: almost inevitably, parents of children born with serious defects experience feelings of shock, guilt, embarrassment, helplessness and inadequacy (MacKeith, 1973). The school can do relatively little to compensate if the child lacks a background of security, though the parents will benefit from expert and sympathetic counselling and guidance, especially during the early years. The school can do more, perhaps, to make up for a paucity of cognitive or linguistic stimulation at home, but in all cases the efforts of the school to give the child a good start in life will be enhanced by parental support. A sense of involvement in decision making, as far as is possible, and of contributing personally to the child's development and education, can transform the attitudes of parents towards a handicapped child, and encourage more positive self-concepts on their own part. Here the school can help by being prepared to listen to what parents have to say, by understanding and respecting their feelings, and by keeping them informed of the child's progress, being careful to point out strengths as well as weaknesses.

The child will benefit, too, if the parents are aware of their own potential as educators. As already mentioned, parental involvement is a crucial factor in the success of compensatory programmes, and evaluation of the experimental use of home visitors to help parents to provide appropriate stimulation has indicated that this is a promising line of approach (Smith, 1975; Donachy, 1976). Even in the case of severe mental or physical handicap, it has been shown that parents welcome and respond to practical instruction and advice on how to assist the development of their children or how to modify difficult behaviour (Clarke and Clarke, 1969; Brinkworth and Collins, 1973). The Portage Project (Weber et al., 1975) provides an example of a systematic programme of early intervention, developed in the USA, which is based on parental involvement. A home teacher pays a visit to the parents of a handicapped child once a week for one and half hours in order to instruct the parents how to present tasks to be learned, how to reinforce the child's efforts and how to record and assess the child's weekly progress. In Britain, Cunningham and Jeffree (1975) have set up workshops for parents of children with severe learning difficulties, and on the basis of their experience conclude that these workshops are worth while and beneficial as long as they meet the needs of the parents. Toy libraries, too, have been found to be a valuable means of encouraging parents to provide suitable experiences for children with special educational needs at home and of giving parents a better understanding of how to interact with their children through play (Head, 1978). As Yule (1975) states, there are many problems in teaching psychological principles to parents, but this is no reason for abandoning experiments in parent education: 'Most of the problems can be regarded as technical, and soluble. . . . The next decade should witness a massive expansion of research and practice in this area.'

In recent years, parents have become increasingly disinclined to remain at the receiving end of services; they have taken strong initiatives in seeking to supplement existing provision. This has been done mainly through the voluntary organisations specifically concerned with the handicapped, acting largely as pressure groups but in many cases establishing educational or parent support groups of their own (Stone and Taylor, 1977), and through the Pre-School Playgroup Association (Williamson, 1972; Crowe, 1983). The latter organisation, based on self-help with some professional guidance and financial assistance from local authorities, has shown a considerable interest in young children with difficulties. It is responsible for 'opportunity groups' in many parts of the country, which are available for children with any kind of difficulty and which, in addition to giving an opportunity for the parents to meet and share mutual concerns, allow the children to have stimulating play and contact with normal children.

Conclusion

In spite of inadequacies in the provision made for young children with special educational needs in this country, much progress has been made in recent years in the identification, assessment and education of these children at the nursery and infant school stages. Considerable advances have been made on the medical side, and there has been increasing recognition of children's social, psychological and educational needs. There is now a greater awareness of the many conditions and factors which may contribute to educational difficulties. Supplementing the work of statutory bodies, voluntary agencies are playing a valuable role in seeking to ensure that the needs of children with difficulties are fully met. Not surprisingly, the multiplicity of agencies concerned, especially during the early years, has led to problems in communication and coordination of effort, but there are many examples of successful cooperation between different professional workers, for instance in the multi-disciplinary pre-school assessment centres operating in a number of regions. While we need to know much more about the most appropriate ways of dealing with learning difficulties in the early years, many fruitful ideas have been suggested by both practitioners and research workers. It is to be hoped that adequate resources will be available for further experiment and evaluation, as well as for the expansion of existing provision where this is urgently needed.

References

Anderson, E. (1973) *The Disabled School Child*. London: Methuen.
Becker, R. D. (1976) The neurology of childhood learning disorders: the minimal brain dysfunction syndrome re-examined. *Therapeutic Education* **4**, 20–31.
Bender, L. and Gurevitz, S. (1955) Results of psychotherapy with young schizophrenic patients. *American Journal of Orthopsychiatry* **25**, 162–170.
Bentovim, A. (1973) Disturbed and underfive. *Special Education* **62**, 31–5.
Bereiter, C. and Engelmann, S. (1966) *Teaching Disadvantaged Children in the Pre-School*. Englewood Cliffs, NJ: Prentice-Hall.
Blackie, J. (1967) *Inside the Primary School*. London: HMSO.
Blank, M. and Solomon, F. (1968) A tutorial language program to develop abstract thinking in socially disadvantaged children. *Child Development* **39**, 379–89.
Brennan, W. K. (1974) *Shaping the Education of Slow Learners*. London: Routledge & Kegan Paul.

Bricker, W. A. (1971) Behaviour modification programmes. In Mittler, P. (ed.) *Psychological Assessment of the Mentally Handicapped*. London: Churchill.

Brinkworth, P. and Collins, J. (1973) *Improving Babies with Down's Syndrome*. London: National Society for Mentally Handicapped Children.

Central Advisory Council for Education (Wales) (1967) *Primary Education in Wales* (The Gittins Report). London: HMSO.

Clarke, A. D. B. and Clarke, A. M. (1969) *Practical Help for Parents of Retarded Children*. Hull: Hull Society for Mentally Handicapped Children.

Cleave, S., Jowett, S. and Bate, M. (1982) *And So To School*. Windsor: NFER–Nelson.

Chazan, M. and Cox, T. (1976) Language programmes for disadvantaged children. In Williams, P. and Varma, V. P. (eds) *Piaget, Psychology and Education*. London: Hodder & Stoughton.

Chazan, M. and Jackson, S. (1971) Behaviour problems in the infant school. *Journal of Child Psychology and Psychiatry* **12**, 191–210.

Chazan, M. and Jackson, S. (1974) Behaviour problems in the infant school: changes over two years. *Journal of Child Psychology and Psychiatry* **15**, 33–46.

Chazan, M. and Laing, A. F. (1982) *Children with Special Needs: The Early Years*. Milton Keynes: Open University Press.

Chazan, M., Laing, A. F., Jones, J. E., Harper, G. and Bolton, J. (1983) *Helping Young Children with Behaviour Difficulties*. London: Croom Helm.

Cooper, J., Moodley, M. and Reynell, J. (1978) *Helping Language Development*. London: Edward Arnold.

Cratty, B. J. (1970) *Perceptual and Motor Development in Infants and Children*. London: Collier Macmillan.

Crowe, B. (1983) *The Playgroup Movement*. London: Allen and Unwin.

Crystal, D., Fletcher, P. and Garman, M. (1976) *A Language Assessment, Remediation and Screening Procedure* (LARSP). London: Edward Arnold.

Cunningham, C. C. and Jeffree, D. M. (1975) The organization and structure of workshops for parents of mentally handicapped children. *Bulletin of British Psychological Society* **28**, 405–11.

Delacato, C. (1963) *The Diagnosis and Treatment of Speech and Reading Problems*. Springfield, Ill.: Charles C. Thomas.

Department of Education and Science (1972a) *Education: a Framework for Expansion* London: HMSO.

Department of Education and Science (1972b) *Aspects of Special Education*. Education Survey 17. London: |HMSO

Department of Education and Science (1973) *Special Education: A Fresh Look* (Reports on Education, No. 77). London: HMSO.

Department of Education and Science (1975) *Educating Mentally Handicapped Children* (Education Pamphlet 60). London: HMSO

Department of Education and Science (1978) *Special Education Needs* (The Warnock Report). London: HMSO

Department of Education and Science (1981) *Statistics in Schools, January 1981*. London: HMSO

Department of Health and Social Security (1976) *Fit for the Future* (The Court Report). Committee on Child Health Services. London: HMSO.

Donachy, W. (1976) Parent participation in pre-school education. *British Journal of Educational Psychology* **46**, 31–9.

Dunn, L. M., Horton, K. B. and Smith, J. O. (1968) (eds) *Peabody Language Development Kit*. Circle Pines, Minn.: American Service Inc.

Edgerton, R. B. (1967) *The Cloak of Competence*. Berkeley and Los Angeles: University of California Press.

Evans, R. and Ferguson, N. (1974) Screening school entrants. *Association of Educational Psychologists Journal* **3**, 2–9.

Finnie, N. R. (1971) *Handling the Young Cerebral Palsied Child at Home.* London: Heinemann Medical Books.

Forrest, A., Ritson, B. and Zealley, A. (1973) *New Perspectives in Mental Handicap.* Edinburgh: Churchill-Livingstone.

Francis-Williams, J. (1964) *Understanding and Helping the Distractible Child.* London: The Spastics Society.

Francis-Williams, J. (1970) *Children with Specific Learning Difficulties.* Oxford: Pergamon.

Frostig, M. and Horne, D. (1964) *The Frostig Programme for the Development of Visual Perception.* Chicago, Ill.: Follet.

Gahagan, G. A. and Gahagan, D. M. (1970) *Talk Reform.* London: Routledge & Kegan Paul.

Galton, M., Simon, B. and Croll, P. (1980) *Inside the Primary Classroom.* London: Routledge & Kegan Paul.

Gillham, W. E. C. (1979) *The First Words Language Programme.* London: Allen and Unwin.

Goodacre, E. J. (1968) *Teachers and their Pupils' Home Background.* Slough: NFER.

Gunzburg, H. C. (1968) *Social Competence and Mental Handicap.* London: Baillière, Tindall and Cassell.

Haskell, S. H. and Paull, M. E. (1973) *Training in Basic Cognitive and Motor Skills.* Harlow: Educational Supply Association.

Head, J. (1978) Toy libraries: a resource for parental partnership. *Occasional Papers of Division of Educational and Child Psychology* **2**, 34–40. Leicester: British Psychological Society.

Hughes, N. A. S. (1972) Developmental physiotherapy in the care of mentally handicapped babies. In Laing, A. F. (ed.) *Educating Mentally Handicapped Children.* Swansea: Faculty of Eduation, University College of Swansea.

Jackson, R. (1975) The education of the physically handicapped child. In Williams, A. (ed.) *Education of Handicapped Children. Aspects of Education*, No. 2. Hull: University of Hull, Institute of Education.

Jeffree, D. M. and McConkey, R. (1974) Extending language through play. *Special Education: Forward Trends* **1**, 13–16.

Jeffree, D. M. and McConkey, R. (1976) *Let Me Speak.* London: Souvenir Press.

Kephart, N. C. (1960) *The Slow Learner in the Classroom.* Columbus, Ohio: Merrill.

Kiernan, C. C., Jordan, R. and Saunders, C. (1978) *Starting off.* London: Souvenir Press.

Kiernan, C. C. and Woodford, P. (eds) (1975) *Behaviour Modification with the Severely Retarded.* Amsterdam: Associated Scientific Press.

Kirk, S. A., McCarthy, J. J. and Kirk, W. D. (1968) *The Illinois Test of Psycholinguistic Abilities.* Chicago, Ill.: University of Illinois Press.

Kirman, B. H. (1968) *Mental Retardation.* Oxford: Pergamon.

Kushlick, A. and Cox, G. R. (1973) The epidemiology of mental handicap. *Developmental Medicine and Child Neurology* **15**, 748–59.

Langan, W. (1970) Visual perceptual difficulties. In Mittler, P. (ed.) *Psychological Assessment of Mental and Physical Handicap.* London: Methuen.

Leach, D. J. (1981) Early screening for school learning difficulties: efficacy problems and alternatives. *Occasional Papers of Division of Education and Child Psychology* **5**, 26–57. Leicester: British Psychological Society.

Leeming, K., Swann, W., Coupe, J. and Mittler, P. (1979) *Teaching Language and Communication to the Mentally Handicapped.* London: Evans/Methuen Educational.

Luria, A. R. (1961) *The Role of Speech in the Regulation of Normal and Abnormal Behaviour.* Oxford: Pergamon.

McInnes, J. M. and Treffry, J. A. (1982) *Deaf–blind Infants and Children.* Milton Keynes: The Open University Press.

MacKeith, R. (1973) The feelings and behaviour of parents of handicapped children. *Developmental Medicine and Child Neurology* **15**, 524–7.

Mittler, P. (1970) (ed.) *Psychological Assessment of Mental and Physical Handicap.* London: Methuen.

Mortimore, J. and Blackstone, T. (1982) *Disadvantage and Education.* London: Heinemann.

National Society for the Study of Education (1973) *Yearbook 72, Pt I: Behaviour Modification in Education.* Chicago, Ill.: NSSE.

Neisworth, J. T. and Smith, R. M. (1973) *Modifying Retarded Behaviour.* Boston: Houghton Mifflin.

O'Connor, N. and Hermelin, B. (1963) *Speech and Thought in Severe Subnormality.* Oxford: Pergamon.

Priestley, P. H. (1973) Educating the mentally handicapped. In Forrest, A., Ritson, B. and Zealley, A. (eds) *New Perspectives in Mental Handicap.* Edinburgh: Churchill-Livingstone.

Pringle, M. L. K., Butler, N. R. and Davie, R. (1966) *11,000 Seven-Year-Olds.* London: Longman.

Pritchard, D. G. (1963) *Education and the Handicapped 1760–1960.* London: Routledge & Kegan Paul.

Quigley, H. (1971) Reactions of eleven nursery teachers and assistants to the Peabody Language Development Kit. *British Journal of Educational Psychology* **41**, 155–62.

Reynell, J. (1969) *Reynell Development Language Scales.* Windsor: NFER.

Richman, N., Stevenson, J. and Graham, P. J. (1982) *Pre-school to School: a Behavioural Study.* London: Academic Press.

Rogers, C. (1982) *A Social Psychology of Schooling.* London: Routledge & Kegan Paul.

Rutter, M. (1968) Concepts of autism: a review of research. *Journal of Child Psychology and Psychiatry* **9**, 1–26.

Rutter, M., Graham, P. and Yule, W. (1970a) *A Neuropsychiatric Study in Childhood.* London: Heinemann.

Rutter, M., Tizard, J. and Whitmore, K. (1970b) *Education, Health and Behaviour.* London: Longman.

Shiach, G. M. (1972) *Teach them to Speak.* London: Ward Lock Educational.

Smith, G. (1975) *Educational Priority, Vol. 4: The West Riding EPA.* London: HMSO.

Sonquist, H. D. and Kamii, C. K. (1967) Applying some Piagetian concepts in the classroom for the disadvantaged. *Young Children* **22**, 231–45.

Stone, J. and Taylor, F. (1977) *Handbook for Parents with a Handicapped Child.* London: Home and School Council.

Tansley, A. E. (1967) *Reading and Remedial Reading.* London: Routledge & Kegan Paul.

Taylor, P. H., Exon, G. and Holley, B. (1972) *A Study of Nursery Education* (Schools Council Working Paper 41). London: Evans/Methuen Educational.

Thompson, T. and Grabowski, J. (1972) *Behaviour Modification of the Mentally Retarded.* London: Oxford University Press.

Watson, L. S. (1973) *Child Behaviour Modification: a Manual for Teachers, Nurses and Parents.* Oxford: Pergamon.

Webb, L. (1967) *Children with Special Needs in the Infants School.* London: Collins Fontana Books.

Weber, S. J. et al. (1975) *The Portage Guide to Home Teaching*. Portage, Wisconsin: Cooperative Educational Service Agency.

Wedell, K. (1973) *Learning and Perceptuo-Motor Disabilities in Children*. London: Wiley.

Wedell, K. and Raybould, E. C. (eds) (1976) *The Early Identification of Educationally 'At Risk' Children*. University of Birmingham Occasional Publications, No. 6.

Weikart, D. P., Epstein, A. S., Sweinhart, L. and Bond, J. T. (1978) *The Ypsilanti Preschool Curriculum Demonstration Project: No. 4, Preschool Years and Longitudinal Results*. High/Scope Educational Research Foundation Monograph. London: Grant McIntyre.

Westmacott, E. V. S. and Cameron, R. J. (1981) *Behaviour Can Change*. Basingstoke: Macmillan Educational.

Westman, J. C., Rice, D. L. and Bermann, E. (1967) Nursery school behaviour and later school adjustment. *Americal Journal of Orthopsychiatry* **3**, 725–31.

Williamson, C. (1972) *Handicapped Children in Playgroups*. London: Pre-School Playgroup Association.

Winchell, C. A. (1975) *The Hyperkinetic Child*. Westport, Conn.: Greenwood Press.

Younghusband, E., Birchall, D., Davie, R. and Pringle, M. K. L. (1970) (eds) *Living with Handicap*. London: National Bureau for Cooperation in Child Care.

Yule, W. (1975) Teaching psychological principles to non-psychologists: training parents in child management. *Association of Educational Psychologists Journal* **3**, 5–16.

Yule, W., Berger, M. and Howlin, P. (1973) Language deficit and behaviour modificaton. In O'Connor, N. (ed.) *Language, Cognitive Deficits and Retardation*. Edinburgh: Churchill-Livingstone.

9

Carrying out Assessment with Young Children

STEVE TYLER

The assessment of a child's work and behaviour is a necessary and inevitable part of every teacher's day, as is the process of making decisions which affect the learning opportunities available to the child. In making these decisions teachers make use of the information gained from their daily contact with each child, their experience of working with young children in general and their knowledge of theoretical issues concerning the education and development of the young child. For some purposes, however, the information immediately available to the teacher may be insufficient, and recourse to a rather more formal and systematic technique of assessment may be required. In this chapter, we shall consider some of the means by which the young child may be assessed and his progress recorded, though we shall not, of course, touch on specialist assessment techniques available only to the educational psychologist.

Some assessments of a child are instantaneous and prompt an immediate decision for a particular course of action. The adult observing a child balancing precariously upon a teetering tower of blocks that he has constructed may recognise that the child is honing his physical skills and increasing his knowledge of the physical world. It may be the first time he has managed to construct such a structure and it therefore represents a particular achievement. However, the adult will also recognise that the child will need careful supervision and that a rapid intervention may well be required for his physical safety. Most situations that occur in the nursery or infant school are, however, less immediate and require more subtle evaluation. What provision should be made to extend the child's learning? What assistance should he be given and when? The answers to these questions come from the teacher's evaluation of particular details of classroom activity and upon a considered reflection of the needs of the individual child. Assessment is a process requiring the teacher to find out and reflect upon the experiences the child has had and the stage in his learning that he has reached, in order to decide where and how he may be assisted to go further.

The idea of making a detailed assessment of the progress made by a child or student has long held currency within educational circles. Accordingly, numerous different methods, involving sophisticated techniques and varying degrees of formality, have been devised to assist the teacher in the process of making the assessment and recording the information obtained. In the infant school informal tests and checklists associated with reading and mathematics schemes have appeared, as well as more formal standardised tests. However, until comparatively recently, little attention had been paid to the means of assessment suitable for use within the nursery by teachers. Traditionally, pre-school estabishments have adopted a relatively informal, child-centred approach in which the emphasis has been placed upon the encouragement of self-paced learning through play. Within this tradition, teachers have undoubtedly been involved in the process of making assessments of the children but these have tended to be informal. In the main, formal testing of the child has been the method adopted by colleagues in other disciplines concerned with the welfare of the young child, such as psychologists and doctors. Although the information obtained from such testing is obviously of value to teachers, it may not answer some of the questions teachers need to ask. In both infant and nursery schools there are benefits to be gained from the teacher developing her own assessment skills.

Types of individual assessment

An assessment may be made for many purposes, although any single procedure may fulfil several of these. In general, it is possible to distinguish two types of individual assessment: formative evaluation, which is concerned with the collection of information as a basis for action in the promotion of the child's development, and summative evaluation, which occurs at the end of a period of teaching and is concerned with the collection of information which summarises the stage the child has reached. This information is often used as the basis for comparisons between children. One may also distinguish between assessment procedures which concentrate upon a specific aspect of the child's development (e.g. reading tests) and procedures which give a more general overview of his developing abilities. The form of assessment used will depend upon the purpose for which it is being made.

Most teachers will encounter children who appear to be experiencing difficulties in one or several areas of their development. Assessment may help not only to confirm the teacher's original opinion of the child's levels of functioning but may serve also to identify the particular areas in which he or she requires special assistance. Within a system of assessment, clues as to how that assistance might be provided may also be obtained. However, assessment should also be of benefit to those groups of children who, although progressing satisfactorily, still require to be monitored and considered. A general system of appraisal applied systematically ensures that consideration is given to each child's needs. At a more specific level, where the objectives for a child are closely defined, a process of assessment is necessary in order to judge the child's progress towards meeting these objectives. Within the learning process it is important that the task set matches the child's stage of learning. As Harlen (1982) points out, this does not mean giving children more of what they can already do. Rather it implies the provision of materials and experience which yield the right challenge for the child and help him to take the correct size of step, using and extending his existing ideas. Assessment, including reflection upon the results of the process of assessment, is an integral part of matching educational provision to the child. Although we are concerned with the assessment of the individual child, the process of making the assessment may not only be of benefit to a specific child. A system of assessment may also help staff to evaluate the effectiveness of a particular programme they are running and to communicate information about the child more efficiently to colleagues concerned with his education.

Assessment may be carried out by a variety of procedures used either singly or in combination, and may involve either consideration of the *process* of learning or of the *products* produced. Thus a teacher may wish to examine the way in which the child tackles a task or the piece of recorded work that results from this task. Whereas the infant teacher may, after the initial reception period, be able to adopt the latter approach by basing her evaluation of the child's progress upon his written work and the stage he has achieved on the various schemes employed in the school, the nursery teacher rarely has such an option. In most nursery classes, little recording by the child occurs other than in the form of his drawings and paintings, and the teacher must make her assessment by observation of and contact with the child himself. What he will be doing, essentially, in this context is playing. Play also forms an important, though sometimes underrated, part of the infant school curriculum.

Assessment and play

What young children do is 'play'. Whereas at later stages 'play' may be contrasted with 'work', at the earliest stages of the child's education such a differentiation carries little validity. That learning occurs through play is a central tenet of early education and is supported by some empirical evidence. For example, Sylva et al. (1976) describe the role of play in the problem solving activities of pre-school children. They found that children who were given opportunities to play with equipment before being asked to use it to solve a problem fared better in the quest for a solution than those who did not engage in play beforehand. The play described here was of the exploratory kind since the equipment was relatively novel. Other authors caution, however, that certain forms of play may preclude learning (in the sense of acquiring information from a novel or unfamiliar source) if those forms appear prematurely and as a distraction before exploration of the source is complete (Hutt, 1970). Thus it may be argued that not all forms of play necessarily promote learning.

Any discussion of 'play' is fraught with difficulty since so many differing and conflicting definitions of the term exist. It encapsulates many and various forms of activity, all of which may serve some useful function for the child under particular circumstances (see chapter 16). Indeed, Sylva et al. (1980) comment that they found teachers loath to deprecate the value of any child's play, and by selective recourse to the numerous theories of play this position may be justified. Thus, for some practitioners, all that a child does in his play may be construed as valuable and necessary to his development. Yet it is also generally recognised that superficially similar activities may have different qualities associated with them. According to Parry and Archer (1974): 'There are two levels of play. One merely keeps children occupied: the other contributes to their educational development.'

The question is how to distinguish between these two levels. This is not easy since any attempt to measure the value of play in a wide variety of settings requires the development of criteria by which types of behaviour as different as pouring water into a bottle and playing mothers and fathers may be compared. Lomax (1977) suggests that as an integral part of the process of assessing and recording the progress of the individual child in the nursery, staff should observe and note the proportion of time dedicated to each type of activity by the child. In this way a record of how long the child devoted to play in, for instance, the Wendy house as opposed to play at, perhaps, the collage table would be obtained. In the infant school play periods tend to be rather more structured and the child has fewer choices of play materials available at one time, but recording of play preferences may still serve a useful purpose since (as in the nursery) play reveals the nature of the predominant experiences to which the child is exposed. Also of importance is the fact that, while indulging in a particular activity, the child's play may be exploratory or repetitive, attentive or desultory. What is required is a means of analysing the play which will enable us to place a value upon it. Once we have done this we may take steps to ensure that the child benefits from the experiences we provide.

How, then, are we to distinguish between different forms of play at this age level? Hutt's (1979) taxonomy of play forms a useful starting point in any attempt to answer this question. Hutt's model distinguishes between 'epistemic' and 'ludic' aspects of play. Whereas epistemic behaviour is concerned with the acquisition of information and knowledge, ludic behaviour involves the rehearsal of material already accommodated. Each of these two categories of play may be further subdivided into component categories. Thus Hutt divides epistemic behaviour into those patterns concerned with (a) problem-solving, (b) those relating to exploration, and

E

(c) those which are productive activities designed to effect a change, altering either the state of the material played with or the performance of the individual child. Hutt's dichotomy between epistemic and ludic patterns of play resembles Piaget's distinction between 'accommodation' and 'assimilation' (Piaget, 1951). However, Hutt's model permits us to go further since it allows us to categorise common activities within a theoretical framework. Figure 1 shows how activities might be placed upon the epistemic to ludic continuum.

Figure 1 shows that conceptual games and tasks requiring auditory or visual discrimination are more typically biased towards the epistemic end of the play spectrum, whereas fantasy play and physical play are more usually loaded towards the ludic end. Construction toys and manipulative play (which has been distinguished from play with jigsaws by the latter's dependence upon often complex visuo-spatial abilities) occupy an intermediate position in this model together with activities such as drawing and painting.

Hutt (1979) would argue that the ludic activities are typically mood-dependent, requiring the child to be relaxed for their appearance, while epistemic behaviours are elicited by novelty and challenge in the environment. Although most activities will contain both ludic and epistemic elements – the predominance of one over the other depending upon the exact conditions prevailing – Hutt's taxonomy suggests that there is a need for a balance to be struck between the two. If a child exhibits predominantly epistemic behaviour patterns, there is a danger that, although learning is occurring, generalisation through the application of the skills and concepts to different contexts is not. Similarly, if a child spends an overwhelming proportion of his time engaged in ludic behaviour, it is difficult to see how the child is acquiring much fresh information to act upon, although he may, of course, be refining his skills of social interaction. Thus an excessive predominance of any one form of play in the child's repertoire for an extended period of time seems unlikely to be conducive to his development.

Hutt (1979) also considers that play which involves a great deal of repetition is often undesirable. A great deal of thumb-sucking, rocking or other self-manipulatory or self-stimunatory behaviour patterns would soon be noticed by the teacher, but other perseverative patterns are rather less obvious. The repeated patterns of scooping and pouring continued endlessly with little or no accompanying social contact exhibited by some children at the sand and water trays are examples of such patterns. In many cases it is difficult to argue that this repetition constitutes the useful rehearsal or practice of a skill. It may be correctly claimed that children need occasionally to retreat from the stimulus of the environment and that repetitive activites assist them to do this, but if a child devotes considerable time to the repetition of elementary movement patterns long since acquired it may be construed that his play is generally of poor quality.

A similar but alternative means of classifying play activities, based as with

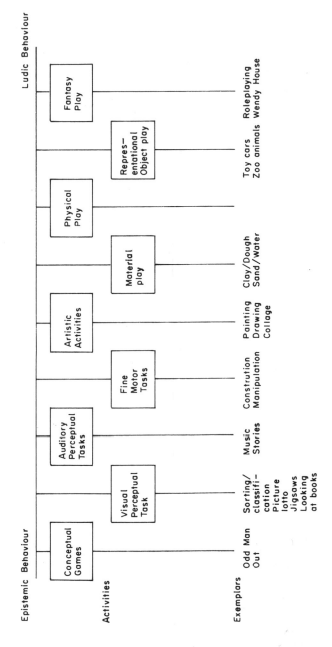

Figure 1   *Classification of children's activities.*

Hutt's taxonony upon direct observation, is seen in the work of Sylva et al. (1980). In this study the level of cognitive challenge typically present within play activities is identified, and again it is made clear that one cannot determine the quality of a child's play simply from the fact that he is engaged in a particular activity or expresses a preference for this activity. Examination of Sylva et al.'s (1980) classifications and of others presented in the literature suggests that there is a consensus that the following *specific features* of the activity must be taken into account:

1 The degree of concentration shown by the child upon the activity engaged in.
2 The complexity of the sequence of elements in an episode of play.
3 The degree of social participation inherent in the activity.
4 The degree of symbolism incorporated in the child's play.
5 The language content of the play.

These features should be taken together, since to take each in isolation may provide equivocal results.

In general, play involving sustained attention to the activity or task is viewed as superior to play in which the bouts are of short duration and concentration is fragmented. However, the duration of play episodes is a measure which is very variable both within age groups and for individual children and may be dependent upon a variety of factors relating to the child and his environment. Moreover, it is also true that prolonged episodes in which the play is unvaried represent an indication of play of poor quality. Within a bout of play it may be argued that the more elements or action patterns that are combined within the given episode, the greater the complexity and hence the quality of the play, provided that the sequence of the elements forms a coherent unit. Yet individual, brief play episodes may nevertheless show startling imagination and be worthy of being classified as play of high quality (i.e. high quality in the sense that it indicates and encourages satisfactory all-round development).

In general, it is assumed that high-quality play is associated with high levels of social contact and symbolism. The classic studies of Parten (1932) suggested that 'solitary play' (wherein the child plays independently with toys which differ from those being used by other children) is the least mature form of play, and that 'cooperative play', in which all children are working towards a common goal with some evidence of social organisation, is seen as the most mature form. Recent work suggests, however, that this position may be oversimplified and that solitary play may subserve different functions at different ages (Smith, 1978). For instance, an older child may *prefer* to work on his own for some periods in order to work out a problem with, perhaps, a construction toy, without interference from less mature children. In general, in assessing the child's social behaviour we should therefore be careful to distinguish between the level that a child is *capable* of and the level that he happens to *prefer* at any particular time.

Teachers generally appear to regard forms of symbolic play as being of inherently high quality, a view which is also supported by the literature on play. For example, a number of studies (Smilansky, 1968) support the view that through tutoring children in fantasy play linguistic facility is substantially raised. However, Smith (1977) argues that most of these studies fail to demonstrate the effectiveness of fantasy play *per se* in the raising of levels of performance, and it seems that any claim that the presence of symbolism itself necessarily indicates that the play episode in which it is contained is of high quality requires substantiation.

The use of language in the course of play generally has been the subject of much attention over the past decade. Tough (1976) argues that the use of language for certain purposes is a critical feature of the child's functioning within the pre-school. She defines seven different purposes for language: self-maintaining; directing; reporting on present and past experiences; towards logical reasoning; predicting; projecting; imagining (see chapter 4). Tough argues that all children tend to use language for the first three purposes, but only a minority of children frequently employ language for the last four. It may be argued that since these purposes are of importance in later schooling where logical reasoning, prediction and projection are frequently demanded of the child, the facility to employ language to fulfil these purposes is something that should be encouraged in the nursery and infant school. Tough's analysis might be seen to provide a useful tool for looking at the language content of play and as such might be incorporated into a system of assessment. But an overdependence on the analysis of the language content of play in the assessment of its quality would seem to be a mistake. Some play by the nature of its focal material would seem to encourage or discourage social interaction. Moreover, because a child is functioning well linguistically, it does not necessarily follow that he is capable of performing equally well in all spheres. In order to establish a child's customary pattern of language usage, it would appear to be necessary therefore to sample his speech in a number of different play settings.

Estimation of the quality of a child's play is therefore a complex matter and each of the aspects listed above needs to be considered in detail and in varying play contexts before a final judgement can be made. It is clear that the assessment of the quality of the play of an individual child necessitates careful observation and interpretation. Consider the following two examples of children at play:

John is pushing a pram around the edge of the garden. At a distance, this behaviour appears comparatively simple and repetitive and might be categorised as play of low quality. Closer observation reveals that the child's motor behaviour is accompanied by a 'brr-brr' vocalisation, and that he is moving in a systematic pattern across the field. Subsequent discussion reveals that he is pretending that the pram is a lawnmower, his actions imitating those of an adult cutting the lawn.

Thus his play contains elements of imitation, symbolism and for the particular child novelty since he has not played in this way before.

Paul and Lucie are in the nursery playroom, while most of the other children are outside. The two have been playing at 'keeping-house' for approximately half an hour, not in the Wendy house but in a house they have constructed together from items of nursery furniture and large bricks. They have adopted roles of 'mummy' and 'daddy' and the episode has involved different sequences. Observation of this play in isolation would suggest that the level of play is high by the criteria already cited. However, this is a pattern of play which has been repeated often by the two children with little variation. Moreover, the children concerned seldom engage in other forms of play, especially those forms which also involve adults.

The first example shows the need to look at each play episode carefully and to avoid hasty judgements. The second example illustrates that we need to examine our observations of children within the overall context of our knowledge of them. Superficial judgements might have led us to attribute greater value to the play of the second example, and led us to intervene in the first episode. Closer observation and more detailed consideration would lead us to opposite assessments of the situation in each case.

Observation and assessment

Observation of a child, whether he is playing in the nursery class or engaged in a task within the infant school, is frequently an essential component of making an assessment. Observation is particularly useful in the evaluation of aspects of the child's social behaviour and his use of language. These are, of course, important characteristics of which the teacher should be aware, and we know that teachers themselves give emphasis to the development of these areas (Hutt et al., 1984). On the negative side, detailed observations are time-consuming, and many periods of watching the child may elapse before particular insights into the child's behaviour are gained if the environment is not structured to elicit the behaviour in which we are interested. For example, in the nursery we may wait a long time to see the child at play in the Wendy house if we do not encourage him in some way to engage in this activity. Similarly, in the infant school, if we do not set up the task correctly we may not see certain uses of language. Behaviour patterns that occur fairly infrequently may still be present in the child's repertoire, may be elicited by the appropriate stimuli and may be of significance in the interpetation of his overall level of performance.

Not only is observation of unstructured activity time-consuming, however, it may also present the teacher with serious difficulties of execution. Whereas the researcher may observe with only limited interactions between herself and the target child, such a situation is difficult for the teacher to maintain within her own playroom or classroom. Adults who are customarily seen as the focal point of the classroom may find it difficult to switch their role to a non-interactive one. All teachers are only too aware of the demands children make on them! Nevertheless, these difficulties are not insuperable. Various method chosen being dependent on the particular question we wish to answer. method chose being dependent on the particular question we wish to answer. If we wish to examine the child's performance in a very specific area, it may be possible to follow him and watch his performance for the duration of the activity or task, provided this is not too extended. However, if our concern is for a more general evaluation of the child's performance or play, we may use a sampling technique, in which we look at what he is doing or saying at periodic intervals. In her discussion of how to make an appraisal of the child's use of language, Tough (1976) gives clear illustrations of how such a process might be carried out. Sampling observations depend on the teacher keeping in mind one or two children during, for example, a half-day session. At regular intervals of, perhaps, a quarter of an hour, the teacher looks at the child and notes details of what he is currently doing. What is actually recorded will depend upon the purpose of the assessment, and recording may take several forms. The teacher may write a quick long-hand account of what the child is doing, thereby building up a *diary* of his day. Alternatively, she may use a *checklist* of predetermined categories, a tick by one of them indicating that this behaviour pattern occurred during the observation period. In either case, the teacher must be clear about the things she wishes to note and must be close enough to the child to observe and hear clearly.

Practising teachers, as we have already said, make observations all the time, whether these are formal in the manner just described or informal. The results of observations of either kind are often summarised in the form of rating scales. For example, if we are interested in how well the child concentrates on a task, we may wish to rate him on a scale which extends from 'low' to 'high' powers of concentration. Rating scales are a relatively quick and simple method of recording information but their validity and reliability depend to a large extent upon how clearly and specifically we can describe the child's behaviour. Some rating scales adopt simple descriptions such as 'good', 'fair' or 'poor'. Alternatively, they may rate the occurrence of a behaviour from 'frequently' to 'occasionally' or 'rarely'. Such descriptions are vague and although they may be used consistently by the individual teacher, it is not clear that their meaning will be interpreted in the same way by her colleagues. This point is of particular importance if the record which results from the process of assessment is to be passed on. A solution to this problem is provided, in part, by the provision of a comprehensive definition of each point on the scale. In some instances this definition is supplied for the teacher, as in the *Manual for Assessment in Nursery Education* (Bate and Smith, 1978). An alternative approach adopted in the *Keele Pre-School Assessment Guide* (Tyler, 1980) is to require all members of staff who have contact with the child to confer before rating the child on a scale whose end points are specified and divided from each other by gradations (e.g. high concentration to low concentration). Upon positioning the child on the scale the assessor is required to make a written description of the child's behaviour, thereby defining the meaning of the point on the scale. Both these approaches may serve to increase the validity and reliability of a scale. Nevertheless, points on a scale should be considered relative rather than absolute and scales are best used for recording progress in areas related to, for example, the individual child's concentration and confidence rather than for comparisons between children.

Observation alone, however, is unlikely to tell us all we need to know about a child. It serves to indicate what he does, but not necessarily what he *can* do. As Tizard et al. (1976) point out:

> As measures of cognitive development. . . , observations of play proved considerably less reliable and more time-consuming to carry out than standardised tests. Further, because play is self-initiated, it is not usually possible by observing play to see the limit of the child's capacity. With no pressure upon him he does not work to his optimum.

Although the child's customary level of functioning is important, the teacher must also be concerned with the *extent* of the child's learning. Moreover, the two levels of functioning, the customary and the highest currently possible, need to be distinguished since the actions of the teacher should be consequent upon a knowledge of both. In the case of the child who functions at the highest level of which he is presently capable, staff responses may be principally concerned with the facilitation of learning. In the case of the child who habitually functions at a similar level, but which is much lower than that which he is able to achieve, the implications for action are different. Here the teacher may feel inclined to concentrate upon aspects of the child's motivation or upon his perception of staff expectations. Observation alone is unlikely to enable staff to distinguish successfully between the two children.

Although comparatively brief periods of observation may serve to highlight the problems of particular children whose behaviour shows excessive tendencies in a specific direction, in almost every assessment procedure we need to know what it is that the child has gained from the experiences we have provided. Observation alone is unlikely to tell us this, as we will usually have to provide a structure either in the shape of a formal test or, more informally, in a particular classroom activity.

Structured assessment

Superficially, it may seem that standarised tests developed by psychologists and educationalists furnish the teacher with an effective and efficient means of assessing the child's current level of functioning. In practice, however, the usefulness of such tests within the classroom is limited. There are several reasons for this. First, many of the tests need to be administered and interpreted by someone with special training. Thus some of the better standardised tests may be unavailable to teachers. Secondly, there are many difficulties associated with the testing of young children. Young children are notorious for their distractibility and they are frequently poorly motivated by tests and the situation in which they are tested, despite the best efforts of the test designers to make the items attractive. Thirdly, there are problems relating to the classroom environment. Most tests, unless they are specifically group tests, require the child and the tester to be separated from the other children. Some nurseries and schools do not have such a suitable room, and even if they do some children may fail to respond at their best as a consequence of being withdrawn from their normal environment. It should also be pointed out that some tests are very time-consuming and it may be impracticable to administer them to all the children in a class. A fourth difficulty is that tests tend to be summative rather than formative in nature. Thus, although they will usually enable a teacher to compare a child and his classmates and even a child and the average of a large sample of children of his own age, it is unlikely that the test results will provide a genuine indication of the next step the child should take in the learning process unless the test is very specific. And with such highly specific tests, teachers must be very clear that they understand what it is that the test is really testing. Different skills are employed in a word recognition test and a sentence completion test, although both may masquerade as a reading test.

Where tests are employed, and there is undoubtedly a case for their use in particular circumstances, individual children should be subjected to them only infrequently, and care must be taken not to teach test items. It must also be recognised that tests may be more successful in the examination of some areas of the child's development than in others. For example, the Bullock Report (Department of Education and Science, 1975) (see chapter 11) expresses doubts about the general use of tests for word recognition, and refers to their unsatisfactory nature in relation to the holistic nature of language learning and the range of skills the infant teacher is trying to develop.

A further important point is that standardised tests are generally formal and require a set method of presentation to the child if we are to ensure that the test is the same for all children. Such uniformity is not always achieved, however; for example, even though questions may be posed in the same way for each child they may not necessarily have the same meaning, due to ethnic or socioeconomic differences in individual children's backgrounds. Certainly the procedures involved in testing are often alien to the classroom teacher who is accustomed to modifying her questions until she is certain that the child genuinely understands what is being asked of him, even if he still doesn't know the answer.

An alternative to testing, therefore, is to examine the child's performance in a semi-structured situation. The distinction between structured and semi-structured is not always clear cut, but it rests primarily upon the higher degree of flexibility present in the latter. Tough (1976) gives examples of ways in which the teacher can use a variety of semi-structured situations to assess language development in young children. She suggests that since looking at pictures and books is a common activity in both the nursery and infant classroom, it may be a particularly appropriate situation in which to commence an appraisal. The teacher may first attempt to establish whether the child is aware of the central meaning of the picture or story, and whether he can link particular elements with the overall theme. In subsequent questioning the teacher may ask the child to predict what will happen next in the story or to empathise with the characters by telling her what they are feeling. What the child says in response to these questions will provide important clues to his understanding of and ability to use language. Throughout the situation the teacher is able to adjust her questioning in response to the child's replies. This technique could be applied to other areas of development or of the curriculum as well. Semi-structured situations appear to have more to offer the teacher attempting to assess the young child, but the teacher should be careful in these situations not to provide unnecessary clues to the answers to her questions nor to make unnecessary assumptions about the child.

Systems of assessment

In the course of making an assessment of an individual child a variety of methods and procedures may be used within an overall system of assessment. The components of the system may be few or many depending upon the particular purpose for which it has been designed. Various sources of assistance to the teacher interested in the assessment of the young child exist in the form of tests and guides (Jackson, 1971; Bate et al., 1976), but the teacher needs to be aware that in some instances these may not meet her purpose exactly, and although some guides lend themselves to adaptation, most tests do not. In addition, all will furnish results requiring some interpretation. How then should we judge the usefulness of an assessment system?

Where all-round assessment is required, it is obvious that the system should evaluate the child's develpment in as many ways as possible in order that a complete picture of the child may be obtained. Table 1 shows a possible breakdown of the areas which might be appropriate for examination in the assessment of a nursery child, taken from the *Keele Pre-School Assessment Guide* (Tyler, 1980). To the areas listed might be added those of 'social knowledge' and 'aesthetic awareness', athough both of these areas provide particular problems for assessment. Similarly, in the infant school it might be decided to break down the child's development into areas of reading and language skills, mathematical skills and physical skills, social behaviour and scientific knowledge. Subdivisions of these areas would be closely identified with the particular schemes of work used in the school, since in both the nursery and the infant school it is obvious that the system of assessment adopted must be congruent with the general curriculum, with the specific aims and objectives of the teacher and with the means by which these aims and objectives are achieved. It is also important that the system should contain a degree of flexibility to allow for future curriculum develpment.

Table 1   *Summary of items included in the Keele Pre-School Assessment Guide (Tyler, 1980)*

General biographical details and description of hand preference

Section I: Characteristic behaviour: rating scales
    1 Tends to play alone – mixes well
    2 Aggressive – timid
    3 Cautious – confident
    4 Initiates activities – follows lead of others
    5 Low concentration – high concentration
    6 Imaginative – unimaginative
    7 Other characteristics (unspecified)

Section II: Specific skills and concepts acquired in four areas (each subsection of an area contains five items)

Cognition:
    C1   Space and time
    C2   Properties of objects
    C3   Sorting and classification skills
    C4   Memory
    C5   Number
    C6   Problem solving

Physical skills:
    P1   Drawing and writing
    P2   Manipulative skills
    P3   Coordination

Socialistion:
    S1   Self-help
    S2   Play patterns

Language:
    L1   Language use
    L2   Speech
    L3   Vocabulary
    L4   Comprehension

Most systems of assessment involve the use of a record form. This form should present the necessary information as clearly as possible while minimising ambiguity, in order that staff may be encouraged to consult it. It should also allow for and facilitate comparisons between areas of the child's development since frequently the child's performance in one area may be explained by reference to his abilities in another. Thus if the child has a short attention span, is this the cause of his failure on a particular number task rather than a lack of the concepts required? Our record should help us to examine this question. The meaning of the entries on the record should also be plain to all those who may have access to it. The assessor may be clear in her own mind what she means when recording or ticking the phrases 'knows colours' or 'can add to 20' but the phrases contain many shades of meaning. Statements such as these may therefore require elaboration. Within the record, various fine gradations may also be possible, revealing how far the child has progressed towards acquiring a particular concept or skill. Thus we may wish to note whether the child has been exposed to the particular experiences required for learning this skill or concept, whether he can use it occasionally or whether he has consistent and complete mastery of it and so on. Alternatively, we may care to record only when the last stage has been reached, thereby losing information but gaining in simplicity and clarity.

The nature of the school day requires that the system adopted should require a minimum of time to complete while providing the maximum amount of useful information. In addition, the system should be sufficiently detailed to enable us readily to identify particular areas which may subsequently require more specific assessment procedures. Where possible, the activities and materials used by the child in the assessed tasks should be readily accessible and familiar to him, and the surroundings in which assessment takes place should also be familiar. The work of Donaldson (1978) clearly suggests that children perform well in settings that are familiar and where the form of the questions make 'human sense' to them.

Most systems of assessment will have strengths and weaknesses, and few will meet all possible requirements without being excessively unwieldy. The teacher must therefore be clear why an assessment is being made and, crucially, whether the information that is obtained is of genuine assistance in determining the appropriate action to be taken in assisting the child's development.

References

Bate, M. and Smith, M. (1978) *Manual for Assessment in Nursery Education*. Windsor: NFER.

Bate, M., Smith, M. and James, J. (1976) *Review of Pre-school Tests*. Windsor: NFER.

Donaldson, M. (1978) *Children's Minds*. London: Fontana.

Harlen, W. (1982) *Evaluation and the Teacher's Role*. London: Macmillan/Schools Council.

Hutt, C. (1970) Specific and diversive exploration. In Reese, H. W. and Lipsitt, L. P. (eds) *Advances in Child Development and Behaviour*, vol. 5. New York: Academic Press.

Hutt, C. (1979) Towards a taxonomy of play. In Sutton-Smith, B. (ed.) *Play and Learning*. New York: Gardner Press.

Hutt, S. J., Tyler, S., Hutt, C. and Foy, H. (1984) *Play, Exploration and Learning*. In the press.

Jackson, S. (1971) *A Teacher's Guide to Tests and Testing*. London: Longman.

Lomax, C. M. (1977) Record-keeping in nursery school: a two-year study. *Educational Research* **19**, 192–8.

Parry, M. and Archer, H. (1974) *Pre-school Education*. London: Macmillan/Schools Council.

Parten, M. (1932) Social participation among pre-school children. *Journal of Abnormal and Social Psychology* **27**, 243–69.

Piaget, J. (1951) *Play, Dreams and Imitation in Childhood*. London: Routledge & Kegan Paul.

Smilansky, S. (1968) *The Effect of Socio-dramatic Play on Disadvantaged Pre-school Children*. New York: Wiley.

Smith, P. K. (1977) Social and fantasy play in young children. In Tizard, B. and Harvey, D. (eds) *Biology of Play*. London: Heinemann.

Smith, P. K. (1978) A longitudinal study of social participation in pre-school children: solitary and parallel play re-examined. *Developmental Psychology* **14**, 517–23.

Sylva, K., Bruner, J. S. and Genova, P. (1976) The role of play in the problem-solving of children 3–5 years old. In Bruner, J. S., Jolly, A. and Sylva, K. (eds) *Play: its Role in Development and Evolution*. Harmondsworth: Penguin.

Sylva, K., Roy, C. and Painter, M. (1980) *Childwatching at Playgroup and Nursery School*. London: Grant McIntyre.

Tizard, B., Philips, J. and Plewis, I. (1976) Play in pre-school centres. I. Play resources and their relation to age, sex and IQ. *Joural of Child Psychology and Psychiatry* **17**, 251–64.

Tough, J. (1976) *Listening to Children Talking*. London: Ward Lock Educational/ Schools Council.

Tyler, S. (1980) *Keele Pre-School Assessment Guide*. Windsor: NFER.

Further Reading

Bate, M. and Smith, M. (1978) *Manual for Assessment in Nursery Education*. Windsor: NFER.

Haslen, W. (1982) *Evaluation and the Teacher's Role*. London: Macmillan/Schools Council.

Hutt, C. (1979) Towards a taxonomy of play. In Sutton-Smith, B. (ed.) *Play and Learning*. New York: Gardner Press.

Sylva, K., Roy, C. and Painter, M. (1980) *Childwatching at Playgroup and Nursery School*. London: Grant McIntyre.

Part II

10

Learning and Teaching Mathematical Skills

GEOFFREY MATTHEWS

Many teachers (and others concerned with young children) in the past have run a mile at the mention of 'number' or perhaps worse still 'mathematics'. There are unfortunately very good reasons for this. Until the 1960s, school mathematics was often a dreary subject with a strange language and a set of rules of its own, divorced from reality. Tricks had to be learnt to 'get the answer' and the teacher had finally failed when the child would ask 'What sort of sum is it?' The choice was an add, take-away, a times or a 'gozinta' (goes into) and it was indeed tragic that only a lottery could determine which one worked for the particular sum. Things have changed slowly since the reforms started in the 1960s, and we owe it to the children to see that the old horrors are permanently banished. Even if some of us suffered ourselves, we must make a real effort to see that mathematics can actually be enjoyable, and we must start by convincing ourselves if we are to have any hope of communicating the excitement to the children.

Many of the past woes stemmed from a desire to get the stuff over as quickly as possible, no doubt to pass on to happier activities like painting or milk, or to be able to report that the class had 'done' money sums or fractions or whatever might seem to impress. For whatever reason, there was an appalling mismatch between what the children *could* do and what they were *asked* to do. We therefore have to ask two questions in this chapter. First, what *is* mathematics for children up to the age of about seven? Secondly, how can we find out where each child is in his development of mathematical thought, so that we can provide him with relevant experiences to help him forward?

It will be convenient to deal first with the infants (age range five to seven). Later, there will be discussion on how the seeds for the ideas concerned are planted in younger children, who for convenience will be described as 'nursery', though of course they may be in a playgroup or at home. This order may seem illogical, but it will help to give a clearer picture, if only because so much more is known about the capabilities of infants. It must be emphasised that each child exists in its own right on a particular day: a nursery child is a nursery child and not a 'potential infant'.

Content and method

The reforms in mathematics teaching over the past 20 years have been two-pronged, concerned with *content* and *method*. Infants' teachers have been able to point the way to junior, and even secondary, teachers on method. They were the first to realise that children are individuals. This does not mean that each child should have his own programme and be tucked away in a corner never communicating; in fact, just the reverse. Children learn much from each other and from discussing their activities with their friends and their teacher; but each child can be helped forward with an occasional activity specifically aimed at extending his frontiers (if this happened continuously all day, the child would burst, but there is no danger of this). This implies a very different approach from sitting in rows all doing identical sums. Of course, children must eventually be able to calculate, and even know their tables, but it is a question of timing. If drills are learnt early and blindly, there can be no understanding or pleasure and little hope of later numeracy. The central discovery on how young children learn is that it is through *doing* something; only later will they talk or write about it.

The rationale for learning mathematics by *doing* is simple. Mathematics is an abstract subject and the very word 'abstract' suggests there should be a variety of concrete experiences from which a particular idea can be abstracted. For example, numbers themselves are abstract. No one has ever seen a three. The symbols 3, three, III etc. are just names for the number. The idea of 'the threeness of three' is an abstraction which can only be made after handling a large number of trios of things. Children can *see* three birds, three beasts, three crayons, three brushes, a miscellaneous collection consisting of one ship, one shoe and one stick of sealing wax (three things altogether) . . . and eventually they distil what all these sets have in common, namely the number three.

Turning to content, mathematics for young children may be considered as a set of concepts and skills. The younger the children, the more emphasis should there be on the concepts, for there is so much to understand before the simplest 'sum' can have any meaning. To write 'two cows, four legs each, altogether eight legs' may record something which perhaps a six-year-old has discovered spontaneously looking at a farmyard picture, but at this stage it is not helpful for the teacher to write brightly underneath $2 \times 4 = 8$. Some children going on from their first school at seven or eight will undoubtedly be ready for the beginning of tables, but by this time they will have had many experiences: two rows of four soldiers, two children each with four biscuits, two trays each with four paint-pots and so on, so that just as with the numbers themselves so their products (2 × 4 etc.) are abstracted from concrete experiences. 2 + 4 = 6 of course comes similarly, but if these 'facts' are presented too early, + and × can easily become confused and neither will have any meaning for the child.

Returning for the moment to the 'sixness of six' (or the 'threeness of three'), it is not enough to recognise the 'sixness' in many sets of six objects. Six must also be seen in its place as one more than five and one less than seven, and this involves the *ordering* of numbers: 1, 2, 3, 4, 5, 6, 7 etc. It is necessary also to appreciate that if six things are moved round the table to form a different pattern, there is no need to recount – there are still six. This is called the 'invariance of number' or sometimes 'conservation of number'. (The word 'conservation' is sometimes used very loosely. It is always necessary to ask *what* is being conserved, and *under what circumstances*.) Again, if one set is known to contain six objects (i.e. spoons) and another set can be seen to match these (i.e. one fork to each spoon) then, again without counting, there are six forks.

This idea of matching is sometimes called one-to-one correspondence (to each spoon there corresponds one fork). Finally, if there is a set of six objects and another set of eight objects, then eventually children must be able to compare the sets (probably by pairing off as far as possible) and so begin to appreciate that six is less than eight.

Simply looking at some of the things to be known about numbers has produced quite a catalogue of concepts: the previous paragraph has mentioned ordering, invariance of number, matching and comparisons. These concepts are fundamental and clearly not only concerned with numbers (sticks can be ordered for length, objects compared by weight and so on).

There are many concepts to be acquired by children aged three to seven, and it is worth emphasising the word *acquired*. A concept cannot be taught, it comes to the child at a certain stage when he is ready to grasp it, but the teacher can help enormously by providing relevant experiences to encourage the child at his frontier. Some concepts depend on others, so that it is no use jumping the gun and expecting the child to understand something 'further up the list' than his current thinking allows. A partially ordered tree of concepts is shown in figure 1 which depicts Form C, a progress record.

Progress records

Form C was devised (together with Form I which will be described below) by Julia Matthews as a way of recording the progress of young children in the infants' school, i.e. rising five to seven. A copy of Form C is kept for each child. It gives general information including his special interests, and his progress in reading, and a few examples of his recent written work are kept with the form. All this takes up comparatively little space compared with the

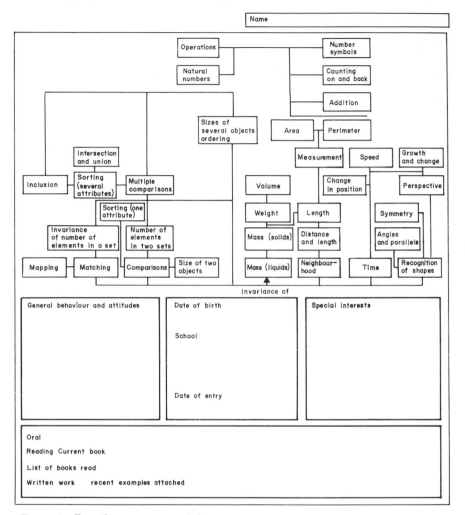

Figure 1   *Form C, a progress record form.*

recording of progress in mathematical and scientific concepts simply because it is easier to record. The concepts under discussion start at the centre of the page and work upwards: for example, invariance of number of elements in a set comes after matching. The left-hand branches of the tree lead towards number; the right-hand branches (often grossly neglected in the past) lead towards spatial ideas. In the middle are various 'invariances' (mass, weight, volume). The tree is partially ordered in the sense that one child may be well ahead along the spatial branches but right at the beginning of the numerical ones. This makes it vital to keep such a record, to make sure that each child's stage of understanding is known; otherwise the experiences provided will be haphazard and the child will be confused by some things he can do and others he cannot. Teachers devise their own way of keeping such a record; for example, a concept might be marked with one tick if the child is reasonably confident and two if he has grasped it thoroughly. The question of how to check up on which concepts he has acquired will be discussed below.

Although the 'concept tree' is invaluable, it is still only a guide when it comes to planning activities. For example, the idea of conservation of weight comes relatively late, but this does not preclude a five-year-old from playing with an improvised balance comprising a coat-hanger with a bag of sand attached at each end. He can have fun exploring why one end goes up and the other goes down, what happens if he changes them round or adds a third bag, and so on. All this is leading towards an eventual understanding of balance and weight. There are stages to be passed through when learning about weight, and indeed other quantities to be measured (length, volume, area). First the child will play freely, getting the idea that one thing is heavier than another: ordering objects according to heaviness, guessing which one will be heavier than another and then testing physically. Later comes crude measurement with improvised units: 'that bag of sand balances seven conkers'. Eventually the need for standard units will become apparent ('we need something better because my seven conkers didn't balance your seven conkers') and a kilogram weight happens to be in the neighbourhood. The art of the teacher is to recognise where the child is in his thinking so that he is not kept on with conkers when he is ready for kilograms or, worse still, pushed on to kilograms before the idea or need for a standard is apparent. It is easy to trace a similar progression through, for example, length (straight comparison of two bits of ribbon, 'measuring' with sticks which are not really the same length, need for standard).

Returning to the ideas needed towards an understanding of number and space (matching, ordering etc. as discussed above), some 'snapshots' will now be given showing how these can be introduced in classroom terms.

Number and space

Relations

The whole of mathematics has been described as the study of sets and relations. Examples of relations are 'is brother of', 'belongs to', 'has the same given name as', but many of the interesting relations at the present level are concerned with comparisons: 'is longer than', 'has more elements than', 'weighs less than' etc. Children can be encouraged to compare in this way. Who is the taller? Which piece of string is the longer? Which stone is bigger and how could we find out? Are there the same number of beads in these two piles? Sometimes the children will record their findings: 'there were more shells than pieces of seaweed'. Such activities, of course, involve comparisons and matching (see Form C in figure 1). 'Mapping' is a so-called many-to-one correspondence. For example, several (or many) children have the common property of having brown eyes, others blue.

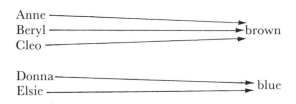

Sorting

Sorting is a fundamental human activity, not confined to mathematics: sheep/goats, men/women, odd numbers/even numbers and so on. At first, children will sort a set of objects into a large number of piles without much apparent reason. Later, they can be asked if they can sort into two piles, perhaps splitting up a set of toy vehicles into cars on one hand and lorries on the other. Finally, they will be able spontaneously to re-sort so that instead of cars/lorries they will sort according to red/other colours, British/foreign. 'Can you sort them by colours, dear?' is giving the game away; 'Good. Now see if you can find another way to sort them' is giving the child an opportunity to think.

Sorting is concerned with sets (e.g. the toy vehicles) and picking out subsets (e.g. those that are blue); it has been pointed out earlier that the idea of a set is crucial for an understanding of number. 'Partitioning' a set into subsets is a further relevant experience. For a partition, each subset must have at least one element and no element can belong to more than one subset. In case this sounds like a legal document, return to the vehicles. It would not be a partition to sort them into cars/lorries if there happened to be no lorries; on the other hand, it is not allowed to consider a particular vehicle to be a car and a lorry at the same time.

There may be seven toy cows in a toy field and a child has put in a fence so that there are three on one side and four on the other. The teacher should resist the temptation to write $3 + 4 = 7$ as this notation is only appropriate after many experiences such as the present one. However, it is laborious to get the children to write 'three cows here, four cows there, seven altogether' so other forms of shorthand have been suggested, e.g. 3, 4 $\rightarrow$ 7. By placing the fence differently, the children can build up more of the story of seven.

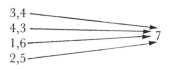

Forms of recording

It is, happily, difficult to separate mathematics from all the other activities going on in infant classrooms. As an example, play at the water tray may well lead to a discussion on which things float and which things sink, and later attempts to determine why. Whenever a group of children engage in such activity, they are encouraged to record their findings. Whether all this is 'mathematics', 'writing' or 'science' is best forgotten.

The search for different ways of recording is itself a very profitable activity; discussion can follow on which way is the easiest to read. Perhaps the simplest record of float/sink, for example, is a straight list:

Things that float	*Things that sink*
cork	nail
pencil	safety pin
bead	pebble
cotton reel	shell
	button
	penny

Another, more vivid, representation is to place the items in a hoop and place a stick across the middle, literally separating the floaters from the sinkers.

The objects could then be replaced by their names.

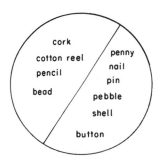

The same information can be recorded as a block graph.

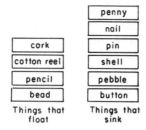

	penny
cork	nail
cotton reel	pin
pencil	shell
bead	pebble
	button

Things that float   Things that sink

It will at some stage be realised that this method is not efficient unless the labels for the different items are the same size. This leads eventually to the use of graph paper with standard grid.

Mapping provides another way of recording.

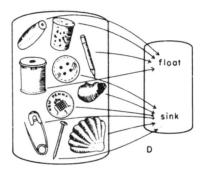

Finally, it is possible to list the objects down the page and mark off for each one a cross in the appropriate column ('float' or 'sink').

	float	sink
cork	X	
nail		X
cotton reel	X	
pin		X
shell		X
pebble		X
penny		X
pencil	X	
button		X
bead	X	

This last way is based on the method of feeding information to a computer, which can only accept such simple imformation as 'yes' or 'no'. The other methods described above cover mapping, partition of sets shown in a diagram, and the block graph leading towards statistics: thus the very representations themselves lead to different mathematical topics.

Measurement

The stages of progression common to all forms of measurement have been mentioned earlier. An illustration of a stimulating activity is afforded by a family-grouped class of five- to seven-year-olds in an English school. Their teacher had asked them somehow to record the width of their classroom. They were not, of course, to use a standard measure, for which they were not ready, but also she stipulated that they should use materials which could be left there to examine, and so foot-lengths and handspans were also banned. The children used five sheets of newspaper, six sticks, four matchboxes, five individual matches, but still there was a small elusive gap between this collection and the far wall. Eventually one child suggested cutting someone else's hair and counting the hairbreadths (an idea which the teacher did not take up!). This was a superb lesson on counting and measuring, with first ideas of limit and the notion that no measurement is ever exact. It was worth hours of meaningless 'instruction' with a graduated ruler.

Model making

Making models from junk can give early experiences in the ideas of volume, space-filling, shape, length and perhaps even area and weight. The model may be *taller* than its creator, but if the child climbs on a chair to paint the top, he is then *higher* than the model. Model making is a natural activity, being in the three-dimensional world into which the child is born. Only later is he familiar with two dimensions; the time for the transition is about the age of seven when the child is ready for the idea of a right angle. At that stage it is more difficult to see right angles at the corner of a room (or even a box) than it is to see them by folding a handkerchief or spotting them at the corner of a postcard or of other objects with squared-off corners.

Checking up

The partially ordered hierarchy of concepts is set out in Form C (figure 1). Often a teacher can see as she goes by or in the course of the day's activities when a child has reached a certain point. For example, a child may have spontaneously sorted some rectangles, squares and circles into separate piles and then re-sorted according to colour. Clearly, he has reached the stage 'sorting, several attributes' and no special check is necessary. However, if the teacher finds herself asking 'I wonder if . . . ', a series of check-ups, devised by the Nuffield Mathematics Teaching Project and recently modified and extended (Inner London Education Authority, 1979) may help her answer her question. The following are examples.

Intersection

The idea behind intersection is that of having more than one attribute. For example, if there are a set of cars and a set of red toys, then a red car will belong to both, i.e. the 'intersection set'. This is an important concept leading to the idea of 'and' (it is both red *and* a car) and later to tables, even multiplication tables (the fifty-six belongs in the number square to both the seven and the eight). An early check is to have two sets of carboard strips, one lot having pictures of miscellaneous objects of the same colour and the other lot objects of different colours but the same family (one might have leaves, another cups, another cats etc.). One strip from each set is chosen, perhaps red things and leaves, and the child is invited to pick from a large pile of cards the one which wi!l 'go with both', i.e. one with a red leaf on it. There are progressively more difficult tasks on intersection, which is unlikely to be thoroughly mastered at our present level. It is therefore particularly important with this concept to find just how far the child has progressed so that he may be encouraged forward rather than made to feel frustrated.

Neighbourhood

At this stage neighbourhood means simply being 'next door to'. Objects are placed in a line in a different order. The teacher makes two washing lines, one under the other, and provides three sets of 'washing' (paper cutouts) each consisting of, say, nine objects (a dress, a pair of shorts, a cardigan etc.). An odd number, say seven, is hung on the top line and the child is asked to copy the contents on the second line. If this is done successfully, the child is then asked to copy in 'reverse order', that is starting say with the dress at the left-hand end instead of the right-hand one as on the top line. The trouble comes halfway along when (because there is an odd number) one garment happens to correspond to itself. If a child successfully completes this task, then he is ready for experiences higher up the tree, i.e. towards an understanding of distance and length; if he does not, then the teacher will from time to time provide relevant similar experiences from which the idea of neighbourhood may eventually be abstracted.

Form I. The organisation of work for infants may be greatly assisted by the second of the two forms of the Progress Records for Young Children, namely Form I (figure 2). While Form C (for Child) is kept as a record, Form I (for Centre of Interest) has a limited life. A class may develop a centre of interest (for example Christmas toys, the market – the range is endless). The teacher writes on the form various ideas for construction, games, reading and all the other everyday classroom activities which could be related to the current project.

The top half of the form looks like that of Form C, and here she will also write various possibilities. For example, if the interest is the coming of Christmas, matching might be a halo for each angel, comparison of sizes

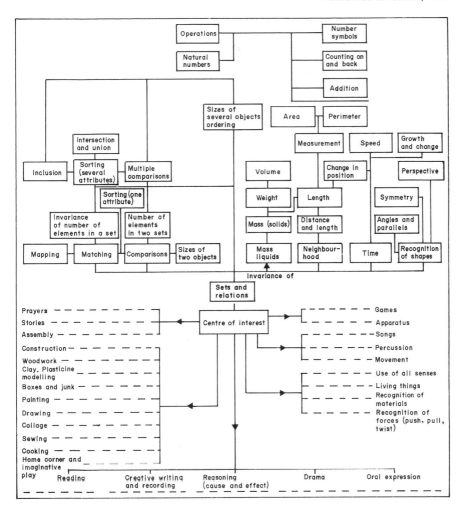

Figure 2 *Form I, a 'centre of interest' form.*

might be between two wrapped presents, numbers of elements in two sets might be between two collections of crackers, multiple comparisons might be between one tree which is tall, slim and light green and another which is short, squat and dark green, distance might involve different routes for Cinderella to take to the ball and so on.

By turning to Form C, noting where the ticks are, and comparing with Form I, the teacher can rapidly assign tasks to each child or group directly linked to their stage of understanding. In this way, at some time during the project anyway, each child is given a task at his threshold and may be ready to acquire a new concept and its associated skills.

Nursery

It has been shown that much is known about how infants learn mathematical concepts and skills: the order of events, how to find out where children are and match them to relevant activities. This background was available at the start of the English Schools Council (1974–7) project Early Mathematical Experiences, concerned with three- to five-year-olds. The aims were:

1. To identify and classify relevant experiences leading to mathematical ideas by observing nursery classes and relating their work to the theoretical development of early mathematical concepts.
2. To produce guides for teachers to help them to stimulate the development of mathematical concepts in young children.

There was little theory to work on at first, and so the first 15 months were devoted to gathering information and anecdotes from nursery teachers and others. Gradually a nexus of information and ideas was built up which could be of use to any adult coping with pre-school children. Of course, the concepts mentioned earlier found their way 'downwards':

Matching: one child to one milk bottle.
Sorting: cars/lorries and indeed (perhaps with some prompting) re-sorting in other ways.
Comparisons: heights of different children.
Ordering: dolls' clothes according to size.

These are, of course, just examples chosen from literally hundreds. The publications of the project have given guidance for eliciting mathematical activities and subsequent conversation from the following areas:

1. Water play.
2. Shape and space.
3. Home corner.
4. Comparisons.
5. Outdoor play.
6. Towards number.
7. Time.
8. Raw materials.
9. The family.
10. The environment.
11. Apparatus, toys and games.
12. Rhymes and stories.

In addition, videotapes have been made to show progression over a year and a film-strip has been produced illustrating mathematics within everyday activities.

It does not appear that the 'concept tree' is of great value at the nursery stage. Things are all happening at once, and the gradual abstraction of concepts at this level is even more relatively important than the acquisition of skills. All the same, it is essential for the adult to know where the children are going later and to make sure their play is purposeful and within their range.

Eliciting mathematical activities

How are these activities elicited? Sharply divided opinions have been expressed at meetings of the Early Mathematical Experiences working groups. At one end of the spectrum, it has been suggested that adults should never intervene with the young children, who should discover their own capabilities and develop their own skills entirely through free play. At the other extreme, there has been a demand for something like a syllabus, with a highly structured daily programme.

There is no 'best' way of proceeding, but children will flourish somewhere between these two violent extremes. Like it or not, 'teacher intervention' exists by simply providing the room and the presence of a teacher, let alone any apparatus which may be set out. On the other hand, talking away at the children as if giving a commentary for the Grand National will not lead to either comfort or progress. It is horribly easy to find oneself doing all the talking: 'Come-on-now,-we're-doing-some-cooking-today.–How-many-are-we?–1,2,3,-that's-right.-How-many-spoons-shall-we-need,-one-for-you,-you-and-you,-yes-3,-jolly-good,-now-what-about-basins-. . .?'

One general principle is not to *impose* mathematics and so risk wrecking a carefree exploration. The mathematics are there all the time. For example, if a child is making a collage he is exploring the use of different shapes and the business of fitting them together. It would be criminal to barge in with 'How many circles have you used so far?' just as the tractor is taking shape, but when it is finished the child may delight in pointing out its components.

The mathematics will often be brought out in this way, at the end of an activity. Sometimes, however, the teacher may start a line of thought. For example, at the water tray, 'If you pour the water from that jug to this container, do you think there will be enough to fill it?' This could lead to similar experiments initiated by the children and perhaps on to sharing problems ('Is there enough to fill all those cups?').

Again, the opportunity to introduce some mathematical idea may crop up unexpectedly. For example, in the home corner, 'Do you think you could give each teddy a plate and a cup and saucer?'.

At other times, the situation may be much more structured. For example, a whole roomful of children may be happily engaged in singing 'When Goldilocks went to the house of the bears' and quite painlessly making comparisons with appropriate miming:

A bowl that was huge,
A bowl that was small,
A bowl that was tiny
And that was all,
She counted them 1,2,3.

In short, there are no rules on how to elicit mathematical activities: it is a matter of awareness and senitivity on the part of the teacher.

The flavour of nursery possibilities is best given by some examples. Each of these illustrates at least one concept already mentioned in connection with infants but turning up naturally in the nursery setting.

Matching

Fiona (4.7) made four biscuits and took them home. The next day she said, 'I couldn't give one to Daddy because there weren't enough. I had one, Justin had one, Joanna had one and Mummy had one, so I gave Daddy a bit of mine.'

Comparisons

Emma (3.10):	I've made a bunny but he won't fit into his house because his ears are too big. They stick out.
Teacher:	What could you do to make him fit in?
Emma:	The house will have to get a bit bigger.
Teacher:	Or what else could you do?
Emma:	I'll give him some smaller ears.
	(She removes ears and replaces them with thinner ones which are of a similar length.)
Teacher:	Is that better?
Emma:	No, he still won't fit in.
Teacher:	What shall we do about that then?
Emma:	I'll make a new house for him, because he still won't fit in.
Teacher:	Why won't he fit in?
Emma:	I don't know.
Teacher:	Are these ears (indicating the replacement ones) any smaller than the round ones? (original ones)
Emma:	(Measures the two types against each other for comparison.) Yes, but only a bit. (She then reconstructs the house from a triangle shape to a circle shape into which the rabbit does fit.) Now look at his house – he fits in now, and he can look out.

Number comparisons

Teacher:	Would you like to tell me about your picture, Clare?
Clare (4.0):	That's the chicken and there's the egg, and the chicken goes in the egg.
Teacher:	How many eggs have you painted?
Clare:	Two eggs, but that's the one the chicken came out of (Clare

points to the larger egg), because that one is too small, the chicken won't fit in that one.

Teacher:	Could you paint a chicken for the other egg?
Clare:	Yes, I'll paint a baby one to fit in the small egg.
Teacher:	How many chickens have you got now?
Clare:	Two, and two eggs.
Teacher:	That is one chicken for each egg.
Clare:	Yes, the big chicken could fit in the little egg if he bends all his legs up, but the little chicken is too small for the big egg.

Shapes

The children are forming their chairs 'into a circle' for milk time.

Lisa (3.6):	That's not a circle, it's got corners.
Simon (3.11):	It's a square 'cos it's got corners.
Alison (4.1):	No, it's not. A square has four corners. Miss C said so and this has three. One, two, three. (All counted in turn.)
Lisa:	So it's not a square
Natalie (3.11):	It's a triangle if it's got three corners.
Alison:	So it's not properly.
Lisa:	Well it's not a circle 'cos a circle is a round ring and it doesn't have corners.

Perspective

Theresa (4.7) drew a picture of Rupert Bear. When asked why he only had one eye, she replied, 'He is standing sideways and you can only see one.'

References

Inner London Education Authority (1979) *Checkpoints Assessment Cards*. London: Learning Materials Service.

Schools Council (1974–7) *Early Mathematical Experiences. Set of guides* (also published as single volume 1982), *pack of slide-transparencies and videotape*. Published for the Schools Council by Addison-Wesley.

Further Reading

Department of Education and Science (1979) *Mathematics 5–11*. London: HMSO.

Department of Education and Science (1982) *Mathematics Counts* (the Cockcroft Report). London: HMSO.

Matthews, G. (ed.) (1972) *Mathematics Through School*. London: John Murray.
Matthews, J. (ed.) (1975) *Trends in Primary Education*. London: Peter Owen.
Nuffield Maths 5–11 (1979) *Teachers' Handbooks 1 and 2*. Harlow: Longman.
Parry, M. and Archer, H. (1975) *Two to Five*. London: Macmillan Educational.
School Mathematics Project (1984) *Pointers*. Cambridge: Cambridge University Press. In the press.

11

Learning and Teaching Reading Skills

PETER HORNER

The Bullock Report (Department of Education and Science, 1975) is based upon the principle that 'reading must be seen as part of a child's general language development, and not as a discrete skill which can be considered in isolation from it'. This means that reading must be looked upon as one of the language arts (the others being hearing, speaking and writing), with each art complementing the others.

Young children are dependent for their learning upon the environment into which they are born. The places, the people, the objects and the activities in this environment provide the experiences by which they learn. In a good home, these experiences will include observing other people making rich and varied use of all the language arts. In the case of reading, this will mean seeing them read not only books, but also newspapers, magazines, cookery recipes, shopping lists, car manuals and a range of other written and printed material. In addition, the child from such a home will possess his own story and picture books, which loving parents will read to him in conditions conducive to the idea that reading is something enjoyable and useful. Less fortunate children, however, may well be brought up in environments where books are hardly to be found, where little reading of any kind is done and where all the language arts are restricted.

Children coming to nursery or infant school will thus be at different stages on a continuum. At one end some may already be reading, while at the other will be children with little or no conception of what reading is. The task of the school is to provide linguistic experiences for those children who lack them and to foster development in those who have made a beginning. To help her in this task, the teacher will want to form some assessment of the linguistic achievements of each child, and without resorting to sophisticated methods of testing, she can do this by observing: the child's general attitude to school; the interest with which he tackles new tasks; his powers of concentration; his use of words and his understanding of what is said to him; his interest in the written words around him; the amount of time he spends in the book corner; his persistence in asking for help in reading.

G

Reading stories

Children are natural imitators, and it is important that they should see others reading. Often they will attempt to copy this activity without prompting, pointing to words on a page and making up a story. Story time quickly becomes of great importance in their day, and the teacher should choose the stories she offers them with great care. Young children are often not equipped to cope with the fantasy world of witches and ghosts, which can arouse fear in impressionable minds, and lead books to acquire unpleasant associations. Such children needs stories about the world they know, the world of birthdays, seasons and weather, or about children who are recognisably naughty, stories to give vicarious experience of toothache and visits to the doctor, or to overcome their feelings of smallness and insignificance in an adult world, stories about race and colour, riches and poverty, stories to arouse compassion, stories where people encounter and overcome the problems of everyday life.

Fortunately, many books dealing with these themes exist in children's literature, and the problem facing the teacher is more often to do with selection than with availability. There are many excellent journals which specialise in giving information about books for children, together with source of supply. Notable amongst these are *Growing Point* (six issues per year from Ashton Manor, Northampton), *Books for Your Children* (four issues per year from Anne Wood, 90 Gillhurst Rd, Harborne, Birmingham 17), *Children's Book Review* (four issues per year from Five Owls Press, Wormley, Herts) and *Children's Literature in Education* (four issues per year from B. Collinge, 2 Sunwine Place, Exmouth, Devon).

In addition, when reading to young children, the teacher should not neglect nursery rhymes. These contain a wealth of language and imagination, and are part of the child's linguistic heritage. The rhythms and repetitions which they include – to say nothing of the simplicity of the rhymes themselves – are easy for young children to remember, as well as being a happy way of introducing them to new words and grammatical structures. Further, many of the traditional nursery rhymes convey specific pieces of information (such as counting, the letters of the alphabet, the days of the week, the order of the months, the difference between right and left and so on) in a context of play which often calls for physical participation on the part of the child. Many children come to recognise individual words in print through the repetition of these well-loved nursery rhymes, whilst an acquaintance with sound units through rhythm and jingle helps them when they come to learn phonic analysis and word recognition later. Thinking ahead to the wider application of the skills of reading, these nursery rhymes (with their special language, historic characters and bizarre content) offer, in the words of Walter de la Mare, 'a direct short cut into poetry itself'.

Another source of reading material in the nursery or infant classroom is the writing produced by the children themselves. In the early stages, this writing will consist of captions written by the teacher beneath a child's drawing or painting, using the words dictated by the child concerned. Later, the child may be asked to trace over the teacher's writing, and later still to copy it out underneath. Gradually, the child will thus take over more and more of the task of writing the caption, until eventually it becomes entirely his own work. These captions (or 'books', since this is what they really are) become part of the reading resources of the classroom. Sometimes they are the work of individual children, sometimes the work of a group with a shared interest. With older children, they can be typewritten to give them a more professional appearance, and they can be used to describe pictures cut from newspapers and magazines or photographs taken by the children themselves. What is important is that in all cases these early efforts written in the children's own language form a bridge between the spoken word and the language of books.

Reading readiness

The provision of a stimulating environment, though important, will not by itself teach a child to read. It should be remembered that reading is a skill developed by societies in an advanced state of civilisation, and cannot be compared to physical skills like walking and talking. Walking is a normal physical development in a healthy child, and talking is an accomplishment that a child will acquire by imitation through living in a social community. But reading, like writing, has to be taught, which gives rise to the question at what age should formal reading instruction commence? The answer is found in the concept of 'reading readiness'.

Reading readiness is defined by Downing and Thackray (1971) as 'the stage in development when, either through maturation or through previous learning or both, the individual child can learn to read easily and profitably'. Such readiness (and indeed all subsequent reading progress) is thought to depend upon a combination of the following factors.

1 Psychological factors, including growth and maturation, cerebral dominance and laterality, neurological considerations, visual acuity, auditory acuity and the correct functioning of the speech organs.
2 Environmental factors, taking into account the linguistic background of the child and his various social experiences.
3 Emotional factors, including personality traits and motivation towards reading.
4 Intellectual factors, including general mental ability, visual and auditory discriminations, and problem-solving abilities relating to language.

In America, various reading readiness tests, based upon these and other factors, are available commercially, but in Great Britain the usual practice is for judgements to be based on the teacher's observations. A useful 'Reading Readiness Inventory' to help guide these observations is to be found in chapter 7 of Downing and Thackray (1971), and its use is strongly recommended. Careful monitoring of chldren's behaviour along the lines suggested by the Inventory will help teachers to identify obvious weaknesses and to take steps to provide compensatory exercises. The need for such experiences is evidenced by the fact that both Reid (1972) and Downing (1972) have found that many children starting school have little notion of what reading is about. Not only do they have difficulty in understanding the purpose of written language, they have only a vague idea of what other people are actually *doing* when they read. Further, Reid and Downing both found that all young children have a particular difficulty in understanding the technical – and often abstract – terms which adults use to talk about language (e.g. 'word', 'letter', 'sound'). Such findings are, of course, in keeping with the work of Piaget, who in his theory of cognitive development (see chapter 2) puts the child below the age of seven or eight into an egocentric mode of language and thought which is qualitatively different from that of adults. They also accord with the work of Vygotsky (1962) who concludes that: 'it is the abstract quality of written language that is the main stumbling block . . . the child has little motivation to learn writing when we begin to teach it. He feels no need for it, and has only a vague idea of its usefulness.'

The above research findings should not be used, however (as they have been by some educationalists), to support *delaying* the teaching of reading until the child shows clear signs of reading readiness of his own accord. Rather they should be used to reinforce the need for the teacher actively to help the child to move towards this readiness. She does this not only by the measures already suggested (and particuarly by reading frequently to her class and helping them to associate reading with pleasure), but also by making clear to them what she is doing when she *is* reading. This means making clear to them that books contain words as well as pictures, that words contain letters that represent different sounds and that to read one commences at the top of the page and proceeds from left to right across and down the page. Further, the teacher should reinforce these facts by providing the children with practical exercises in letter and word discrimination, in sequencing (i.e. arranging first pictures and later words in the correct order to tell a story), and in moving from left to right and down the page. She should also give them practice in listening carefully to individual words and sentences in order to improve their sound distinction. (Suggestions for exercises of this type are found in the books listed at the end of the chapter.)

Reading methods and schemes

When satisfactory progress has been made with these pre-reading experiences, the next step is for the child to be introduced to a reading scheme. There are enormous numbers of published reading schemes available, and they keep on coming! It is important that teachers should be able to assess the value of individual schemes, and their suitability for their children. This assessment should be based on three main criteria:

(a) the method used,
(b) the content (including linguistic structures as well as story content), and
(c) the general appearance and layout.

So important are these, that we need to examine each of them separately.

The method used

The two main methods of teaching reading are 'look and say' (which embraces both the whole word and the whole sentence approach), and the 'phonic method' (both synthetic and analytic). To take the second of these first, the phonic method traditionally meant the alphabet-syllabic system. Using a hornbook (a device which lasted for three centuries in English schools), children first learnt the alphabet by naming the letters, and then learnt syllabaries (i.e. each consonant joined to each vowel in turn, as in 'ab', 'eb', 'ib', 'ob', 'ub', 'ba', 'be', 'bi', 'bo', 'bu' and so on). These were learnt by rote, and when known perfectly children were put directly onto the Lord's Prayer. By the end of the eighteenth century, the hornbook began to give way to books of simple graded exercises using first two-letter words, then three-letter ones and so on. These were combined into nonsensical sentences such as 'As ye go', 'We go up', 'He is at it' and 'The fat pig in a wig did a jig in the bog'. Although this particular approach was displaced by the look and say method in the years before the Second World War, phonic teaching was never completely abandoned, and made something of a comeback after the publication of two Ministry of Education surveys of reading standards (1950 and 1957). These surveys revealed a disquieting number of school leavers and adults who, at least in terms of the society in which they lived, were functionally illiterate. Casting around for a scapegoat, many people were quick to blame these findings upon the use of look and say methods in infant schools.

In its comeback, the phonic method took on a more realistic form. In 1954, Daniels and Diack published *The Royal Road Readers*, based on what they called a 'phonic-word method'. This method observed the old phonic principle that letters stand for sounds, but differed from it in one important respect, namely the belief that children should be taught to hear these sounds (known as sound units or 'phonemes') within words rather than in the isolation imposed by learning each letter of the alphabet separately. Since the 1950s, many publishers have added phonic sections to their look and say schemes, and other phonic-based schemes have been published such as

Racing to Read and *Sound Sense* (E. J. Arnold), *Sounds and Words* (University of London Press), *Sounds for Reading* (Nisbet), *Step Up and Read* (University of London Press) and *Language in Action* (Macmillan Educational).

The look and say method, which as we have indicated came into prominence in the 1930s, differs from the phonic method in that it is based upon the assumption that children recognise words by 'wholes' rather than by breaking them down into their individual letters. It makes the further assumption that when these words are put into sentences with meanings, children will find enjoyment in them and so be motivated to want to read. The first of these assumptions stems in part from the theories of Gestalt psychology (which stress that in our general perception of the world we recognise things primarily in terms of their outline shapes and patterns), while the second owes much to the growth of child-centred education (which stresses 'learning' rather than 'teaching', and emphasises that interest is a prime motivator). It would also be fair to say, however, that look and say received something of a boost from publishers themselves, who found that the whole sentences which it employed gave greater scope for artistic expression and attractive book production than the single word and meaningless sentence approach of much of the traditional phonic method.

Basically, the look and say method presents children with words incorporated into simple, interesting sentences, which they learn to recognise by associating their appearance with the sound made by the teacher as she reads the word to them. So-called 'content' words such as 'rocket', 'elephant', 'rabbit', and 'aeroplane' are learnt relatively easily because of their high interest value, while so-called structure words such as 'said', 'once', 'the' and 'as' are instilled by their frequent repetition in the text. Unfortunately, however, many of the look and say schemes employ a stilted language which has little or no connection with the child's speech patterns, and look and say as a whole makes tremendous demands upon the child's memory and gives him no equipment to deal with new words. Where publishers have tried to remove the last of these difficulties by adding phonic material, this is too often in the form of supplementary activities which offer little help with the unfamiliar words in the primer itself. There are many look and say schemes on the market; amongst them may be mentioned *Time for Reading* (Ginn), *Griffin Pirate* and *Dragon Pirate Stories* (E. J. Arnold) and, of course, *Janet and John* (Nisbet).

Finally, there are some schemes that claim not to follow predominantly either a phonic or look and say method, but to use instead a combination of the two (the so-called mixed method). The most widely used of these is the *Ladybird* scheme (Wills and Hepworth), which is based upon the most frequently used words in the language (the 'key words') as established by the research of McNally and Murray (1962). It consists of twelve stages, with three books at each stage, two of them parallel primers (labelled 'a' and 'b' respectively), and the third (labelled 'c') designed to introduce phonics by means of exercises based upon material in these primers. Other mixed method schemes are *Dominoes* (Oliver and Boyd), *Beacon* (Ginn) and *Kathy and Mark* (Nisbet). A recent development in published reading schemes has been the production of total language schemes. Such schemes not only contain graded reading books but also a variety of related language activities. Two such schemes are *Ginn 360* and *Language Patterns* (Holt, Rinehart and Winston).

The content

As already indicated, the content of primers must be thought of in terms of both the message conveyed (in words and pictures) and the linguistic structures used. To take the message first, research (Zimet, 1976) has shown that many values and attitudes are transmitted to children, either consciously or unconsciously, through the text and illustrations of their reading books. This only becomes a problem, of course, where such values and attitudes are out of keeping with the realities of the child's experience. For example, many primers are rigidly sex-typed, which is incongruent with a contemporary society in which mothers often go out to work and fathers frequently help with the washing up and the shopping. Again, many are socially-typed, and depict a vanishing middle-class world in which well-dressed children play aimiably with pedigree dogs in large and well-kept gardens. Clearly, all this is alien to many children from inner city areas and high-rise flats, and attempts have been made in recent years to produce material with a wider appeal. The *Nippers* series (Macmillan) is an example of one such scheme.

Turning to the linguistic structures employed in primers, it is important to remember that research indicates that children draw on their knowledge of spoken language in order to decipher print. Thus the more closely the sentence structures in these primers are related to those used by the children in their normal speech, the easier it wil be for them to begin to read. Equally important is the research finding that the child needs to acquire the skill of *prediction* if he is to read with any fluency. By prediction, we mean that he becomes able to 'guess' what letters and words come next without having to fix his eyes upon each one. One way in which the teacher can help him acquire this skill is by familiarising him with the likely letter sequences in the English language. For example, there are some sequences that never occur, such as xb, zd, wpxt, while others are extremely common (qu, br, str, ion). Word games where children are asked to guess the next letter in a gradually exposed word are of great help here, for instance t. . . . , tr. . . , tra. . , trai. , train.

Just as they can be helped to recognise likely letter sequences, so children can be helped with likely sequences of words. In the English language there are many of these sequences, such as 'eggs and . . . . . ', 'once upon a . . . . ', 'how do you . . ?' These sequences are easily completed by children in verbal – and later written – games.

Another help with prediction is offered by syntax. This is not so difficult a skill for children to learn as it might seem, since studies of young children indicate that they often show a correct knowledge of grammatical sequence even though the content of what they are saying appears to be meaningless in our terms. (Chomsky provides an illustration of this with his well-known sentence 'colourless green ideas sleep furiously', a sentence which indicates that syntax and meaning are not necessarily inter-dependent.) To help them with this skill, primers should employ a wide range of sentence stuctures which reflect the language actually spoken by children.

Finally, of course, meaning itself helps prediction. It has been estimated that the most common 500 words in English share between them some 14,050 meanings. Faced with this ambiguity, the reader can often only interpret the writer's meaning by making reference to the context cues in the passage he is reading. With practice, this reference becomes automatic, and is an important aid to prediction. Such practice can be given to children through well-structured sentences in their primers, which phase in new words whose meaning is apparent from the words around them, and the teacher can supplement these by presenting the children with carefully chosen sentences of her own (verbal at first, but later written).

The current emphasis on 'meaning' in children's reading matter has led some teachers to abandon commercial reading schemes and teach children to read from the beginning with 'real books'. The work of Bennett (1982) has been influential in this approach. She emphasises three points in her use of real books:

1 The teacher should expect children to enjoy reading new books. In this the example and enthusiasm of the teacher is infectious.
2 The children themselves should expect to be able to read the books offered.
3 The teacher should not expect complete accuracy, but meaning is vital. Children should be given time to realise and correct their own mistakes.

Turning to the linguistic structures used in primers, mention must be made of two schemes which are based upon linguistic theory: *Breakthrough to Literacy* (Longman) and *Link-Up* (Holmes McDougall). The crux of *Breakthrough to Literacy* is a piece of apparatus called the 'sentence maker' (see chapter 12 for a full description). This consists of a triptych of card with a selection of words and affixes on two folds, with the third fold left blank for the personal word collection of the child. There are also a number of cards on which the same selection of words is printed. The child matches these cards with the words on the triptych, placing each card on top of the matched word. The purpose of this is to introduce children to the making of sentences. As the child makes a sentence, so he reads it over to the teacher, who keeps a record of it in a special book until such time as the child is able to do the recording for himself. The sentence maker is accompanied by a series of printed books based upon the language patterns, experiences and interests of young children, and there is an excellent teacher's manual explaining the authors' linguistic theory and the practice of teaching initial reading and writing.

Link-Up is a book-based scheme with a variety of linguistic support material. The authors have used the insights into language and language learning which have been provided by linguists in the past decade. The sentence structures used are based on the spoken language of five- and six-year-olds. Both in the text and in the illustrations, they have drawn on written language in the environment, and the programme brings in street signs, traffic signs, names on shops and on vehicles, names of people and pets and names and labels for common articles of food. There is a manual by the authors (Reid and Low, 1973) which sets out the rationale for the scheme as well as giving guidance on its use.

The general appearance and layout

It goes without saying that books for children should be colourful and attractive, and that the illustrations in reading primers should serve a specific purpose. In the early stages of reading, this purpose will be to reinforce the text, allowing the child to see that something which is shown in a picture can also be 'talked about' in print. Used thus, illustrations provide support for the context, and children can often be seen searching them for clues when they come across an unknown word in their reading. Additionally, illustrations have the advantage at all reading stages of providing material for discussion.

The typeface used in primers should be similar to the print children use when they begin to write. There is evidence that there is a direct relationship between size of print and reading ability. Another important point is that sentences should not be poorly constructed. In many of the recent reading schemes, these important details are taken into account, bringing the schemes more in line with current linguistic theory.

Modified spelling systems and cueing techniques

The inconsistency between sound and symbol in the English writing system has led to many attempts over the centuries to achieve regularity by some other means. These reforms fall into two classes: changes in the spelling system itself, and the addition of cues (such as colour or diacritical marks) designed to help the child's understanding of the existing system. These must be examined separately.

Changes in spelling

The best known attempt to provide a modified, more logical spelling system is the *Initial Teaching Alphabet* (i.t.a.) devised by Sir James Pitman. I.t.a. was designed to overcome the deficiencies and complications of the traditional alphabet (referred to as traditional orthography or t.o.), in which we use 26 letters to represent the 40 sounds of spoken English. In place of t.o., i.t.a. uses a simpler and more regular code. It consists of 44 written characters, each symbolising a constant sound. Twenty-four of these characters are taken from t.o. (the remaining two traditional letters, 'x' and 'q' being omitted altogether), while most of the 20 additional characters are combinations of two letters which usually occur together in t.o. to form digraphs (e.g. 'ie' and 'th'). Finally, instead of having their own form, capitals are simply written as enlarged versions of lower case.

Since its inception, i.t.a. has been subject to a great deal of evaluation, culminating in an enquiry sponsored by the Schools Council (Warburton and Southgate, 1969). The findings of this enquiry were generally favourable to i.t.a. as a medium for the initial teaching of reading, but in spite of this, after a peak of interest in the 1960s, the use of i.t.a. has declined rapidly and i.t.a. is now really only of historical interest.

The addition of cues

The idea of cueing is to provide children with marks of some kind on the script to help them with pronunciation. The two best known methods of doing this are the use of colour and the addition of what are called diacritical marks. To take colour first, *Words in Colour* was devised by Gattegno (1962), who had already tried the use of this medium in mathematics with his Cuisenaire rods. In his reading system, he identifies 47 sounds in English, and to each of them he designates a colour. Whenever one of these sounds is introduced, it is printed in the same colour, however it may be spelt. For example, the 'ee' sound is represented by bright red, and accordingly bright red is used for the letters which represent this sound in such words as 'k*ey*', 'dr*ea*m', '*peo*ple' and 'bel*ie*ve'. Gattegno's scheme is known as a total one, in that it discourages the use of other material in the initial learning stages. It is too detailed to go into fully here, but it is comprehensively described in Gattegno (1962). Other systems using colour are only partial colour-codes, and amongst these may be mentioned *Colour Story Reading* (Nelson) and *Reading by Rainbow* (Moor Platt).

There are as yet no reading schemes published in this country which use diacritical marks, but the best known system of marking is that of Fry (1967), and some teachers add the marks that he suggests to existing reading schemes. Like *Words in Colour*, Fry's system is too lengthy to explain in detail here, but something of its rationale will be apparent if we say that long vowels have a bar over them (e.g. 'gō', 'mē'), unaccented vowels have a comma (e.g. 'ªago'), silent letters are crossed out (e.g. 'mādє', 'māɟd'), long 'oo' sounds have two dots over them (e.g. 'rüle', 'möon') and so on.

As an indication of the extent to which the different systems described above were used in schools in the mid 1970s, the Bullock Report (Department of Education and Science, 1975) found that 10% of classes were using i.t.a, 6% were using colour and 2% were using diacritical marks. Of course, not all schools stick exclusively to any one of these systems, or to any one reading scheme. Many use several, the idea being that it is valuable for children to have reinforcement on parallel texts in several schemes before going on to the next reading stage. (It also means that children who move to new schools are more likely to have had some experience of the schemes they find there.) Where a variety of schemes is used, however, it is vital that the schemes are carefully matched so that confusion does not arise and progression can be maintained. It is also of particular importance that the teacher devotes adequate time to organising the class reading, and to keeping records of chldren's progress.

Organisation

Organisation may be thought of in terms of timetabling, grouping of children, and the use of space and materials.

Timetabling

Many nursery and most infant schools operate a system whereby, apart from such activities as using television the radio or the hall, the work of the children is planned over the whole day rather than being divided into separate lessons. This means that the children have time to work at an activity for as long as their interests are held by it. This has many advantages, but it makes it essential that the teacher is aware of how each child spends his time, so that she can ensure that all her class have experience of essential activities such as language and number.

Grouping

There are many different ways of grouping children. Some schools employ a class system which groups by age, while others use vertical or family grouping. The advantages of the latter are that there is opportunity for older children to help with younger ones, and the teacher is able to set the more advanced children work to do on their own while she gives time to those who especially need her help. As far as reading is concerned, this means, for example, helping the pre-readers on word and picture matching exercises, and on word recognition, as well as looking at books with them and helping them with left to right orientation. While the teacher is doing this, children who have made a start on books can read individually or in pairs, helped at times by an older reader.

In whatever manner the class is grouped, however, the teacher will need to spend a great deal of time listening to individual children read, whether they are beginners or fairly fluent readers. To be really successful, much depends upon how this activity is carried out. If teachers only listen to children stumble over their books, correcting every mistake or hesitation for them, it is doubtful whether they are providing the best kind of help. Listening to children read should be an opportunity for the teacher to diagnose the child's progress, using his own reading material for the purpose. The *kind* of mistakes that children make provide valuable clues to their stage of reading development, and it should be noted that these mistakes fall into set categories. Relying upon the context to guide them, they will often *substitute* a known word for an unknown (e.g. 'dog' for 'puppy'). Sometimes they will make a *non-response*, either waiting to be prompted or asking the teacher what the word says. Other errors are *additions, repetitions, mispronunciations, omissions* and *reversals.* If teachers keep a record of the type of mistakes that children make when reading, a clear picture of the type of help which individual children most need emerges. Hearing children read should also be an opportunity for helping them with the context cueing referred to earlier. This means that rather than correcting children immediately, the teacher should encourage them to look for cues in the context, and thus correct their own mistakes. This has a positive effect upon their reading development, as shown by Goodman (1970), who found that if encouraged to re-read a passage children supply the correct word three times out of four.

This type of individual work with children is time-consuming, and the busy teacher would find it difficult if not impossible to hear all her children read every day in the manner described. On the other hand, the undoubted value of this constructive learning makes it worth while even if it is done less frequently than every day. Not all children will need the same treatment, and careful record keeping will ensure that no one is overlooked.

Use of space and materials

The whole environment of the school conveys messages. The entrance hall and the corridors can be areas for displays of various kinds, as well as the classroom itself. Everywhere in school the child should see written language. Wall charts, posters, nature and interest tables should all have their signs and labels. In a sense, the classroom is the child's first 'book'. It is important that this book should be well written, with labels and captions presented in a script that the child can recognise. Many teachers make considerable use of labels such as 'door', 'window', 'chair', but it is probably better to extend these labels into sentences, e.g. 'this is the door into the playground', 'in this cupboard we keep paints and paper'. Labels of all kinds should be changed frequently, otherwise they become like wallpaper to the children. It is also important that use is made of the knowledge that children already have. For example, their own names and addresses can be a fruitful starting point for work on phonics, as many such words have phonic patterns, e.g. 'street', 'road', 'avenue', 'close', 'lane', 'way', to name but a few.

It goes without saying, of course, that books should be attractively displayed. Many infant classrooms now include a library corner where a piece of carpet on the floor and some cushions or an easy chair or two encourage the idea that reading is pleasurable. Since young children usually choose books by their appearance, most teachers also take care to display those books with their front covers foremost. All this is excellent, but it must be remembered that displays of books should not be confined to book corners. They should be used around the room on nature tables, discovery tables, and in connection with whatever topics happen to be under consideration.

Whatever reading scheme or schemes are used, it is important that they are carefully graded for difficulty. This can be done through the use of a simple colour code, with the easiest books marked, for example, in red, the next hardest in blue, and so on. This code can be extended to cover the reading card apparatus that is in use in the classroom, and since books and apparatus should be stored in such a way that they are easily accessible to children, this means that the latter can be taught to get out and put away material for themselves (particularly if the shelves or cupboards where they are stored are coded in the same way).

Attainment and diagnostic testing

It is a relatively simple matter to grade all the reading material in use by means of what is called the 'cloze procedure'. In this system, every tenth word in a passage of about 100 words is deleted, and if the child can still make sense of the passage, it is within his range of ability (for a full discussion of this procedure see Moyle, 1972.) However, as time goes on, a more structured system of observation and recording is called for. One such system is the Informal Reading Inventory (IRI). This is an extension of the suggestions put forward in the discussion above on hearing children read. It consists of the teacher systematically noting the child's errors as he reads aloud from his primer, and then questioning him on his understanding of a piece that he is asked to read silently. Where there is 99% accuracy in word recognition and 90% accuracy in comprehension, the child is said to be at the 'independent level' of reading skill. Where the child has a success rate of 95% in word recognition and 75% in comprehension, he is said to be at the 'instructional level', while if word recognition falls to 90% accuracy rate or below, and comprehension falls to 50% or below, the child is said to be at the 'frustration level', and the material is clearly too difficult for him. (A full account of IRI and a suggested checklist is given in Strang, 1972.)

Some local education authorites have devised 'screening' tests to identify children at risk in learning to read. These tests can be applied before the child starts to read, and consist of developmental assessments based on the recognition that developmental lags and anomalies in any area of functioning may prevent the child from easily acquiring the skills of reading. These tests examine behaviour in such areas as speech and communication, perceptual/ motor skills, emotional/social behaviour and response to learning (see e.g. the *Croydon Check-List and Guidelines for Teachers No. 1* by Bryans and Wolfendale, 1973).

Many schools, as an alternative, make use of published reading tests. These are of two main types: attainment and diagnostic. Attainment tests are of two kinds, namely single word recognition and sentence completion. The most widely used single word recognition test (used, in fact, in 73% of the sample of primary schools studied by he Bullock Committee) is the *Schonell Graded Word Recognition Test* (published by Oliver and Boyd), while other similar tests are the *Burt Graded Word Reading Test* and the *Vernon Graded Word Reading Test* (both published by the University of London Press). The advantages of tests of this kind are that they are easy to administer, obtain immediate results and cover the whole range of abilities likely to be found in primary schools. The disadvantages are that they make no measurement of comprehension, present the child with words in isolation rather than in the phrases and sentences in which he usually meets them and give no information of a diagostic nature. Sentence completion tests avoid the first two of these disadvantages by presenting the child with incomplete sentences which he is asked to finish by selecting from a range of possible endings (e.g. 'My dog can *talk, sing, fly, bark, draw*'). Sentence completion tests have a further advantage in that they can be used as group, as well as individual, tests with the child being asked simply to underline the correct word. Examples of sentence completion tests are the *Holborn Reading Scale*, the *Young Group Reading Test*, the *NFER Reading Test AD* and the *Southgate Group Reading Test*.

For diagnostic information (that is, for information on the *precise nature* of a child's reading disability and *why* he is experiencing this difficulty), however, we need to turn to diagnostic tests such as the *Neale Analysis of Reading Ability* (published by Macmillan). This test consists of three sub-sets of six passages of prose, each illustrated by a picture. The record form provided with the test classifies reading errors under six headings: mispronunciations, substitutions, refusals, additions, omissions and reversals. The passages of prose are reproduced vertically in single words on the record form used by the teacher so that she can keep a running record of the child's performance. In addition to the main passages, the test contains three further diagnostic tests, i.e. names of letters, knowledge of letter sounds and phonic blends, the whole building up into a detailed profile of the child's reading performance.

Another battery of diagnostic tests is contained in *The Standard Reading Tests* by Daniels and Diack (published by Chatto and Windus). The basic test in this battery is the *Standard Test of Reading Skill*, and on his performance in this test the child is given what is called a 'reading standard'. This standard suggests to the teacher which diagnostic tests it would be appropriate to use with the child in question from the further eleven tests in the battery, all of which serve to reveal particular difficulties that he may have. On the basis of this knowledge, the teacher can plan the necessary remedial exercises.

There are other tests which assess the child's specific reading knowledge, such as *The Swansea Test of Phonic Skills* (published by Blackwell) and *The Domain Phonic Test Kit and Workshop* (published by Oliver and Boyd). The latter is an interesting attempt to link testing to remedial work. It involves a series of oral word recognition tasks which have been systematically chosen to provide comprehensive coverage of phonics. For each phonic configuration tested, there is an accompanying remedial worksheet. Cloze procedure has also been used for testing purposes in the *Gap Reading Comprehension Test* (published by Heinemann).

It is not within the scope of this chapter to go into detail about remedial methods, even if the term is appropriate to children in this age group. Reference to the books listed at the end of this chapter will give comprehensive guidance to those who wish to pursue this subject.

The Bullock Report

Reference has already been made in this chapter to the Bullock Report, *A Language for Life* (Department of Education and Science, 1975). This report, and its official endorsement, are landmarks in the history of education in Britain, and it is appropriate to end by summarising something of its scope and main conclusions.

The Bullock Committee was appointed in June 1972, under the chairmanship of Sir Alan Bullock, following a report by the National Foundation for Educational Research (NFER) on reading standards in schools (*The Trends of Reading Standards 1972*). Its terms of reference were to consider in relation to schools: (a) all aspects of the use of English, including reading, writing, and speech; (b) how present practice might be improved, and the role that initial and in-service training might play; (c) to what extent arrangements for monitoring the general level of attainment in the use of English can be introduced or improved; and to make recommendations. The main recommendations which have a direct bearing upon the nursery and infant school are:

1. A system of monitoring should be introduced which will employ new instruments to assess a wider range of attainments than has been attempted in the past, and allow new criteria to be established for the definition of literacy.
2. There should be positive steps to develop the language ability of children in the pre-school and nursery and infant years. These should include arrangements for the involvement of parents, the improvement of staffing ratios in infant schools, and the employment of teachers' aides whose training has included a language element.

3. Every school should devise a systematic policy for the development of reading competence in pupils of all ages and ability levels.

4. Each school should have an organised policy for language across the curriculum, establishing every teacher's involvement in language and reading development throughout the years of schooling.

5. Every school should have a suitably qualified teacher with responsibility for advising and supporting his colleagues in language and the teaching of reading.

6. There should be close consultation between schools (including the transmission of effective records from one school to another) to ensure continuity in the teaching of reading and in the language development of every pupil.

It is no great exaggeration to suggest that the implementation of these recommendations would take us much nearer to achieving the goal of a literate Britain.

Since the Bullock Report, a number of further documents have been published bearing on the teaching of reading. In 1981 *Extending Beginning Reading* appeared (Southgate et al., 1981). This is a detailed account of a project carried out from 1973 to 1977 for the Schools Council which focused on children of seven years who had attained average reading standards and on what happened to their reading in the next two years. The report contains some interesting descriptions of current practice.

In 1982 the Department of Education and Science (1982a) published *Education 5–9*, an illustrative survey of 80 first schools in England. Not surprisingly, the teaching of reading was regarded by teachers as having the highest of priorities in virtually all of the schools, though in many of them there was an unduly prolonged concentration on the basic reading scheme when many able readers could have profitably spent their time extending their skills by reading more demanding books of reference and fiction. This criticism is echoed in the discussion document, *Bullock Revisited* (Department of Education and Science, 1982b), where it is stated that 'in a good many schools graded reading schemes represent a major part of pupils' reading experience; time for individual reading of books which are interesting in themselves is often limited to spare minutes when other tasks have been completed. The message of these surveys is that reading must be made meaningful and enjoyable, and the teacher's role in ensuring that this ideal becomes a reality is clearly all important.

References

Bennett, J. (1982) *Learning to Read with Picture Books*, 2nd ed. Stroud, Gloucester: Thimble Press.

Bryans, T. and Wolfendale, S. (1973) *Guidelines for Teachers No. 1*. Croydon: London Borough of Croydon.

Department of Education and Science (1975) *A Language for Life* (the Bullock Report) London: HMSO.

Department of Education and Science (1982a) *Education 5–9*. London: HMSO.

Department of Education and Science (1982b) *Bullock Revisited*. London: HMSO.

Downing, J. (1972) How children think about reading. In Melnick, A. and Merritt, J. (eds) *Reading: Today and Tomorrow*. London: University of London Press.

Downing, J. and Thackray, D. (1971) *Reading Readiness*. London: University of London Press.

Fry, E. B. (1967) The diacritical marking system. In Downing, J. and Brown, A. L. (eds) *The Second International Reading Symposium*. London: Cassell.

Gattegno, C. (1962) *Words in Colour*. Reading: Educational Explorers.

Goodman, Y. M. (1979) Using children's reading miscues for new teaching strategies. *Reading Teacher* **23**, 455–9.

McNally, J. and Murray, W. (1962) *Key Words to Literacy and the Teaching of Reading*. London: Schoolmaster Publishing Company.

Moyle, D. (1972) Readability; the use of cloze procedure. In Melnick, A. and Merritt, J. (eds) *Reading: Today and Tomorrow*. London: University of London Press.

Reid, J. F. (1972) Learning to think about reading. In Melnick, A. and Merritt, J. (eds) *Reading: Today and Tomorrow*. London: University of London Press.

Southgate, V., Arnold, H. and Johnson, S. (1981) *Extending Beginning Reading*. London: Heinemann Educational/Schools Council.

Strang, R. (1972) Informal reading inventories. In Melnick, A. and Merritt, J. (eds) *Reading: Today and Tomorrow*. London: University of London Press.

Vygotsky, L. S. (1962) *Thought and Language*. Cambridge, Mass.: MIT Press.

Warburton, F. W. and Southgate, V. (1969) *I.t.a.: An Independent Evaluation*. London: Schools Council.

Zimet, S. G. (1976) *Print and Prejudice*. London: Hodder and Stoughton.

Further Reading

Bennett, J. (1983) *Reaching Out*. Stroud, Gloucester: Thimble Press.

Clark, M. M. (1976) *Young Fluent Readers*. London: Heinemann Educational.

Horner, P. H. (1972) *Reading: an Introduction*. London: Heinemann Educational.

Pumfrey, P. D. (1976) *Reading Tests and Assessment Techniques*. London: Hodder and Stoughton for the United Kingdom Reading Association.

12

Learning and Teaching Writing Skills

SHEILA LANE

Of the four components of the language arts, writing is the most difficult for the child to acquire. In the pre-school years, listening and speaking have been learned together, but with reading and writing, some word recognition has to be mastered before the productive skill of writing can be attempted. Many children will have composed scribble stories and made picture writings, but when reading begins, even the making up of stories in the oral tradition may regress. Children can, quite suddenly, become aware of the difficulties of producing written language unaided. Teachers must not, however, become overwhelmed by the difficulties because children do want to write, and when given positive teaching, they become confident and proud of their achievements.

According to Rosen and Rosen (1973), 'a few children bring to school a cultivated literacy from home which makes writing (usually for them) very easy and profitable'. One of these few is Patrick, the writer of a story called, *Roy the Boy* (Mackay and Simo, 1976). This five and a half year old is able to sustain a long and complex narrative for over 1000 words. He handles characters with confidence and gets his story down on paper with remarkable competence and skill. But for every Patrick there are many others who arrive in school with little understanding of the differences between words and pictures. Some may not connect spoken language with the marks on the page of a book. To understand about written language, children have to come to terms with patterned behaviour. It is the job of the teacher to make writing profitable and pleasurable across the whole range of ability.

There is much that is good in the traditional methods of teaching the first stages of writing and reading. When the child has made a picture or illustrated his news, the teacher will say, 'Now tell me about your picture.' As the teacher writes down the child's comments, the child *sees* what he says being transmitted to the page in exactly the way he has spoken. He traces over the words written by the teacher. Later, he is able to copy this 'sentence' underneath the teacher's writing. A beginning has been made. Soon the teacher will encourage the child to write a little independently, will seek ways to extend his thinking and will help him with vocabulary. At this stage the teacher will also be assisting the child to do something crucial to his development as a writer: to move away from making the picture the focal point of the page. This may need to be done slowly and very sensitively, but the eventual aim is for the writing to stand alone, without the *need* for the picture, as the prime means of communication.

In 1970 came the publication of *Breakthrough to Literacy* (Mackay, 1970). This was an important landmark in language development because the best in traditional methods were brought together and integrated with sound linguistic knowledge. *Breakthrough to Literacy* gives children the opportunity to compose and record as manipulative skills develop. This is done through the use of a device called the 'sentence maker'. The extensive use of the sentence maker, which is also used in the teaching of reading (see chapter 11), ensures that each child can *use* written language on his own before handwriting has been mastered or even started. It is essential that children who are at an early stage with handwriting should have opportunities to 'tell', on paper, the stories which they are capable of composing in their minds. The teacher must make stepping stones for the learning of handwriting by devising ways for the children to record their stories in a permanent form. Naturally, much of the telling will be recorded in pictures, but the skilful teacher will also give scope for the setting down of the written word. We can illustrate this by looking at a First Stage *Breakthrough to Literacy* book, *The Bird, the Cat, and the Tree*. This book begins by showing the place and the two characters. It then sets out, in words and pictures, a sequence of events. This sequence is moved along with the use of simple prepositions: 'up', 'in', 'under', 'to', 'down', 'at', 'from', 'out', 'upon', 'away'. Children find a natural affinity with this kind of

Figure 1   *Zig-zag folder.*

flow when making their own story books or zig-zag folders. An advantage of a zig-zag folder over an exercise or note book is that it can be shortened or lengthened very quickly, enabling the child to display or take home a complete piece of writing (see figure 1) Two other useful *Breakthrough* First Stage books are *My Mum*, which has a biographical approach, and *A Cup of Tea*, which has a recipe-type formula which can be used for other domestic activities.

Developing writing skills

Once children have made a start with recording in words, teachers need to think clearly about the variety of writing skills they intend to foster. Very young children should always be encouraged to write freely about anything which interests them, but the teacher needs to apply professional insight to the analysis of objectives. Specific help needs to be given with: inventing characters; ordering events to make a simple 'plot'; creating settings; using past experiences as a base for the invention of new ideas; taking on new roles; using enriching experiences; developing the ability to hold thoughts in the mind while writing; and vocabulary and spelling. It is likely that there will be, for some children, considerable unconscious plagiarising, which need not be condemned as it is a breakthrough to easy sequential writing.

Inventing characters

Most of the 'stories' young children write are modelled on ones they know. For this reason it is essential that they should hear a variety of well-written stories. Many children have few models to start with and need to meet a large number of characters displaying different qualities, so that the stylistic features of dragons, witches, giants, dwarfs etc. are gradually developed in their minds. Two of the books in *Breakthrough to Literacy* Second Stage (*My Story* and *People in Stories*) can be used to introduce children to traditional make-believe characters (see figure 2).

The teacher and children, together, can also make *Picture Pages* for wall display or for big class turn-over books. The use of thinking clouds and speech balloons helps to reinforce the relationship between the spoken word and the written word in children's minds.

The teacher never, of course, ignores *any* positive stimulus for writing. The background of knowledge which the child has acquired from the streets and playground, from parents and older siblings and from nursery school, provides a known and yet, sometimes, neglected starting point. For example, nearly all children know a version of the singing game, 'The Princess was a Lovely Child':

Figure 2   *Introducing children to make-believe characters.*

Verse 1   *The Princess* was a lovely child.
Verse 2   She dwelt in a high tower.
Verse 3   *A Wicked Fairy* cast a spell.
Verse 4   She (the Princess) fell asleep for a hundred years.
Verse 5   A great big hedge grew giant high.
Verse 6   *A Gallant Price* came riding by.
Verse 7   He cut the hedge down with his sword.
Verse 8   So everyone is happy now.

A wall story book can be made with the children's pictures mounted beneath the captions (i.e. the theme sentence of each verse). Then the teacher draws the children together and talks about the story, which they know so well, because they have already played and made pictures about it. The teacher can say, 'Help me to tell the story of the Princess.' 'Once upon a time there was a lovely Princess called Princess . . . Her hair was like . . . and her eyes were the colour of . . . She wore a beautiful . . . and she had . . .' The children can exchange ideas on how to decorate and embellish each verse. They can make up the Wicked Fairy's spell, and talk about the Prince's horse, before joining in the celebrations on the wedding day. Later, when they are writing their own stories, the captions will give support to those children who need it and will give unobtrusive help in organising the events which, arranged in sequence, constitute 'the plot'. A version of 'The Princess', with very simple accompaniment, is in *Okki-tokki-unga* (Harrap, 1975). *The Lore and Language of Schoolchildren* (Opie and Opie, 1959), provides teachers with a wealth of ideas which can be used in this way.

When adults ask young writers 'And what is going to happen next?', the answer can be, 'I don't know yet because it hasn't happened.' It is therefore unrealistic to ask very young children to think up a whole plot before they pick up a pencil: most children need help if they are to achieve a sequential flow of writing.

Teachers can provide this help in a variety of ways. A traditional method is to use a picture or series of pictures (figure 3) which tell a story when placed in sequence:

Authors who have recently made a welcome contribution to this field are: Raymond Briggs (*Father Christmas* and *The Snowman*: Picture Puffins), Shirley Hughes (*Up and Up*: Bodley Head) and David McKee (*The Magician* series: Piccolo Picture Books; and *King Rollo* series: Arrow Hutchinson). The work of Briggs and McKee has been developed in *Approaches to Writing and Language* (published by Ward Lock, 1981) Book One. Teachers may find it useful to make a collection of pictures from old story books, which can be mounted on cards and used in this way, for oral and written story telling.

ALL the way down the tree he slipped and slid and slid and slipped.

Example: Before:
Guess why King Rollo climbed the tree.
What do you think happened *before* King Rollo slipped?
What might he say?

After:
What do you think happened *after* King Rollo slipped?
Then what did King Rollo say?

Figure 3   *Example of story-telling pictures, adapted from The Adventures of King Rollo by David McKee (Arrow Hutchinson).*

Creating settings

It is worth encouraging children, from the beginning, to place their characters in a setting. Creating a setting helps children who are doubtful about their ability to go on with a story after the initial stimulus. Making *Turn Over Tales* is an idea in which the actual manipulation of the paper strips supports the less confident writers. The procedure is for the teacher to give the class a verbal instruction or question, and to write on the blackboard the first word or two of a possible reply to help them. The children then write their own replies, folding their paper strips over as they do so. For example:

The teacher says:	*The teacher writes:*	*The children write:*
Think of a name		Fluff
Who/what was it?	was ,	was a skeleton,
Say where your character lived	who lived ,	who lived in a tree,
What else was near the place?	near .	near the chip shop.
Was it day time or night time?	Now one ,	Now one dark night,
What was the time exactly?	at ,	at 2 o'clock
What was the weather like?	when ,	when it was foggy,
Now bring someone or something else into your story	along came.	along came a policeman.

This device helps with sentence construction, assists recall, provides a specific 'starter' and creates an amusing context in which to write. A development is for children to exchange strips halfway through or after each turn-over, and then to use them as material for writing *My Funny Story*.

Using past experiences

We all tend to stretch out a spontaneous hand to that which we know, and the use of children's previous experiences as a base for the invention of new ideas needs to be exploited. Although teachers value play experiences and use them to extend children's talk, there seems in general practice to be little planned interaction between these play experiences and the early stages of writing. By organising some of these play experiences, we can see how easily they make natural starting points for writing:

1 Constructional play: bricks, Lego (people and animal bricks are now available), Poleido blocks, roadmakers.
2 Domestic play: Wendy house, shops, hospitals.
3 Imaginative play: puppet making, dressing up.
4 Creative play: collage pictures, junk models.

The Roadmaker (obtainable from Idea, PO Box 63, Amersham, Bucks) provides a ready-made floor layout of roads, junctions, crossings, round-abouts, bridges and movable road signs. Each child in the group can choose a Matchbox toy vehicle (police cars and ambulances are very popular) to 'drive' over the route of their choice. Children are quick to impose restrictions on other drivers and on themselves and are happy to give appropriate priorities where necessary. The Green Cross Code is remembered, and there is much incidental learning about road safety. Model buildings can be added. The writing (or verbal description in the case of nursery school children) which follows can be a straightforward description of a route from a given starting point to a destination. Later, the teacher can use these accounts for playing 'Follow the Road' or for guessing games by reading them out without giving the starting points and destinations. Some children enjoy writing accident stories with graphic telephone calls to police, ambulance and fire station. An imaginative progression is to suggest that children take their vehicles on 'a country drive'. They can listen to a story such as *The Little Car has a Day Out* (Berg, Piccolo Picture Books), and be encouraged to introduce similar elements of surprise into their own writing, e.g. The Little Car 'thought he could see a field that was full of paper bags. But they weren't paper bags. They were white birds.' Later he 'saw something on the road in front of him' "It's a ball," he said to himself . . . It was a hedgehog.' This use of a road plan ties in very happily with *The Village with Three Corners* reading scheme (Hart Davis).

Taking on new roles

During the early stages, children derive pleasure and profit from retelling stories they have heard. Some children can maintain a consistent role, but others move in and out of their characters in a confused way. Others have difficulty in writing, except in the first person. Help may need to be given in a sensitive way so that the flow of writing is not hindered. The teacher can help by creating some situations in which there is a deliberate change of role, using more play experiences and puppet making. A short poem can be used in a prescriptive way e.g.:

> *In My New Clothing*
>
> In my new clothing
> I feel so different
> I must
> Look like someone else.

Basho (From *An Introduction to Haiku* by Harold Henderson)

After drawing pictures of themselves in their new clothes, the children can complete the poem for themselves:

> In my new . . .
> I feel . . .
> I must
> Look . . .

Next, after choosing from the dressing-up box, they can complete:

> When I put on . . .

Children can wear their own home-made simple masks or an item such as a hat when writing. They can listen to *Who Took the Farmer's Hat* (Scholastic Publications), and then retell the story, adding their own ideas about different uses for a farmer's hat, or they can adopt the role of the farmer and write the story of their search in the first person.

Using enriching experiences

Teachers strive to enrich the lives of the children they teach. This 'feeding' needs not only to be of immediate value, but also to become part of a reservoir of knowledge and imagination upon which children can draw.

Children go out of school on visits and excursions far more frequently now than in the past, but it is a pity if they always return to base feeling, 'And now I've got to write about it.' To avoid this, a new first-hand experience, such as a visit to the zoo, can be followed up with information about new facts and with art and craft activities. After this has happened, a story or a poem can be used as a revitalising agent, and only after this need creative writing begin. For example: *The Animal's Lullaby* by Alberti (Bodley Head & Picture Puffin); *The Enormous Crocodile* by Dahl (Picture Puffin); *Prayers from the Ark* by Godden (Macmillan); and *Trouble in the Ark* by Rose (Kestrel).

Music, as a means of communication, seems to have a special appeal to children who are withdrawn and to those whose backgrounds are generally impoverished. A teacher does not have to be gifted musically to give a child a name in simple musical terms:

Tom –my

Glor–i– a

Children who have had little storying at home need to hear a few stories over and over again, so that they have a store of old favourites. One way of holding the children's interest is for the teacher to tell traditional tales with an added ingredient. For example, she can substitute musical notes for the main characters. The story of 'The Miller, His Son and Their Donkey' can be developed in this way:

Seb-as-ti–an

Once upon a time there was an old miller called Sebastian. Here is Sebastian.

The miller had a son called Jake. Here is Jake.

Jake

Now one day  and

were driving their donkey called Hee Haw . . . Listen . . .

Hee – Haw

to market. They walked along

In this fable, Sebastian, Jake and Hee Haw change positions frequently, and so the children need to *listen* carefully if they are to know who is walking and who is riding.

Developing the ability to hold thoughts in the mind while writing

Teachers with experience of supplying spellings for story writing will know only too well that many children forget even the *word* they need before they have moved two steps from their writing tables. We need to teach children, from the beginning, ways of helping themselves. Collecting words and ideas 'in chunks' has an immediate appeal if each child's store is put inside an interesting shape. This method, incidentally, gives teachers an opportunity to correct the collection before the child writes, and enables a first draft to stand without the need for laborious rewriting.

As the idea of the comic strip is familiar and its associations are pleasurable, it provides a stimulating technique for doing this. It is a pity if some teachers feel that such material is not suitable for the classroom; they could, perhaps, be reminded of Southey's remark, 'The truly literate man is never fastidious.' As already suggested, the careful use of thinking clouds and speech balloons helps to underline the interaction between thinking and speaking and reinforces the relationship between spoken and written language (figure 4). Children can be given duplicated copies of a sequence from a story or poem with simple figures and empty thinking clouds and speech balloons drawn in. After listening, the children can embellish the drawings and fill in the clouds and balloons. Completed work can stand in its own right, or it can be corrected and used for orthodox story writing later on.

Figure 4 *When children can use thinking clouds and speech balloons confidently, some will show a mature grasp of human relationships (adapted from a comic strip produced by a Deptford schoolboy).*

Picture making, or even 'colouring in', can act as a useful bridge between the initial stimulus and the actual story writing. Illustrating gives children *time* to be drawn into the subject and to add extra dimension and colour to their own thoughts. Patterns and shapes can be added as an integral part of the picture and used as containers for written ideas, e.g. leaves on trees, smoke rings near monsters, and clouds in the sky, as in figure 5.

Figure 5 *Clouds in the sky provide containers for written ideas.*

When they are pleased with their ideas, children usually incorporate them into their writing straight from the shapes. Others may 'look around,' which creates an early and natural opportunity for cross-fertilisation. Some will change their ideas, and may be gently encouraged to do so, for this can be the beginning of the rethinking and revising which is often difficult to teach at a later stage.

Vocabulary and spelling

Many children may have a greater vocabulary of passive words than their active vocabulary implies. Some children lack confidence in articulation or, as is more usual, in spelling words on paper. From the beginning the teacher needs to alert children to the delights of language; to encourage them to collect words; to choose from their own known vocabulary; and to seek ways of extending and enriching their word store. Young children have a squirrel's enthusiasm for making collections and enjoy filling up various shapes with the results of their scavenging. In the story *Zeralda's Ogre* (Ungerer, Picture Puffin), Zeralda avoids the ogre's potential designs upon her as a dainty morsel by providing him with delicious cooked food. Menus can provide shapes for food collections and can be orthodox or inventive (figure 6).

During the odd few minutes at the end of a session, a group of children can be gathered together for a variation of 'The Memory Shopping Game'. This is often played thus:

First Child: I went shoping and I bought a ball.
Second Child: I went shopping and I bought a ball, and a tin of baked
                 beans.

Third Child: I went shopping and I bought a ball, a tin of baked beans and
              a bag of bulls' eyes.

A variation:

First Child: The pirate had a face.
Second Child: The pirate had a frightening face.
Third Child: The pirate had a scarred, frightening face.

In the early stages, teachers are quite properly more concerned with encouraging an easy flow of words than with syntax and spelling. Children who have been using the sentence maker (*Breakthrough to Literacy* materials) will have developed some conception of syntax, but spelling may still cause problems. Children will be eager to write, but will be inhibited by the spelling of the words they want to use. There is a permanence about the written word which militates against the child's acceptance of the teacher's simple advice to 'write it as it sounds'. Though children will want to use in their written work the words they have encountered in reading, even fluent readers may restrict themselves to only those words which they can spell confidently. This preference for a word which is spelt correctly over a more appropriate but mis-spelt one is natural in children, and must be understood by the teacher. We need to make children literate as well as fluent writers. So help with spelling is obviously one of the things to which the teacher must turn her attention. The words which young children need to spell in order to make their writing coherent may be divided into: (a) those words which are key words to literacy and need to be permanently displayed and positively taught; (b) those words which have particular relevance to the current writing and which need to be written up quickly and displayed in a place where all can see; (c) those words which may be classified as being personal to the writer.

Figure 6   *Menus are a useful medium for the collection of food spellings.*

Teachers need to be free to supply, in the way they think best, words in the third category. Some teachers are anxious that, from the beginning, children should formalise their knowledge of the alphabet and have their personal spelling dictionaries open at the appropriate page when they are asked for 'a spelling'. Other teachers find it difficult to resist building up a word with a child, even when he is engaged upon an exciting piece of writing. An alternative to thumbing through a personal dictionary in a search for the right page is for each child to be given a simple 'helper' strip of paper for use when writing. They can be asked to attempt to spell the word they need on the strip (which at least means that they arrive for help without having forgotten it). It is urged that, whatever stragegies are used in the surmounting of spelling problems, they should be: (a) known and understood by all, and (b) capable of being used very quickly. Speed is paramount if concentration on content is not to be spoilt.

Conclusion

Although it is accepted infant school practice to teach reading to small groups, writing groups are less often seen operating 'close-up' to the teacher. Some of the activities which support writing are easily organised and flourish happily with large numbers, e.g. a whole class. But young children also need short periods of ten to 15 minutes when they are working in a small group of six to eight children. Having the teacher available in this way can ensure that the child has a personal, almost secret rapport with her which has an enormous influence on ideas and the use of language.

At the end of the school day, young children want to take home evidence of 'what I did in school today'. It is important that writing, as well as art and craft, should make the journey from school to home. It is often asked, however, whether there is any point in teachers using red pencils on pages of writing. Paintings do not suffer in this way. The answer is that it is important that words which are destined to be looked at, read and, it is to be hoped, shared with members of the family should be correctly spelt. However, it seems only reasonable to hope that teachers use the same writing tool as that used by the child when making such alterations to the page.

Above all, the teacher needs to *say* something on the page which the child can cherish as personal and positive. Very few teachers would care to justify numerical evaluation as a way of 'marking' the writing of young children. The awarding of stars is an easy way out, but carries no literary significance and makes for no true interaction between writer and reader. The best way to show appreciation is surely to *write back*. This simple act underlines the need to write. When acquiring what is a difficult and artifical skill, children must feel this need. Family and teachers together can provide that which all writers need most, an interested, involved and admiring audience.

References

Harrop, B. (1975) *Action Songs for Children*. London: A. & C. Black.

Mackay, D. (1970) *Breakthrough to Literacy*. Harlow: Longman.

Mackay, D. and Simo, J. (1976) *Help Your Child to Read and Write and Move*. Harmondsworth: Penguin.

Opie, I. and Opie, P. (1959) *The Lore and Language of School Children*. London: Oxford University Press.

Rosen, H. and Rosen, C. (1973) *The Language of Primary School Children*. Harmondsworth: Penguin.

Further Reading

Lane, S. and Kemp, M. (1981) *Approaches to Writing and Language*. London: Ward Lock.

Opie, I. and Opie, P. (1969) *Children's Games in Street and Playground*. London: Oxford University Press.

13

Movement Education with Young Children

BARBARA J. LEWIS and DEREK CHERRINGTON

The normal pattern of motor development

There is a growing need for teachers and parents to gain an understanding of how and at what rate normal children increase their physical competence, a need which has become progressively more acute as attempts are made to produce a pre- and first-school movement curriculum. This area of child development is discussed in chapter 1, but some of the most important points can be summarised here.

The first of these points is that, although the *sequence* in which each child passed through the main stages of physical development is relatively fixed (e.g. crawling precedes walking, walking precedes running), the *rate* at which the child passes through them is very much a personal thing. Each child, it seems, has his own timetable.

The second point is that we are still not sure of the degree to which each child's timetable can be advanced as a result of special training. Does special training in, say, skills like throwing and catching enable children to master these skills at an earlier age than otherwise they individually would? In the light of present knowledge, the answer seems to be that such training does not appear to accelerate the rate of acquisition before maturational readiness (i.e. no child can acquire a skill before he is physiologically, anatomically and psychologically mature enough to do so). However, where special training does help is in improving the *quality* with which a child can perform a skill once he has reached the required stage of physical readiness.

The third point is that an impoverished environment in which the child, quite apart from the absence of special training, is denied even the most basic opportunities for practising skills when he is ready for them, may permanently impair his ability to master these skills now or in later life. Not only this, his whole subsequent learning programme could be affected. Thus it is conceivable that a child's reading, writing or social problems could have their roots in his failure to acquire certain physical coordination skills at critical stages in his earlier development.

What is movement education?

In education, it is customary to group *gross* (as opposed to *fine* or *manipulative*) movement into three main categories. Examples of the motor skills involved in each of the categories can be identified in children's early, unsupervised play and, as the child grows older, these skills become more and more clearly defined. The three categories are:

A Action directed, through efficient body management, towards mastery of certain kinds of physical challenge. This includes movement such as climbing, balancing, leaping and rolling, and leads to 'gymnastic type' movement as the child grows older.

B Trials of strength and speed, and movement concerned with projectiles and/or implements, either in cooperation or competition with other children or with a standard. This leads to athletics and to sports skills and games.

C Movement emphasising rhythm and phrasing, often using sound accompaniment and giving expression to ideas. This leads to dance.

The teacher's role in helping the child to master movement skills differs somewhat in each of the three categories. In category A her aim should be to structure an enriched movement environment which provides the necessary stimulation and challenge, and which not only gives the child the opportunity to practise his skills, but also helps him build up movement schema (i.e. internal representations of well-defined sequences of physical actions which together make up a particular kind of movement, such as rolling) and concepts. In category B, she should provide him with the pieces of small apparatus, and with encouraging activities, that are appropriate to his developmental level. These help him develop the kind of perceptual motor abilities involved in activities like catching, bowling hoops, throwing and skipping or jumping over objects. She should also appreciate his need to experience maximum effort in terms of strength, speed and distance. Finally, in category C, she should provide the child with opportunities to build up rhythmic movement patterns in response to a variety of stimuli (music, rhyme, percussion and so on). We shall be looking at each of these in more detail later in the chapter.

The child and movement education

One of the most significant aspects of the first seven years of a child's life is the sheer amount of movement activity he packs into them. His capacity for

H

movement, of course, begins to manifest itself even while he is still in the womb, and from birth onwards he gains increasing control over it. By the age of two, he is already a miracle of muscular coordination, with good posture control and flexibility, good mobility and relatively well-developed eye and hand coordination. After the age of two, development is less obviously dramatic, but remains rapid. In the years from three to seven, the child translates many of his early, simple movement skills into more complex ones (e.g. walking develops into running, stair climbing becomes more controlled, falls become less frequent), while the accuracy and speed with which movement is accomplished greatly increase. Concurrently, more complex movement schema such as those for hopping and jumping begin to develop.

We have already suggested that all this movement activity may play a part in helping the child to develop the physical coordination skills necessary if he is to tackle many of the more academic tasks of his education successfully. Some psychologists go further than this and hypothesise that it may also be a forerunner to, and subsequently an adjunct of, intellectual development. The child uses movement and play in order to learn. As a consequence, his capacity for conceptual development can be influenced, either positively or negatively, by the quality of his movement experiences during these early years. His attitudes towards the objects around him, his capacity for explaining their behaviour, his self-confidence in dealing with them, his readiness to pursue his natural bent for exploration, his body image and self-concepts, all may be directly linked to the kinds of movement opportunities given him in the home and in the school in the first seven or eight years of his life. The relationship between movement education and overall development is well illustrated in figure 1, adapted from Gallahue (1976).

It is important to stress that these opportunities should not consist simply of the child being forced to copy what grown-ups do. Young children do not learn best by being made to adopt adult patterns of games or movement activity (as when a teacher insists on demonstrating everything to children before they are allowed to have a go for themselves). Instead, they need to be free to develop their own basic patterns of movement behaviour in an environment which stimulates and challenges, and in an atmosphere of active encouragement.

Observing children's movement

The teacher's first step in providing the right kind of movement environment for her children is to familiarise herself with their level of development. In this way she will avoid the mistake of presenting them with activities or with pieces of apparatus inappropriate to their needs. Simple observation of her children in informal settings will tell her much, but it will tell her even more if she has a conceptual framework into which it can be fitted.

Such a framework should indicate to the teacher what to look for in

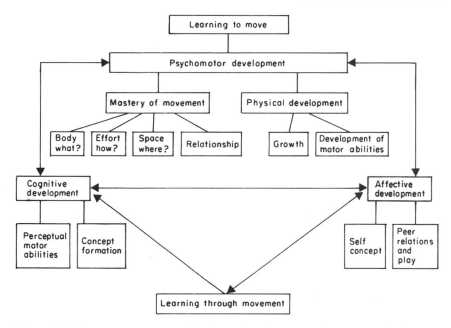

Figure 1   *Schematic representation of the relationship of movement education to psychomotor, cognitive and effective development (adapted from Gallahue, 1976).*

children's movement, should provide her with a vocabulary for describing that movement and should give her a structure from which she can derive a programme of teaching activities. The most widely used framework that satisfies these criteria is that of Rudolph Laban (1960). It involves a classification of movement into four areas, and can be summarised as follows:

1 *What* parts of the body and what class of activity is involved in the movement?
2 *Where* does the movement take place?
3 *How* is the movement performed?
4 What is the *relationship* of the movement to other people and to objects?

In the first (or *what*) area, the body can be used as a whole, either to produce symmetric (with both sides of the body stressed equally) or asymmetric (both sides stressed separately) movement. Alternatively, individual limbs, the head or the trunk can be emphasised, with the rest of the body contributing, as when body parts take weight (i.e. support the body), gesture, counter-balance or initiate and lead whole body movement. The basic *classes of activity* in which the body can indulge are bending, stretching and twisting; these can be combined to produce travelling, jumping, turning, balancing, transferring weight and gesturing.

In the second (or *where*) area, movement can take place in personal space (i.e. in the space immediately around the individual) or in general space (i.e. space shared with objects or with other people). The size of the movement can change, and the movement can vary in direction and can be performed at different levels (i.e. low on the ground or reaching high into the air), thus leading to the formation of pathways which can be straight or curved, and to patterns which can be aerial or floor-based.

The aspects of the third (or *how*) area which we will be most concerned with here are speed (faster and slower movements), strength (stronger and lighter movements) and moving and stopping.

In the fourth (or *relationship*) area, movement can involve individuals in meeting and parting, in surrounding or in being surrounded, in being close or far apart and so on, and can involve them in similar relationships with objects. Laban's classifications can be summarised in chart form (figure 2).

Armed with these classifications, the teacher is better equipped to observe her children. Do some children habitually use the same parts of their bodies and the same class of activity? Do some move less freely in space than others? Do the boys constantly go for movements involving strength whilst the girls go for those involving grace and fluency? Do some children tend to crowd in on others or to work habitually alone? And what do these things tell her about the children's developmental level or about the nature of their previous movement experience?

Of equal importance, what do they tell her about the kind of movement experience she needs to devise to help children improve their performance? And having devised it, how successful does it appear to be? Are the children beginning to use their bodies and to explore space in the imaginative and uninhibited way she had hoped for? If not, how can she help them further? (e.g. in a task requiring travelling on hands and feet the children may perhaps move only forwards, and in her check under the 'where' heading the teacher should notice this and encourage backwards and sideways travelling as well).

Providing the necessary movement experience in categories A and B

Once she is familiar with the need to observe children's movement, and with some of the ways in which this can best be done, the teacher is ready to start devising movement programmes for them. If we look back at the first two categories of movement given on page 215, we can deduce that the experiences which they demand in terms of Laban's four classifications are:

What. *Travelling*: running, skipping, sliding, crawling, creeping, hopping, slithering, walking.
Balancing: taking weight on different body parts, hanging from different parts, tipping out of balance.

BODY			
What?	Whole		
	Part		
	Action	bend	
		stretch	
		twist	
	Activity	travel	(including weight transfer)
		balance	
		jump	
		turn	
		gesture	
SPACE			
Where?	Personal	close to and around the body	
	General	all the space in the area	
	Body shape	round, broad, thin, twisted	
	Size of movement	small or large	
	Directions	forwards, backwards, sideways	
	Levels	high, low, medium	
	Pathways	on the floor or in the air	
EFFORT			
How?	Time	sudden	sustained
		quick	slow
	Tension	firm	fine
		strong	light
	Flow	smooth	hesitant
		going	stopping
	Space	direct	flexible
RELATIONSHIP			
Relationship?	Proximity	near, far, approaching, retreating, surrounding	
	Sequence	canon, matching, opposing	
	Spatial relationship	above, below, beside	
	Supporting	lifting, lowering, pushing, pulling, carrying	

Figure 2   *Laban's (1960) classification of movement.*

Jumping: bouncing, bounding, leaping and, since these involve jumping as well as travelling, hopping and skipping.

Turning: spinning, wheeling, rolling, twisting, tumbling.

Gesturing: reaching, waving, bending.

Where. Moving in different directions, moving at different levels, climbing up and down, making varied use of personal space (i.e. taking up different body shapes – round, wide, thin, twisted, curled and so on), taking straight or wavy pathways through the air or along the ground.

How. Moving quickly or slowly, strongly or lightly, smoothly or jerkily, stealthily or loudly, fluently or restrictedly.

Relationship. Interacting with another child, with other children or with an object. Pushing, pulling, lifting, lowering, touching, stroking, receiving and imparting force, striking and catching.

When planning movement experiences, it is vital to remember that the above list is not a set of four different kinds of experiences, but four interrelated classifications which all enter into each single activity that the child performs. For example, if we take an activity such as travelling, the child may be *creeping* in one *direction*, doing so *stealthily* and on a course which takes him *towards* other children. Unless this point is kept firmly in mind, the teacher will be unable to help the child explore all the possibilities of a particular movement.

Turning to the physical context in which this movement takes place, the teacher needs to provide:

1 Surfaces which are variously straight, inclined, bumpy, flat, smooth, textured, soft, hard, slippery, narrow, broad, high, low and of medium height.
2 Gaps and holes which are variously large, small, round, square, tall and thin, long and thin and which can be jumped over or squeezed through.
3 Objects which can variously be climed over or on, which can be jumped over or on or off, which can be held on to or twisted around, which can be pushed and pulled and crept into.
4 Bars and poles which can be hung or swung from, or which can be crept under or jumped over.
5 Balls which are of various sizes and weights (also bean bags).
6 Bats of various weights and grip sizes.
7 Ropes of different lengths and thicknesses.

Providing the necessary movement experience in category C

The kind of experience involved in category C on page 215 is very largely dealt with elsewhere in this book (chapter 14), and all that we need say here is that they should be thought of as appealing to the child through his senses. Thus he may be given *auditory* experiences, such as music, percussion, words (poems, stories, verbal descriptions) and body sounds (clapping, hissing, stamping and so on); *visual* experiences, such as paintings, sculptures, mobiles, machinery, photos of the sea or of the effects of the wind, the movement of animals or of other children; or *tactile* experiences, such as roughness, smoothness, spikiness, malleability, stickiness (bread, paste, clay etc.). These experiences can be presented to him during the movement lesson itself or he can encounter them on outings and give them expression when he returns to school (e.g. a windy or snowy day, autumn leaves, traffic, a railway train, aeroplanes).

The movement lesson

Having learnt something of the skills involved in observing children's movement, and having mapped out a general programme of the kind of movement experiences which she needs to provide for them, the teacher is now ready to go on to the business of planning the movement lesson itself. Since the nature of this lesson will differ with the age of the children concerned, we shall look at the three to five age group (the nursery child) first, and then the five to sevens (the infant child).

The nursery child

The three- to five-year-old child, whether in a nursery school or in a nursery unit attached to a primary school, is unlikely to have a purpose-built space for physical activity (although outdoors there may be fixed apparatus of some kind, such as a climbing frame). These children are usually free to wander around an area set out with a variety of learning materials, and the apparatus for gross motor play may simply occupy a corner of the room to be used when children choose. This organisational set-up usually coincides with a teaching method whereby the teachers and nursery assistants deliberately avoid directing children's activities for much of the school day, and concentrate instead upon encouraging, reinforcing and developing what the children themselves choose to do.

For this reason, the term movement 'lesson', within the context of the nursery child, must not be taken to imply anything set and formalised. Though the teacher may wish to allocate short blocks of time here and there for working with children as a group, she must avoid the kind of organised lesson appropriate to an older age group in which children change their clothing and are taught in a specially designed area (hall, gym or playground). Such a lesson is not really suitable for the very young as it involves their having to understand and obey verbal instructions, and to work together in large groups.

In place of verbal instructions, the child should have his movement activities initiated by the environment itself. The time to use words is when the child is actually engaged in these activities, and needs help from the teacher to describe what he is doing and to name the objects with which he is working. Obviously, once he shows her that he is beginning to form movement schema, and to build up the concepts associated with them, the teacher can allow herself to introduce a limited amount of verbal direction, thus helping the child to reinforce what he has learnt and to test it in new situations, but she must avoid ever using these directions as an alternative to providing the right kind of stimulating and enriching environment.

Such an environment can only be created if the child is given the kind of apparatus that simulates the natural environment and that can be used in a number of different ways and levels of difficulty. He can then select what is suitable for him, or rearrange things to his own liking. Wherever possible, the apparatus should also contain built-in methods of reinforcing the child, so that he can monitor his own progress without external comments, and proceed to set some of his own standards (e.g. this can be achieved by colour coding the rungs of climbing frames or ladders, or by auditory cues). It is also advisable that in her arrangement of the environment, the teacher concentrates upon the three categories of movement discussed earlier one at a time, thus allowing a progress from natural movement to the more stylised movement of gymnastics or games or dance.

Category A: Movement leading later to gymnastics. Suppose that the teacher has decided to structure the environment to provide the child with experiences of climbing (and thus to help him build up concepts of high and low, up and down). Some or all of the following pieces of apparatus would be suitable:

Climbing frame	Steps
Slide	Vertical plank
Inclined ladder	Inclined plank
Vertical ladder	Low pole for going under
Stackable boxes of various sizes	Suspended ball to jump and touch

Alternatively, suppose she wants to provide opportunity for stepping with big or little steps (and thus help the child build up some concepts of distance). In this case, she would choose:

Small carpet squares or mats with varying gaps between them
Two ropes arranged to form a 'river' of varying width
Hoops or ropes laid in an interesting pattern
Small boxes to step over or onto
Low benches
A sheet covered with large coloured spots and anchored to the floor

To take a third example, suppose she wants to provide balancing experiences (and thus help the child to build up concepts of weight and equilibrium). She would then choose:

Planks of varying width, directly on the floor or slightly raised
Chalk or tape lines on the floor
Thin rope laid on the floor in a wavy pattern
Carpet squares made into a track for maintaining balance while changing direction at speed
A balance board (made by supporting a board on a raised rib down the centre so that it tips from side to side)

Basic (and inexpensive) equipment of this kind can be used by the teacher in various permutations to give the child experience of all the activities listed in category A. The cardinal steps for the teacher to remember are in this order:

1 Choose the topic (climbing, stepping, balancing etc.)
2 Select and arrange the apparatus.
3 Observe how the children use the apparatus, meanwhile helping them to verbalise their experiences and to relate them to their environment.
4 Where necessary, make suggestions as to how this usage can be further developed.

Category B: Movement leading later to games and athletic skills. For the nursery child, this category can be divided into two: (a) body management, and (b) ball handling, with or without an implement. This, in turn, can be divided into receiving, carrying and sending away. If the teacher decides to give the children experience of body management, then ideally she needs to take them outside so that they can feel free to move as fast as they like. This movement consists of running, jumping, swerving, turning, twisting, in fact all those body movements implied by a category of movement that later leads to games and athletic skills. The teacher should set out objects like traffic cones, boxes, mats, hoops (in fact any apparatus of the appropriate height or width, and flimsy enough to be knocked over without the children falling and hurting themselves), and the children should be encouraged to run and dodge and jump at speed.

If the teacher decides to concentrate upon ball handling, then the children may need rather more immediate help and guidance from her. In this sub-category, *receiving* implies absorbing the momentum of an object and gaining control of it (e.g. catching with the hand or trapping with the foot), a thing which small children have difficulty in doing due to their poor judgement of speed and flight. They need to start with a large ball which is rolled to them along the ground, and only to proceed to catching as they become more confident. Even then, it is necessary to help the child avoid 'head aversion' (i.e. turning the head away at the moment of catching through a fear of being struck in the face), and for this reason bean bags are often preferable to balls. *Carrying* implies travelling with the ball (either holding it in the hand or keeping it in intermittent contact with the feet). Again, it is better to start with large balls. *Sending* implies throwing or striking, and here the child is better off with a small ball (or bean bag), which he finds easier to control. Initially, he should be encouraged to throw for distance ('as hard as possible'), though later he can be given something to aim at, such as humpty dumpty faces painted onto a sheet or old curtain. Children should not be encouraged to throw from behind a line as this tends to retard their development necessary beyond the immature stage of throwing with the feet together.

As with body management, ball handling is best practised outside when possible. This also makes it rather easier for the child to practise striking the ball with an implement, such as a bat. If the teacher provides bats, she should remember that nursery children are more successful in striking stationary than moving balls, and in addition to allowing them to hit balls on the ground, she should also try to supply balls suspended above the ground on string.

Category C: Movement leading later to dance. Imaginative play, drama and music all become interwoven here (see chapters 14 and 16); however, the teacher without much background in these subjects will find it useful to remember that dance-like activity can be achieved in children through the use of rhythmic phrased movement using contrasting ideas like rising and falling, going and stopping, large and small, fast and slow. The teacher should emphasise the qualitative differences in movement experiences between the contrasting words she is using (there is a link with language here; also with number concepts).

The teacher's starting point for work of this kind is often a musical instrument. A drum is ideal, and her rhythmic tapping upon it will quickly attract the interest of her children. Once a group has gathered around her, she can beat the drum faster to suggest acceleration, and then slower to suggest deceleration, and the children will quickly want to express this in movement. Once this happens, the teacher can encourage the use of words to describe this movement, aiming to bring out the expression of contrasts (fast and slow, loudly and softly) and of imaginative action (darting, rushing, creeping). Essentially, the teacher aims to help children develop an understanding of the overall pattern of a phrase of sound (i.e. the idea of going and stopping, accelerating and decelerating, in response to sound). However, she can also give opportunities for 'keeping in time' (marching, skipping, walking), which help children to develop a feeling for the rhythm itself.

Another starting point is a poem or a story which the chidlren have just heard. The suggestion that they act out the giants or the trains or the water is usually enough to provoke imaginative movement. Alternatively, the stimulus can come from the movement of raindrops or the snowflakes or the leaves or the wind experienced on a recent outing. In every case, the principle is the same: the teacher presents a carefully selected and well thought out stimulus, helping the children to go beyond their initial movement response by observing others and listening to her suggestions. The teacher aims to increase the range of movement responses of which the child is capable and to encourage better performance (figure 3). She must remember, of course, that there is nothing to be gained (and much to be lost) by forcing children into movement or by keeping them at it once their interest has begun to wane.

The infant child

Movement lessons for infant school children usually take place in a specially equipped hall, and the children are required to remove their shoes and socks

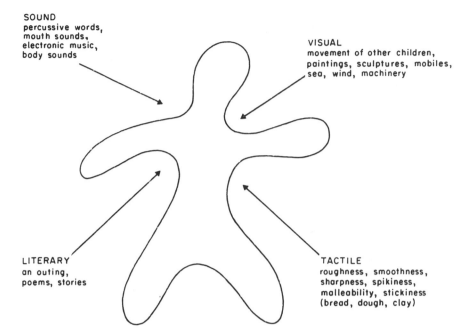

SOUND
percussive words,
mouth sounds,
electronic music,
body sounds

VISUAL
movement of other children,
paintings, sculptures, mobiles,
sea, wind, machinery

LITERARY
an outing,
poems, stories

TACTILE
roughness, smoothness,
sharpness, spikiness,
malleability, stickiness
(bread, dough, clay)

Figure 3   *Stimuli for dance.*

and outer clothing. These lessons normally possess a definite structure, and are centred upon a specific theme or topic. Children have to learn to listen to the teacher's directions, and to stop and start when asked. They learn how to move some of the large apparatus themselves, and how to work with other children, and they are taught to become increasingly safety conscious.

As with nursery children, however, lessons in the three different categories do not each take the same form, and for this reason it will again be helpful to look at them separately.

Category A: Movement leading to gymnastics. In this category, the lesson usually starts with a general activity, such as travelling and stopping, during which the children get used to moving together in a big space and listening to the teacher. The lesson topic is then introduced in the form of a number of tasks which the children are asked to explore under the teacher's guidance. An example of a complete lesson will be given below, but, first, it is important to stress that in presenting these tasks, the teacher's role is still mainly one of providing the children with the opportunity for movement, rather than of instructing them precisely in what they have to do. Thus she will frequently give the tasks to her class in an open-ended form, rather than in a limited one (e.g. 'travel using both hands and both feet' instead of 'do bunny-jumps'). From time to time, she will stop the class, drawing attention to good work, pointing out ways in which work can be improved in variety and quality, and perhaps asking a child to demonstrate to all the rest.

These tasks normally occupy the first half of the lesson, and in his exploration of them the child builds up movement sequences by allowing each of his movements to flow easily into the next (consequently forming what is sometimes called a 'sentence of movement'). In the second half of the lesson, the child is then usually encouraged to apply his earlier movement experiences to fixed apparatus (thus, in a sense, using these ideas to solve fresh, environmentally imposed tasks). A lesson devised along these lines is as follows:

> *Lesson topic*: Travelling and stopping, using different parts of the body.
> *Introduction*: Running and stopping, running and stopping, avoiding each other and using all the space available.
> *Floorwork*: Finding ways of travelling on different parts of the feet (e.g. toes, heels, sides of the feet). Finding different ways of travelling using both hands and feet (e.g. hands moving together or one after the other, feet moving together or separately, one foot off the ground, one hand off the ground). Finding different body surfaces on which to travel (large and small).
> *Apparatus*:
> 1 Two mats. Moving across the first mat using the ideas for travelling on different body surfaces developed in floorwork. Pause in between mats, and repeat on second mat.
> 2 Bar. Travelling along the bar using hands and feet.
> 3 Two inclined forms, supported in the middle by a bar, a box or form stand. Running up the first form, stopping at the top and running down the second.

The layout of this apparatus is shown in figure 4. It will be noted that the three pieces of apparatus are duplicated on either side of the room, giving six sets of apparatus in all. Such a layout would be suitable for 30 children, divided into five groups of six. The teacher should assign one group to each piece of apparatus, then move them on after a few minutes, so that each group has the opportunity of working on each of the three different kinds of apparatus. The teacher's role is to move from group to group, encouraging and suggesting, and from time to time, as with floorwork, stopping the class so that they can watch one child demonstrate his movement ideas (there is no need to stress that *all* children must be given a chance for this individual demonstration at various times, and that demonstration should always be for the purpose of praise and encouragement and never for negative reasons).

In planning her work, the teacher should concentrate upon one topic for several lessons at a time, only moving on to something new when children have developed their schema to an appropriate level. Changing topics too frequently only leads to confusion, to work of a low standard and, ultimately, to loss of interest by both class and teacher. However, within the chosen

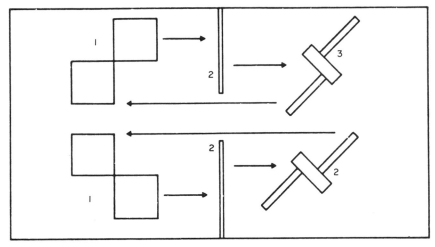

Figure 4   *Simple apparatus arrangement.*

topic, there is every reason for the teacher to vary the tasks and the apparatus which she offers to her class. As children grow older, they can also be exposed to apparatus offering more scope. A list of such apparatus, still within the topic of travelling, and together with the tasks which children might attempt upon it, is as follows (see figure 5):

1 Inclined forms: climb up using hands and feet, slide down using a large body surface.
2 Form, box, mat: find different ways of travelling on the form and box, stopping on the box before jumping off and rolling on the mat.
3 Climbing frame with ladder: climb using hands and feet.
4 Climbing frame with ropes: climb and swing.
5 Two mats and two forms: travelling and stopping, without using the feet.
6 Plank, trestle and mat: bounce up the plank using feet only or hands and feet, stop at the top, jump down and travel on body surfaces.

For other topics which she can use in this category, in addition to travelling, the teacher is referred back to the list on pages 218, 219. She should also look frequently at Laban's classification (page 217), so that she comes to use this automatically in her observation and guidance of her children.

Category B: Movement leading to games and athletic skills. As for the under-fives, this category includes body management and ball handling, but in addition the over-fives should experience some fundamental games principles, the structure of games and their rules, cooperation and competition, and how to score. Some children will want to compete in individual activities, and to compare themselves with others in tests of speed or distances thrown or

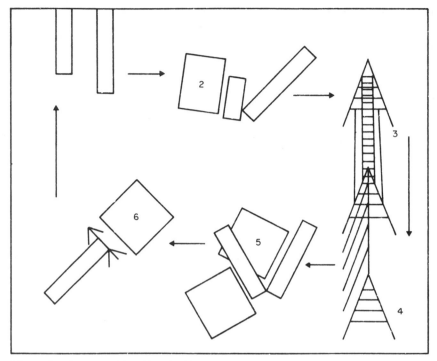

Figure 5   *A more complex apparatus plan.*

jumped. They will be able to invent ways of scoring in simple activities, and also construct complete games for themselves. Such games are often more suitable than the games that adults impose upon them.

The category B lesson, like that in category A, commences with an introductory activity. For example, each child may be given a ball or a bat and a ball, and asked to follow some common activity such as bouncing the ball, hitting it with the bat or throwing it up in the air and catching it. Alternatively, the teacher may concentrate upon footwork and orientation in running and in turning activities (e.g. all children running and changing direction at each word of command). Even in these introductory activities, the teacher should not miss the opportunity to introduce teaching points, such as reaching towards the ball with 'open' hands and 'giving' with the hands when catching.

After the introductory activity, the children are usually divided into groups, and each group then assigned to a set of equipment and given an activity to perform with it. The emphasis, particularly with children at the lower end of the infant age group, must be upon *small* groups with plenty of equipment. Suitable equipment includes: small balls, bats, bean bags, skipping ropes (one for each child in the class), medium balls, large balls, canes, shinty sticks, targets (old cans), hoops, skittles (sufficient to equip several small groups). In addition, if the lesson is taking place in the playground, targets and lines can be drawn in chalk on the walls and on the playground surface to increase the scope of the equipment. An example of the plan of the hall or playground when organised for this kind of small group work with equipment is shown in figure 6 (five groups of six children each). The activities suggested for each group are:

1 In twos, bouncing a medium-size ball into a hoop and allowing the partner to field it.
2 Each child bowling a hoop, then trying to jump through or over it.
3 Each child kicking a medium size ball against a wall and trapping the return.
4 Each child jumping over the canes resting on the skittles (this can be allowed to develop into an obstacle race).
5 Two teams facing each other in lines, with a large ball midway between the two lines, and attempting to drive the large ball towards the opposing team by throwing small balls at it.

The number of different activities that the children experience in one lesson will depend on the length of the lesson, the nature of the activities and

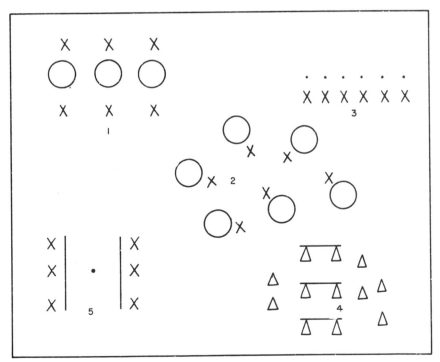

Figure 6   *Possible plan of playground.*

the age of the children. Normally, each group should be allowed to get round at least two or three of the five activities on offer. With older infants, it might then be possible to bring the whole class together for a short team game. At the end of the lesson, it goes without saying that the children should be made responsible for returning equipment to the appropriate boxes or cupboards.

Category C: Movement leading to dance. The spontaneous skipping and jumping of children is often regarded by adults as being dance-like. It is often accompanied by sound (clapping, singing), and is clearly movement for the sheer enjoyment of moving. The teacher's task is to incorporate this kind of movement into the more structured experience of dance itself. Dance differs from this undeveloped movement in that it emphasises rhythm, it contains phrased movement in which the rhythm is built into longer patterns and it emphasises the quality of movement.

The structure of dance is summarised in Laban's classification of movement (page 217), while the classes of possible stimuli for arousing dance in children are illustrated in figure 3. Here, however, we must introduce a note of caution. Too often, when seeking stimuli for dance, teachers simply ask children to 'be' something (e.g. a tree, a flower opening, the wind). This is inadequate. If children's dance is to contain *rhythm, phrasing* and *quality*, the teacher must first discuss with them some of the attributes of the stimulus being presented. These attributes must then be related to the children themselves, using Laban's four categories. With very young children, the theme for a lesson may be selected from activities that emphasise any one of these categories more than the other three. Here are some examples of topics which do just this:

Topics emphasising the body (*what*)
1 Actions using the whole body.
2 Actions using parts of the body (fingers, toes, elbows, knees etc.).
3 Actions with particular parts of the body leading.
4 Actions emphasising the shape of the body: curved, angular, spiky, long and thin, spread wide.

Topics emphasising space (*where*)
1 Personal or general space.
2 Extension into space: near to and far from.
3 Patterns in the air and on the floor: straight, angular, curved, twisted.
4 Levels: high, medium, low.
5 Directions: in front, behind, to the sides.
6 Size: big or small.

Topics emphasising body quality (*how*)
1 Weight: with varying degrees of tension, ranging from firm and powerful to gentle and light.

2 Time: with varying speeds, from sudden and quick to slow and sustained.

3 Space: with varying degrees of plasticity from straight and direct to flexible and roundabout.

4 Flow: with varying degrees of fluency from restraint and withholding to ease and fluidity.

Topics emphasising relationship with whom or with what (*relationship*)

1 Individual child with teacher.

2 Whole class with (or against) teacher.

3 With partner, trio or group.

4 Leading, meeting, following, copying, mirroring other children.

Suppose, for example, the teacher decided to take a *where* topic, then her lesson might proceed as follows:

Lesson Topic: Size (big and small).

Accompaniment: Drum and/or cymbal.

Introduction: Moving with sound of drum, and stopping when drum stops (repeat each drum phrase several times before changing its length, so that children can anticipate). Rhythms of nursery rhymes are a useful source of ideas.

Movement training:

1 Travelling using small steps (the rhythm can be speeded up to produce a prancing step).

2 Using larger steps, the children being encouraged to move their legs backwards and sideways as well as forwards.

3 Change of body shape using small or large steps at the same time.

Dance form: Blend the ideas developed above into a dance that has a beginning and a satisfying end. There are various ways of doing this, working in each to the rhythm tapped out by the teacher. For example:

1 From a large spread shape use small steps and sustained body movement to become rounded and folded-in to a small ball.

2 From a large spread shape use long steps and sustained body movement to become rounded and folded-in to a small ball.

3 From a starting position that is small use long or small steps to spread gradually and take up as much space as possible.

The above should be repeated two or three times, with the teacher drawing attention to good work, and occasionally inviting individual children to demonstrate. Subsequently, the children can be asked to link their movement phrases together, going, for example, from big to small and back to big again, and then experimenting to produce the same sequence of movement in different ways.

Finally, with older infants, an alternative starting point would be to take action words that have occurred in a story or poem. Words such as 'dart', 'swirl' or 'explode'. But, as with our earlier warning that children should not simply be asked to 'be' the stimulus object without adequate preparation, so we must again warn teachers not just to present these words to children and see what happens. The teacher should first analyse them carefully to determine their movement potential. Since words of this kind are usually likely to emphasise the *how* topic, the teacher will find it useful to remember that this topic can be explored using the concepts of time, weight, space and flow. Thus words like 'explode' and 'swirl' could be analysed as follows:

Explode   *time* sudden
              weight strong/firm
              space direct

Swirl   *time* sustained
              weight firm or fine touch
              space flexible

An analysis of this kind would quickly show the teacher that exploding and swirling could be used in combination to develop a dance phrase. Thus, using her voice as the stimulus this time, she could give the class 'swirl, swirl, swirl and explode', or 'swirl, explode, swirl, swirl, explode, explode', the two movements flowing into, yet contrasting with, each other.

References

Gallahue, D. L. (1976) *Motor Development and Movement Experiences for Young Children.* New York: Wiley.
Laban, R. (1960) *The Mastery of Movement.* London: Macdonald and Evans.

Further Reading

Mauldon, E. and Redfern, H. B. (1969) *Games Teaching. A New Approach for the Primary School.* London: Macdonald and Evans.
Morison, R. (1969) *A Movement Approach to Educational Gymnastics.* London: Dent.
North, M. (1973) *Movement Education. A Guide for the Primary and Middle School Teacher.* London: Temple Smith.
Slater, W. (1974) *Teaching Modern Educational Dance.* London: Macdonald and Evans.

14

Making Music

AVRIL DANKWORTH

'I run a playgroup in my locality. As much as I should like to include music as one of the many activities for the under fives, I have no knowledge of the subject, and wouldn't have an idea about launching music activities; anyway, with plenty to do already, I'm not even entirely convinced of the necessity to do so.'

Words of this kind come from many devoted playgroup leaders, helpers and nursery and infant teachers. Stimulating words to a musician! However, one is almost spoilt for choice in the amount of material which can provide an answer. My first advice is, 'You do not have to be a musician to be musical.' That is, you do not have to be a good instrumentalist or a good singer to make music with your children; all you need is the desire to have fun, and share your enthusiasm and sincerity. If you really want to do it, you will. Secondly, so far as musical equipment is concerned, the greatest demand made upon you is the ability to press the button or turn the knob of a record player, tape or cassette recorder. And hey presto! The door is open to innumerable possibilities:

1 Recorded music (instrumental and/or vocal) can provide incentive for movement, playing and painting.
2 Recordings can teach you the repertoire of songs, poems and singing games you need. They can also teach the children and serve as accompaniment to their singing.
3 Recorded stories leave you free-handed (and free-minded!) to share the enjoyment of active participation with the children. (A tape or cassette recorder makes available the additional possibility of recording 'sounds around us', and the children's experiments as well as their own performance.)

If you have no funds for purchasing this basic equipment, plan to devote the proceeds of your next coffee morning or white elephant sale to that very end.

Thirdly, the only other apparatus you need you can acquire for yourself: any objects or materials which will make 'sounds' in their own right or which can be used to imitate other sounds. These can be dug out from your own home at no, or little, expense.

Last – but not least – you must take upon yourself the responsibility of 'having a go', 'taking the plunge', 'letting your hair down', developing a healthy streak of 'insanity'; in short, becoming a child. All this is confessedly easier if you can work together with your adult colleagues as a team, so that no one will feel self-conscious or out of the picture.

The conviction

If we take seriously the fact that the first five years of life are vital, formative ones in which the seeds for all future development are laid, then nursery teachers carry a heavy responsibility indeed, far beyond that of simply being child-minders. What with social training, creative activity in its broadest sense and the development of the five sense, there is plenty to keep us busy.

Of the five senses, what about the senses of taste, smell and hearing? Do we really come to terms with these so well as we do with the senses of sight and touch? If we set out to provide an environment which will arouse curiosity, stimulate interest and inspire creativity, these three senses must be provided for as much as the other two, especially in a world full (and overfull) of sounds to the extent that we close our ears to them.

You may well ask, 'What connection have sounds to music?' Sounds of every description are the grass roots of music, music being, indeed, the organisation of sounds. The constantly quoted teaching adage, 'Start where the child is, and work from there', was never truer than when applied to music. Further, sounds are not graphic art; they are not sculpture; so they have to be classified under music, however arbitrary that may be! Sounds are an important, familiar part of life, just as valid and exciting as all the things we see. It is just as thrilling to recapture a sound as it is to recapture a sight; often the two go together anyway.

Stage 1a: Activities with record player

Pulsation games: 'Follow m'leader'

Where to begin? Well, get the record player going with some bright music, which has consistent pulsation, catchy melody and attractive instrumentation: folk dances, folk songs (including nursery rhymes, the folk heritage of the children), ballroom dances, Latin American/Afro Cuban music, marches, waltzes, the occasional current pop tune. Then get the children around you to play 'Follow m'leader' games, using any kinds of movement or mime which comes into your head. Start by sitting, but soon get everyone standing and moving around.

Body movements

First use each part of the body on its own. Head: nod, shake, tilt from side to side, roll clockwise, roll anti-clockwise, develop a 'nervous twitch'. Eyes: blink, wink, stare, cross, roll; use the fingers to produce Chinese eyes, bloodhound eyes, clown eyes. Then try shoulders, elbows, hands, fingers, hips, legs, knees, feet, toes, trunk.

Mime

Next include work on mime. Here are some ideas: cookery, carpentry, household chores, household decorating, toiletry, gardening, boats, swimming, sport, vehicles, musical instruments. Let each adult take a turn at being leader, and eventually (on a much later occasion) let the children take a turn, too, if they wish. This should all be done in an informal, party atmosphere, with everyone joining in. In a larger nursery let each teacher take a small group of her own.

So you have taken the plunge, and the water is not so cold as you thought! You will find that for much of the time you will all perform many of these actions in time to the music, that is, subconsciously reacting to the underlying pulse (or throb) of the music, an invaluable experience in itself. As you go on, try to extend the range of movements by performing them while you jump, hop, turn or even move across the floor. Use a variety of speeds of music, which will bring slow, quick and medium speeds of movements.

Stage 1b: Recorded songs

Next acquire a recording of children's songs or poetry. Switch on the music and sing/speak with the record, encouraging the children to help you. Fingerplay and actions will often assist children to memorise the song, as well as develop coordination. Bear in mind that it is better to repeat one or two items from the record than to play the whole of one side. Try not to cram. Children love repetition anyway, and it helps memorisation and builds their confidence.

Songs and poems appeal to the imagination, extend vocabulary and help develop speech. Often they become the basis for discussion and conversation. When using recorded songs and poems, always mouth the words with the performer to help the children memorise them. Often the children do not realise that the recorded voice is not yours!

Stage 1c: Games with sounds

Music corner

Having launched the movement and singing ideas, the next challenge is to make a music or 'sounds' corner. Have available here (with constant and regular changes, additions and replacements) all kinds of materials for experimentation in making sounds and for making into simple rhythm (non-pitch) instruments (Dankworth and Priestley, 1973):

> *Drums*: Round plastic fridge containers. Tins with tight-fitting plastic lids. (Remove the base of the tin and seal rough edges with adhesive tape.)
>
> *Gongs*: Pieces of metal and pottery which can be suspended, then struck to set them vibrating.
>
> *Jingles*: Small objects mounted in such a way that they dance and jingle against each other.
>
> *Shakers*: Containers (of varied material, shape and size) with fillings (also varied) which rattle against the sides of the container when shaken. The contents may be seeds, soil (sand, stones, pebbles etc.) or metal. Children are always curious to know the contents of shakers, so it is often a good idea to make a number of shakers from transparent plastic containers.
>
> *Clappers*: Two like surfaces clapped together: stones, bones, shells, sticks, plastic ointment boxes.
>
> *Scraper*: Anything with ridges on its surface: notched stick, cheese grater, comb, metal washboard, corrugated cardboard.
>
> *Crackly paper*: Tissue, cellophane, plastic wrappings, plastic egg boxes.
>
> *Tearing material*: Paper and cloth of varied textures.
>
> *Water*: Containers for pouring, straws and tubes for blowing bubbles, stones for plopping. (This can be included in waterplay.)

These materials can be put out as (a) a cross-section of various sounds or (b) a variety of one type. Invent all the games you can to encourage listening and evaluation. The element of colour can be introduced usefully too. 'Listen to this green shake. Listen to this white shake. Now shut your eyes, listen, and tell me which I'm shaking now.'

If we accept that children's art is a reflection of their experience and imagination, then just as surely we can accept their experiments with sounds as equally valid. If we agree that visual collage is acceptable to the eye, then why not sound collage, too? As ever, the point at which we, as adults, comment on the children's efforts, and the moment at which we suggest developments from the initial idea, is left to our discretion. By and large, though, the experiments of the music corner are worth while in their own right, but may well have the bonus of being incorporated later into the 'Follow m'leader' games, into song accompaniments and into songs, poems, stories and plays as sound effects.

Already the seeds are sown, aimed at developing the child's curiosity and consciousness of the sounds around him: on the one hand, non-pitch everyday sounds and, on the other, pitch sounds in the form of recorded songs and instrumental music, sounds that have surrounded him and been subconsciously assimilated from the moment he was born. All the elements for future development are there: sing, play, listen, move, create, notate (in pictorial representation of the object which produces the sound). The child loves to express himself in these elements.

Stage 2a: Activities with record player

'Follow m'leader' games

'Follow m'leader' games are the ideal start for developing a feeling for pulsation, phrasing and pattern. Try to choose a great variety of types, speeds and moods of music. There is no need to buy special recordings; just explore those you and your friends already possess.

As the leader, you will quickly come to realise your responsibility for 'keeping the pot boiling', never *stopping* to think what to do next, but imagining your next move while you keep the activity going; also, anticipating the moment of change, and remembering what has been done, so that you can repeat or avoid repeating, as you wish. Here the leader is, in fact, performing a first-class piece of improvised movement. You may like to start by playing the game in a sitting position, but as soon as possible get everyone standing, to extend the repertoire of movements.

Introducing the four body sounds

The next stage is to get the children performing the body percussion sounds: finger click; hand clap; knee pat; and foot stamp. In the first instance, they are just performed pulsatingly, reflecting the underlying heartbeat (or throb) of the music. The leader changes from one to the other informally, and the followers obey the visual command, the challenge being to observe and instantly imitate the leader. Later, use little repeated patterns of four beats.

As the leader, always meet the eyes of your followers with a smile; this is a happy moment. Communication is vital, music being the most social of activities. Communication must be established before you can hope for cooperation, concentration and coordination. You *must* become one of and with them.

The body sounds game is a more disciplined exercise than the freer body movements and mimes, and serves as a stepping stone towards acquiring the feeling for formal rhymes, comparable with moving from scribble drawing to the manipulation of a pen for writing.

Introducing rhythm instruments

Extend the whole 'Follow m'leader' idea by using home-made rhythm percussion instruments, making the opportunity to use all the space around the body. Play the instruments at high, low and middle levels, in front of and behind the body, to the left and right of the body, under each knee, drawing zig-zags, circles, snakes, figures, letters in the air. Shakers, jingles and clappers are the easiest instruments to manipulate for this game. The resulting movements are wonderful experience for developing awareness of the body and the space around it.

Never underestimate the vital importance of the pulse games, developing in children their inherent feeling of response to the underlying heartbeat, throb of the music. Everything in musical performance depends upon this feeling, so it is up to us to dream up all possible varieties of response to it. Consider, too, that recent research would indicate that children with the best sense of rhythm are often the first to read.

Stage 2b: Songs

Songs are best caught rather than taught. Pop songs are never taught; we just catch them as easily as measles, by hearing them over and over again. So this is our technique, too. Remember that children are not concerned with prima donna achievement; they are ready to accept your natural singing voice just as they accept your natural speaking voice. Sing your new song at least four times:

1 Get the children to listen.
2 Sing and add some fingerplay or actions.
3 Repeat 2, inviting the children to do the actions with your.
4 Invite the children to help you sing the song as well as doing the actions.

Prime favourite is *This Little Puffin* (Matterson, 1969), which also lists further useful references. There are numerous books on the market which combine songs, poems and other activities, often linking in theme.

Music is half melody, half rhythm, so never neglect poetry, rhymes and jingles; they are invaluable for developing a sense of rhythm and everyone can cope with poetry, even if they are modest (or immodest) about their singing voices.

Stage 2c: Games with sounds

Dramatic sound effects

Who has *not* had the experience of reading or telling children a story, reaching the point where a sound suggests itself, and somebody well involved in the drama of the situation starts to make that sound? In no time at all everyone is doing it! It is the most natural response and is really a compliment to the story-teller.\But we adults usually tend to quell the sound effects. What a pity! (especially when they are frequently a far better imitation of the sound than we could make ourselves). After all, radio and television could not exist without sound effects, as well the children know, however tiny. Be prepared to allow time for such descriptive sound effects; in fact, use the idea by practising the sounds first, if you like. Keep a lookout for stories which lend themselves to this kind of treatment, and even invent some for yourself.

Other opportunities for using dramatic sound effects occur in puppet plays, songs and poems. Make a note of songs, poems and plays which have a common theme. Once you launch the idea, the children will beat you at your own game.

Illustrated story books are a must for children; so always let them see the pictures as they hear the story. This is invaluable as eye training, especially when it shows a picture of something which produces the sound they are imitating. The process can later be reversed, asking the children to make the noise suggested by the picture.

Stage 3a: Activities with record player

Improvised rhythms

Using knee pats only, get the children to follow you through the changes between slow, quick and very quick sounds; also include silences where the hands flap in the air. Silences are most important to music. For slow sounds, pat both knees; quick sounds are patted on the left knee, very quick sounds on the right knee (thus producing whole-, half-, quarter-beat sounds and one-beat silences). These can be introduced by stories like the 'Lion hunt' (*Juba this and Juba that*, Penguin) and 'One day a little Indian boy' (*This Little Puffin*, Penguin) and by modifications of them; and subsequently practised with recorded music.

Finally, get everyone to make up their own hand dance, mixing slow, quick and very quick sounds and silences. The very quick sounds will not be marvellously performed by the under-fives, but they love to have a try. Later, include the other three body sounds in the improvised hand dance. Improvise means no more than, 'Make it up as you go along'.

Formal rhythms

When you feel that you and the children are ready, introduce the formal rhythms: accent, weak beats, pattern and rhythm ostinato, and keep these in practice alongside the pulsation 'Follow m'leader' games.

Accent. Just as the heartbeat of the music falls regularly, so do the accents or strong beats. A march brings accents on every two or four beats, following the 'left, right' marching pattern:

Two-time: Strong weak Strong weak Strong weak Strong weak
Four-time: Strong weak weak weak Strong weak weak weak

Waltzes have accents on one in every three beats:

Three-time: Strong weak weak Strong weak weak

The music itself will tell you where the accents occur.

So, having got the recorded music playing, begin by getting everyone's arms jigging up and down with thumbs up, to the pulse; then, get everyone counting to the music in threes or fours (I overlook two-time at first, since the quick change from strong to weak beats can be confusing; just call it four-time!).

As soon as everyone can do this, pat the knees on every count of one.

Four-time:	S	w	w	w
	1	2	3	4
	Pat	thumbs	thumbs	thumbs
Three-time:	S	w	w	
	1	2	3	
	Pat	thumbs	thumbs	

Weak beats. This is the complementary game. Get everyone 'flapping their wings' to the pulse; then count in threes or fours (as before). As soon as everyone can do this, flap the wings on every count of one and click the fingers on the weak beats:

Four-time:	S	w	w	w
	1	2	3	4
	Flap	click	click	click
Three-time:	S	w	w	
	1	2	3	
	Flap	click	click	

Combining accent and weak beats. Pat knees on the accent and click fingers for the weak beats, counting aloud all the time. (Click the tongue, too!)

Pattern. You need a vocal record for this game. This involves us in patting on the knees the time pattern, word pattern, syllabic pattern (call it what you will), that is, every syllable of every word of a song or poem. 'Play me every little bit of every word.' It works with simple songs, because there is a new note of melody for every syllable of the lyrics. Many children find this far easier to perform than the pulse, since their hands move on their knees to match the way their lips are moving.

It is possible, even with tiny children, to combine two of these ideas, especially if you have adult leaders for each group. First, set the recorded music going, then try:

A Group 1 performs Pulse
   Group 2 performs Accent
B Group 1 performs Accent and Weak Beats
   Group 2 performs Pattern
C Group 1 performs Pulse
   Group 2 performs Improvised Hand Dance.

Plenty of practice in all these ideas is vital; little and often is the motto and let the practice include improvised hand dances *and* formal patterns.

Rhythm Ostinato. This involves us in playing the syllabic pattern of a word, or short group of words, over and over again with obstinate repetition (*ostinat* is the Italian word for obstinate). One-syllable words produce long sounds, two-syllable words the short ones:

For example, the words: 'cof - fee   tea'
produce the rhythm ostinato: 'short   short   long'

Everything suggested in this section is, of course, transferable to rhythm instruments, both the improvised and the formal rhythms.

Stage 3b: Songs

Song/poetry accompaniment: improvised rhythm

The hand-dance idea (mixing slow, quick, very quick sounds and silences) can also be used to make backings for songs and poems. The four body sounds make an effective backing in their own right, but bear in mind that the improvisation can (and should) be transferred to rhythm instruments, first with random choice, but later on a more selective basis, effects being chosen:

1 According to their suitability for the mood and character of the music and words, e.g.:
Marches: footstamping, drums, gongs, clappers
Quiet rhythmical songs: fingerclicks, jingles, shakers, scrapers
Spanish effect: fingerclicks, handclaps, footstamps, clappers, jingles
Schuplattler effect, as used in Austrian dancing: four body sounds.
2 For their possibility as dramatic sound effects, e.g.:
Drums for soldiers, Red Indians, marches
Gongs for church bells, clock chimes
Jingles for Christmas music, horses, gipsies
Shakers for rain, sea
Clappers for clocks, horses, Spanish music
Scrapers for machines, frogs, crows.

Stage 3c: Games with sounds

Listening to stories and poems on record

This is the direct extension of the games for stage 2. Most often the adult needs to speak to the children before playing the record; she must tell, in her own words, what is to come on the record. Then, during the playing of the record, she will involve the children in active participation: finger play, actions, speech. By contradiction, the children listen more attentively this way than if they just sit with arms folded, though there *are* moments in the day when this, too, is desirable and necessary.

Taped and recorded sounds

Make tape recordings of familiar sounds: indoor noises, outdoor noises, animals, birds. Encourage the children to recognise and imitate all with their voices, together with materials from the music corner. Get hold of sound-effect recordings (there is a whole range of them listed in the BBC record catalogue) and use these for guessing games.

The 'mouth music' can be developed as much as you like. Let the children try some of these ideas:

> *Birds*: Chicken, turkey, sparrow, cock, cuckoo, duck, dove, owl, chaffinch, rook, swan, woodpecker, yellowhammer, seagull, parrot.
> *Animals*: Cat, dog, horse, cow, donkey, sheep, lion, mouse, pig, wolf, monkey, hyena, coyote, snake, goat, giraffe.
> *Humans*: Yawn, snore, hiccough, scream, shout, pant, sigh, hum, sing, sniff, talk, sneeze, blow, munch, sob, gargle, suck, whistle, laugh, giggle, cry, stutter, speak, moan, yell.
> *Outdoor sounds*: Rain, wind, hailstones, thunder, sea.
> *Out of doors machines*: Clock, pneumatic drill, train, dumper, aeroplane, siren, motorcar, motorbike, police car, ambulance, helicopter.
> *Indoor machines*: Telephone, egg whisk, small electric drill, kettle, vacuum cleaner, shaver, sewing machine, dishwasher, spindryer, hair dryer, washing machine, floor polisher, electric toothbrush, TV before programme begins, clock, watch.

Recording sounds

Later, some of the children can make their own tape recordings (this is best done in twos and threes).

Children's own guessing games.

1 Make tape recordings of their own mouth music; finally, use about three examples for others to guess.
2 Similarly, let the children themselves tape some of the sounds around them; again, finally select about three of the best for presentation.

Sound collage. Two children build and tape a sound collage to last about one minute at the most. For example:

They choose two well-contrasted mouth music sounds and arrange them in a little programme:

> (a) Sound A
>   Sound B
>   Sounds A and B together   *or*

(b)   Sounds A and B together
      Sound A
      Sounds A and B together
      Sound B
      Sounds A and B together

Stage 4a: Record player activities

Free movement response

As a start, especially in limited space, the very simplest form of movement response is the old game of musical bumps. For as long as the music plays, the children jump, hop, skip, wave warms, but immediately the music stops they must sit on the floor and not get up again until the music tells them to continue moving.

The next stage is to let every child move in his own way, the call *only* being given by the adult: 'Move your head however you like.' 'Now move your fingers however you like', slowly or quickly, as the music suggests. Finally, every child responds entirely freely to the music, dancing (that is, moving) as the music tells him, making the changes himself between movements of arms, legs, whole body, staying on the spot, moving across the floor and so on.

This freer kind of response presents no problems when children have been encouraged from the start to respond to recorded music; the vocabulary of movement and mime used in the 'Follow m'leader' games gives every child some ideas for response.

All the movement games, besides their musical value, have the incidental bonus of developing the use of the body, gaining control and coordination of the various parts. The games also aim to develop initiative and confidence in trying movement ideas, combining them and using them in various situations, all invaluable assets to be reflected in creativity generally, as the young child develops.

Fundamental movements

With adequate floor space, another form of movement response is by walking, running, skipping, swaying, as suggested by the music.

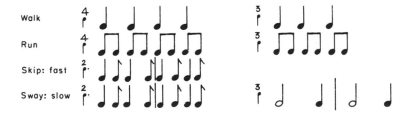

These movements can also be linked with song material, for example:

Walk: Baa baa black sheep
Run: Polly put the kettle on
Skip: The Mulberry Bush
Sway: Hush-a-bye baby

The rhythm of every song suggests one of these movements, so the singing of a song can be followed by its suggested movement; alternatively, the two can be performed simultaneously, the footsteps being underlined by a rhythm instrument, played by the adult leader.

Painting to music

This is a movement–visual game, best done with coloured crayons or felt-tip pens rather than paint. Two large sheets of paper are required for each child (newspaper will do perfectly well), so that there is plenty of space for the resulting art. Choose two well-constrasted pieces of music. For example, very quick/very slow; very smooth/very jerky; or very loud/very soft.

Play item one while the children scribble-draw all over sheet one, then change to sheet two for the second item. Compare the results for colour, shape, texture. Keep the best of these, and later use them as picture music, getting the children to play on their home-made instruments in the manner suggested by each of the pictures.

The children can also try making pictorial illustrations of sound effects as they listen to them played on recordings. This is admittedly a more challenging exercise: trying to make a picture of the *sound*, as distinct from the *object* which makes it.

Singing games

These are the oldest and most well-tried form of movement, linking singing with dancing; they are marvellous inasmuch as the voices tell the body what to do. Valuable, too, as communal and social activities, they survived for years as adult party games, before ballroom dancing took over.

Although these are ultimately best performed without instrumental accompaniment, you may well find the record player motivates everybody very well to start with, and leaves you (the adult) free to lead proceedings from the movement point of view, until you are launched.

Band conducting

When everyone in the group can manage to play a home-made instrument, one of the hardest things to do is stop! Re-apply the musical bumps idea to instruments, everyone stopping and starting with the music.

Another game for developing control is band conducting, where the children follow a visual signal. At first, the conductor is an adult, but later individual children can take it in turn to lead. First, set the music going. When the conductor waves hands above the head, everyone plays; when the hands go behind the back, everyone stops.

The next development is to have two groups of players, one following the waving of the conductor's right hand, the other following the left. There are thus four possibilities: (a) right-hand group plays alone; (b) left-hand group plays alone; (c) both groups play together; (d) both groups silent. With large groups of children, the band can be divided into four groups, but this is very demanding on the conductor!

Stage 4b: Songs

Song/poetry accompaniment: formal rhythms

Take the formal rhythms of pulse, accent, weak beats, pattern (learned in stage 3 as activities with record player) and, as soon as possible, perform them with body sounds during the singing of songs, each child singing and moving at the same time. It is not difficult. However, the rhythm ostinato is *very* difficult to do at the same time as you sing; better, by far, to delegate it to a small group of children to maintain as the backing (i.e. accompaniment) to the song or poem being performed by the rest of the children. For example, a small group speaks the rhythm ostinato 'Coffee tea', meanwhile patting on the knees the syllabic pattern. The rest of the children concentrate on singing or saying the rhythm, 'Polly put the kettle on'. The next vital step forward is to transfer the formal rhythms to rhythm (non-pitch) instruments.

Song accompaniment with chime bars

The formal rhythms can also be used on a single chime bar to make a drone-note accompaniment to absolutely any song. The best choice is usually the final note of the song; alternatively, five steps up from there, or a combination of the two. Example: 'Polly put the kettle on' – final note G (alternatively D, or G and D together).

Stage 4c: Games with sounds

Create stories with sounds

Having experimented with sounds, added sounds to existing material, listened to recordings of sound effects and stories with sound effects, it is high time (if it has not happened already) to make up some stories of your own, getting the children to help.

The plot should be very simple indeed: just a beginning, a middle and an ending. The middle is the place for the happening or happenings; aim at first for one happening, then later two, and certainly never more than three. This puts a tight limit on the budget of ideas and concentrations. This activity is best tackled, initially anyway, very informally with a small group of three or four likely customers.

The bonus, of course, is for the children to illustrate the characters and events in the story. The adult must be extremely careful not to reject pictures simply because they in no way compare with the commercially produced illustrations you have been enjoying together. Pictorial illustration is an important part of rudimentary ear-and-eye training, and should be encouraged regularly.

Wall charts

Another easy way of linking ear and eye is to construct charts and big picture books of creatures and objects associated with pitch, volume, speed and musical 'colour'. This is probably best done by producing pairs of large wall pictorial charts with the children's own illustrations, each picture clearly labelled with its name. For example: high and low sounds; loud and soft sounds; quick and slow sounds; quick and slow moving creatures/objects; sounds I like/sounds I dislike. Other charts to show 'colour': crackling sounds; tearing; watery; scraping. Later, the charts can be used for 'reading', that is, for recognising each picture and reproducing the sound it makes. Another popular venture is to think about the five senses and produce appropriate wall charts.

Pictorial notation

The rudimentary notation can now well be extended to link with the listen and move activities of stages 1–3.

From Stage 1a. Instead of the adult leader performing in front of the children for body movement activities, she points to a wall chart (or blackboard) to indicate which *part* of the body is to be moved (children's free choice of actual movement). A vocabulary of about four ideas is ample. The same applies to mime. For example, the pictorial chart could show:

Carpenter's saw	Boat
Toothbrush	Teacup and saucer

As the leader points to the different pictures, the children perform the mime suggested.

From Stage 2a. The body sounds should be illustrated vertically:

Finger click
Hand clap
Knee pat
Foot stamp

by picture, diagram or secret sign; use a different system each time you play the game; sometimes mix the three ideas and as soon as possible use the children's ideas and illustrations. In performance, the teacher works as in stage 2, but pointing on the chart instead of performing. It is a good moment now for working more at the repeated patterns (the rhythm ostinatos) of four beats and splitting them in a variety of ways:

$$2 + 2 \qquad = \left\{ \begin{array}{l} 2 \text{ claps } + 2 \text{ stamps} \\ 2 \text{ clicks } + 2 \text{ claps} \end{array} \right.$$

$$2 + 1 + 1 \quad = \left\{ \begin{array}{l} 2 \text{ stamps } + 1 \text{ pat } + 1 \text{ clap} \\ 2 \text{ pats } + 1 \text{ clap } + 1 \text{ click} \end{array} \right.$$

Another visual representation, e.g. $1 + 1 + 1 + 1$ could be performed as follows:

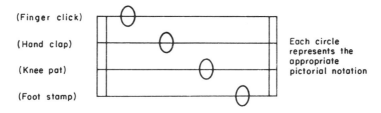

(Finger click)
(Hand clap)
(Knee pat)
(Foot stamp)

Each circle represents the appropriate pictorial notation

From stage 3a. Using knee pats only, get the children to follow your pointing instead of your performance, mixing slow, quick, very quick sounds and silences. Again, it is probably best to illustrate these vertically, inasmuch as eventually the visual aids can show the relationship between whole-, half- and quarter-beat sounds and one-beat silences. Think of animals or objects which move in these different ways.

Notational equivalent	*Speed*	*Examples for pictorial notation*
♩	slow	snail, tortoise, chameleon
♫	quick	trotting horse, trotting dog
♬	very quick	greyhound, ostrich, cheetah
𝄽	silence	owl flying, snake, animal paws

The game is best performed with knee pats *only*, since it is very difficult to perform the very quick sounds with the other body sounds.

J

Illustrations for formal rhythms are probably best done on a basis of small, medium, large sizes of something associated with the lyrics; the illustration for silence should be associated, likewise, with the lyrics. They should be arranged in lines of three or four pictures, as the music indicates.

For example: 'Baa, baa black sheep' (four-time).
Sounds are shown pictorially by sheep, lambs and tufts of grass.

Pulse	4 medium-size sheep	
Accent	1 sheep + 3 tufts	
Weak beats	1 tuft + 3 lambs	
Accent + weak beats	1 sheep + 3 lambs	
Rhythm ostinato	1 sheep + 4 lambs (2 are very tiny!)	One for the ma — ster

Rhythm ostinatos can, of course, also be pictorially associated with their performance as song accompaniments. The first line of the lyrics can serve as a long rhythm ostinato:

Baa,   baa   black   sheep, have you a –ny wool -------?

Rhythm ostinato games

More important by far, at this stage, is the business of actually performing these games with the use of speech, body sounds and instruments to develop the feeling for pulsation and the vocabulary of short phrases. In addition to their use as an accompaniment device, we can play all kinds of little games with words and short phrases. Take a theme, e.g. the names of people, animals, fruits, flowers, sweets, breakfast cereals, places, cars, football teams, pop groups, railway stations, etc.; the titles of songs, poems, stories; or short phrases like sayings, proverbs, football yells. The theme should spring from its association with a topical event, the adult using the children's contributions. For example, using the names of the children:

Group 1

Bil–ly   Smith
short short   long

Group 2

Val– er –ie   Plun·kett
2 very short short   short short

The teacher conducts with right hand waving for group 1, left hand for group 2, and both hands for combined performance; sometimes the groups perform individually, sometimes together. The rhythm ostinatos can be performed:

1 Speech only.
2 Add body sounds performing the syllabic pattern.
3 Add rhythm instruments performing the syllabic pattern.
4 Perform on chime bars: (a) one note, (b) two notes, (c) three or more notes.

If you prefer, this can all be done against a background of recorded music.

Melody making

Most of the melodic work with the under-fives is concerned with the singing of jingles and rhymes caught from recorded and live voices. As and when possible, the chime bars can be introduced as drone-note accompaniments, and the more ambitious adults may like to introduce melody ostinato accompaniments, even if they only perform these themselves.

Certainly, if funds will stretch, some chime bars should be available to children in the music corner. They make a delightful, pitched sound, in direct contrast to the rhythm effects. Put out five which make the pentatonic scale starting on C: C D E   G A and the children cannot fail to produce a pleasing combination of sounds. They can (a) freely doodle tunes for marching, running, skipping, swaying; (b) play rhythm ostinatos on any choice of sounds; (c) invent new tunes to familiar rhymes by playing the time pattern on to these five sounds. For the musically precocious children, at least, this provision should be available whenever possible.

Stage 5a: Activities with Record Player

Word games

Much beneficial vocabulary work can be done by taking a topic and getting children to play word games by collecting together all words of one, two, three or four syllables, then grouping these to make rhythm ostinato accompaniments for poems, songs and recorded music. The one-syllable words match exactly each pulse of the music, while the two-, three- and four-syllable words fit *over* the basic pulse. For example, taking the topic 'trees':

one syllable	oak
two syllables	willow
three syllables	sycamore, crab-apple
four syllables	elderberry

Any one of these words can be used for a one-word ostinato, while any combination can be used for a two-, three- or four-word ostinato, for example:

> Two-word ostinato: willow, sycamore
> Three-word ostinato: oak, sycamore, willow
> Four-word ostinato (used separately or combined):
> (a)   elderberry : willow   : crab-apple : oak
> (b)   oak   : oak   : willow   : sycamore

Echo games

The leader (teacher or child) performs a rhythm ostinato once and immediately the class echoes. This process is repeated, each time with a new ostinato. It can be performed with any rhythm effects, against an accompaniment of recorded music or completely unaccompanied.

Stage 5b: Songs

Accompaniments using chime bars

If rhythm ideas are aimed at developing an awareness of 'sounds around', then melody ideas must aim at developing consciousness of pitch: the height and depth, the rise and fall of sounds (Dankworth, 1973). The simple formal accompaniment techniques of drone, melody ostinato, bass line and melody doubling can be performed by any number of children on any instrument and played at any octave: they are virtually all playing the same thing at the same time, their parts being learned in the quickest possible way, often initially by rote and memorised with the help of any visual aid the teacher and children can devise, such as a blackboard, chart or notebook summary.

To each of these ideas, of course, may be added some of the rhythm backing ideas and movement too. Percussion instruments, both rhythm and melody, should be made available on the music table or in the music corner, where the children can practise, prepare and experiment. Several rhythm ostinatos can be combined to make an effective accompaniment to a song or poem, the words being derived from the subject of the lyrics, or indeed, actually using parts of the lyrics.

Five-note (pentatonic) tunes are useful for part-singing/playing. The five notes are actually the first, second, third, fifth and sixth degrees of the major scale:

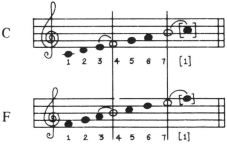

The pentatonic scale contains no semitones, and for this reason any pentatonic tune can be performed canonically, at any distance apart and in any number of parts, accepting, of course, that some tunes sound more effective than others treated in this way.

All pentatonic tunes can be successfully accompanied by drone-notes, and 'do-it-yourself' melody ostinato backings can be devised from tune extracts or random choice of notes used in the line.

Certainly at this stage, if not before, staff notation should be used to show an exact picture of what the children have learned by rote. This measures up precisely with the 'look and say' method of reading (see chapter 11) where the reader sees the word/s for familiar objects and phrases, and later has to recognise them in new contexts. Furthermore, a freely improvised 'doodling' on these fives notes (mixing slow, quick, very quick sounds and silences) produces a truly improvised backing comparable with a freely improvised rhythm backing.

Stage 5c: Games with sounds

Notation–rhythm

Having worked on the idea of pictorial notation, it is not too long before the need for a common symbolic system becomes obvious, and the universal rhythm notation is quickly assimilated.

As soon as the children are ready, French time names can be used as an abstraction of the colloquial words used so far; but for some children the everyday words remain more meaningful, and the teacher should always be prepared to move between the two methods. Somervell rhythm shorthand is also an extremely useful first step towards full notation, for example:

Remember, word patterns should be built around any topic of current interest to the children.

Sounds lasting more than one beat ever remain a challenge when you use colloquial words, because a particular one-syllable word must be agreed upon to represent the sound which is longer than all other one-syllable words.

whereas the French time names get round the problem very neatly:

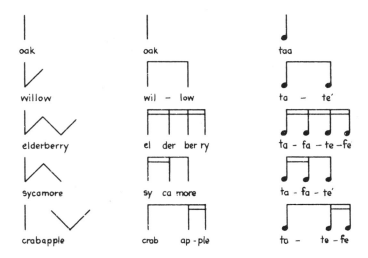

Development from the rote-playing of one-, two-, three- and four-syllable words (see stage 5a) can be in the form of rhythm notation, now linked with whole, half and quarter divisions of the beat, for example:

oak

oak

taa

willow

wil – low

ta – te′

elderberry

el der ber ry

ta – fa – te – fe′

sycamore

sy ca more

ta – fa – te′

crabapple

crab ap – ple

ta – te – fe

Set the recorded music going. The teacher points to each word in turn, first indicating four repetitions of each word; then two repetitions; then once only. Meanwhile, the children speak the pointed words and knee pat the syllabic pattern. Finally, the teacher dodges from one word to another, always moving the pointer slightly ahead of the pulse beat.

Rhythm ostinatos can then be built from these words by the children and practised in the same way:

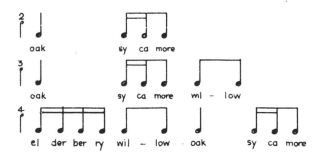

Another presentation:

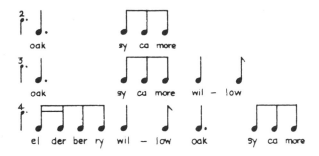

The final test: write several bars of time pattern utilising the units practised, and get the children to recognise and read them in the new context.

Notation–melody

The beginning stages of developing pitch consciousness (whatever the age of the children) are surely in the recognition of widely differentiated high and low, then high, low and middle pitch sounds; the smaller children can show their recognition in movement, the older ones by use of hands. This leads naturally onto the use of the hand moving up and down to show higher and lower sounds in a melody, making 'in the air' a tune ladder, the teacher leading, the children copying; this technique is especially useful in the teaching and learning of a song. Ultimately, the children should be able to do these movements with eyes closed, showing their conscious memorisation of height and depth, rise and fall of sounds.

It is then an easy step to tune shapes, where a broken or continuous line indicates the approximate rise and fall of a melody, making a rough graph or diagram. The line can be drawn in the air, on a blackboard, chart or paper. The character of the tune determines whether the line is broken or continuous. Children can be encouraged to draw their own tune shapes.

Staff notation is an exact picture of the music. A line represents a sound. Small characteristic tune extracts (tune snaps), stepwise and leaping, are a most useful introduction to melody reading, especially the opening and final phrases of songs and tunes familiar to the children.

Currently popular signature tunes of radio and television programmes, together with commercial jingles, can be transcribed and written on wall charts for the children to follow, recognise and even play on their recorders, if the key is suitable.

All this kind of work, done regularly and often, springing from the song and listening material in hand, gives children a very real awareness of the link-up between seeing, hearing and doing. The staff notation learned in this way can immediately be given letters names and/or tonic solfa names, and

Tune shapes showing pitch and duration

Staff Notation

a) Solfa (Singing Names)

b) Letters (Playing Names)

linked with the work of Dalcroze, Kodály and Orff, according to the interest and experience of the teacher.

The notes used in such tune extracts can then be arranged in a different order, and used for reading practice, thus calling upon recognition of known material in a new context. It is all a matter of moving from approximation and guessing to exactitude, and if teachers bypass the duty of teaching their pupils to read and write, the dots will remain a secret to their pupils, who will ultimately be reliant, for ever, upon rote learning.

Music corner: individual and group assignments

Experiments in pitch can be made by the children (as a class or in groups) with different vibrating lengths: pluck a rubberband stretched to varying lengths, make a one-string fiddle and pluck it with finger-stopping, fill a bottle to various levels and blow across the mouth of the bottle and so on.

Pentatonic tunes are useful for the discovery and learning of melodies because they are based on the limitation of five notes instead of the customary seven of a major or minor melody. Recorder tutors offer a good repertoire of tunes using three or four notes only. If the children are going to pick these out for themselves, it is worth considering doing this in stages; tell them or give them the notes/bars used in the melody and (a) the starting note; (b) the finishing note; (c) no further clues.

The 'Aladdin' game is to play on pentatonic bars the time patterns of familiar tunes, thus producing 'new tunes for old'. At first this amounts to little more than random selection, but eventually, with further practice in the music corner, some children learn to be very selective about which sequence of sounds is the most effective and satisfying. Some even find the five-note scale too limiting, and demand all seven notes and more!

The pentatonic approach is, recognisably, the principle used as the basis of Carl Orff's system of music teaching, and melodies built in this way have the added advantage of being easily and effectively accompanied by drone-note/s combined with rhythm and melody ostinati (in Schott's *Music for Children*, Book I, there are many examples of the type which can be invented). Once the pentatonic principle is launched on pitch percussion, other melody instruments can be incorporated; the idea makes children very ready, willing and able to do improvisation and original composition as individual and group assignments which may even include composing poems too.

Conclusion

The imaginative and emotional outlet of participating in movement and informal singing is, in itself, a vitally important reason for including it in the programme for under-eights, possible budding musical talent may be frustrated if we fail to encourage it at the grass roots level of sing, play, listen, move, create, notate. Above all, there is the spontaneous enthusiasm, involvement and fun of it all, to be enjoyed as a personal and social experience. Refuse the invitation to make music, and we deny ourselves and our children this supreme pleasure. Don't forget: making music *is* the child's natural heritage.

References

Dankworth, A. (1973) *Voices and Instruments*. London: Hart Davis.

Dankworth, A. and Priestley, L. (1973) *Make Music Fun*. (Available from A. Dankworth, 56 Station Road, Long Marston, Tring, Herts.)

Matterson, E. M. (ed.) *This Little Puffin: Finger Plays and Nursery Games*. Harmondsworth: Penguin.

Further Reading

Ainsworth, R. (1969) *Look, Do and Listen*. London: Heinemann.

Chatterley, A. (1969) *70 Simple Songs with Ostinato*. London: Novello.

Fletcher, M. I. and Denison, M. C. (1950) *The High Road of Song*. London: Warne.

Shephard, M. (1973) *Playgroup Music*. London: PPA.

Shephard, M. (1982) *Music with Mum*. London: Allen and Unwin.

Southam, W. (1967) *Play Songs*. London: Feldman/EMI.

Wiseman, H. and Northcote, S. (1957) *The Clarendon Book of Singing Games*, vols. I and II. London: Oxford University Press.

15

Learning and Teaching Art and Craft Skills

HENRY PLUCKROSE

The need to create

In recent years it has become fashionable for anthropologists and zoologists to present learned papers on the similarity of man and ape. From these studies much useful material has resulted. We know, for example, that young chimpanzees learn through play. We know that they possess a high degree of intelligence, can communicate through sounds and bodily postures, and can solve simple problems. However, research has also highlighted the divide which separates man and ape. One of the most significant differences, in my opinion, is that man can communicate in line and the ape (despite many attempts by researchers to prove otherwise) cannot.

From earliest times man has been a maker of marks. Wherever we find evidence of man – in China, in southern Europe, in Central America, in the Middle East, in the Pacific Islands – we find evidence that he was an artist. The whorls and spirals in the burial caves at Paola (Malta) and on the stone monuments in Anglesey might suggest to some scholars that such definitive mark making had a deep religious significance; for me, on a less intellectual level, it confirms my belief that man needs to make marks, to pattern and to fashion the artefacts of his everyday life.

To appreciate the power of this innate drive we have only to watch a three-year-old at play. With equal facility he can construct a car or an aircraft from commercially produced wooden blocks or from junk. His imagination overrides the restrictions imposed by space, time or by the materials that are available. He constructs because he has to.

As teachers and parents we can, of course, deepen and extend construc-tional play during the early years of childhood by ensuring that a range of tactile material is available. Paints and crayons, chalks and pastels, card, scissors, glues and adhesive tape will allow imaginative physical play to be extended so that the child's own constructions can be naturally incorporated into it. Thus John, building a station with wooden blocks, might well demand to make a train . . . and a toilet roll mounted on cotton reels is for John just as real a train as one purchased from a school supplier. Indeed, it probably has greater significance; he made it himself.

With just as much intensity the young child makes marks. The paintings of the nursery school child are invariably creations of the moment, immediate and intense. They often change in content as they are being worked; a picture which began as a fire engine ends up as a roadside crash, or a princess ends up as 'my Mummy'. At this stage the concentration span is often brief, the handling of the paint and the making the marks having greater appeal than the finished picture. Thus the making of the marks seems to have more significance than what the marks say to the onlooker (a characteristic which does not apply to eight- and nine-year-olds).

Mark making, which might be repeated several times during one school day and many times during one school week, helps children to develop manipulative skills. It also develops their ability to communicate through marks which other people can appreciate and understand. The scribble made by a two-year-old in paint and called 'Daddy' is undoubtedly a human response to a human need. The three- or four-year-old will not bother whether his 'pictures' are appreciated by his fellows. They are individual and personal. As he moves through the infant school, however, picture making tends to become more representational, the marks more identifiable, the desire for his peers to understand his picture more pronounced.

This period of growth deserves careful and sympathetic handling by all the adults in the child's life. The need to decorate is innate and the role of the adults will be largely supportive. Not every child will handle paints easily; for some wax crayons provide a better alternative, for others felt pens or chalk. Some children will find painting with large brushes (size 12) on newsprint the most satisfying method of making a picture; others will prefer to use fine brushes (size 4) on small sheets of coloured paper. As each individual is unique, possessing specific gifts, the teacher has to try to provide as wide a range of art orientated activities as possible to ensure that each member of the group has the opportunity to discover what his particular gifts are.

It is this variety of approach that many teachers find most difficult to handle. A class of seven-year-olds will have within it some children who emotionally, intellectually and manipulatively function little better than four-year-olds. These children will be living and working alongside children who possess ability beyond their years as well as those whom we could describe as typical of their age group. To meet the needs of all these children in the confines of one classroom and in all areas of the curriculum is a daunting task. In the visual arts a partial solution is to provide a variety of activities each week (e.g. painting, printing, collage, dyeing, junk model making, clay, woodwork) so that each child can respond to a selected activity at his own level.

Let me illustrate this with a specific example. Let us assume that puppets are being made, perhaps as a follow-up activity to a performance given in school by adult puppeteers or with the specific aim of developing spoken English. The gifted seven-year-old could be shown how to build a glove puppet on a Plasticine core, while other less capable children are making stick puppets with paper plates or 'sock' puppets from paper bags. Each child will grow from his involvement with the materials; each child will be able to contribute something to the group activity which follows upon it; each child will be challenged to give neither more nor less than that which might be expected of him (and which he expects of himself).

Just as we should recognise that there will be a different level of response from individual children engaged in any group activity (be they of nursery or infant age), it is also important to appreciate that each child needs to feel that his skills are being developed and extended, that he is learning.

Thus art practice in the early years needs to encompass variety and growth. The nursery child who has printed with a vegetable requires of us that printmaking is continually extended in the years that follow. Wood, paper, card, fabric, leaves, hands, lino, plaster can all be used to produce an image. By the time the child is seven this principle should be so well established that in the years that follow printmaking is seen not in terms of 'what shall I use?' but 'what will best give me the effect I require?'

I am here suggesting that the early years of childhood should involve developing awareness, not the mastery of sophisticated techniques and skills. This can only be done by helping each child relate the process which he has mastered to the ones which follow upon it. Again, let me clarify this by an example. Athough most six- and seven-year-olds can easily cope with paper batik (a wax paper picture cracked and charged with dye), the children would be helped to understand the process by first attempting simple wax resist (or candle pictures). Development in the presentation of experience is as vital in the arts as it is in the mastery of mathematics or reading.

However, whilst the teacher of nursery and infant children needs to have some idea of the direction in which the art activities might move, she must also allow for those moments of spontaneous response which are characteristic of the young child. There will always be at least one child in a class who needs to 'paint out' a fear, a tension or an experience. As maturity is reached such tensions are often resolved through words (spoken or written) or through considered action. For the very young, for whom these avenues are closed, symbols often take the place of words.

The teacher therefore has to satisfy a number of needs at a variety of levels. The need for experiment and experience has to be set against the need for spontaneity; the development of skills against the response which individual children make to specific materials. All of these factors have to be considered against the various abilities and disabilities of the children who comprise the group undertaking the art programme.

The teacher can best meet these contrasting (and perhaps conflicting) needs by providing art experience both as an individual and as a group activity. Individual experience (be this in clay, collage or paint) is there for children who (for whatever the reason) just want to create. Individual experience allows for consolidation of activities that have gone before (e.g. printmaking), for experimenting with new materials (e.g. a collage from leaves and found objects), as well as providing support for the tense, the withdrawn and the isolate. Group experience, where the teacher takes a leading role, gives the opportunity to create situations which enable children to learn how materials behave as well as to develop ideas which have been thrown up in other areas of the curriculum (e.g. a visit to the local market might well result in making a group model or a large wall frieze).

Group activities, of course, are more appropriate to children of infant age than to nursery school children. The nursery school child is very much of an individualist, working and playing in the company of other children but not necessarily with them. The five- and six-year-old is independent, but is prepared to share and contribute towards a known and understood end. By seven, social development should be such that group activities, to which all the children contribute, are an accepted and integral part of the school day.

With so much emphasis upon individual response to materials, with the feeling amongst many educationists that a chid 'plays with materials and thereby learns them', it would be excusable for the teacher to regard her role as largely passive: a provider rather than an initiator, one who watches rather than one who does. This would be to undervalue and to underplay her role. It would also suggest that she misunderstood her function.

Art education also involves developing the senses through looking, touching, listening, smelling and even tasting. Thus young children must be helped to look at their world: at the colours of the countryside, the patterns of bricks, slate and stone. They must be helped to appreciate the texture of different surfaces, to assimilate through all their senses the peculiar qualities of the things that surround them. Sometimes this will involve taking groups out of school. Feeding the ducks (and noting the shape of their heads and the colours of their plumage) can be just as much an art experience for a four-year-old as is a visit to a toy museum for his seven-year-old brother. The sensitive teacher will draw upon such visits so that activities within the classroom bear some relationship to the world outside its walls.

At the same time an effort should be made to bring the outside world into school. Displays of interesting objects, natural and man made, should be mounted throughout the school. The language which will flow from handling them is not necessarily the language of art, but mastery of words (and an appreciation of what they mean) will help deepen the child's sensitivity to such things as colour, pattern, texture and shape.

In writing this chapter, I am conscious that I have not defined activities and approaches as perhaps was expected of me. It is not easy in the years from three to seven to define stages in art and craft. The three-year-old would see himself as a worker, a maker, a doer. So would his five-year-old sister and seven-year-old brother. What the teacher has to do is to create a climate in which making and doing can flourish, however mature the child, however gifted, however diffident, however slow.

Essentially what is required of the adult is that she respects each child's work, handling storing and displaying it with thought and care. Time must be made to allow children to finish their pictures and their models for it is impossible to be creative when the clock (or the timetable) is the determining factor. As adults we feel the tensions which grow when we work against time. For children, such tensions are just as real, particularly as their paintings and their plays are, for them, their 'work', their reality.

The visual arts play a vital part in the education of the young child because they form a bridge, unifying the child's direct experience of the world and the symbolism of the written word, science and mathematics. But art practice is more than just this. It links the child across time, drawing upon instincts which are as old as man himself. 'The first picture,' observed Leonardo, 'was nothing but a line which surrounded the shadow of a man made by the sun upon the wall.' Through art, the young child explores and, using techniques as old as civilisation, comments upon himself and his world.

Successful art practice helps prevent our schools from becoming places where technique and subject content dominate childhood. Where children are encouraged to express themselves freely in paint and paper, clay and card, a curriculum which hitherto had been somewhat mean, meagre and mechanical will begin to flower, and with it the children and the teachers with whom they work.

Art with young children is not simply about method. It is also about the quality of life in the classroom, in the school and in the world beyond. Through the purposeful coordination of eye, hand and brain, it enables the child to express those qualities which make him human – and totally separate him from the higher apes.

Organisation of the classroom

Let me now turn to the more practical aspects of art activities with young children. First, we must decide what type of activity will best fit into the limits imposed by the size, abilities and interests of our group and the space we have available (both for working and storage). Then we should decide how we propose to organise the activity: as group work (four or five children) or with each child working individually. For some activities (e.g. painting with heated wax crayon), group work under the guidance of an adult is essential for success and safety; for others (e.g. paper and fabric collage), a child could be encouraged to work alone.

Secondly, we must make sure that the activities we let the children attempt are within their capabilities. A newly qualified teacher can only learn this from experience and by watching and listening to more experienced colleagues. Thus, whereas printing on fabric often succeeds with children of junior age, it will largely end in frustration for the child in the infant school.

Another important fact to remember is that all the materials necessary for the activity in hand must be readily available. To start on wax and wash work without preparing the stain to be applied over the wax is to court disaster. If children are working on individual activities, make sure that they know where materials are stored. Brushes in different sizes, charcoal, papers, scissors and paints should be readily available for the children's use. Part of the art lesson's value lies not only in the work produced but in the care of tools and materials.

When working at any craft – whether modelling or painting – try to see that each child enjoys what he is doing and wants to do it. For me, this means trying to fit the task to the child. A child who enjoys working on small sketches in crayon is encouraged to follow this bent, while his more extrovert classmate may well be doing bold murals in another part of the room. This means that, on the whole, children produce better work because they have given more time to the medium of their choice. Nevertheless, we must be sure to give our children a variety of experiences so that they can discover what they like doing best.

Try to organise the lesson so that the activity fills the time available. It is not satisfactory for the children to be torn away from something in which they are engrossed because the timetable demands it. The larger the block of time you have available for some craft activities, the more successful will be the finished work.

Finally, there is one other factor which is often overlooked. Children sometimes fail with their work because the size of the material on which they are working is wrong. At times, the teacher needs to encourage the child to work on a larger scale. On other occasions, the child's idea may be too ambitious to succeed. If this is the case, the teacher may have to intervene and suggest other media for the work in hand.

In practice, all this means is that the teacher's role is continually to vary the tools and materials which are made available to the group (see below). In addition to painting equipment (which should always be available), tables could be prepared for some of the following activities: dry colour (e.g. pastels, chalks), clay, junk modelling, collage, resist techniques, print making, constructions with wood, wire or found materials. The alternatives given at any one time should not be too extensive; the aim is not to so excite the children with possible activities that none is undertaken.

Even young children should be encouraged to complete that which they begin, although it must be stressed that we are not trying to produce works of art but to help each child discover something of the nature of materials. When the teacher feels that a child has not fully explored the possibilities of the activity at a level appropriate to him, then she should guide him towards that fuller understanding, by demonstrating, by encouragement and by individual attention.

As Gombrich suggests in *The Story of Art* (Phaidon), 'There is no such thing as Art. There are only artists.' If we, the teachers, could remember this and respect the personality and individuality of each child, then we will see children as *artists* involved in a voyage of discovery and a flowering of personality. There is no telling what riches they may gain from such an experience.

Materials and tools

Colouring materials. Paints, e.g. poster colour, water colour (tubes and blocks), powder colour, oil colour, polymer acrylic paint, stains, dyes. Pastels, e.g. oil pastels and oil crayons, chalk, wax crayons.

Drawing materials. Lead pencils, ink (black and white), charcoal sticks and pencils, felt- and fibre-tipped pens, coloured pencils, coloured inks.

Paper. Sugar, cartridge, pastel, tissue, crêpe, cellophane, kitchen, newsprint, metallic, transparent and sticky: in as wide a range of colours as possible.

Card. Strawboard, manilla board, cardboard – smooth and corrugated.

Fastenings. Pins, tacks, nails, paper clips, coldwater paste, balsa cement, impact adhesives, gum, acrylic resin, Sellotape, masking tape, brown sticky paper.

Cloth and fabric scraps. Felt, rick-rack, braid, thread, crash, imitation linen, cotton, Vilene, velvet, needlecord, net curtaining, towelling, ribbon, wool, tape.

Other materials. Polystyrene blocks and tiles, metal foil, candles, Plasticine, wire, plaster, flour, cement, wood offcuts, dowelling, nails, tacks, screws, cottons, lino and other floor coverings.

Natural materials. Chalk and sandstone for carving, sand, clay, cane, raffia, rushes, raw wool, fruits and seeds, twigs and bark, feathers, scraps of weathered wood, stones and pebbles, shells.

'Junk' materials

In addition to the scrap materials listed, the class should be encouraged to bring a wide variety of 'junk' to school. Plastic detergent bottles, scouring powder packets, matchboxes, packing straw, egg trays, wood and plastic offcuts, pipe cleaners and chicken wire scraps can all be used for experimental craft activities. I find the following 'junk' materials particularly useful: raffia, packing straw, string, sweet wrappers, cotton, rug wool, hair, wood shavings, newspapers and magazines, old cardboard boxes, card strips, wallpapers, sandpapers, fabric and leather scraps, cotton reels, matchboxes, card tubes, drinking straws, cotton wool, feathers, silver paper, foil, corrugated card and papers, 18-gauge wire.

Storage of this material is often the most difficult problem the teacher has to face. Small rooms, large classes and restricted cupboard and shelf space mean that either the teacher has to improvise or the children have to go without valuable creative experience. The tea-chest or large cardboard box in which all this material is haphazardly dumped is one solution. This does not, however, develop a respect for materials in the children, neither does it encourage them to be tidy. If there is some shelf space available, the most successful method is to have a series of cardboard boxes, each clearly labelled to show the contents, e.g. wire scraps; glues; fabric oddments; string; cotton and wool; wood offcuts; nails; pins; screws and eyehooks. It is also possible to store material in bags hung on the sides of cupboards, either in carrier bags or in wall-pockets made from hessian.

Tools

For teacher's use: shears, punch, sharp craft knife, guillotine, awl, wire-cutters, electric glue pot, wall staple gun, range of woodwork tools – saw, hammer, screwdriver – electric iron.

For children: small scissors suitable for cutting paper and cloth, needles (large eyes), metal rulers, hammer, pliers, brushes in a variety of sizes (2 to 16) palette knives, lino-printing rollers.

Further Reading

Marshall, S. (1970) *Aspects of Art Work*. London: Evans.
Pluckrose, H. A. (1972) *Art*. London: MacMillan.
Pluckrose, H. A. (1978) *A Source Book of Picture Making*. London: Evans.
Read, H. (1958) *Education through Art*. London: Faber.
See also the *Introducing* series published by B. T. Batsford (London), which covers a wide range of basic art techniques, and *Art and Craft in Education* (published monthly; London: Evans).

16

Understanding and Encouraging Children's Play

ALICE YARDLEY

The nature of play

At any stage in life, being caught up in something more important than oneself, merely for its own sake and free of obligation, is a most refreshing experience. Such experience, so hard to come by in adult life, is how the child at play spends most of his energy and time.

The spontaneous play of early childhood involves the child completely, and he invests all of his faculties and resources in pursuit of it. As a result, play becomes an act of concentration at times so completely absorbing as to render the child oblivious to all else. Play is also developmental, and from babyhood to maturity it follows a pattern as clearly defined as any other aspect of the child's development. It is, moreover, orchestrated in relation to all other developmental patterns, and what affects the child's play experiences affects his total growth.

Studies of play emphasise its essential nature; the child's play needs are no less important than his need for food and love and shelter. The young of many animals play, and there is a firm connection between the length of the play period, its range and quality, and the intelligence of the animal. Kittens and puppies play, so do foals and lambs, but it would be difficult to decide whether young worms play or not.

Movement is one of the first signs of life. It occurs long before the individual is born, and remains an essential characteristic of his person until the day of death. The child moves because he must, and we expect him to move vigorously and continuously during his waking hours. Even during sleep, movement continues both inside and outside the body.

In the earliest stages of life movement is often involuntary and random. Even so, it brings the child into contact with his environment, and stimulated movements of a more intentional nature begin to fuse with involuntary activity. Watching the baby, we notice how growing control of the muscles which activate his head and arms leads to his noticing people and objects, followed by attempts to grasp and hold them. Such casual encounter does not satisfy the curious infant, and movements of an exploratory nature soon follow. Play has begun. It brings pleasure and satisfaction which reinforce the child's efforts to investigate the unfamiliar until he makes some sense of it (Yardley, 1970a). Under favourable circumstances, the tool of play will continue to serve the child as he learns to live by playing at living. It is through his play that we know the child really lives.

It seems astonishing in view of these readily observable facts that the child's need to play has so often to be justified. The child does not need to prove why he breathes and eats, yet as he grows older his need to move and to play are frequently questioned by those adults who seem to think that learning is a transformation which takes place 'only in the head'. Sometimes parents and even teachers are difficult to convince, and the way they talk about play provides many clues as to the concept they hold of it. 'I give him a piece of pastry dough to play with,' says one mother, 'because it keeps him quiet.' 'Can't you find something to play with?' a father complains to his son, 'You're forever under my feet when I'm at home.' One infant teacher explained, 'They come into my class from the nursery, and the first thing they have to learn is that there is more to school than playing all day.' The trouble does not lie so much in what these adults expect children to do, as in the ideas to which they apply the label of play. The concept of play has a long and interesting history which has its roots in the early origins of man.

Attitudes to play

Before the invention of writing, education was the responsibility of the adults who reared the child, and it took place mainly in the home where the child learned by experience and imitation what would fit him for the life he would be expected to lead as an adult. Once man learned how to write, teaching demanded skills which were beyond those the home could provide. Thereafter, education became increasingly divorced from the life the child experienced outside school, and it is only in recent times that the aridity of a purely academic education has been brought into question.

Great educators through the ages have been mindful of play, though sometimes their conception of it differed widely from that of modern educators. Plato saw play as a means of teaching children the skills of adult work, and 'the teacher should endeavour to direct the children's inclinations and pleasures, by the help of amusements, to their final aim in life' (Plato's *Laws*). 'Would to God we had more of this child's play' wrote Martin Luther. Three hundred years ago, Comenius recommended education based on learning by doing: 'Whatever children delight to play with . . . provided it be not hurtful, they ought rather to be gratified than restrained from it' (*The School of Infancy*, 1633).

The first book on education to focus on the child was written by John Locke in the seventeenth century. *On Education* (1693) is a plea for children to be accepted as they are and to be allowed to learn through play which comes naturally to them. Rousseau, likewise, understood play as a means of learning, and recognised the degree of effort invested by children in self-chosen activities (*Émile*, 1762). Robert Owen's methods emphasised the need to keep children happy while learning. He advocated plenty of outdoor play, and in school 'with these infants everything was made to be amusement' (*Life of Robert Owen by Himself*, 1857).

It was Froebel, however, who was the first to penetrate the real significance of play. 'Play', he wrote in *Education of Man* (1905) 'is the purest, most spiritual activity of man at any stage.' It should, he believed, receive our most serious consideration. Dewey, in *Democracy and Education* (1915) differentiates between 'mere activity' and experience, and he believed that play which failed to lead to educative growth was no more than amusement. School he saw as 'an environment in which play and work shall be conducted with reference to facilitating desirable mental and moral growth'.

Maria Montessori was the first educator to recognise the contribution of movement to all aspects of learning, and her work with handicapped children in the slums of Rome was based on the principle of freedom to grow by one's own activity (Cass, 1966). She noticed the concentration of children engaging in self-chosen activity which involved the use of all their senses. The present-day emphasis on children learning rather than on the teacher teaching owes much to her influence.

During this century, the study of childhood has developed into a recognised science, and the works of such educators as Susan Isaacs (1929), Charlotte Bühler, Anna Freud, Dorothy Gardner (1956 and Gardner and Cass, 1965), Piaget, Bruner and others has helped to probe the mysteries of children's play (Cass, 1971). Through her work at the Malting House school at Cambridge, for example, Susan Isaacs (Isaacs, 1930, 1933) provided ample evidence of the child's ability to learn through self-chosen activity and first-hand experience. She writes (1930) about 'the strength of the child's spontaneous impulses towards understanding', and she is convinced that the child's own doing and his own thinking and talking are the chief tools by which he learns. She differentiates between three main types of play activity: (a) play related to the development of bodily skills, (b) play which leads to the exploration of the physical environment and to understanding the world around, and (c) play as an imaginative pursuit associated with inner desires and a developing sense of perspective. The three, of course, interact.

Piaget (1951, 1972; Piaget and Inhelder, 1974) interprets play in relation to the changing structures of the child's mental activity. During the sensorimotor stage of intellectual development, practice games predominate and involve physical activity rather than thought. During the next stage, the emergence of symbolic games provides evidence of thinking activity and an intense interest in making one thing stand for another. The third kind of play revolves around games with rules and is essentially social; the group decides the rules and these are communicated to all participants. Piaget firmly believes that thinking skills develop as a result of internalised action, and that mental operations become available to the child through his own manipulation of objects and materials in the environment.

A comprehensive study by Bruner et al. (1976) brings together a 'body of literature emphasising the crucial role of play in the development of the individual human child as well as in the evolution of the primate order'. The scope of this study is enormous, including as it does observations ranging from chimpanzees playing in their natural environment to nonsense verse and other forms of language play. It is packed with references and constitutes a veritable bible on play for all serious students.

Play has also fascinated many distinguished observers who, while not necessarily interested in education as such, have put forward various explanations or theories of play. One of the earliest of these was the 'surplus energy' theory (Spencer, *Principles of Psychology*, 1835), based on the notion that parental care relieved children of responsibility and they therefore had spare energy which had to be released. Even today, adults sometimes 'send children out to play to let off steam'. The fact that play revives a wilting child and that energy generated by play has to be used rather than got rid of scarcely fits this theory. Another theory, the 'recreational' theory of play, suggested that play offers a relaxation from work. 'All work and no play makes Jack a dull boy.' If by play we mean the opportunity to follow pursuits of our own choice as opposed to doing what others expect of us, then there is some truth in this idea.

A more interesting theory was promoted by Karl Groos in 1899 (*The Play of Man*) when he suggested that the play activities of childhood were a preparation for adult life, that play was nature's way of providing practice skills which will be needed in later life. The make-believe of early childhood seems to support this idea, though there are other types of play which do not fit the concept.

Stanley Hall (*Youth*, 1928) suggested that in the early years of life the child relives the developmental processes through which man achieved his present evolutionary state. This 'recapitulation' theory is based on the idea that full adult development is reached only if, during the individual's formative years, each developmental stage has been satisfactorily played out. By reliving the behaviour of primitive man, the individual is purged of harmful tendencies and antisocial impulses. When we watch Johnny 'taking it out of the clay' there would seem to be some truth in this.

James Sully (*Studies of Childhood*, 1912), a pioneer of child study, came to the conclusion that the child's play is his means of expressing his ideas. It is imitative and imaginative, and often used by the child as a means of understanding incomprehensible events in the real world.

Each of these theories (see Hartley et al., 1952; Millar, 1968; McLellan, 1970) holds a part of the truth, but none is completely adequate. The influence of these ideas is frequently echoed in current attitudes to play. Even among infant teachers there are those who regard play as a fringe benefit, as something to indulge in once the serious business of the day has been completed. Schools still exist where young children are expected to earn the right to spend time in creative pursuits or self-chosen activities, and 'choosing time' or 'free play' or 'creative activities' appear as periods on the weekly timetable. That play begins with life itself, and is the right of every child (Pringle, 1974), is not universally acknowledged.

Learning through play

The child's life goals are to survive, to make what he can of himself and to contribute in a unique way to the community in which he is reared. His curriculum is to learn about and understand the physical world surrounding him, and to develop a sense of empathy and communion with the people he meets in it. How he accomplishes these tasks depends on the relationship between what he brings to life in the way of personal resources and what the environment has to offer. Adults responsible for him during his years of dependency can help or hinder according to the way in which they modify his environment, but he must do his own learning. The child is naturally creative, and will devote much of his energy to creating himself as a person. Where the child's natural resources are activated in a beneficial environment, his unique potential as a person has the best possible chance to develop.

The child begins his life in the limited confines of his cot, his pram, his mother's lap and his bath. He plays with his fingers and toes and feels the shape of himself; he comes by the notion of his separateness, and eventually discovers where he finishes and the rest of the world, including other people, takes over (Stallibras, 1974). Within the envelope of his skin resides an entity which later becomes labelled 'self' (Winnicott, 1964).

As he becomes more mobile, so his world expands within such limits as adults impose on him. As his movements bring him into contact with objects and materials, his senses are stimulated and by means of his skin, his eyes, his mouth, and his muscles he extracts information with which to feed his mind (Yardley, 1970a). Each sensory experience affects his emotional state, and the impressions he receives and retains are a synthesis of sensory and emotional reaction (Sheridan, 1975).

As a small child he lives much of his waking time near the ground, and the things he picks up from it become his first playthings. He is also intensely interested in what constitutes his own body and person. Learning about the world outside himself and learning about self proceed side by side.

Of the objects he picks up from the ground, by far the most fascinating belong to the crust of the earth itself. Soil, stones, rocks, shells, sand and water, the plants which the earth supports and the insects it harbours – these are the first play materials which introduce the child to the study of his natural environment. They are the same materials which fascinated and challenged primitive man. In order to live, the cave man had to gain control over his environment. Two of his feet became hands (and therefore tools) and an upright posture enabled him to use these hands to manipulate materials. This was merely the beginning of a challenging combat. Adequate as fingers are, they make little impression on rocks, or water, or wood, and the ingenuity of man gave him access to such extensions as sticks and hammers and containers. Today, man has extended the use of his hands, his ears and his eyes until he can reach the moon or Mars and beyond, always discovering with each fresh conquest that more is to be discovered.

The simple materials which helped develop man's intelligence are the ones which remain highly educative through the individual's lifetime. The child begins his exploration of these materials through playing with them, and he continues to learn more about them at different levels in his intellectual growth. He does not 'grow out of them', and there is never a stage when he has learned all he can from them. The notion that children of six or seven should stop playing with sand or water in order to turn their attention to something more worth while arises when play situations deteriorate because they have not been kept alive by responsible adults. Any adult who works for a road construction company will confirm the fact that as each type of natural material is treated in fresh ways, so it produces fresh problems which add further challenge to man's ingenuity.

In his handling of these materials, the child goes through several observable stages (Marzollo and Lloyd, 1974). At first his manipulation of sand, for instance, is purely exploratory. He handles it dry and discovers how it will sift, scatter, spray, pour, fill up containers, yield and resist. With the addition of water, its behaviour takes on fresh characteristics. It now holds a shape and can be moulded. As it dries out again it falls away, and the shapes made with it may be easily modified. These and many other characteristics become known to the child. He frequently repeats a process, such as pouring sand through a funnel and watching it sift out in the shape of a cone, until he knows without a shadow of doubt that one event follows another. The range of his discoveries at this stage will depend on the variations in the material itself, and on the apparatus available for manipulating it. He will have more to learn from sand which ranges from fine silver sand to coarse black volcanic sand and with apparatus which includes a range of tubes and containers as well as levers and scoops, than he will from a small heap of damp sand and a bucket and spade.

Once a level of satisfaction has been reached, the child often abandons his material. Adults, who are inclined to understand effort only in terms of an end product, may wonder 'What was all that about? He's been messing about for days and there's nothing to show for it.'

During this apparently passive period, the child is assimilating the discoveries he has made about his materials, and the processes he has observed are being internalised. Then there comes the day when he is stimulated to return to the sand. He has perhaps been given a farm set. He goes immediately to the sand, wets it and moulds it into the landscape on which his farm is arranged. In doing this he applies knowledge previously gained to a new situation. His understanding of the material is now used to serve his purposes. Imagination and knowledge now combine to bring about some creation which is the outcome of a partnership between the child and the material. This is one of the reasons why it is so important for the child to make his own relationship with materials, free from the kind of over-intrusive adult suggestions or instructions that can sometimes come between him and his experience.

Each of these stages is accompanied by a certain tension which may take the form of excitement as the child's efforts lead him on in his discoveries. Often a further stage may be observed in which the child handles the material in a more relaxed way merely for the pleasure it brings. As adults, we try to recapture this pleasure stage, and our behaviour during a seaside holiday is expressive of this. We also retain the satisfaction of meeting the challenge presented to us by this material, and we continue to learn from it, which is one of the reasons why gardening is such a widespread leisure pursuit. Faced with the prospect of creating a new garden or moving into a newly built home, we feel similar emotions to children as we shovel the soil and rocks about until they take the shape we have in mind.

Through playing with materials the child discovers much about himself, particularly when he is able to compare his own efforts with those of other children. He can lift the biggest bucket of sand, he can push a heavy plank into position, he can reach the other end of the field first. He is big and strong for his age, just as mother has told him he is.

From about the age of two onwards, imagination plays an ever increasing role in his play pursuits. Not only can he do things with objects and materials, he can, in imagination, *be* these things. He can be other people as well. Reality can be translated into symbols and, irrespective of time, place or real properties, he can in imagination learn about objects and about other people through taking on their characteristics as his own. He also knows enough about self to have some judgement of other peoples' selves.

About the age of three the child makes one of the most exciting discoveries of life. The idea that he possesses an inner world of reality into which no other human being may enter except by his cooperation; that he can, for example, think what he likes about his angry mother and she need never know, opens up for the child the domain of inner delight which will remain his personal citadel until the day he dies. The psychological self is based on what the child thinks and feels about himself.

Eventually, often with the help of social play, the child develops notions of right and wrong behaviour, and the ideal self is born. This ideal or watchdog self (variously called the conscience and the super-ego) helps to determine the behaviour of the conscious self (Klein, 1959). Once it becomes established, it not only helps the child to evaluate his own behaviour, it helps him to form judgements and concepts about other people, judgements and concepts that teach him that these people can be both difficult and unpredictable. What he learns about the clay through playing with it remains reasonably constant, but other people are sometimes devious and changeable, and seem governed by minds often apparently quite unlike his own. Other people will indeed remain the most problematic of his learning experiences, and from now on playing with them will be one of his deepest needs, and the most educative aspect of his life (Holme and Massie, 1970).

The intelligent and imaginative child who finds himself denied playmates of his own age, or who fails to get satisfaction out of such companions as are allowed him, may create his own imaginary playmate. 'Nicky', or 'Kelly', or 'Poopoo' (as the case may be) is imagined with such clarity that he or she takes on a separate identity. 'Nicky' can provide the means of playing out many fantasy situations, a means of enabling the child to explore his own mind and to try to fathom the minds of others. 'Nicky' normally disappears as the child finds satisfaction in flesh and blood companions, but he can persist if the pattern of development is hindered by emotional conflict. One boy of six, whose parents were on the verge of separation, kept 'Nicky' alive until home circumstances settled down.

As a result of these different kinds of learning, the child is constantly forming ideas about the world and about the way in which it works. Eventually these ideas become labelled and constitute basic concepts. The quality of concepts formed during these early years determines the quality of much later learning, and it is through play experiences that many important concepts are formed.

The child with his finger under the kitchen tap, for example, will learn how to make the water drip, dribble, squirt, gush, flow, cascade and flood rather than merely run out of the tap. When at a later stage he is able to use these terms, he brings a personal image to each of them, and so understands them in a way that no amount of telling could achieve. What he later learns to read about in books is endowed with what he retains from this first-hand experience. 'Reading the words makes the pictures come' as one child of six explained.

The child playing with a piece of Mum's pastry dough discovers that he can change it in appearance without altering the amount of it, that there is a way of cutting out round shapes leaving very little pastry over, that ingredients react on one another and respond to water and heat, that accuracy is important in achieving desired results, and that eating too much is as detrimental to his person as eating too little. The child pouring water from his teapot onto the lawn again and again watching it disappear learns that b inevitably follows a, but that by adding or subtracting certain factors the sequence may be modified. Once this process has become internalised, the child has acquired a thinking skill which enables him to reason.

In this way he formulates ideas about the world which later combine to give him a mental model into which he can fit each fresh discovery. He is also discovering the mathematical and scientific principles which control the way his materials behave (Lovell, 1961). If he is denied the play experiences in early childhood, it may be difficult to develop adequate concepts later. The idea of compensatory experience at a later stage is fraught with insurmountable problems. We cannot provide at the age of five the play experiences from which the child may learn at the age of two or three, simply because the child is no longer two or three and at a stage where basic concepts are being formed. We may perhaps help to improve upon the concepts he has acquired, but missing out on foundational experience leaves its mark for ever.

In a literate society, the ability to communicate ultimately determines the individual's degree of social survival. However intelligent he may be, he is unlikely to make his mark unless he is articulate. Long before the child has mastered the various uses of words, he has ideas and impressions which he needs to communicate. Given the right materials he can be highly articulate. Using paint, crayon, charcoal, pencils and other marking media, he can fashion on paper symbols which represent his impressions. Using modelling materials, he can give a third dimension to his symbols. Using his body, he can create an even more realistic representation. The spontaneous dramatic play of young children provides them with a highly articulate vehicle through which they exercise the skills of communication both with self and with others.

Children provided with adequate play opportunity master many skills which later may be transferred to the uses they make of words. Experience gives rise to the need to communicate. The ability to invent and handle symbols provides a means of representing experience, or rather of representing the child's impressions of experience.

The vehicles of marking and modelling media, and of the various uses of his own body, serve as means for conveying the symbols. The development of listening skills and the spoken word (Lewis, 1963) grows out of non-verbal communication, and words act as linking elements which hold action together (Tough, 1976). Eventually reading and writing words may be grafted onto the child's uses of listening and speech. If highly complex uses of words such as reading are thrust to the child's attention at the expense of foundational understanding, he is bound to miss many chances of becoming accomplished in his personal use of words at a later stage (Yardley, 1970b).

Early and varied play contributes in a most positive way to all aspects of human growth and development. Physically, it enables the child to develop muscular strength and control, along with balance and confidence in using his own body. Through the use of creative materials he discovers much about himself and his own disposition, and so learns to handle his own behaviour by learning how to use in creative ways energy generated by such drives as aggression and destruction. Through play which brings him into contact with others he learns about other people's behavior and how to handle it (see e.g. Dansky, 1980). Through play with materials and people he develops concepts and learns to use thinking skills. Moreover, his discovery of the physical world and of people in it affords him an infinite variety of wonderful experiences, and the exercise of his imagination opens up for him that other dimension of life which borders on the spiritual. It is mainly through his play that he becomes a person in the fullest sense of the word.

Provision for play

Provision for adequate play is decided by the play needs of the child himself (Roberts, 1971), and we should not fall into the trap of believing we meet these needs by making use of the child's interest in play to satisfy some goal of our own. We do not set out to make a prescribed curriculum more palatable by presenting it in play form. We start by paying sincere respect to those needs which arise from the child's most effective means of doing his own learning in his own way.

The first requirement for play is space and freedom with safety and with access to out-of-doors. Congested flats, particularly high-rise flats, formal gardens, tiny playgrounds and busy roads restrict the child severely and often give rise to misbehaviour (Newson and Newson, 1963, 1968). Children need access to simple materials in generous quantities, to creative materials, to simple equipment which leaves plenty of scope for imagination (Allen, 1968). Play facilities need to cater for both boys and girls; equally important is the emotional climate in which play takes place. The attitude of adults in charge should positively encourage play as desirable and respectable. Children at play also need a supervising adult who understands what the child is experiencing, who knows when to withhold and when to intervene, and to whom children can refer when the need arises (Matterson, 1965). Provision for play is made in a number of different environments, the most obvious of which are the home, community play spaces, the nursery and infant school and playgroups.

Provision for play in the home is subject to wide variations, some of which depend on the socioeconomic group to which the family belongs (Newson and Newson, 1976). It is well nigh impossible to find space for vigorous physical play, for paste and scissors, for paint and clay, for a corner to call one's own, in the tiny cluttered home of a large impoverished family. The bath makes a good place for water play, but it is usually full of clothes left to soak. The little ones must be minded, there are errands to run, Dad's on night shift and must be allowed to sleep during the day, time itself is in short supply for the five- to seven-year-old. Meanwhile, the more affluent family has the security and natural surroundings of a garden. Mum may have time to take children to the park. Dad has a car, and play can occur in the fields or on the seashore.

Playgroups offer supervised play, and most of the adults in charge are eager to learn more about what should be provided and about the children's needs and of how they learn from play (Crowe, 1971). Yet playgroup facilities exist mainly in middle-class areas and are run by middle-class Mums; fewer groups exist in the more deprived social areas where they are most needed.

The community generally, however, is gradually becoming better equipped to meet the needs of children. Some shopping precincts, for instance, have play equipment and interest areas, and even a playgroup or crèche. Here and there are playparks. Yet the equipment to be found in places of this kind is often unimaginative, while adventure playgrounds are not suitably equipped for young children, and are often dominated by older boys and girls. In a few districts we find roads closed to traffic, and play spaces created between blocks of flats, but too often these are out of sight and hearing of parents, who understandably feel unable to let young children play freely when beyond recall.

Theoretically, nursery and infant schools base much of their education on play. In most nursery schools the provision is good, and learning is based on well-planned play pursuits. Sometimes, however, although the necessary play facilities may be provided, it is not necessarily the case that they are best used. Is play simply a subject allowed for in the timetable or is it how the child lives and learns in school? In spite of current knowledge of how children learn (Smith, 1980), there is much to be done before that knowledge becomes understanding, and beliefs about play are translated into classroom practice.

Even more doubts occur in some infant classrooms. In one classroom, for example, simple materials such as sand, water, clay and shells may be available, but the sand tray is small and the diminutive heap of sand it contains is well damped down. 'I don't give them dry sand,' the teacher explains, 'because it gets all over the floor.' There are a few containers, a scoop and a couple of jelly moulds in the sand. 'The children soon lose interest,' the teacher continues. 'They grow out of it and need something more challenging.' So she gives them writing patterns to copy or trace, and all the exciting properties of sand remain unexplored.

In another classroom, the house corner looks trim and attractive. Dressing-up clothes are neatly suspended on coat-hangers along a rail, the little stove has knobs which turn and a row of shining pots and pans. On the dresser there are cups and saucers and cutlery. The dollies sit obediently in their prams. Why is it that the house seems so deserted? The children know. 'It's fiddly to put all the dresses back' one girl explains. A little boy has another reason: 'You just get a good game going, then they stop you at it.' Meanwhile, one seven-year-old looks up from her workbook. 'I'm seven,' she says. 'You don't use Miss's house corner when you're seven.' Perhaps the fastidious young teacher has no idea that the children regard the house as her territory, or that it is she rather than the children who is responsible for the way it is used and maintained.

In another classroom things are different. Natural materials are available in good supply. There is a wide range of marking media. This is an imaginative collection of junk material. Creative materials are available in an area designed for messy activities. There is an interesting collection of objects on the investigation table. Dramatic play is well provided for. The mathematical activities look interesting. There is a window box for growing plants and a pet corner just outside the classroom door. A music-making area, books attractively displayed, a writing table well stocked with marking tools and paper, and a woodwork bench, occupy appropriate areas of the classroom. The teacher is trying to base learning on play pursuits, but 'Why is it,' she complains, 'that after a good beginning some of the activities seem to come to nothing and children finish up messing about with this and that, rather than learning from what they do?'

Close study of the classroom suggests two reasons. The first lies in the way the room is arranged, and the second in the way each activity has been structured. While each activity appears to occupy a suitable position in the room, the juxtaposition of the activities needs attention. The young child takes a global view of the classroom, and his mind does not hold a picture of each situation in relation to the others. Thus, because he is easily diverted, he may intend to paint the model he has just completed, but if the paint is at the other side of the room he will very likely get caught up in a rival interest and 'forget' to do so. Similarly, the child constructing with bricks finds he is right in the path of traffic in and out of the classroom, and soon gives up in the face of the constant disruption which this entails. Nor is it difficult to discover why water play has come to a standstill. There are plenty of containers for exploring the pouring properties of water, but what is there to help a child discover its use as a solvent or the way in which it supports some objects while others sink? Where is the equipment which allows him to observe the relationship between water and air? Has any thought been given to the way water can be modified, or to ideas for exploring its wetness? In short, where is the careful thought about the educational ends which water is meant to serve?

If situations for informal learning are to remain educative, they need to be kept alive. Knowledge of the child's developing powers of understanding provides the teacher with a knowledge of the stages through which the child proceeds in his grasp of an idea. She is then in a position to provide the right equipment to make this understanding possible. By applying developmental knowledge to a learning situation, she ensures that the child is able to proceed from a grasp of simple notions towards a deeper understanding of the ideas inherent in a situation. She does not teach him to weigh by introducing him to a set of scales and the standard measures. She first gives him objects which he can balance in his hands, and leads him through a sequence of stages in discovering balance and the use of units towards the idea of weight as the effect of gravitational pull.

The term structured play has recently crept into the nursery and infant school terminology. It can mean a number of things. By some it is interpreted as closely supervised play in which the adult plays a positive oral role. Others think of it as play more definitely directed by an adult. But, ideally, it means play carefully planned along developmental lines, constantly under review and frequently revitalised, and allowed to serve as a means towards the achievement of appropriate educational objectives. We must now look at the adult's role in bringing about this structure.

The role of the adult

As play is the child's response to an inner need, his play behaviour is very revealing, and the adult can often learn more about the child through observing it than by submitting him to a battery of tests. Detailed coverage of the ways and means of assessing the quality of children's play is provided in chapter 9, and trained observation of play is an essential part of a teacher's professional preparation. It tells her not only the degree of control and coordination the child has acquired over his body, but also much about his temperament and his potential for intellectual development. Through observing play, it is easy to identify, for example, the habitually aggressive child, or the one who rushes headlong into each fresh adventure, or the one who hovers uncertainly or who hesitates. Then, because play produces endless problems for the child, the teacher's observation of how he deals with these problems gives her a good insight into his intelligence.

In his imaginative play, particularly in dramatic and role play, the child gives the teacher insights into his innermost thoughts. He does not merely imitate (e.g. in his role as father, teacher or postman), he reveals his own impressions of the way other people behave. In a sense, he uses his body as a means of reflecting upon this behaviour, and in his drama he shows us what he thinks about it. Further, through dramatic play, he discloses the inner conflicts, desires, aspirations and emotional experiences which threaten him, or fill him with joy and satisfaction. The anger he feels when thwarted by a powerful adult finds outlet in the way he beats up the pillow as he makes the doll's bed, or stamps about in the all-powerful role as the policeman.

The child as a social being is much in evidence when he plays with other children. Whether he is likely to become someone who has good ideas or someone who carries them out, someone who makes the rules or someone who breaks them, becomes evident to the observer. By the way he manipulates objects or handles materials, it is easy to see whether a child has a sense of order, or the ability to estimate, or the wit to perceive relationships.

In addition to observing play, a prime concern of the nursery or infant teacher is to provide the right facilities for it, and these may be grouped under the following headings:

1 The social situation. The opportunity to learn from other children by sharing experiences with them. The challenge of interaction with adults outside the home.
2 Play materials. Natural materials (e.g. sand, water, shells, clay). Modelling and marking media. Dressing-up materials. Large blocks.

Construction toys. Musical instruments. Big play apparatus. Wood-work. Needlework and cookery. Domestic implements.

3 Objects to delight and excite the senses, e.g. unusual or beautiful objects such as silk, copper vessels, feathers, bones, pottery, carved wood etc.

4 Books and other literary materials.

5 Events, such as a visit to a bakery or airport, which stimulate dramatic and creative expression.

6 A stable atmosphere in which children feel free to explore and learn through play pursuits supported by adult approval.

Provision is, however, merely a starting point; the teacher and other adults in the classroom are the most essential part of the child's play experience and do, in fact, determine to a considerable extent the quality of the child's play and the degree of learning which takes place in it.

There is no blueprint for adult participation, however, and great sensitivity is needed in deciding when to join in and what kind of contribution may be helpful. When dramatic play is in its stride, for example, adult intervention can bring it to a halt. Of course, sometimes the children invite an adult to participate, but he or she is only expected to play a subordinate role which allows for little initiative. An adult-sized doll introduced into the house corner seem sometimes to satisfy this need equally well. Play with materials which leads to investigation and discovery offers the adult more scope, and encouraging a child to talk out what he is doing helps him to establish concepts and to acquire a vocabulary which enables him to crystallise experience and make it part of his thought processes. 'Sand and water both pour,' said Jane, 'but the water pours through the sand.' Talking to her as she experiments can help her to identify the differences between continuous and discontinuous matter.

Sometimes children understand an idea or principle, yet lack the vocabulary to express it. 'Every time I put sugar in the water,' Mark explained, 'it all goes away.' 'Yes,' replied his teacher, 'it dissolves doesn't it? Sugar dissolves in water. Do you know anything else which dissolves?'

A more subtle form of intervention is through the introduction of new avenues of interest to maintain a child's motivation in an existing learning situation. Philip and Paul cut an apple across and were so delighted by 'the pattern inside' that they forgot their intention to eat it. 'Lot's of things have things inside,' Philip observed. Their teacher set up a table containing an old tap, a nut, a rubber ball, a cabbage, a flashlight, a pencil and a felt pen. She put a notice on the table 'What's Inside?' and this caught and held the attention of Philip and Paul and two or three of their companions for several days. Each day she changed some of the objects on the table. Occasionally she provided objects which communicated a single idea, e.g. fruits with seeds inside.

Mary watched water spouting from a vertical row of holes in a container.

'They're different,' she said, 'from big to little,' obviously puzzled by the differences in the jets. Her teacher put the same container in the dry sand. She also provided other perforated objects. Mary filled these again and again, watching the size of the jets and the level of the sand in relation to her pouring. She continued to experiment with sand and water until she came to a number of conclusions about their behaviour.

The role of the adult in organised games becomes important as children reach the top end of the infant school. By the age of about seven, when children recognise the need for rules, they frequently apply to the adult for decisions as to what is fair (but see Opie and Opie, 1959, 1969 for interesting insights into lore and games developed by children themselves).

Conclusion

Recent developments in pre-school and early school education have brought the play of young children under the microscope. In a time of financial stringency, expenditure on education tends to be justified in terms of what is produced. The play of young children in nursery and infant schools is acknowledged as the basis of learning at this stage, but increasing emphasis is now being placed on the role of the adult in determining the quality of that play. Structure and intervention are often key ideas in devising programmes designed to make play more profitable, and many useful insights and strategies have been provided by the Schools Council Project on the *Structuring of Play in the Infant and First School* based at the University of Sussex (see, for example, Manning and Sharp, 1977). While this should help to improve both the teacher's understanding of the true educational purposes of play and the nature of the provision she makes for it, we must beware of ever using play simply as a masking devise for tuition based on specific objectives which satisfy adults rather than children.

There is much about children's play we do not understand. Indeed, being no longer children, we may lack the wherewithal to understand its full purpose for the child. We must guard against that form of intervention which leads to the domination of play for our own purposes, and instead concentrate on providing the best possible facilities for the child to do the job he understands so well.

Play is a universal activity. In every country in the world children play, and their play has comparable characteristics. Children using paint and other marking media adopt the same kind of symbols. Children of Gurkha troops stationed in Kowloon use the same symbols for the sun, a bird, a tree, even houses, as children in Britain. Rhoda Kellogg (1970), who made a study of thousands of drawings and paintings by children aged two to four in the Golden Gate Nursery Schools in San Francisco, identified six basic designs of which the magic circle or mandala, a circle combined with a cross, predominated.

Play is also influenced by culture and fashion. House play, for example, in Egypt takes place in the shade of a fig tree, with 'Mum' busy baking round flat cakes thrust into her imaginary mud oven on a wooden spade. In South Africa, 'Mum' spends hours on the telephone inviting people to cocktail parties. Among the high-rise flats in Nottingham there are innumerable weddings, often with the bride pushing a pram. Children in Northern Ireland or in parts of Africa or the Middle East, play out the conflicts of their parents, experiment with the routines of adult life, imitate adult officials, and thus come to terms with the business of living in their difficult or dangerous environments.

Wherever man has made his home he has tried to control the natural materials around him, and these materials, in turn, have become the playthings of his children. The infant scooping up the mud of the Nile explores it in exactly the same way as a child on the banks of the Derwent, although the objects he will later fashion from it will characteristically be different. Graphically, this juxtaposition of similarities and differences illustrates the subtle way in which inheritance and environment make their respective contributions to the patterns of play we witness in the children we teach.

References

Allen of Hurtwood, Lady (1968) *Planning for Play*. London: Thames & Hudson.

Bruner, J. S., Jolly, A. and Sylva, K. (1976) *Play: its Role in Development and Evolution*. Harmondsworth: Penguin.

Cass, J. E. (1966) *Montessori in Perspective*. Washington, DC: National Association for the Education of Young Children.

Cass, J. E. (1971) *The Significance of Children's Play*. London: Batsford.

Crowe, B. (1971) *The Playgroup Movement*. London: Allen & Unwin.

Dansky, J. L. (1980) Cognitive consequences of sociodramatic play and exploration training for economically disadvantaged preschoolers. *Journal of Child Psychology and Psychiatry* **20**, 47–58.

Gardner, D. E. M. (1956) *The Education of Young Children*. London: Methuen.

Gardner, D. E. M. and Cass, J. E. (1965) *The Role of the Teacher in the Infant and Nursery School*. Oxford: Pergamon.

Hartley, R. E., Frank, L. K. and Goldenson, M. (1952) *Understanding Children's Play*. London: Routledge & Kegan Paul.

Holme, A. and Massie, P. (1970) *Children's Play: a Study of Needs and Opportunities*. London: Michael Joseph.

Isaacs, S. (1929) *The Nursery Years*. London: Routledge & Kegan Paul.

Isaacs, S. (1930) *Intellectual Growth in Young Children*. London: Routledge & Kegan Paul.

Isaacs, S. (1933) *Social Development in Young Children*. London: Routledge & Kegan Paul.

Kellogg, R. (1970) *Analyzing Children's Art*. Palo Alto, Cal.: National Press Books.

Klein, M. (1959) *Our Adult World and its Roots in Infancy*. London: Tavistock.

Lewis, M. M. (1963) *Language, Thought and Personality in Infancy and Childhood*. London: Harrap.

Lovell, K. (1961) *The Growth of Basic Mathematical and Scientific Concepts in Children*. London: University of London Press.

McLellan, J. (1970) *The Question of Play*. Oxford: Pergamon.

Manning, K. and Sharp, A. (1977) *Structuring Play in the Early Years at School*. London: Ward Locke/Drake Educational.

Marzollo, J. and Lloyd, J. (1974) *Learning Through Play*. London: Allen and Unwin.

Matterson, E. M. (1965) *Play with a Purpose for the Under-Sevens*. Harmondsworth: Penguin.

Millar, S. (1968) *The Psychology of Play*. Harmondsworth: Penguin.

Newson, J. and Newson, E. (1963) *Patterns of Infant Care in an Urban Community*. London: Allen and Unwin (Penguin ed., 1965).

Newson, J. and Newson, E. (1968) *Four Years Old in an Urban Community*. London: Allen and Unwin (Penguin ed., 1970).

Newson, J. and Newson, E. (1976) *Seven Years Old in the Home Environment*. London: Allen and Unwin.

Opie, I. and Opie, P. (1959) *The Lore and Language of School Children*. London: Oxford University Press.

Opie, I. and Opie, P. (1969) *Children's Games*. London: Oxford University Press.

Piaget, J. (1951) *Play Dreams and Imitation in Childhood*. London: Routledge.

Piaget, J. (1972) *The Child and Reality*. London: Muller.

Piaget, J. and Inhelder, B. (1974) *The Child's Construction of Quantities*. London: Routledge & Kegan Paul.

Pringle, M. K. (1974) *The Needs of Children*. London: Hutchinson.

Roberts, V. (1971) *Playing, Learning and Living*. Oxford: Blackwell.

Sheridan, M. D. (1975) *Children's Developmental Progress*. London: NFER.

Smith, P. K. (1980) Play and its role in education. *Educational Analysis* **2**, 15–24.

Stallibrass, A. (1974) *The Self-Respecting Child*. London: Thames and Hudson.

Tough, J. (1976) *Listening to Children Talking*. London: Ward Lock.

Winnicott, D. W. (1964) *The Child, The Family and the Outside World*. London: Penguin.

Yardley, A. (1970a) *Senses and Sensitivity*. London: Evans.

Yardley, A. (1970b) *Exploration and Language*. London: Evans.

Further Reading

McKenzie, M. and Kernig, W. (1975) *The Challenge of Informal Education*. London: Darton, Longman and Todd.

Newson, J. and Newson, E. (1979) *Toys and Playthings*. Harmondsworth: Penguin.

Parry, M. and Archer, H. (1974) *Pre-School Education*. London: Macmillan (Schools Council Pre-School Education Project).

Sylva, K. (1977) *Play and Learning*. In Tizard, B. and Harvey, D. (eds) *The Biology of Play*. London: Heinemann.

Yardley, A. (1974) *Structure in Early Learning*. London: Evans.

17

Teachers and Parents Working Together

TERESA SMITH

Pre-school education is curiously out of fashion. The heady days of the expansion of nursery education following the 1972 White Paper *Education: a Framework for Expansion*, with its proposals for 'a new polity for the education of children under five', are long gone. Pessimism about the effectiveness of pre-school provision has been widespread, following the early negative findings concerning the American Head Start and other early education programmes which were published at the end of the 1960s. Yet recent studies, most notably the Consortium for Longitudinal Studies' *Lasting Effects of Early Education* (Lazar and Darlington, 1982), with new data on the long-term effects of intervention programmes for disadvantaged children, should lead us to rethink our map of the field of pre-school education and plot in rather more firmly some of the contours of parental involvement.

'Parental participation', one of the key phrases of the 1970s, has turned into a major debate on 'parents as partners' and 'parents as educators'. This chapter is about that debate: the complex relationship between home and school, the link between parents' understanding of their role in their children's development, the 'educational climate' of the home and the development of what Bruner (1980) called the 'competent next generation'.

Parent involvement in practice

Parents in schools

The Plowden Committee (Department of Education and Science, 1967) hoped that the relationship between home and school, between parents and teachers, would become 'a closer partnership between the two partners to every child's education'; to which Parry and Archer (1974) added the further hope that 'the good school should become an extension of the child's home or family rather than a substitute, and therefore it should cooperate positively with the parents. Lack of understanding and communication between home and school often lies at the root of children's poor school adjustments and performance.' Parent assemblies, open days, parent evenings, parents' rooms for a cup of coffee and a chat, parents staying to settle their children, parent–teacher associations (PTAs), parent governors, parents helping in the classroom – all demonstrate the intention of creating open and accessible schools where parents can be involved in their children's learning and can have some say in the organisation.

A recent survey of parental involvement in primary schools (Cyster et al., 1980) suggests that Plowden 'good practice' is indeed on the increase. One-third of the schools surveyed in 1976–7 had formal PTAs compared with 17% in the Plowden survey in 1964. A total of 55% of the primary headteachers reported an increase in parental involvement, and 63% believed that parental attitudes had changed markedly as a result, with parents finding it easier to visit the school to talk to teachers or the headteacher, and appreciating teachers' difficulties more easily, and with greater understanding between parents and teachers. Wolfendale's overview (1983) further illustrates good practice with a variety of examples of innovation and initiative: school-based 'outreach work' by home visitors or liaison teachers, parents' resource centres, such as the Newham Parents' Centre, toy libraries and home-based reading programmes. What staff, and parents, think about involvement is illustrated by a recent study of parents in pre-school groups in Oxfordshire (Smith, 1980). The views of staff clearly varied. Some teachers emphasised the warmth and friendliness of the school for both parents and children, accessibility to parents wanting to talk about problems and the importance of information about the home for staff and their work with the children. Others emphasised how parents learnt through involvement in the school group, whether this prompted new insights into child development in education or a new self-confidence in their own abilities; yet others saw involvement as potentially therapeutic for the parents. Some saw parents as partners, others saw a clear boundary between parent and professional, with parents as willing 'pairs of hands' when they could see the need and possessed the confidence. Some thought parents learnt more about children and had ideas for activities to do with them at home. But the strongest feeling was the importance of continuity and shared experience between home and school, of access to the group and the child's experience there.

Involvement in schools, however, is not universally welcomed or practised. Staff in one-quarter of the primary schools surveyed by Cyster et al. (1980) were unwilling to have parents in their classrooms; one-third expressed anxiety about parents gossiping and the 'lack of confidentiality'; one-fifth thought that parents in the classroom caused behaviour problems in the children, and that parents' failure to understand the aims of the school led them to criticise the teachers. In more than half the schools, working mothers were seen as the major obstacle to involvement; and in nearly half the schools staff spoke of the 'apathy and ignorance' of parents who were either unwilling or unable to visit. However, it is clear from the Oxfordshire study that there are very many parents who wish to know more about their child's development at school and are willing to be involved, but feel excluded.

Parents and the voluntary sector: playgroups and self-help

Voluntary provision of pre-school facilities, such as playgroups, crêches or community nurseries, depends on parental involvement. This has an economic aspect in that parents organise and run a service, and also a participatory meaning, in that parents have rights and responsibilities for how that service is organised. In many areas playgroups are the main, or only, experience of pre-school education for both parents and children; figures for the under-fives in this country suggest that more than half the pre-school provision is provided by the voluntary sector (Hughes et al., 1980). The Pre-school Playgroups Association's figures show that the majority of playgroups are managed by a parent committee, and that parents help with the children in most groups.

What does involvement mean for parents in playgroups? Mothers in playgroup studies (Palfreeman and Smith, 1981; Gray and McMahon, 1982) talk about what they have learnt; 'many feel they have gained a wider perspective of their children and greater confidence in themselves in bringing up their children; "time to call my own" is valued not just for its own sake but for the mutual relief from the intensity of the mother–child relationship.' Involvement is seen as an important way of making friends and building a community network, and bringing about change both in the mothers' own lives and in the community. The strongest sense here is of parents as providers/initiators of a service for themselves and other parents, and as members of a self-help group.

Home visiting and children with special needs

Both home visiting, as a strategy of intervention for families with young children, and intervention schemes with handicapped children emphasise the crucial importance of the home as the child's environment and of the parents' role in their children's development. Starting from small beginnings in the West Riding Educational Priority Area Project in the early 1970s (Armstrong and Brown, 1979), home-visiting approaches vary. Some home visitors, and their employers, see their task essentially as preparing the child for school, by instructing the parents how to teach the child concepts such as colours and shapes. For others, the essential task is to encourage parents' own self-confidence and help them to realise the educational context of the home and the role they play in their interactions with their child. This range is illustrated vividly by examples of school-based schemes in Lothian and Coventry, adult education-based work in London, 'drop-in centres' such as the South Harringay Pre-school Centre and volunteer schemes such as Scope and Home Start (Aplin and Pugh, 1983). Poulton (1980) traces the broad historical development of home visiting from an 'educational' focus on the child's early learning in the home, to a wider concern with adult and child education, to a community-based 'family support' approach focusing on parents' own needs and coping capabilities as the context for the child's learning. Despite the differences in emphasis in different schemes, however, Poulton summarises common aims broadly as helping parents 'to feel that they have an important part to play in their own children's development'.

The notion of parents as educators runs throughout intervention schemes with handicapped children (Pugh, 1981). There is a strong emphasis on parents learning to use professionals' tools, whether learning to break down behaviour into specific sequences as in the Portage schemes or watching a health visitor's assessment and talking through what she was looking for, as in the Haringey Health Visitor Home Visiting Project. The focus is on the professional 'package': 'training parents to use some of the techniques restricted to professionals and regarding them as "co-therapists" or "co-teachers" ' (Mittler and McConachie, 1983). There is also a strong element of parents themselves defining what they want for their handicapped children and what are the problems that need solving, and then selecting professionals to work on these problems with them. One example is Kith and Kids, a group of families with handicapped children in north London. In a neat reformulation of the usual power relationship, we here have professionals as partners instead of as leaders.

Clients or consumers?

For Wolfendale (1983), the distinction between parents as 'clients' or 'partners' is the touchstone which divides traditional from innovatory ways of working with parents. The language of 'client' or 'consumer' is familiar from social work with families and young children. In the Social Services field there is growing interest in preventive work with families which tackles problems before they reach crisis proportions, in outreach work and day-care rather than in residential work separating children from parents, and in working with families rather than providing care for children on their own, a mixture of approaches increasingly tagged with labels such as 'family centres'. In addition, the development of 'drop-in centres', where parents with young children can meet and share experiences or problems and make friends, together with the shift in the focus of traditional child care voluntary organisations (such as the National Children's Home, Dr Barnardo's and the Children's Society) from residential work to 'outreach work' with families in day-care, can all be seen as experiments in service provision which may simply have the objective of more effective work with hard-to-reach families and young children but which may in time shift the focus of work from therapeutic programmes for 'clients' to services for 'consumers' in the community. So, indeed, can the attempts to integrate services for families with young children by combining 'education' and 'care' elements, by attaching a teacher to a day nursery, by extending the hours of a nursery class to open earlier and close later, and by running parents' groups alongside a children's group in a building which is open for community use.

However, the debate about parents as clients or consumers tends to run on a different track from the debate about parents as learners or parents as educators. Many social workers are reluctant to see teachers' skills as relevant for the problem families they spend most of their time dealing with; 'teachers know little about working with the under-fives, and nothing about working with parents' is a not uncommon view. Both teachers and social workers may regard those families at the problem end of the spectrum as incompetent in dealing with their children: teachers because parents seem unable to appreciate their children's efforts or to use educational skills or knowledge in their relationship with their child; social workers because they may view parents as too overwhelmed by their own problems to have the time, energy or confidence to think about their child's development. The starting points for thinking about the educational context of social work intervention with families are consequently often missed. For example, although much family work is based on 'contracts' between family and social worker, with the learning of specific pieces of behaviour or interaction patterns between parents and child as explicit goals ('diversionary tactics' at mealtimes or bedtime, praise, reinforcement and so on), these contracts are rarely seen as educational strategies or interventions, that is, as strategies which involve adult learning as well as child learning, and strategies to which the teacher could also lend guidance and expertise.

Adult education and Pre-school provision: parent education or parent support?

Community education, like parental involvement, is one of the fashionable notions of the moment: everybody is doing it, yet there are probably as many definitions of community education as there are of parental involvement. Not surprisingly, therefore, community education offers some strange paradoxes. For example, the large-scale concentration of resources in community schools such as the Abraham Moses Centre in Manchester, or in Nottingham's Sutton Centre, or in Stantionbury Campus in Milton Keynes, squares oddly with the small-scale local focus peculiar to the notion of community. Similarly, the role often assigned to parents as mere *learners* and *consumers* of the resources of community schools squares oddly with the partnership and participation which are also peculiar to the notion of community.

The key question about parents in community education is the following: are we talking about 'parent education' (parents as consumers) or 'parent support' (parents as participators)? The distinction is often blurred because the shift in focus from work with children on their own to work with parents, whether in an educational or therapeutic context, that characterises parent education has accompanied a parallel shift in focus from the institution to the home and community. It is increasingly obvious that parents want more resources to help with their children at home: they want books to read to their children; they want books about child development; they want paper and paints; they want the opportunity to borrow or share toys. And increasingly, adult education programmes and community work projects are getting into the business of providing resources for parents. The growth of toy libraries based in schools, adult education institutes, clinics or people's homes, is one example. The success of schemes like the Newham Parents' Centre, with its book shop and network of groups and courses, is another. Packs of materials for parents' groups published jointly by the Pre-School Playgroups Association and the Open University's Community Education Department is a third.

The notion of 'parent support' has, however, proved an even more useful device for bringing together a range of different projects with parents; for example, family centres, mothers' groups, whether set up by outside workers such as teachers or health visitors or by parents themselves, and schemes such as Scope, Home Link, Family Groups and Home Start (Knight et al., 1979; Poulton and Poulton, 1979; Poulton, 1981; Palfreeman, 1982; Pugh, 1982; van der Eyken, 1982). Home Start and Scope, to take just two examples, both describe themselves as family support schemes. Neither provides services for children such as playgroups; neither works directly with children; both take the parent, usually the mother, as the focus, and work directly to improve the mother's self-confidence and coping ability. Both work with what might be called the most isolated, depressed and hard-to-reach families, in significant contrast to self-help groups of the playgroup kind. Yet Home Start and Scope are also self-help schemes, in that they depend on volunteers, local people often with similar experiences. The difference between Home Start and Scope is that the former works on an individual basis, volunteer and mother matched one-to-one, while the latter works through the group, where all the mothers are volunteers on a self-help basis. Both schemes, however, agree on two basic points. The first is that helping mothers to learn confidence through self-reflection and discussion is more effective than simply operating a helping or educational service on its own. The second conclusion is that, although parents learning about themselves, about their families, about their capabilities and about their children are the fundamental features of the scheme, this learning is nevertheless informal and arises out of experience. It is not formal 'parent education' in the sense that parents are the recipients of knowledge and information passed on to them by 'experts' in the field.

Parent involvement and parents as educators: research findings

There are two questions to ask about research into the relationship between home and school. First, what does the research tell us about the importance of the home background? Secondly, what is the evidence for the effectiveness of intervention strategies to change some of the patterns of the home?

We have abundant evidence concerning the link between children's development and educational achievement on the one hand, and parents' attitudes and expectations and what we might call the 'educational climate' of the home on the other, in the classic longitudinal studies by Douglas (1964; Douglas et al., 1968), the Plowden Committee (Peaker, 1971) and the National Children's Bureau (Essen and Wedge, 1982). But the evidence for the effectiveness of parent involvement strategies is sparse and scattered, and has to be gathered together from different sources; much of the recent research deals with the impact of early intervention programmes with parents and children rather than the element of parent involvement as such. The usual question has been 'does pre-school work?' rather than 'does parent involvement work?'. As Wolfendale points out (1983), there is no 'overall theory of parental participation, established and tested by proper investigation in the tradition of the behavioural sciences'. One of the key questions for pre-school research – left unanswered by the most robust recent evidence from the Consortium of Longitudinal Studies (Lazar and Darlington, 1982) – must be whether parent participation or 'enriched curriculum' is more effective in promoting children's development and educational progress. It is indeed true that as yet there is 'no easy prescription', no easy answer, as Lazar and Darlington (1982) point out in their summary of 11 very different early intervention programmes in the United States. But the picture is not too bleak. It can be argued that, at the very least, we have some very strong clues about both the impact of parent involvement and the nature of the process.

Returning to the relationship between the home background and child development, for sociologists the explanatory link is social class: parental attitudes are powerfully affected by position in the social structure and all the factors that go with it of differential access to employment, housing, space and other amenities. For psychologists, the notion of class obscures the differences in the fine detail of the parent–children interaction observable *within* social class groups. The sociological argument does not explain individual variations within groups: why some children in some families are so much more successful in their educational performance than others in the same social position. These are broad generalisations, but class differences clearly do continue to operate most powerfully throughout a child's school career, affecting the choices he makes at each 'rung of the educational ladder' (Halsey et al., 1979). The question is how to unpack the notions of 'class' and of parental 'attitudes' to gain a better understanding of the factors and processes that make the difference.

In his study, Douglas (1964) found a close and consistent relationship between social class, children's educational achievement and parents' attitudes. Parental interest in their children's development was associated with high attainment, good examination results and staying on at school; low interest was associated with poor performance and early leaving, findings which were consistent both for the population as a whole and also within each class group. Douglas' 'parental attitude' scale included measures of parents' own educational aspirations (whether either parent had wanted to pursue further education after leaving school), their interest in the child's progress (as demonstrated by the father visiting the school to discuss the child's progress on at least two occasions or as assessed by the teacher), and their aspirations for the child's further education or occupation. His conclusion in the second study (Douglas et al., 1968) is that home influences are crucial throughout the school career, but greatest at two points: during the pre-school years and at the school-leaving age.

Douglas' approach was followed closely by the Plowden Committee in their national survey of parent attitudes and subsequent analysis of the relationship between parents' occupation and attitudes and children's achievement (Department of Education and Science, 1967): 'how much parents influence children's achievements at school and how their influence operates'. As in Douglas' study, there is a strong link between attitudes and behaviour and social class. For instance, middle-class children read more at home than working-class children, and borrowed books from libraries; fewer working-class children had homework, and middle-class parents were slightly more likely to help their children with it, although there were no social class differences in parents' desire for children to have work to do at home; more middle-class parents visited schools and talked to the teacher and the headteacher, went uninvited to the school and expressed worries about teaching methods.

The Plowden study distinguished six associated clusters of parental attitudes and behaviour which have bearing upon children's school progress:

1 The extent to which parents took responsibility and the initiative for their child's education (whether they had visited the school, asked for advice on how to help their child etc.).

2 The relations between parents and teachers (whether parents thought it was easy to see the teachers whenever they wanted, and did not feel they were interfering if they went to the school uninvited etc.).

3 Fathers' interest and support.

4 Mothers' time and attention to their children's development (whether parents felt 'they should leave it all to the teacher').

5 Parents' interest in and knowledge of the child's work at school (whether the child talked to his parents about his school work and took books home; whether parents spent time with their child in the evenings and weekends; whether they were satisfied with his progress and the school's teaching methods, and thought they were given enough information and consulted sufficiently by the teachers).

6 The level of literacy in the home (whether parents belonged to a library and had books at home; whether the child used the library and read at home).

On these six clusters, class differences again showed up consistently, with the slight exception of teacher–parent relations, where middle-class parents were more likely to express dissatisfaction than working-class parents.

The Plowden Committee concluded that 'attitudes could be affected in other ways . . . than [by] parents' occupation, material circumstances, and education . . . and could be altered by persuasion'. Their recommendations were essentially for a 'minimal programme' to win 'cooperation from parents' and 'support from the home' for school-based communication and information; for example open assemblies, parents' evenings, parents as extra pairs of hands in the classroom and so on. In post-Plowden orthodoxy, this is now the standard list of good practice in home–school relations. Lack of understanding and communication between home and school is seen as the fundamental problem to be tackled by more information for parents about school and its objectives, and greater involvement of parents in the school and its activities.

Critics of Plowden have, roughly speaking, taken three lines of attack. The first is the ambiguity of the notions 'parental interest' or 'parental attitudes'. For example, whether a father visits the child's school or not may depend more on the flexibility of working hours than 'interest'; similarly, taking children on outings may depend on financial circumstances. There is abundant evidence that working-class parents are as interested and as anxious to promote their children's education as middle-class parents. In the Newsons' data from their Nottingham longitudinal study (Newson and Newson, 1977), 82% of working-class parents of seven-year-old children helped their child with reading.

Secondly, critics such as Bernstein and Davies (1969) argue that class is consistently underestimated, that measures of parental interest and attitudes in fact measured class-linked behaviour patterns, and that the task of changing attitudes might therefore turn out to be the far more complicated task of changing patterns of behaviour with associated attitudes. The third line of attack is to ask for the evidence that the Plowden recipe of better understanding and communication between home and school, leading to a change in parental attitudes and children's educational performance, actually *works*.

There is plenty of evidence that parents do learn from their involvement with schools, as earlier quotations about work in progress demonstrate. But the difficulties inherent in strategies to increase parents' contact with schools and understanding of their work are illustrated clearly in the following two action research studies. Young and McGeeney's study (1968) *Learning Begins at Home* was designed to test out some of the ideas of the Plowden Committee (of which Michael Young was a member). Their programme of open meetings, talks between parents and teachers, and discussions on teaching methods produced some changes. Parents felt they knew more about the school's work and how they could help their child at home, and appreciated teachers' interest more; teachers learnt more about parents' views and the children's home conditions; and children's performance in school improved slightly but significantly. The value of this study lies in its perceptive account of parents' and teachers' mutual ignorance of each other's views and situations, and of the small steps necessary for a strategy for change in parent–teacher relationships. Barbara Tizard's more recent study (Tizard et al., 1981), of two years of intervention trying out new ways to involve parents in nursery schools and classes, illustrates this gap in understanding even more clearly: even when teachers made determined efforts to give information, parents did not necessarily understand any more about the school's objectives or methods, or change their views about teachers' efforts.

Whether or not this line of criticism is too pessimistic, it should, however, focus our understanding of the processes at work underlying parents' attitudes about education, their role as parents and their behaviour with their children. Information and knowledge may be a necessary, but not a sufficient, ingredient in this process. What is missing is the sense of active participation implied in the notion 'parents as educators'.

The history of the American early education programmes takes us into this different perspective. Beginning from the same starting point in the concern of sociologists like Douglas about the mis-match between children's potential and performance, particularly in Black and poor groups, and merging with the shift in psychologists' thinking about the nature and development of intelligence and early learning and the impact of the environment on early experience, there was a tremendous surge of optimism in the early 1960s that policies of early intervention would solve all problems of under-achievement and poverty, encapsulated in phrases like 'how to raise your child's IQ 20 points'. Launched with enormous enthusiasm as the 'War on Poverty', programmes and project expanded dramatically, ranging from Head Start schemes in local community centres to carefully designed university-based demonstration projects run by trained professionals. With the usual time-lag, Britain's home-grown 'poverty programme' was launched in the shape of the five Educational Priority Area Projects in 1968.

The standard pattern of results from early intervention programmes both here and in the United States is well known: an initial 'boost' to children's performance at school entry followed by progressive 'wash-out' after the first few years in school. But Lazar and Darlington (1982) give us a completely new picture some ten years on.

Their data are drawn from 11 different projects which collaborated in the Consortium for Longitudinal Studies, drawing on a range of work with pre-school children and their parents, at home, in pre-school centres or a combination of both. All the projects conducted their own pre- and post-programme evaluation throughout the 1960s and early 1970s. New material was collected in 1976, when the children were aged between nine and 19 years (some still at school, others now in the employment market) on a variety of measures, including school performance, and children's and parents' attitudes and aspirations. The results can be summarised briefly. Children with pre-school experience were less likely than those without to require remedial teaching throughout their school career (in American terms, special education classes and grade retention), and they did better in mathematics and reading, although there were no differences between the two groups on intelligence scores. When interviewed in 1976, pre-school 'graduates' had more positive attitudes about themselves and about school, and were more likely to give school- or job-related achievement as reasons for feeling proud of themselves. Likewise, parents of pre-school 'graduates' interviewed in 1976 had higher aspirations for their children, and were more satisfied with their children's school performance, than mothers of children without pre-school experience. What is the significance of these findings?

First, as Lazar and Darlington (1982) point out in discussion of the results, they demonstrate that 'relatively small inputs into . . . children's total lives' affected 'low income children in ways that were both statistically and educationally significant'. Early intervention is no longer hailed as the panacea for problems of poverty, yet on the strength of this carefully conducted re-analysis it can certainly be 'advocated as one effective policy that may some day take its place within a coordinated set of public policies and private initiatives designed to redress the needs of low income families'.

One of the Consortium programmes, the High/Scope project developed at Ypsilanti, is even more specific. On the basis of follow-up data on children up to the age of 19, major economic advantages have been claimed for pre-school programmes: reduced delinquency, reduced costs for special education and increased earning power for those participating in the programmes (Schweinhart and Weikart, 1980; Weikart, 1982).

Secondly, the results give us some clues to the *process* involved in the journey from initial intervention to long-term results. Can we tell precisely what it is that works in the programmes? The answer is that we cannot, from the Consortium data, as Lazar and Darlington (1982) are careful to point out. However, they do take us through their conclusions so far, and then go on to offer a hypothesis.

Drawing on Weikart's analysis of the Ypsilanti programme, Lazar and Darlington (1982) construct a path diagram from their data in which early intervention is shown to affect later school competence directly and also indirectly via children's performance on intelligence tests at the age of six. They argue that intelligence test scores reflect what they term 'developed abilities', that is, problem-solving skills, verbal ability and general knowledge, as well as motivation, attitudes and skills such as persistence. So it is not surprising to find a link between performance in these areas and later performance in school. They also argue that attitudes and values relevant to successful performance – for example, self-esteem and attitudes towards school, authority, achievement and so on – were often goals of intervention programmes anyway, and indeed provide some of the post-school measures collected by the Consortium. The data thus indicate that long-term effects were the result partly of changes in broadly speaking educational skills and knowledge (cognitive functioning) and partly of changes in attitudes and expectations and motivation (non-cognitive characteristics).

Now for the hypothesis. We know from the data that parents' motivation and attitudes were affected by involvement in pre-school programmes, but what effect does this have on children's performance? Lazar and Darlington (1982) talk of an interactive process between parents and children:

> Although we have little information at present on family processes and outcomes, it seems possible that mutual reinforcement processes occurred between the early education participants and their parents. Perhaps the children's participation in a program raised the mothers' hopes and expectations for their children. Pooled consortium data indicate that the mothers of early education participants continued to have higher aspirations for their children than the children had for themselves and thus presumably exerted more pressure to achieve. We also found that parents of the program group reported more satisfaction with their children's schoolwork than did parents of the control group. Perhaps children interpreted these parental attitudes as a belief in a support of their efforts, and it served to spur them on.

On the face of it, the notion of a 'mutual positive reinforcement process' is perfectly sensible: a positive feedback loop between parents and children, with children's better performance leading to more parental interest and encouragement which sustains the performance and so on. And there is no difficulty in relating this to the 'clusters' of positive parental attitudes identified by Douglas and the Plowden Committee.

The crucial question is whether the long-term impact of programmes such as those included in the Consortium is due primarily to the child component (the work done directly with children, whether in a pre-school centre or in the home, or both) or primarily to the component of parental involvement (that is, mediated through the work done with and by parents). It could, of course, be the result of both together, each factor acting on the other. Lazar and Darlington (1982) are scrupulous in pointing out that the Consortium data do not as such answer this question. Parental involvement varied greatly across the 11 projects. Most, but not all, projects included home visits of one sort or another in the programme, and project staff worked with the parents at home, usually the mother. Some wrote parental involvement in the centre-based group into the programme. Some of the programmes (for example, Ira Gordon's Florida Parent Education Program, and Levenstein's Mother–Child Home Programs) were entirely home-based. Results of these in terms of children's development and attitudes and mothers' attitudes were as satisfactory as the centre-based programmes. But it is impossible from these results to say which are more effective: home-based or centre-based programmes, programmes for younger or for older children, programmes using 'professional' or local people as 'para-professionals', programmes with parent involvement or programmes without.

Although the Consortium material cannot provide us with hard comparative data on parent involvement, there are several studies that we can put together to give us clues on both impact and process.

First, let us consider the impact of parent involvement on both parents and children. The latest figures from the Weikart project contain data on one year-group of children whose parents were not included in a home-visiting or involvement programme because the staff were busy writing the curriculum. The preliminary results suggest that children's scores are well below those of their colleagues in other year-groups whose parents had been included in the programme (Weikart and Radin, personal communication, 1982). Then there is Donachy's study (1979) in Scotland of a programme with mothers and three- to four-year-old children in nursery classes and school-based groups, showing that a programme of even a few months with mothers reading and carrying out activities at home with their children produced changes in children's performance and mothers' responses.

Radin (1972) describes a project in which a school-based programme for four-year-olds ran alongside home visits by a teacher to work with parents and children together, plus a programme of discussion groups for mothers. Children were divided into three experimental groups. The first group had the whole programme: the pre-school programme for four half-days a week for nine months, plus the 'home tutorial' sessions with the classroom teacher and the mother, plus weekly small group meetings for the mothers organised by a social worker focusing on child-rearing practices. The second group had the school-based programme plus the 'home tutorials'. The third group had the school-based programme, but this time the 'home tutorials' were conducted by the teacher without the mother. Radin looked at the children's educational performance, and their school behaviour as rated by the teachers; she also looked at parents' child-rearing attitudes and the levels of stimulation in the home. By the end of the year's programme, all the children had made educational gains and displayed more curiosity and motivation in general; but the gains lasted, at the one-year follow-up, only for those children whose mothers had been involved. Mothers' attitudes about how to control their children changed significantly for those in the small group meeting; and mothers' thinking about educational materials in the home seemed to be changed by their involvement in the 'home tutorial' sessions. Radin's conclusions were that a pre-school programme plus parental involvement clearly can boost children's development, with gains that last beyond the programme itself; that the maximum potential for change is clearly associated with maximum parental involvement; and that a small group programme clearly can change parents' styles as educators. Thus involvement can 'enhance mothers' perceptions of themselves as educators of their children and of their children as individuals capable of independent thought'

Finally, there is a more recent programme with older children, the Haringey Reading Project (Tizard et al., 1982), an experiment designed to assess the effects of parental involvement in the teaching of reading. A previous survey had found that in working-class families children whose parents said they heard them read at home were markedly better at reading at the age of seven and eight than children who did not receive this kind of help from their parents.

Six schools in Haringey were selected. In two schools, one top infant class was selected for parent help with reading at home, with the rest of the classes in the year acting as controls for comparison; in two schools, one class was selected for extra teacher help at school, with similar control groups; and the remaining two schools acted as controls. The programme lasted for two years. The researcher with the class teacher met the parents individually at school to discuss the project; parents welcomed the project and agreed to hear their child read at home as requested and complete a record card. The researcher visited homes two or three times each term throughout the two years to observe the children reading to their parents. At one school, other reading activities were sent home from school, and parents were given advice on these by the researcher. Apart from this, parents were given no training in how to hear their children read. The results show that the children in both the parent participation classes and the groups with extra reading help from a teacher improved their reading in comparison to the control groups. But the children who received help at home showed greater relative improvement than the children receiving extra help at school, as they ended up with fewer extremely poor readers and with more able readers. There were other spin-offs: teachers clearly found working with parents worth while and continued this after the programme ended, and they thought the children were better behaved and keener at school; while parents clearly welcomed involvement with the schools. Because of the small numbers of groups in this study it probably needs further replication; nevertheless, the conclusions are another piece in the jigsaw.

The importance of these studies lies in their evidence for the 'parents as educators' approach. Programmes for parents to work with their own children, without any formal 'training', clearly can affect both parents' behaviour with their children and the children's competence. Two questions remain: first, what do we know about the *process* of this parent–child interaction and of parents' sense of their own role?

The follow-up study of a home-visiting programme in the West Riding Educational Priority Area Project (Armstrong and Brown, 1979) can illuminate something of the process:

Five years after the end of a home visiting programme in the West Riding EPA, parents and children were contacted to get a picture of changes that had occurred. The interesting finding of this study is that while after three years of school there were minimal differences in performance between the group of 'home visited' children and a second group who had not been visited, there were substantial differences in attitude between the two groups of parents. The differences lie essentially in the parents' view of education and of their own role in relation to their children's development. Mothers in the 'visited' group were more likely to have helped to prepare the child for school. They felt that talking to the child was preparation in itself. They 'told her what she'd be doing', 'told him he'd be painting like at playgroup'; 'her older sister talked about it'. The few mothers in the comparison group who said they had prepared the child laid more stress on 'teaching him things' – they had 'taught him to write his name', 'told him not much playing, more reading and writing'; and one mother said she had not prepared her child 'because you're told not to teach anything now as all the methods are different'. Again, when the mothers were asked what they thought were the most important activities at school for five-year-olds, those in the visited group talked about 'playing and learning in preparation for work', while those in the comparison group were more concerned with formal educational skills like 'learning to read and write'. Mothers in the visited group were far more likely to say that they had tried to help with their child's education; and they put this in terms of 'answering questions and explaining things' to the child, while the comparison group again stressed formal reading and writing. Although both groups had visited the school with equal frequency, the visited mothers were far more likely to wish for greater involvement in their child's schooling. They wanted to 'go and see more about teaching methods so if I want to help him I could do so', and 'wouldn't like to live there but would like to know more about what the children are doing'. The comparison mothers did not understand 'new methods' and said they were 'quite happy with the present set-up' and 'preferred it as it was'. And finally, more of the visited mothers hoped their child would have further education or training when he left school as it would 'help to get a better job'.

A considerable difference in parents' sense of their own role as educators, and in their understanding of what might be called educational processes, is demonstrated here. Mothers in the home-visiting programme came to hold a much wider view of education and early learning, and their role in this; while mothers in the comparison group tended to see education as something that happens only in school and involved formal skills above all else. A small comment in McCail's study (1981) of the Lothian home-visiting schemes illustrates a similar shift when mothers began to discover 'how interesting their children were . . . They began to believe that it was more possible to influence the sort of person their child would become.'

We can find further illumination in the classic study of parent–child interaction by Clarke-Stewart (1973). Her research was designed to explore the critical variable for development in mothers' behaviour with their young children. Clarke-Stewart focuses on actual behaviour rather than attitudes, feelings or personality. Her findings emphasise two points: first, the interactive nature of the mother–child relationship as the prerequisite for the child's development of motivation and competence; and, secondly, the importance of the mother as mediator. She isolates a pattern of behaviour which she labels 'optimum maternal care' or 'general maternal competence', a pattern of warm accepting, stimulating interaction, responsive to the child's behaviour, adaptive as the child gets older, closely related to the mother's willingness to experiment and be imaginative, and to her language skills and knowledge about child rearing and development. The child's competence – language ability, cognitive and intellectual functioning, motivation in new situations – is significantly related to the mother's general competence. Her important and illuminating hypothesis is that the mother acts as mediator. To give one specific example from her study, the fact that toys were available in the home did not seem to be related to the child's level of play: what mattered was the amount of stimulation with toys and objects that the mother gave the child at home in their play together. Perhaps then we can take Clarke-Stewart's data as an illustration of the process of 'mutual reinforcement' in the interactions between mothers and children hypothesised by Lazar and Darlington (1982): a clear pattern of warm, responsive, challenging behaviour on the part of the mother towards the child. It is also reminiscent of Bronfenbrenner's (1974) description of the home environment and the parent role as both 'catylist' and 'fixative' of the child's experience.

It is important to note that Clarke-Stewart herself relates her findings to the notion of class. She finds significant differences in the groups she studied between Black and White families in their children's development and competence and mothers' patterns of interaction. Black and White mothers were equally positive in their views about their children in the initial interviews, and seemed to be equally accepting towards their own children during the study's observations. As Clarke-Stewart notes, 'they spent the same amount of time with their children, held them as much, were as responsive to their distress.' However, Black and White mothers were increasingly likely to do different things with their children while they were together: 'White mothers looked at their children, talked to them, played with them more, and were more openly affectionate; Black mothers, by contrast, were more restrictive and spent more time caring for children's physical needs.' As Clarke-Stewart comments, 'Black mothers emphasised the physical aspect of childcare; White mothers emphasised the educational aspect.' Her point is that these patterns are similar to those observed between mothers of different social classes; here we have two groups of mothers, who, although occupationally and educationally apparently equivalent, 'are products of very different histories, traditions, social, and perhaps economic, pressures', which goes to make up an explanation for mothers' different expectations and patterns of behaviour in preparing children for the future.

There is a separate tradition of child development research which is relevant here, that of the impact of day-care. It has often been commented that compensatory education research look for positive effects in the form of educational performance, increased motivation on the part of the child, and so on; while day-care research tends to look for the presence or absence of harmful effects on the child from care away from the mother. Recent studies suggest that the important factor for the child's development is not the fact of day-care, nor the fact of a working mother. Working mothers may spend no less time with their children than at-home mothers, and may play and talk more with their children at the end of the working day. The important fact may be whether a mother is happy working or not. In one American study of kindergarten children and their mothers (Clarke-Stewart, 1982; Farel, 1980), mothers working did not appear to affect the children's competence or adjustment to school. However, children did badly if they had mothers who did not work but would have liked to and who thought that working would have benefited the child. Children whose mothers worked but thought this was bad for the child did slightly better, possibly because the children were compensated by good child care arrangements. Again, the conclusion is surely that an interactive process is at work: the mother's confidence about her own role as mother or as breadwinner partially affects the child's development and competence. As Farel (1980) concludes, 'the mother who works but feels she would rather be at home with her child is making a judgement about working. A mother who does not work but is not satisfied with this status is making a judgement about the mothering role.' Farel's argument here is that her study provides evidence that a psychological variable (i.e. the mother's attitude towards employment) acts as a mediating variable between the fact of maternal employment and the effect on the child as expressed in his behaviour and development. This is not simply a point about attitudes, but a point about the complex pattern of interaction between parent and child, of which the mother's self-confidence and feelings about working or not working form a part.

Is our conclusion, then, that parents' attitudes and interests are all that matter? It depends, of course, on the meaning of the terms. These studies surely demonstrate that attitudes are an integral part of the patterns of response between parents and children, in turn bound up with economic and social factors. What appears to matter most is parents' sense of confidence and competence and their expectations in relation to a realistic appraisal of the possibilities, as Clarke-Stewart's material suggests. If this material gives us some clues about the process of parent–child mutual reinforcement, the second question is how to encourage it. Does parent involvement in the current debate mean 'parent education' or 'parent support'?

The confidence/competence debate is not new. Bruner in the early 1970s was pointing out the connection between a mother's sense of being in control of her own life and her child's development (Bruner, 1972). And it is clear that pre-school programmes can have striking effects on parents' confidence in their abilities to become involved in activities beyond the home. A recent review (Zigler and Berman, 1983) of American pre-school programmes provides an illustration. In one Head Start programme in the county of Wisconsin, nearly half of the parents continued to be involved in other community organisations years after the pre-school programme for their children had finished; and this was a group to whom, in the authors' own words, 'organised volunteer work is usually quite foreign'.

There is no doubt that parent programmes which set out to develop skills and knowledge relevant for child development can be successful in doing so and in increasing parents' enthusiasm, motivation, self-confidence and sense of their own competence. Trained professionals working in the home or in centres with parents can clearly help parents to learn, but there has been a substantial shift in focus from 'professionals' working with parents (by definition 'non-professionals') to parents (whether we call them 'volunteers' or 'para-professionals') working with other parents.

The Ypsilanti Infant Education Project began as a straightforward home-visiting scheme with trained staff visiting homes once a week to work with the mother and child on child development activities. Results were as predicted, with the exception that the control group in this study, who were simply given the same tests as the experimental group to check children's progress and mothers' expectations of their offspring, clearly thought that these tests were in themselves a programme and used them as such. The logic of home-based intervention shifted the project increasingly to the use of volunteers in the programme: local mothers who had been through similar experiences, and were willing to be trained to work on a parent-to-parent or peer-to-peer model. However, the focus has also shifted from the cognitive/child development emphasis of the early work to one of support in family crises, housing problems, income maintenance and so on: that is, from an *educational* to a *parent support* model, a similar shift to that described earlier in many of the home-visiting schemes in this country. Scope, Home Start and Cope's Family Groups similarly rely on local people as workers, rather than trained outside 'professionals'. All these schemes demonstrate the development of self-confidence and competence on the part of isolated and depressed mothers with young children, very much the clientele described in Brown and Harris' (1978) study of young mothers and depression, and in Shinman's (1981) analysis of mothers who fail to make use of the opportunity of pre-school provision for their children even when it is on the doorstep.

The 'parent education' or 'parent support' dilemma is neatly posed by the American educationist, Hess (1980). Describing the enormous success of popular books written for parents on how to learn to 'handle their children's problems', he argues:

Parent-education programs thus seem to convey three messages to parents: First, they probably do not have the competence needed for child-rearing; second, knowledge and techniques for dealing with children are available; third, if they wish, they can acquire these skills. A fourth message is implicit but unavoidable – if parents are not successful, it is their own fault.

The answer he suggests is to look for a different approach based on a recognition by parents of the importance of 'learning on the job' from other parents, and of 'self-help and mutual support'.

Van der Eyken's (1982) study of Home Start in Leicester indicates that on measures of parental confidence, reduction in family stress and children at risk the project is judged a success, but it is clear that such work has shifted its focus from children's educational development and has come to be directed at the parents. We probably do not have enough information as yet about different approaches to helping parents develop their confidence and competence, and about the impact of such different approaches on children's development, to make firm claims about comparative effectiveness. It is clear, as Lazar and Darlington (1982) point out, that different approaches to parent involvement work to some extent. They argue in their conclusions for the force of 'non-cognitive variables' on children's educational development, that is, children's attitudes and motivation, parents' self-confidence and skills. Yet they do not include these variables in their path diagram of the effects of early intervention on children's school performance, for lack of evidence. These, then, are surely the crucial questions to add to the path diagram: how do parents' motivations, confidence and skills affect children's development and performance, and how do 'parent education' or 'parent support' programmes help parents develop confidence and competence?

What should we conclude from this overview of parent involvement? First, that both American and British evidence shows clearly that programmes involving parents with their children can affect both parents' confidence and competence and their children's development. Secondly, the crucial component seems to be the parents' role as educators of their children, with active participation. Thirdly, if the process of adult–child interaction is essentially one of mutual responsiveness, with parent and child mutually reinforcing each other, then the question is how to initiate and maintain this as a positive cycle for the developing child. Fourthly, a possible hypothesis from Lazar and Darlington's (1982) findings is the strength and continuity of this mutual responsiveness, once established, throughout the child's school career. Fifthly, the process of parental participation is essentially to do with adult education: how and where adults learn. And finally, we should note that the key questions remain to be answered. Is parent involvement or the best possible pre-school programme more effective in promoting the child's development? And is parent education or parent support more effective in helping parents to learn?

Bronfenbrenner's comments in his review of early intervention programmes remain today as provocative and challenging for both policy and research as when they were written in 1974:

> The family is the most effective and economical system for fostering and sustaining the development of the child . . . The involvement of the child's family as an active participant is critical to the success of any intervention programme . . . Without such family involvement, any effects of intervention, at least in the cognitive sphere, appear to erode fairly rapidly once the programme ends . . . The involvement of the parents as partners in the enterprise provides an on-going system which can reinforce the effects of the programme while it is in operation, and help to sustain them after the programme ends.

References

Aplin, G. and Pugh, G. (eds) (1983) *Perspectives on Preschool Home Visiting*. London: National Children's Bureau, and Coventry: Community Education Development Centre.

Armstrong, G. and Brown, F. (1979) *Five Years On: a Follow-up Study of the Long-term Effects on Parents and Children of an Early Learning Programme in the Home*. Oxford: Social Evaluation Unit, Department of Social and Administrative Studies.

Bernstein, B. and Davies, B. (1969) Some sociological comments on Plowden. In Peters, R. S. (ed.) *Perspectives on Plowden*. London: Routledge & Kegan Paul.

Bronfenbrenner, U. (1974) Is early intervention effective? Facts and principles of early intervention: a summary. Reprinted in Clarke, A. M. and Clarke, A. D. B. (1976) *Early Experience: Myth and Evidence*. London: Open Books.

Brown, G. W. and Harris, T. O. (1978) *Social Origins of Depression*. London: Tavistock.

Bruner, J. S. (1972) *The Relevance of Education*. London: Allen and Unwin.

Bruner, J. S. (1980) *Under Five in Britain*. London: Grant McIntyre.

Clarke-Stewart, A. (1973) *Interactions between Mothers and their Young Children: Characteristics and Consequences*. Monographs of the Society for Research in Child Development, No. 153.

Clarke-Stewart, A. (1982) *Day Care*. London: Fontana.

Cyster, R., Clift, P. S. and Battle, S. (1980) *Parental Involvement in Primary Schools*. Slough: NFER.

Department of Education and Science (1967) *Children and Their Primary Schools* (the Plowden Report). London: HMSO.

Donachy, W. (1979) Parental participation in preschool education. In Clark, M. M. and Cheyne, W. M. (eds): *Studies in Preschool Education*. London: Hodder and Stoughton for the Scottish Council for Research in Education.

Douglas, J. W. B. (1964) *The Home and the School*. London: McGibbon and Kee.

Douglas, J. W. B., Ross, J. M. and Simpson, H. R. (1968) *All Our Future*. London: Peter Davies.

Essen, J. and Wedge, P. (1982) *Continuities in Childhood Disadvantage*. London: Heinemann Educational Books.

Farel, A. M. (1980) Effects of preferred maternal roles, maternal employment and sociodemographic status on school adjustment and competence. *Child Development* **51**, 1179–86.

Gray, M. and McMahon, L. (1982) *Families in Playgroups*. London: Preschool Playgroups Association.

Halsey, A. H., Health, A. F. and Ridge, J. M. (1979) *Origins and Destinations: Family, Class, and Education in Modern Britain*. Oxford: Clarendon Press.

Hess, R. D. (1980) Experts and amateurs: some unintended consequences of parent education. In Fantini, M. D. and Cardenas, R. (eds) *Parenting in a Multi-Cultural Society*. London: Longman.

Hughes, M., Mayall, B., Moss, P., Perry, J., Petrie, P. and Pinkerton, G. (1980) *Nurseries Now: a Fair Deal for Parents and Children*. Harmondsworth: Penguin.

Knight, B., Gibson, M. and Grant, S. (1979) *Family Groups in the Community*. London: London Voluntary Service Council.

Lazar, I. and Darlington, R. (1982) *Lasting Effects of Early Education: a Report from the Consortium for Longitudinal Studies*. Monographs of the Society for Research in Child Development, no. 195.

McCail, G. (1981) *Mother Start*. Edinburgh, SCRE.

Mittler, P. and McConachie, H. (eds) (1983) *Parents, Professionals and Handicapped People: Approaches to Partnership*. London: Croom Helm.

Newson, J. and Newson, E. (1977) *Perspectives on School at Seven Years Old*. London: Allen and Unwin.

Palfreeman, S. (1982) Mother and toddler groups among 'at risk families'. *Health Visitor* **55**, 455–7.

Palfreeman, S. and Smith, T. (1982) *Preschool Provision: Voluntary Initiatives and Integrated Services in Cheshire*. Cheshire: Cheshire County Council Education Department.

Parry, M. and Archer, H. (1974) *Preschool Education*. London: Macmillan.

Peaker, G. T. (1971) *The Plowden Children: Four Years Later*. Slough: NFER.

Poulton, G. (1980) The educational home visitor. In Craft, M., Raynor, J. and Cohen, L. (eds) *Linking Home and School: a New Review*, 3rd ed. London: Harper and Row.

Poulton, L. (1981) Bassett Green first school family education project. In Community Education Development Centre *Outlines: a Source Pack for Community Education*. Coventry: CEDC.

Poulton, L. and Poulton, G. (1970) Neighbourhood support for young families. *Early Child Development and Care* **6**, 1–2.

Pugh, G. (1981) *Parents as Partners: Intervention Schemes and Groupwork with Parents of Handicapped Children*. London: National Children's Bureau.

Pugh, G. (ed.) (1982) *Parenting Papers*. London: National Childrens Bureau.

Radin, N. (1972) Three degrees of maternal involvement in a preschool program: impact on mothers and children. *Child Development* **43**, 1355–64.

Schweinhart, L. J. and Weikart, D. P. (1980) *Young Children Grow Up: the Effect of the Perry Preschool Program on Youth Through Age 15*. Ypsilanti, Mich.: Monographs of the High/Scope Educational Foundation No. 7.

Shinman, S. M. (1981) *A Chance for Every Child? Access and Response to Pre-School Provision*. London: Tavistock.

Smith, T. (1980) *Parents and Preschool*. London: Grant McIntyre.

Tizard, B., Mortimore, J. and Burchell, B. (1981) *Involving Parents in Nursery and Infant Schools: A Source Book for Teachers*. London: Grant McIntyre.

Tizard, J., Schofield, W. N. and Hewison, J. (1982) Collaboration between teachers and parents in assisting children's reading. *British Journal of Educational Psychology* **52**, 1–15.

Van der Eyken, W. (1982) *Home Start: a Four Year Evaluation*. Leicester: Home-Start Consultancy.

Weikart, D. P. (1982) In Breedlove, C. and Schweinhart, J. (1982) *The Cost Effective-ness of High Quality Early Education Programmes*. Ypsilanti, Mich.: High-Scope Educational Research Foundation (Report prepared for the 1982 Southern Governors' Conference).

Wolfendale, S. (1983) *Parental Participation in Children's Development and Education. Special Aspects of Education*. London and New York: Gordon Breach.

Young, M. and McGeeney, P. (1968) *Learning Begins at Home: a Study of a Junior School and its Parents*. London: Routledge & Kegan Paul.

Zigler, E. and Berman, W. (1983) Discerning the future of childhood intervention. *American Psychologist* **38**, 894–906.

Further Reading

Bruner, J. S. (1980) *Under Five in Britain*. London: Grant McIntyre.

Cyster, R., Clift, P. S. and Battle, S. (1980) *Parental Involvement in Primary Schools*. Slough: NFER.

Pugh, G. (ed.) (1982) *Parenting Papers*. London: National Children's Bureau.

Shinman, S. M. (1981) *A Chance For Every Child? Access and Response to Pre-School Provision*. London: Tavistock.

Smith, T. (1980) *Parents and Preschool*. London: Grant McIntyre.

Tizard, B., Mortimore, J. and Burchell, B. (1981) *Involving Parents in Nursery and Infant Schools: A Source Book for Teachers*. London: Grant McIntyre.